AMERICA'S
WORKING
WOMEN

AMERICA'S WORKING WOMEN

COMPILED AND EDITED BY ROSALYN BAXANDALL, LINDA GORDON AND SUSAN REVERBY

VINTAGE BOOKS A DIVISION OF RANDOM HOUSE
NEW YORK

First Vintage Books Edition September 1976

Copyright © 1976 by Rosalyn Baxandall, Linda Gordon and Susan Reverby

All rights reserved under International and Pan-American Copyright Conventions. Published in the United States by Random House, Inc., New York, and simultaneously in Canada by Random House of Canada Limited, Toronto. Originally published by Random House in September, 1976.

Designed by Charlotte Staub

Library of Congress Cataloging in Publication Data

Main entry under title:
America's working women.

Includes bibliographical references.
1. Women—Employment—United States—History—Sources. 2. Women—Employment—United States—History—Addresses, essays, lectures. I. Baxandall, Rosalyn. II. Gordon, Linda. III. Reverby, Susan.
[HD6095.A662   1976b]   331.4'0973   76–10575
ISBN 0–394–72208–6

Manufactured in the United States of America
9 8 7 6 5 4 3 2

ACKNOWLEDGMENTS

Please note that footnotes have been deleted from all articles reprinted here. Grateful acknowledgment is made to the following for permission to reprint previously published material:

Arno Press: Excerpts from *Homestead, the Households of a Mill Town,* by Margaret F. Byington (Charities, 1910). Reprinted by Arno Press, Inc., 1969.

Association for the Study of Afro-American Life and History, Inc.: Excerpts from "Letters from Negro Migrants, 1916–18," *Journal of Negro History,* Vol. 4, No. 3 (July 1919).

Beacon Press: Excerpts from *Rank and File: Personal Histories of Working-Class Organizers,* edited by Alice and Staughton Lynd. Copyright © 1973 by Alice and Staughton Lynd. Reprinted by permission of the publisher.

Columbia University Press: Excerpts from *The Ojibwa Woman* by Ruth Landes. Columbia University Press, New York (1938). Reprinted by permission of the publisher.

Robert Ernst: Excerpts from *Immigrant Life in New York City, 1825–1863* by Robert Ernst (King's Crown Press, New York, 1949). Reprinted by permission of the author.

CONTENTS

1865-1890

1890-1920

1920–1940

1940–1955

1955-1975

INTRODUCTION

Work defines who we are. Through labor and its collective organization humans have the power not only to maintain themselves but to accumulate skills across generations, to create beauty as well as usefulness, to elevate the standard of living of whole societies. Human labor also forms culture, not just high art but the shape of our daily lives. In human history the labor of men and women both was always essential to cultural and economic survival and advance.

The organization of this labor, however, has varied under different economic systems. Capitalism, especially after industrialization, transformed labor into a commodity which could be sold to others—the system called wage labor, which is often seen as the only real work. This text defines work comprehensively: wage labor, slave labor, and unpaid household labor.

The fact that we are focusing this anthology on working-class women does not mean that middle-class, professional or even upper-class women do not work or that their work is not significant. But women who have had the opportunity to do professional work are a tiny minority. And their interests, needs and problems are not those of the majority of women. In this text we want to look at that majority, and correct a distortion, a political distortion: the virtual exclusion from history of working-class women's work. The housekeepers, factory workers, secretaries, waitresses and prostitutes belong in the center of history, not along its edges.

Capitalism, through the wage labor system, introduced a new distinction between the sexes. For the first time men began to work for wages outside their homes, while women continued to work within their homes without wages. Despite the drastic changes industrialization brought in the *way* women worked, this new sexual division in the location of labor did nothing to change the type of work women did in precapitalist society: domestic manufacture, family maintenance, re-

production, and the socialization of children. Women's roles continued
to be seen as part of the natural functions of the universe, as instinctive
as an animal building a nest, as little noticed as breathing.

For centuries the social contribution of unpaid housewives has been
enormous. As well as raising new generations and preserving the old,
they have often run their communities as well as their homes, setting
up and maintaining schools, public services and recreation. On farms,
women usually shared in the outside work, tended the animals, planted,
picked, weeded and canned, as well as doing all the indoor household
chores. Yet housewives are commonly considered dependents, contributing neither to their own support nor to the economy. Housework is
not included in the Gross National Product, although nothing could be
more deceptive. Housework and family maintenance are absolutely
essential to the functioning of this or any other economy.

The denigration of housework has been destructive for women: it
has asked them to see themselves as parasites, not only dependent on
but exploitative of their men. In addition, the nature of housework
itself creates severe problems for women's self-consciousness. A housewife works unlimited hours and has no day off; it is not easy for her to
become conscious as a worker of her rights to decent working conditions. So much of housewifery involves serving others that self-esteem
often comes only from self-abnegation. Housework defines the whole
woman. When you are employed, your job is something you do; but a
housewife is something you are.

Even when women did bring in money through their work at
home—by taking in boarders, laundry, or children, for example—their
efforts continued to be invisible, seen as a continuation of routine
household chores. Census-takers normally ignored these often considerable women's contributions to family incomes, which had the effect of
suggesting that working-class families could survive on less money than
was really the case. Women's supplementary earnings were often essential. They did work that let them stay at home because it minimized
their conflicts with husbands or fathers who did not want them in the
outside world and did want to continue to be waited on at home.
Earning money at home allowed women to continue full-time child care
and to perform the exhausting, intangible psychological work of holding their families together.

Until World War II, women living with husbands usually took jobs
outside their homes if they were extremely poor or if a hardship befell
them—a husband sick or hurt or unemployed. Mothers were expected
to remain at home all the time, and if they could not or would not, their

absence was seen as a misfortune and an immorality. For most wives, outside employment meant that their husbands had been inadequate in some respect, and it was therefore a blow to masculine self-esteem. A major exception to this was in the black community, where discrimination in employment meant that frequently only the women could find work, often as servants. Most men of all classes and ethnic groups fought with varying degrees of fervor to keep their women at home if they could possibly afford it. Furthermore, most jobs were so oppressive that men honestly hoped to spare their women the hardships of employment. Most women also preferred full-time housewifery to the alternative— housework plus an exhausting outside job. It was considered more appropriate, however, for single women to work outside their homes, even at a young age, to contribute to the family economy. The expectation of contribution to the family held even when young women moved away from home.

The jobs that were available to women frequently involved work that was an extension of housework—in laundries, canneries, textile and clothing factories. Partly because this kind of production had traditionally been women's, it was poorly paid. In addition, the fact that unpaid housework and motherhood were considered women's inevitable vocation helped keep wages low for all women workers, single and married. Women's employment was expected to be always (a) temporary and (b) less important than their real vocation, providing a justification for employers to offer low wages. The norm that all women were housewives or housewives-to-be was the basis of the myth that all women were supported by men, lived at home, and took jobs for extras, for "pin money."

But these myths were rationalizations. The major reason employers paid women less was that it was profitable. Not only could women be forced to absorb unemployment and seasonal work, and to perform the most tedious jobs, but their availability to do so was used as a threat against men to keep men's wages and resistance down.

Excluded from both skilled jobs and the opportunity to learn skills, women workers accepted low wages and poor conditions because they had few choices. By offering women only the worst working conditions, employers helped continue a vicious circle: the fact that women's jobs were so unpleasant and poorly paid meant that most working-class women naturally preferred housework, especially since they had to do it anyway after their hours of employment; the fact that women were responsible for housework and children perpetuated their seeing themselves and being used as marginal workers.

Women continually tried, individually and collectively, to improve their working conditions, but they faced major obstacles. In many cases male workers sought to discourage female organizing because they wanted to keep women out of the wage labor force, because they considered women's jobs peripheral to the economy, and because women received lower wages and could contribute little to union treasuries. Women were put in the double bind of being told they were unwilling and impossible to organize and finding themselves undercut or ignored when they tried.

The fact that women usually carried the major responsibility for their children also set up obstacles to their struggling for better conditions. Family needs often meant that women literally had no time to attend meetings or at other times participation in collective action meant that women had first to wage individual struggles against their husbands and fathers just to get out of the house. Women's fears for the welfare of their children sometimes made them particularly fearful of being fired for resistance to the boss. Women have been accused of discouraging male militance by their dependence and fearfulness. But in fact it is the discrimination against women and their families' refusal to share household responsibilities that have made them fearful. Men rarely discussed the issues of their workplace with their wives or daughters, nor included in their labor struggles demands that would improve women's lives (such as birth control, sanitation, and housing improvements). When women became involved in the labor movement, their militance and perseverance often exceeded men's.

While collective activity was often difficult for them, women constantly struggled individually against their bosses, both at home and at work, particularly in response to disrespectful treatment. Often they took foolhardy, bravado stances against overwhelming odds and suffered painful defeats. Yet there was often a rationality even to such doomed efforts, for the gains in self-respect sometimes outweighed even such great losses as being fired, deserted, or beaten up. In the long run, however, only collective action would earn women both self-respect and power.

Women both participated in and fought against their own oppression. Working women are neither victims nor heroes exclusively. To celebrate only those few who emerged victorious over sex, class and race discrimination is to suggest that those who could do no more than merely survive were failures. Those who escaped the usual lot of working-class women often had unusual sources of support as well as individual spunk and genius. In fact, mere survival often required great strength, imagination and energy. Furthermore, the specific conditions of women's oppression were always affected by their resistance. While few women succeeded in escaping their bonds entirely, almost every woman has been able to alter in her favor the conditions of her own existence. These changes, in turn, contributed incrementally to reforming the institutions and culture of class and sex oppression itself.

Women also used whatever power they had in their own lives to extract small advantages from their dependent status. As a result they sometimes decided to accept and even support elements of their own subordination. Still, in the long run women never gained much from the small "protections" that accompanied their inferiority.

All men, on the other hand, profit to some degree from their power over women. All men gain some services, however small, and some privileges from sexual inequality. For most men, these gains are small when measured against the disunity in the working class and the distortion of human communication that results from sexual inequality. Some men, by contrast, profit greatly from sex discrimination—both from the low wages and poor working conditions they offer women workers, and from the weakness of the working class that sexual disunity creates. These benefits to capitalists accrue equally from unpaid (housewives) and paid women workers.

Working-class women have not yet been able to build an effective movement to fight for their own interests. One reason for this failure has been a difficulty in understanding fully what those interests are. While men have often perceived women as alike, they are not. Ethnic, religious, geographical and racial differences have divided women. Above all, class divisions have made alliances between women across class lines difficult and sometimes destructive. Working-class women have often been alienated from the feminism of more prosperous women whose focus on sexual equality seemed irrelevant or shallow. Working-class women have resented male supremacy, but they have been painfully aware of the terrible conditions of most working-class men's lives. Their husbands, fathers, brothers and boyfriends have had poorly paid, oppressive, unsafe, exhausting jobs over which they have little or no control. Observing this, women could hardly be attracted by demands for equality with men of their own class. Yet this kind of equality is what the feminist movement has sometimes projected as "liberation." On the other side, working-class women have gained little by tailing the male union movement, where women's needs have been ignored and where men and women alike have often been forced into reducing their hopes to incremental improvements for their own small unit.

Despite these severe limitations, women's traditional responsibilities often give them a deeper understanding of the capitalist economy than their men have. As the major consumers in the family, women often understand that the wage increases men win through their unions are promptly taken back through inflation. Women's experience puts them in a position to see the relationship between job and home life, unemployment and employment, community and workplace, school and work, private and public life. "Bread and roses" has been a woman's demand, and it manifests a fuller understanding of total human needs than has usually been apparent among men's social movements—the need for creativity, respect, beauty and personal self-determination as well as a decent standard of living.

The dream of "bread and roses" cannot be realized in a society in which a few have the power to transform work into unthinking employment, to place control over work in the hands of those who do not do it, and to define social priorities through control of capital. Only the working class can create a society in which people set their own priorities and express themselves through their work and only a workers' movement that includes the needs of all—paid and unpaid, industrial and domestic—can have the power, the daring and the imagination to create that kind of society. Only with a feminist analysis and practice can there be a movement of the whole working class. By feminism we mean sexual equality *and* the eradication of the sexual power relationships which have permeated every aspect of human life. Sexism is an historical relationship which has changed over time and varies among classes, races, ethnic groups. A socialist feminist strategy must take these historical variations into account, and this is one of the reasons that this anthology is historical. The abolition of capitalism in itself does not guarantee, as history has shown, total human liberation. A socialist feminist revolution can produce this fundamental change, and in such a revolution working-class women must play a central role.

This is the reason for the focus of our book. Its focus should not suggest that other social groups cannot make important contributions; we ourselves are professional women and we hope that our skills can be useful to a socialist feminist movement. But the neglect of working-class women has not been accidental. It is part of a systematic exclusion of the working class from the history and cultural records of our country, and an attempt to dissuade the contemporary working class from imagining that it could be in control of its own destiny. We want to challenge this pessimism. We offer this book as a political act. We want to help restore a history to working-class women because we believe they can reconstruct this society.

This does not mean that we consider working-class women as having a monopoly on social vision. On the contrary, our strategic orientation is to see women as half the working class. For all three of us, the women's liberation movement was an outgrowth of our participation in the civil rights and New Left movements. We see in the women's liberation movement the potential for a revitalization of a long and rich socialist tradition. For too long, women's experiences have been peripheral to the Left; women's experiences must be made central both to an analysis of what is wrong with today's world and to a strategy of how to create a better one.

By its nature our book has a limited perspective, as all historical work must, but we particularly regret some of our necessary exclusions. We have, for example, left out child-rearing, a central part of women's work, because we felt it deserved more attention than we could give it. We have not covered every type of even paid work; teaching, which was a working-class occupation at times, has been omitted, for example. Nor have we examples of the work of every ethnic and cultural group in the United States. Wanting to focus this book on the modern United States, we have had to slight the earlier chronological periods. Indeed, we have covered the first half of U.S. history in less than a tenth of our pages, resulting in inevitable omissions and oversimplifications in the first section.

Our material is also limited because most women left no lasting records. They did not have the time to write, or couldn't, or didn't consider their lives important enough to be recorded. We have used a variety of historical materials: union records, short stories, poems, songs, social workers' reports, statistical studies. There is still much more to be uncovered.

Yet we have been able to print only a fraction of the material that we found. Our original inclination, in our desire to be comprehensive, was to produce a book of four times this length. However, the costs of publishing in this country required a shortening so drastic that in many ways this is a different book. Through many painful choices we have had to eliminate much material that we considered vital to an understanding of women in U.S. history. We hope that eventually all the selections that we unearthed will be published. We have placed copies of our full collection in the Archives of Industrial Society in the Hillman Library of the University of Pittsburgh in Pittsburgh, Pennsylvania, for the use of those who would like to pursue this history further. Despite these limitations we hope that readers will be able to find something of themselves and their histories in the book.

Many people contributed time, energy and inspiration to this book. Some gave, in addition, ideas, historical materials, and criticisms. For this vital assistance we wish to thank: Carolyn Ashbaugh, Lee and Finney Baxandall, Marlou Belyea, Janet Bertinuson, Dorothy Rose Blumberg and Albert Blumberg, Jeremy Brecher, Susan Porter Benson, Frank Brodhead, Susan Bucknell, Charlotte Bunch, Nancy Cott, Marlyn Dalsimer, Bruce Dancis, Ellen DuBois, Alex Efthim, Mary Ann Ferguson, Luis Nieves Falcon, Harriet, Lewis and Irma Fraad, Jan Gelderman, Martin and Jesse Glaberman, Sherna Gluck, Ann Gordon, Jim Green, Barbara Grief, Florence Howe, Allen Hunter, David Hunt, Oakley Johnson, Liz Kennedy, Gerd Korman, Paul Lauter, Eleanor Leacock, Susan Lee, Jesse Lemisch, Jonathan Levine, Lanayre Liggera, Marsha Love, Alice and Staughton Lynd, Phyllis Lyons, Del Martin, Betita Martinez, Anthony Mazzocchi, John McDermott, David Montgomery, Maurice Neufeld, Tillie Olsen, Susanne Paul, Clary Perez, Elizabeth Pleck, Helen Rodriguez-Trias, Marvin Rogoff, Roberta Salper, Danny Schechter, Howard Schneider, Meredith Schwartz, Susy Scott, Tim Sieber, Ann Snitow, Joseph Starobin, Dorothy Sterling, Temma Kaplan Weiner, Vera Buch Weisbord and Charles Zunser.

The book would not have been possible without the help and aid of librarians and xeroxers in several locations. We would especially like to thank Ernie Lendler and Dorothy Swanson of the Tamiment Institute Library, and the staffs of: West Virginia University Library (in particular Dave and Sara in microfilm and xeroxing respectively); University of Pittsburgh Archives of Industrial Society; Catholic University Archives; the Library of Congress; Wayne State University Archives of Labor History and Urban Affairs; Howard University Archives; Schlesinger Library of the History of Women; Wisconsin Historical Society; the Health Policy Advisory Center; the U.S. Women's Bureau; the Intitute for Policy Studies.

Ann Froines edited two sections of the book. Lise Vogel went over our materials on early New England textile workers and made vital suggestions, as did Liz and Stuart Ewen about our sections on housework. Sarah Eisenstein contributed considerably to the conception of the 1890 to 1920 period. Maurine Greenwald gave not only suggestions and support, but inadvertently her automobile to a West Virginia

flash flood, in the cause of the book. Evelyn Dershowitz gave generously of her time in xeroxing, typing and doing many other favors too
numerous to specify. Annie Chamberlin and Susan Siens not only
typed the cumbersome manuscript but, most nobly of all, read it as
they went and saved us from numerous mistakes, inconsistencies and
nonsensical statements. Toni Morrison, our editor, and Pat Chu, her
assistant, and Nancy Inglis of Random House, made this a much better
book than we could have done ourselves. Ephraim London helped a
great deal with legal advice.

Two of us began this project in teaching courses on women's history.
The enthusiasm, imagination and intelligence of our students at New
York State College at Old Westbury and the University of Massachusetts at Boston gave us many of the ideas and a sense of purpose for
writing the book. Robb Burlage, Keith Dix, Carol Fuller and other
friends in the labor movement in West Virginia were of great help and
inspiration.

Our greatest debt is to the many women and men who are now
reviving the history of working-class people under the influence of the
renaissance of feminism and Marxism. One of the characteristics of
this new Marxist-feminist history is that it is being developed collectively. All three of us have had the luck to be involved in a Marxist-
feminist conference group to whose members and above all group discussions we owe many of our insights. All over the country we have
acquaintances whose work has taught us much. A network of interested
people has been able to bring to our attention important research and
analysis when the scholarly journals, still dominated by male-suprema-
cist and bourgeois standards of scholarship, will not print them. The
encouragement of the many others confronting the same problems in
looking at women's and working-class history has stimulated in us both
a renewed respect for the analytical tools of Marxism and the awareness of the necessity to sharpen, redesign or reject those tools when
necessary to understand reality better.

The new historiography of which we are a part is very much in
process. Many of the conclusions implicit in our introductory writings
are the product of much debate, and many are still the subject of
controversy. This documentary collection does not allow us to spell out
the issues in these controversies, but it would be misleading if we did
not at least identify the questions. A partial list of some of the issues
that we had to confront in preparing this book might include:

1. How housework fits into the capitalist mode of production, what
benefits it provides to men and to the capitalist class.

2. The continued existence of patriarchy in cultural and behavioral patterns and relationships: to what extent are sexist hierarchies universals, and to what extent have they been modified historically and by different ethnic, racial and religious influences? To put it another way, has capitalism destroyed patriarchy and substituted wholly different forms of male supremacy, or are there significant precapitalist forms that continue?

3. The periodization of history, for events, even events concerning the working class in particular, fall into different patterns when women as opposed to men are made the center of focus.

4. The dividing line between the family and the larger community, for the traditional distinction between extended and nuclear families begins to fade as women's networks of sharing and support are considered.

5. The definition of social class itself, for women's class position cannot accurately be measured by their relationship to the means of production alone nor by their husbands' or fathers' class position alone—in fact, a focus on women shows that class and class consciousness are formed, in individual cases, by a combination of economic and cultural factors.

6. The varied forms of resistance to exploitation, for here too a focus on women reveals that historians have previously focused too exclusively on obvious forms of struggle, neglecting such social activities as boycotts, "gossip," consciousness-raising, etc.

These questions, and many more, are not strictly academic, for the answers to them will affect the development of strategies for changing the society. Furthermore, they are not questions that concern women only. In most cases the impact of women's history has been to reorient analysis of all social history. Many historians of the working class, for example, have attempted to explain men's class consciousness solely in terms of their job experiences. Women's history has reminded us that people's lives are of a piece, that class and sexual power relations take place twenty-four hours a day, in every activity, in every space. A feminist perspective on history makes possible a closer integration of economic and cultural, sociological and individual, factors than ever before. And this unified way of understanding people is essential not only for scholars but also for anyone working for change.

TO 1820

The United States was founded as a European colony on territory deviously and sometimes forcibly taken from its original residents. First establishing seacoast enclaves, then gradually moving westward, the Europeans eventually deprived the Native Americans of all their lands, even though the country was large enough for all to share.

Like all colonial powers, England tried, though unevenly, to keep her American colonies economically dependent upon the motherland. British colonial legislation therefore discouraged manufacture in the New World and encouraged agriculture, which provided England with the foodstuffs she needed and could sell to other countries.

Continuing in America their European traditions, the settlers established a division of labor which usually placed men in agriculture and women in manufacture or in some farm tasks which provided both subsistence and products for local markets. In this preindustrial society, manufacture was confined almost exclusively to the home. Raw materials were usually produced by the family, tools of production belonged to the family, and a large part of the finished product was used by the family. When products were sold, the profit belonged to the family. Men dominated the most skilled crafts, but women's work was visible and highly valued, a value that increased with the shortage of women. As regions matured socially and economically, the excess of men tended to disappear. A shortage of women was characteristic of the early stages of settlement, and was more common in the southern colonies than in New England. By the end of the colonial period, women frequently outnumbered men in the New England cities. Even when there was not a shortage of women, however, the relative fluidity of a society in formation led to the abandonment of some of the traditional restrictions on women's work, and new opportunities were sometimes available. Male settlers looking for wives commonly valued physical strength above all other characteristics. And unlike British women, American women could own land in some areas up until the early 1800s.

The Protestant religions of most of the European settlers were well suited to the needs of a developing country, for they esteemed hard work and condemned idleness as sin. In spite of the fact that they were often victims of religious persecution, the colonists themselves were no more tolerant of others. Though the colonists had a somewhat broader view of the woman's sphere, those women who stepped too far out of it were harshly punished. Women who would not accept conventional and religious definitions of their roles—women who practiced healing, blasphemed, or broke family discipline—were sometimes burned as witches or banished.

The majority of the population were farmers and artisans who often owned their land and tools. Yet by the mid-eighteenth century there was a developing working class—that is, people who sold their labor for wages. Throughout this period there was diminishing equality of economic opportunity and a growing stratification of the society. Political democracy in the form of the right to vote varied considerably from colony to colony and state to state, although increasingly women and blacks were deprived of rights. In the U.S. Constitution, non-whites were accorded less than human status and were counted as three-fifths of a person.

In the South, and to some degree in the North, slave labor provided a major basis for the growing prosperity of the planter and commercial classes. The Europeans first tried to enslave the Indians, but found their resistance indomitable. Blacks were forcibly kidnapped from Africa and were sold into slavery on this continent. Poor whites were enslaved in another way, coming here as indentured servants with an opportunity to work their way to freedom—though due to harsh treatment and perpetual debt, many never made it. Children and widows were often apprenticed; while learning a trade or craft, they too served as unfree laborers for many years. The American class structure was a pyramid: at the top were the landed gentry, merchants and a few early manufacturers; below them were the farmers; then the independent artisans; journeymen and laborers; below them were indentured servants and apprentices; and at the very bottom were the slaves and Native Americans.

Naturally there was resistance. Slave and servant discontent manifested itself most often in individual acts of sabotage and escape. There were some organized slave rebellions, followed by savage repression. The Indians kept up a nearly constant armed resistance, but their weapons were inferior to those of the Europeans and they were often divided by bribery and the colonists' exacerbation of tribal rivalries. The American Revolution itself was a form of rebellion, perhaps the world's first antiimperialist revolution. However, it did not destroy the hierarchical class system; rather, it replaced the British ruling class with an alliance of ambitious colonial gentry and merchants. Within the American Revolutionary period, however, there were several rebellions of small farmers—the "Regulator" movement of 1767–71, for example, and Shay's Rebellion of 1786–88, as well as repeated urban agitation by artisans, laborers, and seamen. These rebels fought regressive taxes, an oppressive debt structure, impressment, and other policies against their class interests imposed by British and colonial rulers. They used traditional forms of collective action, but were frequently defeated after the Revolution by the superior force, organization and political ideology of the new governments. Nevertheless, the American Revolution was not without importance for working people. As part of a tradition of revolutions that began in Britain in the seventeenth century, the American Revolution produced radical democratic thinkers such as Tom Paine, who popularized the idea of democracy here. These ideas were to appear again and again in new forms of protest against economic and political inequality.

The Revolution, like all wars, had an important effect on women. The sense of crisis did help to break down traditional barriers to women's activity. Even before the outbreak of hostilities, women were organizing boycotts of British goods, since as consumers women felt the injustice of the tax laws most keenly. During the war, women took over men's jobs and organized the care of the sick and wounded soldiers. These new opportunities and responsibilities as well as the general ferment of radical ideas inspired a few individual women— mainly from the more prosperous classes—to ask for a share in political power. But these individual demands did not spark a feminist movement, probably because the great majority of women were so challenged and taxed just by doing their traditional work in the harsh conditions of this New World that they had no time to form higher expectations. Furthermore, in this as in other preindustrial societies, while women had a second-class status, they were not excluded from the mainstream of production. Their work was subordinate to men's, but they worked alongside men. Particularly the wives of craftsmen could learn their husbands' trades and often practice them if they were widowed. Women were less isolated than in industrial society, for they did not stay at home with the children while their husbands went out to work—rather their husbands stayed home to work, for there was no distinction between living and working quarters. Women's work—agricultural, manufacturing, child care and house cleaning—was integrated into other forms of production and highly respected.

By the end of this period, however, industrial forms of production began to change the whole society, and women's work in particular. For a period some political leaders of the society tried to discourage the development of industrial manufacturing, preferring an agricultural society. Others, like Alexander Hamilton, perceived that industrial production was an advantageous trend and wanted the United States to lead in this profitable new form of enterprise. Observing that free land made most men reluctant to sacrifice their independence for wage labor, these men thought to use female labor in industry. The Protestant religious values of New England, with their emphasis on the dangers of idleness, encouraged these developments. Though industrial manufacturing did not become a major form of production in this period, its beginnings created new opportunities and new problems for women. Removing them from the control and some of the protection of patriarchal families, it gave a growing minority of women their first taste of independence and exploitation.

THE FIRST AMERICAN WOMEN

ALTHOUGH NOT a Native American herself, Ruth Landes wrote down her own observations, made while doing "field work" in the Ojibwa community, and transcriptions of many life histories of women as told to her by other Ojibwa women.

The Ojibwa were a primarily nonagricultural people of the Great Lakes region. They are but one of many Native American peoples, and we have no reason to believe that their economic and social patterns are in any way typical. But the excerpts illustrate a very important fact: that while there is a strong division between women's and men's work in this as in all societies, there is also a rich lore of women going beyond their prescribed roles.

Ruth Landes's observations were not made in preindustrial America, but in the 1930s when the Ojibwa people had clearly been affected by industrial society despite their distance from big cities.

THE OJIBWA WOMAN

Prescriptively feminine work is extremely varied. It is learned and practised by every girl, no matter to what extent she may supplement it with male work. She sets simple twine traps about the wigwam to catch whatever small creatures may wander into them; these are usually rabbits. She does this regularly, and it is the first lesson in trapping which she teaches her children. The snared rabbit is skinned, the meat and bones thrown into the cooking pot, the fur saved for weaving into rabbit robes. These robes are pretty and warm, and invaluable to hunters. The woman cuts the fur of one rabbit into a long, thin, continuous rope, which is tied onto another such rope made from the fur of an-

Ruth Landes. *The Ojibwa Woman.* New York: Columbia University Press, 1938.

other rabbit; one rope is then used in the weaving as weft, and another rope as warp. They use long strips of grass and cedar bark for weaving also, and make mats out of them to be used on the floor or stood up against the lodge wall. Native or commercial twine is used to crochet fishnets used by women and men.

Women tan deer and moose hides in several different ways, to produce varying grades of fineness and coarseness in texture, and colors that range from brownish tan to a yellowish cream. . . . Moccasins for serviceable wear are made of a leather that is tanned to a rich tan color and to a coarse thick texture, whereas moccasins used at dances are made of leather as delicate and pretty as a European's kid glove. . . .

The "moss-back" cradles in which infants are carried, or were carried until lately, are made in two stages, one of which is men's work and the other women's. The husband makes the wooden frame; the wife makes the leather sack or blanket which is sewn onto the frame, and is laced around the infant. The leather of the sack is now being replaced by velvet, as being more modish. Snow-shoes are likewise made in two stages. The man makes the wooden frame, and his wife or sister or mother weaves or crochets the rawhide (usually moose hide) mesh.

Women of the backwoods still manufacture their own needles and thread, or did until very recently. The needle is made of a marten's penis-bone, or sometimes of tough wood. The thread is made from the long back tendons of moose and deer, sometimes from the tendons of dead horses, occasionally from buffalo tendons, whenever a buffalo strayed into the woods for shelter and was caught there. The tendons are prepared by separating out the component threads, which are then stretched and dried "and they never break." Some plant products are also used as sewing thread, especially for binding together bark blankets and utensils. . . .

Every woman sets out nets for fish, especially during the seasons of open water. Fish is used for the lighter meals, such as breakfast, also to tide over shortages in the meat supply, or to add variety to the diet. It is considered a most important item. The large organs of some large fish are used as storing utensils; oil, for instance, was formerly stored in sturgeon bladders.

A woman often aids her husband in his hunting. While the husband does the actual shooting, she handles the canoe on duck or moose hunts, and is on the watch for game and for signs of danger. She also performs part of the sacrifices her husband must offer after a successful bear or moose hunt. She cleans the skull of the bear, paints it "prettily" in red and blue circles and stripes, adorns it with bright colored ribbons, slings a small sack of tobacco about it, and hangs it on some tree. She handles the "bell" of the moose head with the same respect, adorns it with ribbons, and hangs it aloft with a sack of tobacco. . . .

Women gather herbs for food and medicinal purposes. The food herbs are chiefly tea-substitutes; they are less in demand now than in earlier days. However each woman is still busily occupied collecting medicinal herbs, of which a great variety are employed. The bark of certain trees is used as medicament and nourishment during times of winter starvation.

Herbal doctoring is practised by both men and women. That is, women do not become eligible for the profession as a simple consequence of their sex; but those who are vitally interested in the work apply themselves to it continuously, and the gifted ones are recognized and are in constant demand by patients. The native pharmacopoeia is remarkably extensive; besides herbs, it includes animal products such as bear gall and certain skunk secretions. There are numerous traditional prescriptions for a great variety of ailments, and new prescriptions seem to be invented daily. Pharmaceutics is the interest of older, rather than of younger women; or it may be that older women have become distinguished through long practise. Middle-aged women spend days grubbing in the soil, and return laden with branches and roots. Their wigwams are hung with sacks containing these materials, waiting for the occasion to be brewed into a prescription. Some women are so interested that they trade with individuals in distant groups of Cree, Dakota, etc., to secure herbs that are not indigenous.

Women are the midwives of the Ojibwa. Men are excluded from a childbirth except for a certain brief magical performance which is resorted to in a desperate case. Midwifery is a highly skilled occupation, depending upon an extensive herbal knowledge, detailed knowledge of the female anatomy and physiology, varied massage techniques, and a cool and resourceful intelligence. This profession, too, is not open to all women but only to those who show marked aptitude and interest. Public recognition of a woman's ability is expressed by repeated requests for her services at confinements. . . .

Serious inroads are made upon a fast occupational sex dichotomy because of the Ojibwa respect for ability, and stress upon individualism. There are numerous women with an aptitude for pursuits that are culturally defined as masculine, for they at one time or another engage in these occupations. Everywhere there are some women who hunt, go to war, and doctor as men do. Women who perform masculine work do so with a feeling that they are assuming simply an additional role, one which is defined as unusually difficult but which for them is surrounded by no status aura. People take such women seriously at face value, and explain them as beneficiaries of the supernatural whom their blood discharges did not completely frighten. But the behavior of these women is never taken to be characteristically feminine despite the fact that even the most conservative women usually find it necessary to take up some prescriptively masculine work at one time or another. The cultural view of the normal woman remains unchallenged and finds expression in the training that is usual for girls. Those women whose behavior is exceptional are not judged with reference to the conventional standard but with reference to their individual fortunes only. The conduct of the ideal woman, therefore, and the behavior of any individual woman may be quite at variance. . . .

This is evidenced in the case of Half Sky, a girl visionary. She was her father's eldest and favorite daughter, and his constant companion throughout her youth. "She learned everything by watching him"; her interest delighted him, so he taught her the masculine prerogatives of setting complicated traps and of handling a gun. After his death, her heart-broken sorrow righted itself through an identification with him so that she took up the masculine duties and honors of her widowed mother's lodge. She not only could do the work of men but she also felt the responsibilities of men. . . . Sheeba had also learned a good deal from her father. After her mother's death she undertook to rear her little sister, and taught her hunting in addition to women's trapping and fishing. In time the two girls had a lodge together and lived comfortably by hunting and fishing. The girls ceased hunting, however, after marriage, to follow exclusively feminine work. . . . It is common to find widows living alone with their children, supporting them with the aid of the elder daughter, as a father would. The two women "hunt like men", at the same time that they carry on the women's industries. . . . Gaybay was an only daughter who often accompanied her father. When she was ten or twelve years old, he died. She was then old enough and with enough experience to aid her widowed mother in supporting the lodge; so the two women used to trap all kinds of furs for the trade. After her marriage, Gaybay did less trapping since operating an independent trapping line breaks up the domestic household; but she resumed after her widowhood. . . . If a man's only child is a daughter, it is almost a certainty that he will teach her the work of a man, at the same time that her mother will teach her the work of a woman. This was the case with Iron Woman, the daughter of a famous shaman. She was noted for her "supernatural" ability at all skilled activities: religious performances, games, hunting. Her father had taught her carefully, and had provoked her to prove her superiority over others. She was so interested she never thought of marrying and maintaining her own lodge; besides "she thought no man was good enough for her." Her parents did not coax her to marry; they were interested chiefly in making her their companion in all that they knew and did. . . .

Those women who adopt men's work are characteristically resourceful and untroubled. Their attitude stands in marked contrast to that of the exceedingly few men upon whom necessity has placed the obligation of women's work. Thus, John Henry Prince and his wife Jean Mary once got lost in northern Manitoba at a time when Jean Mary was far advanced in pregnancy. The day of childbirth approached, and still the couple were not rescued. As the birth pains became more severe, the man began to blubber. His wife expected his assistance, but he had to combat the deep-seated tradition forbidding men to act as midwives, even to approach a woman closely while in her travail, or to talk about the details of childbirth. So John cried, but Jean Mary was impatient with orthodoxy in time of urgent need. As the baby was being born, "she said to him, 'Shut up, and don't sit there crying! Come here and help me as much as you can! It's not you that's having the pains.' So the man came, shivering and crying, and he asked his wife, 'Are you going to live?' So finally the baby was born." . . . And again, a Cree man of the White Dog reserve became distracted when his wife was lost in a storm and he was left alone for the night with their nursing infant. He did not think of calling a neighboring woman to nurse the frantic baby, but he fumed and strode up and down, and finally called upon the supernaturals for aid. " 'If there is a god, please show me what to do to stop my baby's crying,' and after he had done everything (by way of invocation), he tried to give it something to drink, but he did not have any milk in the house. He walked back and forth there in the house, and at last he said, 'Oh, *manito,* give me milk in my breast so I can stop my baby's crying, or else it will die!' He sat down and started to nurse the baby. At last towards morning he knew that he had milk in one of his breasts. So the baby nursed, and at last it fell asleep." . . .

Many women undertake men's work only when the men who should be responsible are not available or have defaulted. . . .

The husband of Ice Woman was so shiftless that Ice Woman had to support the household. She chafed under the obligation but remained with her "useless husband" because she had promised her dying father to do so. It may have been that the husband was lazy because he was actually ill, for he died in his sleep in early youth, but, as no critical symptoms appeared he was simply condemned as incompetent, and so his wife's burden was made doubly onerous. "She was a good worker, but her husband was worthless. She did all the work herself alone, and got along fine. He was so useless that even when he tried to do anything, he never did it right. . . . Ice Woman used to wade out in the deep snow, and carry bundles of wood on her back while her husband lay in the wigwam on his back with no moccasins on. She killed rabbits and brought them home to feed her husband. Finally the man got sick. . . . at last he died and she was left a widow. She did not care. . . .

Widows, and other women, frequently choose to support themselves in preference to marrying; and as a matter of course make casual use of the basic masculine techniques as an auxiliary means of livelihood. A woman can always marry and thus share the work with her husband in conventional fashion. Therefore women who prefer to live alone in all probability enjoy, and even seize upon, this manner of life: they desire solitude, or wish to hunt and trap, or delight in complete self-reliance. . . . Ice Woman . . . prolonged her widowhood for obviously personal reasons. It is quite consistent that women so clear-eyed and deliberate . . . should employ male techniques when it seems desirable to do so.

"This is a story of a woman named Gaybay. When she was a girl about ten or twelve years old, her father died, and after that she and her mother, Keeshka, stayed all alone in the bush. Keeshka was a great old woman to make things such as mats, rabbitskin robes, and birch-barks (roof-coverings). Gaybay learned how to do all these things, and to set nets. In the summer time they used to cure a lot of rice, berries, and they also made maple sugar and maple syrup. In the fall they killed lots of fish and rabbits, and they dried meat for the winter (which they must have hunted and trapped for themselves). They lived in a wigwam (*mitigo giwam,* "lodge made of wood") all winter. Gaybay and her mother used to work together. They never lived among people, they always lived by themselves on islands near the Lake of the Woods where they could get rabbits and fish to kill. By now Gaybay was a young girl (i.e., newly menstruating). They also killed weasels and muskrats in the spring. One spring Keeshka found five little baby foxes. They took these foxes and kept them on an island. They fed them on fish, and when fall came, they killed the foxes and sold the fur: black fox, silver fox, and a cross fox, and they got good money for them." Some years later the girl married, and not long after was widowed. Her mother was still unmarried. So the two widows, mother and daughter, lived together again and returned to the economic ways of earlier years. "She stayed with her mother again for a long time. She was like a man. She could kill a deer any time she wanted to." Then she remarried, but her husband died shortly, and she resumed living with her mother. "After that, she stayed single for nearly eight years. She used to snare (like a man) cross fox, and silver and black fox, also rabbits. Foxes meant good money in those days, and so she lived very well." Unlike her mother, who never remarried, Gaybay had five husbands, and during the married intervals functioned like a conventional woman inasmuch as she never hunted, trapped, or fished, but confined herself to the sedentary activities connected with the wigwam and to assisting her husband on the hunt when so requested. But during the periods of widowhood, which were far longer than those of marriage, she found no difficulty in adjusting to the occupational life of a man. . . .

HOME WORK

In PREINDUSTRIAL AMERICA wage labor was rare. For women, household work—housewifery—was the most common form of work, and it was skilled labor.

Nearly all manufacturing was done in the home, some of it under the exclusive jurisdiction of women—such as textiles—and some of it with women assisting their husbands. The presence of skilled manufacture in the home made housewifery a far more varied, challenging and laborious job than it is today, and it meant that housework was done most often with the entire family participating in some way.

In this excerpt from a nineteenth-century description of women's lives in the seventeenth and eighteenth centuries, we get a glimpse of the manufacture of textiles.

HOME MANUFACTURING

ON MAKING CLOTH

The manufacture of the farm-reared wool was not so burdensome and tedious a process as that of flax, but it was far from pleasant. The fleeces of wool had to be opened out and cleaned of all sticks, burrs, leaves, feltings, tar-marks, and the dirt which always remained after months' wear by the sheep; then it had to be sorted out for dyeing, which latter was a most unpleasant process. Layers of the various colors of wools after being dyed were rolled together and carded on coarse wool-cards, again and again, then slightly greased by a disagreeable and tiresome method, then run into rolls. The wool was spun

Alice Morse Earle. *Colonial Dames and Good Wives*. Boston: Houghton Mifflin, 1896.

on the great wheel which stood in the kitchen with the reel and swifts, and often by the glowing firelight the mother spun. . . .

For many years after this, housewives had everywhere flax and hemp to spin and weave in their homes, and the preparation of these staples seems to us to-day a monumental labor. On almost every farm might be seen a patch of the pretty flax, ripening for the hard work of pulling, rippling, rotting, breaking, swingling, and combing, which all had to be done before it came to the women's hands for spinning. The seed was sown broadcast, and allowed to grow till the bobs or bolls were ripe. The flax was then pulled and spread neatly in rows to dry. This work could be done by boys. Then men whipped or threshed or rippled out all the seed to use for meal; afterwards the flax stalks were allowed to lie for some time in water until the shives were thoroughly rotten, when they were cleaned and once more thoroughly dried and tied in bundles. Then came work for strong men, to break the flax on the ponderous flaxbreak, to get out the hard "hexe" or "bun," and to swingle it with a swingle knife, which was somewhat like a wooden dagger. Active men could swingle forty pounds a day on the swingling-board. It was then hetchelled or combed or hackled by the housewife, and thus the rough tow was gotten out, when it was straightened and made ready for the spruce distaff, round which it was finally wrapped. The hatchelling was tedious work and irritating to the lungs, for the air was filled with the fluffy particles which penetrated every-where. The thread was then spun on a "little wheel." It was thought that to spin two double skeins of linen, or four double skeins of tow, or to weave six yards of linen, was a good day's work. For a week's work a girl received fifty cents and "her keep." She thus got less than a cent and a half a yard for weaving. The skeins of linen thread went through many tedious processes of washing and bleaching before being ready for weaving; and after the cloth was woven it was "bucked" in a strong lye, time and time again, and washed out an equal number of times. Then it was "belted" with a maple beetle on a smooth, flat stone; then washed and spread out to bleach in the pure sunlight. Sometimes the thread, after being spun and woven, had been washed and belted a score of times ere it was deemed white and soft enough to use. The little girls could spin the "swingling tow" into coarse twine, and the older ones make "all tow" and "tow and linen" and "harden" stuffs to sell. . . .

The wringing out of this linen yarn was most exhausting, and the rinsing in various waters was no simple matter in those days, for the water did not conveniently run into the houses through pipes and conduits, but had to be laboriously carried in pailfuls from a pump, or more frequently raised in a bucket from a well.

TODAY HOUSEWORK tends to isolate women. But in the Colonial Period the husbands of poor or middling women were usually farmers, artisans or small shopkeepers, and in these cases the men did their work at or near home also. Craft or retail shops were usually part of the home, and women often assisted in their husbands' work. Furthermore, the closeness of communities and absence of mechanical devices made sharing and cooperation, even in housework tasks, necessary.

CHANGE WORK AND THE WHANG

It was the custom both among men and women to join forces on a smaller scale and have a little neighborly visiting by what was called 'change-work.' For instance, if two neighbors both were to make soap, or both to make apple-butter, or both to make up a rag carpet, instead of each woman sitting at home alone sewing and fitting the carpet, one would take her thimble and go to spend the day, and the two would sew all day long, finish and lay the carpet at one house. In a few days the visit would be returned, and the second carpet be finished. Sometimes the work was easier when two worked together. One man could load logs and sled them down to the sawmill alone, but two by 'change-work' could accomplish the task much more rapidly and with less strain.

Even those evil days of New England households, the annual housecleaning, were robbed of some of their dismal terrors by what was known as a 'whang,' a gathering of a few friendly women neighbors to assist one another in that dire time, and thus speed and shorten the hours of misery. . . .

PERHAPS NOTHING is as illustrative of the skilled nature of women's work as the practice of healing. Seventeenth-, eighteenth- and most early nineteenth-century Americans took it for granted that any

Alice Morse Earle. *Home Life in Colonial Days*. New York: Grosset and Dunlap, 1898.

housewife would be an expert nurse, the folk technology of medicine having been taught to her by her mother. The almost exclusively male medical profession began in the nineteenth century to attack the folk traditions of healing as worthless quackery; an "old wives' tale" came to mean a false superstition. Contemporary reevaluation of the tradition of "natural" healing, especially when it is freed of a worshipful and uncritical attitude toward the medical profession, shows that many "old wives' tales" were sensible and effective.

Some women were professionals in healing, most frequently midwifery—"professional" in the sense that they did this work for money, not in the contemporary sense of the word which suggests extensive formal training, licensing and an elite status. More accurately, they were craftswomen.

The source of the following prescriptions is particularly interesting. It is a book entitled *The United States Practical Receipt Book*; though published in 1844, it is a collection of old, traditional recipes. Collected in indiscriminate order are "receipts" for foods (e.g. how to make catsup, vinegar, cheese, flour), household chemicals (ink, dyes, hair-curling liquid, priming powder for percussion caps), and many medicines and medical procedures like those given here. People did not make distinctions between these categories in this period before specialization, professionalization and commercialization; making cheese and curing ringworm was all part of the general category of a woman's household manufacture.

Notice that two of the recipes—for "preventive lotions"—are for birth control. It is not well known that birth control techniques were invented by women, not by chemists or doctors; that birth control practices have been in use in most societies from earliest recorded history; and that many of these techniques were reasonably effective— not as effective as the 98 percent reliability that is available today, but often with as much as a 50 percent likelihood of preventing conception.

HEALING

INDIAN CURE FOR THE HEART-ACHE

Take a piece of the lean of mutton, about the size of a large walnut, put it into the fire and burn it for some time, till it becomes almost reduced to a cinder, then put it into a clean rag and squeeze it until some moisture is expressed, which must be dropped in the ear as hot as the patient can bear.

RINGWORMS

. . . Obtain some blood-root (called also red-root, Indian paint, &c.)
. . . slice it in vinegar, and afterwards wash the place affected with
the liquid. . . .

HOARSENESS

One drachm of freshly-scraped horseradish root, to be infused with
four ounces of water in a close vessel for two hours, and made into a
syrup with double its weight in vinegar, is an approved remedy for
hoarseness; a teaspoonful has often proved effectual; a few teaspoon-
fuls, it is said, have never been known to fail in removing hoarseness.

NEW TEST FOR THE DETECTION OF PREGNANCY

. . . Urine must be allowed to stand for from two to six days, when
minute opaque bodies are observed to rise from the bottom to the
surface of the fluid, where they gradually agglomerate, and form a
continuous layer over the surface. This layer is so consistent that it
may be almost lifted off by raising it by one of its edges. This is the
kisteine. It is whitish, opalescent, slightly granular, and can be compared to nothing better than to the fatty substance which floats on the
surface of soups, after they have been allowed to cool. . . . [Its presence indicates pregnancy.]

HANNAY'S PREVENTIVE LOTION

Take pearlash, 1 part; water, 6 parts. Mix and filter. Keep it in close
bottles, and use it, with or without soap, immediately after connexion
[sexual intercourse].

ABERNETHY'S PREVENTIVE LOTION

Take bichloride of mercury, 25 parts; milk of almonds, 400 parts;
alcohol, 100 parts; rose-water, 1000 parts. Immerse the glands in a
little of the mixture, as before, and be particular to open the orifice of
the urethra so as to admit the contact of the fluid. This may be used as
often as convenient, until the orifice of the urethra feels tender on
voiding the urine. Infallible, if used in proper time.

VOMITING DURING PREGNANCY

Two or three spoonfuls of the following mixture . . . either occasionally, or when the vomiting and heartburn are more continual, im-

*The United States Practical Receipt Book; or Complete Book of Reference . . . by
a Practical Chemist.* Philadelphia: Lindsay & Blakiston, 1844.

mediately after every meal:—Take of calcined magnesia 1 drachm; distilled water 6 ounces; aromatic tincture of rhatany 6 drachms; water of pure ammonia 1 drachm. Mix.

THE FOLLOWING ANALYSIS of women's work in colonial America is from one of the first classic histories of women's work: Edith Abbott's *Women in Industry*, published in 1913. Born in Nebraska in 1876, Abbott received a Ph.D. from the University of Chicago in 1905. She not only wrote on women's history but also on immigration, housing for the poor, and employment conditions. Like many of the best social historians, Abbott was an active reformer, politically and personally involved with the issues of her work. She worked at Hull House, a settlement house in Chicago organized by Jane Addams, and served on many committees and projects for improving working women's lives.

INDUSTRY

Our primary interests during this early period were agriculture and commerce, and there was very little field for the industrial employment either of men or women. Such manufactures as were carried on in these early industries were chiefly household industries, and the work was necessarily done in the main by women. Indeed, it would not be far wrong to say that, during the colonial period, agriculture was in the hands of men, and manufacturing, for the most part, in the hands of women. . . .

It is of interest to note, too, in this connection that in the case of land allotments in early New England, women who were heads of families received their proportion of planting land; and in Salem, Plymouth, and the Cape Cod towns women could not get enough land. Although spinsters did not fare too well, it is a matter of record that in Salem even unmarried women were at first given a small allotment. The custom of granting "maid's lotts," however, was soon discontinued in order to avoid "all presedents and evil events of graunting lotts unto single maidens not disposed of." . . .

And besides the occupations of a domestic kind, there were, in the

Edith Abbott. *Women in Industry*. New York: D. Appleton and Company, 1913.

seventeenth and eighteenth centuries, various other employments open
to them which it may be worth while to notice. . . .

One of the oldest of these was the keeping of taverns and "ordi-
naries." In 1643, the General Court of Massachusetts granted Goody
Armitage permission to "keepe the ordinary, but not to drawe wine,"
and throughout this century and the next the Boston town records show
repeated instances of the granting of such licenses to women. In 1669,
for example, "Widdow Snow and Widdow Upshall were 'approved of
to sell beere and wine for the yeare ensuinge and keep houses of
publique entertainment'," and there are records of the granting of
similar permissions to other women on condition that they "have a
careful and sufficient man to manage the house." Such licenses were
granted most frequently to widows, but occasionally to wives. Thus the
wife of Thomas Hawkins was given permission to sell liquors "by
retayle" only because of "the selectmen consideringe the necessitie and
weake condition of her Husband." . . .

Other kinds of businesses attracted women in this same period. The
raising of garden seeds and similar products seems to have been a
common occupation. Women were sometimes shrewd traders and,
often, particularly in the seaboard towns, venturesome enough to be
speculators. . . .

Among the other gainful employments for women in this period
which were not industrial might be mentioned keeping a "dame's
school" which, though a very unremunerative occupation, was often
resorted to. There were, too, many notable nurses and midwives; in
Bristol a woman was ringer of the bell and kept a meeting-house, and
in New Haven a woman was appointed to "sweepe and dresse the
meeting house every weeke and have 1s. a weeke for her pains." The
common way, however, for a woman to earn her board and a few
pounds a year was by going out to service. But it should be noted that
the domestic servant in the seventeenth and eighteenth centuries was
employed for a considerable part of her time in processes of manufacture and that, without going far wrong, one might classify this as an
industrial occupation. A servant, for example, who was a good spinner
or a good tailoress, was valued accordingly, and advertisements in
eighteenth-century newspapers frequently mention this as a qualification.

There remain, however, a number of instances in which women were
employed in and were even at the head of what might, strictly speaking, be called industrial establishments. A woman, for example, occasionally ran a mill, carried on a distillery, or even worked in a sawmill.

The "Plymouth Colony Records" note in 1644 that "Mistress Jenny, upon the presentment against her, promiseth to amend the grinding at the mill, and to keep morters cleane, and baggs of corne from spoyleing and looseing." At Mason's settlement at Piscataqua, "eight Danes and twenty two women" were employed in sawing lumber and making potash. In 1693 a woman appears with two men on the pages of the "Boston Town Records" "desiring leave to build a slaughter house." But all of these seem to have been unusual employments.

There were, however, a great many women printers in the eighteenth century, and these women were both compositors and worked at the press. Several colonial newspapers were published by women and they printed books and pamphlets as well. Women were also employed in the early paper mills, where they were paid something like the equivalent of seventy-five cents a week and board.

Although there is no doubt of the fact that women were gainfully employed away from home at this time, such employment was quite unimportant compared with work which they did in their own homes.

In considering minor industrial occupations within the home we find that a few women were bakers and some were engaged in similar work, such as making and selling of preserves or wine. But the great majority of women in this group were employed in the manufacture of textiles, which in its broadest sense includes knitting, lacemaking, the making of cards for combing cotton and wool, as well as sewing, spinning and weaving.

Some women must have found knitting a profitable by-employment. Knit stockings sold for two shillings a pair, and occasionally for much more. One old account book records that "Ann" sold a "pare of stockens for 16s." Sewing and tailoring were standard occupations and were variously remunerated,—one woman made "shirts for the Indians" at eightpence each, and "men's breeches" for a shilling and sixpence a pair, and in addition to this work of tailoring she taught school, did spinning and weaving for good pay, managed her house, was twice married and had fourteen children.

Spinning and weaving, the processes upon which the making of cloth depended, absorbed a great deal of the time of the women and girls of the period. . . .

In the seventeenth century, the work was household industry; the raw materials were furnished by the household and the finished product was for household use; but so far as any part of it was marketed or exchanged at the village store, the system became closely akin to handicraft. The commodity that was exchanged or sold belonged to the woman as a true craftswoman, the material had been hers and the product, until she disposed of it, was her own capital. When the article was sold directly to the consumer, as frequently happened, even the final characteristic of handicraft, the fact of its being "custom work," was present.

With the expansion of the industry, especially in the latter half of the eighteenth century, a considerable part of the work was done more in the manner of what is known as the commission system. As yarn came to be in great demand, many women were regularly employed spinning at home for purchasers who were really commission merchants. These men sometimes sold the yarn but often they put it out again to be woven and then sold the cloth.

The most important occupations for women, therefore, before the establishment of the factory system, were spinning and weaving. . . .

In concluding this discussion of the employment of women during the colonial period, some reference must be made to the attitude of the public opinion of that day toward their work. The early court orders providing for the employment of women and children were not prompted solely by a desire to promote the manufacture of cloth. There was, in the spirit of them, the Puritan belief in the virtue of industry and the sin of idleness. Industry by compulsion, if not by faith, was the gospel of the seventeenth century, and not only court orders but Puritan ministers warned the women of that day of the dangers of idle living. Summary measures were sometimes taken to punish those who were idle. Thus the "Salem Town Records" show (December 5, 1643) "It is ordered that Margarett Page shall [be sent] to Boston Goale as a lazy, idle, loytering person where she may be sett to work for her liveinge." In 1645 and 1646 different persons were paid "for Margarett Page to keep her at worke." Among the charges against Mary Boutwell in the "Essex Records," 1640, is one "for her exorbitancy not working but liveinge idly."

Perhaps the best expression of the prevailing attitude toward the employment of women at that time is to be found in one of the Province Laws of Massachusetts Bay for the session of 1692-93. The law ordered that every single person under twenty-one must live "under some orderly family government," but added the proviso that "this act shall not be construed to extend to hinder any single woman of good repute from the exercise of any lawful trade or employment for a livelihood, whereunto she shall have the allowance and approbation of the selectmen . . . any law, usage or custom to the contrary notwithstanding."

It is not, therefore, surprising to find that, in 1695, an act was passed which required single women who were self-supporting to pay a polltax as well as men. That this attitude was preserved during the eighteenth century, the establishment of the spinning schools bears witness. There was, however, the further point that providing employment for poor women and children lessened the poor rates, and the first factories were welcomed because they offered a means of support to the women and children who might otherwise be "useless, if not burdensome, to society."

The colonial attitude toward women's work was in brief one of rigid insistence on their employment. Court orders, laws, and public subscriptions were resorted to in order that poor women might be saved from the sin of idleness and taught to be self-supporting.

How DID women find paying jobs? Communities were not so closely knit in the New World that people could always count on being provided for by their friends and neighbors, nor could employers necessarily find what they needed by word of mouth. Newspapers served as employment agents, and eighteenth-century advertisements also give us a revealing sampling of the jobs that women did. In a preindustrial society like this, the jobs that women did for pay are pretty much the same as those they did without pay. The use of hired wet nurses was still widespread among the wealthy classes. Not only could women who had just finished nursing a baby of their own wet nurse; women who had had a baby at any time in the past could also, for the suckling of any infant could stimulate the flow of milk.

ADS

Any honest industrious Man, that understands the Management of a Saw-Mill, and Farming, with a wife that understands managing of a Dairy, may by applying to John Moore of New York, be employed on very good Terms; and their having a Child or two, will be no objections.

New-York Post-Boy,
January 23, 1748/9

Wanted, a Grave, sedate, sober woman, not exceeding thirty years of age, who understands the management of a family, the care of children, and who may be trusted with the keys, such a one by bringing a recommendation, may hear of a good place, by inquiring at the printer's hereof.

New York Mercury,
July 29, 1754

Wanted. Two White Servant Maids, to serve in a small Family; the one for a Nurse-maid, to take Care of a Child or two; the other to Cook and do the other necessary Work about the House; They must be well recommended and engage to stay a Twelve-Month at least in the Family. Enquire of the Printer.

New York Mercury,
August 27, 1770

A Woman with good Breast of Milk who is willing to go into a Family is wanted.

New-York Post-Boy, September 7, 1747

A Woman with a young Brest of Milk who is willing to go into a is willing to go into a Gentleman's Family.

New York Mercury, September 19, 1763

Samuel McKee. *Labor in Colonial New York,* 1664–1776. New York: Columbia University Press, 1935. Alice Morse Earle, *Home Life in Colonial Days.* New York: Grosset and Dunlap, 1898.

SERVITUDE

INDENTURED SERVANTS

THROUGH THE INSTITUTION of indentured servitude many poor European women and men bound themselves to serve more prosperous colonists for a fixed period of time. They were poorly paid and often treated rudely and harshly, deprived of good food and privacy. Of course these terrible conditions provoked resistance. Living in separate families without much contact with others in their position, indentured servants had one primary path of resistance open to them: passive resistance, trying to do as little work as possible and to create difficulties for their masters and mistresses. Of course the masters and mistresses did not interpret it that way, but saw the difficult behavior of their servants as sullenness, laziness, malevolence and stupidity. One must compensate for that point of view in the following excerpts, written from the masters' point of view, to perceive the responses of women to severe oppression.

OPPRESSION AND RESISTANCE

During the colonial period service of every kind was performed by transported convicts, indented white servants or "redemptioners," "free willers," negroes, and Indians.

The first three classes—convicts, redemptioners, and free willers—were of European, at first generally of English, birth. The colonization of the new world gave opportunity for the transportation and subsequent employment in the colonies of large numbers of persons who, as a rule, belonged to a low class in the social scale. . . .

Lucy Salmon. *Domestic Service*. New York: Macmillan, 1897.

From the very first the advantage to England of this method of disposing of her undesirable population had been urged. . . .

So admirable did the plan seem in time that between the years 1661 and 1668 various proposals were made to the King and Council to constitute an office for transporting to the Plantations all vagrants, rogues, and idle persons that could give no account of themselves, felons who had the benefit of clergy, and such as were convicted of petty larceny—such persons to be transported to the nearest seaport and to serve four years if over twenty years of age, and seven years if under twenty. Virginia and Maryland were the colonies to which the majority of these servants were sent, though they were not unknown elsewhere.

It is impossible to state the proportion of servants belonging to the two classes of transported convicts and redemptioners, but the statement is apparently fair that the redemptioners who sold themselves into service to pay for the cost of their passage constituted by far the larger proportion.

The condition of the redemptioners seems to have been, for the most part, an unenviable one. . . .

The Anglesea Peerage Trial brings out the facts that the redemptioners fared ill, worked hard, lived on a coarse diet, and drank only water sweetened with a little molasses and flavored with ginger. . . .

The wages paid were, as a rule, small, though some complaints are found, especially in New England, of high wages and poor service. More often the wages were a mere pittance. Elizabeth Evans came from Ireland to serve John Wheelwright for three years. Her wages were to be three pounds a year and passage paid. Margery Batman, after five years of service in Charlestown, was to receive a she-goat to help her in starting life. Mary Polly, according to the terms of her indenture, was to serve ten years and then receive "three barrells of corn and one suit of penistone and one suit of good serge with one black hood, two shifts of dowlas and shoes and hose convenient." . . .

Mrs. Mary Winthrop Dudley writes repeatedly in 1636 to her mother, Mrs. Margaret Winthrop, begging her to send her a maid, "on that should be a good lusty servant that hath skille in a dairy." But how unsatisfactory the "lusty servant" proved a later letter of Mrs. Dudley shows:

"I thought it convenient," she writes, "to acquaint you and my father what a great affliction I have met withal by my maide servant, and how I am like through God his mercie to be freed from it; at her first coming me she carried her selfe dutifully as became a servant;

but since through mine and my husbands forbearance towards her
for small faults, she hath got such a head and is growen soe insolent
that her carriage towards vs, especially myselfe is vnsufferable. If I
bid her doe a thinge shee will bid me to doe it my selfe, and she sayes
how shee can give content as wel as any servant but shee will not, and
sayes if I loue not quietnes I was never so fitted in my life, for shee
would make mee haue enough of it. If I should write to you of all the
reviling speeches and filthie language shee hath vsed towards me I
should but grieue you. My husband hath vsed all meanes for to reforme
her, reasons and perswasions, but shee doth professe that her heart and
her nature will not suffer her to confesse her faults. If I tell my husband of her behauiour towards me, vpon examination shee will denie
all that she hath done or spoken: so that we know not how to proceede
against her: but my husband now hath hired another maide and is
resolved to put her away the next weeke" . . .

The trials of at least one Connecticut housekeeper are hinted at in an
Order of the General Court in 1645, providing that a certain "Susan
C., for her rebellious carriage toward her mistress, is to be sent to the
house of correction and be kept to hard labor and coarse diet, to be
brought forth the next lecture day to be publicly corrected, and so to be
corrected weekly, until order be given to the contrary."

WOMEN SERVANTS suffered uniquely from the indignities of patriarchal control over their personal lives. The sexual double standard
often put them literally in a double bind: powerless to resist the
advances, and even the rapes, of their masters and other men, they
were nevertheless given the entire blame for being caught in viola-
tion of conventional sexual morality. At the same time, as the following description shows, women servants were frequently prevented
from having respectability because their employment did not allow
them marriage.

SEXUAL EXPLOITATION

It was to the master's economic interest to keep his women servants
from marriage and to prevent their having illicit sexual relations, very
likely to result in childbearing with consequent interruption of work

and impairment of health and stamina. As a practical matter the guarding of this interest was most difficult. Work in the fields brought women into intimate contact with the menservants. Household duties exposed them to the advances of members of the master's household, perhaps even the master himself. Poor Richard's advice to his readers in 1736 was doubtless well founded. "Let thy maidservant be faithful, strong, and homely," he cautioned. Children born out of wedlock were an all-too-common occurrence in the servant ranks.

In many of the colonies a servant guilty of bastardy was required to pay the fines and fees usually exacted from free unmarried mothers and, in addition, was obliged to indemnify her master for the loss of services he had suffered through her pregnancy and confinement. Few maidservants had funds of their own or sufficiently prosperous friends or relations to pay these charges. Extra service was the only alternative. While both Maryland and Virginia imposed some measure of responsibility upon the putative father, later Virginia statutes merely required him to give bond for the maintenance of the child, but the obligation of extra service was solely the mother's. Pennsylvania and North Carolina followed Virginia in imposing extra service upon female servants guilty of bastardy. . . . The plentitude of illustrations of extra service imposed upon maidservants for bastardy by the courts from Pennsylvania down to the Carolinas point to the inescapable conclusion that in those areas the master was often enriched far beyond his actual losses. They also demonstrate the direct relationship between illicit unions and the prohibition against the marriages of indentured servants without their masters' consent.

To illustrate the amount of extra service thus imposed, let us consider the case of Ann Hardie, brought into the Ann Arundel court by her master in 1747. She was sentenced to serve six months (for an expenditure of 614 lbs. of tobacco for costs of suit), an additional year (for having a mulatto bastard "to the trouble of his house"), and six months of £3 current for a second child. In addition, the second child's father was required to serve six months or pay £3 currency, and to serve an additional nine months for the child's maintenance. As late as 1780 an extra term of seven years was imposed by the Frederick County court upon Fanny Dreaden for having a "base born child." The bastardy prosecutions of servants Nicholas Millethopp and Mary Barton also illustrate the master's interest in keeping his servants from

Richard B. Morris. *Government and Labor in Early America.* New York: Columbia University Press, 1946. (Reprinted New York: Octagon Books, 1965.)

marrying. The servants pleaded marriage in England, were unable to furnish proof by witness or certificate, and were found by the Virginia county court not to have come into the country as man and wife nor to have declared themselves until some months after their arrival. They had concealed their marriage upon the advice of their importer, who sold them into servitude without revealing their status. They were condemned for fornication and enjoined from living together as man and wife until they had served their terms. "Such presidents [precedents] being allowed," the court concluded, "All whores and Rooges might say the like."

Where the putative father of the illegitimate child happened to be the master, there was a danger that he would brazenly assert his rights at law to extra service from his maidservant. A Virginia statute of 1672 confessed that "late experiments shew that some dissolute masters have gotten their maides with child, and yet claime the benefitt of their service." To prevent such scandalous conduct, the legislature deprived such masters of their legal claims to extra service. Instead, the maidservant was to be sold for the extra term by the church wardens or required to pay 1,000 lbs. of tobacco to the parish. However, the determination of the authorities that the master should gain no extra advantage from his own wrongdoing did not preclude their ordering the maidservant to return to her master and serve out her term. Other than an occasional admonition and the requirement that he post security for the maintenance of the child, no punishment was accorded the master under these acts. One maidservant on a Maryland plantation preferred whipping to marriage with her master, the father of her child, on the ground that "he was a lustful, very lustful man." Under Virginia law, if the unmarried mother happened to have had a criminal record, her master was entitled not only to an extra year of service but to the service of the illegitimate child as well, and it must be borne in mind that the services of a minor between the ages of twelve and eighteen had very considerable economic value on a plantation.

Finally, some of the colonies provided servitude for fornication committed by a servant, male or female, and for miscegenation. A Virginia statute fixed a penalty of a year extra whenever a manservant was convicted of having had illicit relations with a maidservant. A freeman convicted of having relations with a woman servant was liable to serve the master a year. This penalty was later reduced to one-half year extra. The penalty was applied to women servants as well as to men. A Maryland act of 1692 provided that any white woman marrying a

Negro would become a servant for seven years; if the Negro were free, he was to become a servant for the remainder of his life.

ALMOST AS SOON as they came to this continent, European settlers tried to create a slave system. It is often forgotten that their first victims were the Native Americans, whom they called Indians. That American Indian slavery never became a stable or profitable system was due to the Indians' powerful resistance.

The most exploited workingwomen in America were surely the slaves. In viewing the enormous cruelty of the institution of slavery, it is important to keep in mind that it was essentially a system of labor, which created for the rulers of the southern United States a great proportion of their wealth. Slavery was not a peripheral, but a central institution in the United States and in the entire capitalist world; indeed, it was originally the basis of the capitalist system. The slave trade and the agricultural exploitation, through slavery, of the European colonies in the "New World" had provided the capital that enabled the capitalist class to create, first, an international commerce and, later, a powerful industrial economy.

The nastiness and brutality of the treatment of American slave women should not be blamed simply on the personal corruption, sadism, and sexism of slave owners. The personalities of the slave owners and the violence they used were both products of the necessity of getting work out of resistant slaves. Historians of slavery have often mystified this process from both sides, emphasizing the evils of slavery as a moral question and the personal relationships between slaves and masters. While both of these issues are important and relevant, they are not the essence of the slave system. When slaves and ex-slaves reflected on their own condition, they did not fall into this mystification. Overwhelmingly they saw their creation of value for their owners as the key to their situation.

We are unusually fortunate to have some access to descriptions of slave life by ex-slaves. During the New Deal, a federally funded writers' project interviewed hundreds of ex-slaves. The women who tell their stories here were very old when interviewed, and their recollections of slavery often dated back to childhood. But despite these limitations, their stories reveal much about the work they did, how they were made to do it, and how they managed to survive their difficult lives. (We have been able to deal with slavery in only one section of the book and we chose to put it in the period of its origins.)

The following are excerpts from the life stories of three women.

BLACK SLAVES

ELLEN BETTS

I got borned on the Bayou Teche, clost to Opelousas. That in St. Mary's Parish, in Louisiana, and I belonged to Tolas Parsons, what had 'bout five hundred slaves, counting the big ones and the little ones, and he had God know what else. . . . Miss Sidney was Marse's first wife, and he had six boys by her. Then he marry the widow Cornelia, and she give him four boys. With ten children springing up quick like that and all the colored children coming 'long fast as pig'litters, I don't do nothing all my days, but nurse, nurse, nurse. I nurse so many children it done went and stunted my growth, and that's why I ain't nothing but bones to this day. . . .

When the colored women has to cut cane all day till midnight come and after, I has to nurse the babies for them and tend the white children, too. Some them babies so fat and big I had to tote the feet while 'nother gal tote the head. I was such a little one, 'bout seven or eight year old. The big folks leave some toddy for colic and crying and such, and I done drink the toddy and let the children have the milk. I don't know no better. Lawsy me, it a wonder I ain't the biggest drunker in this here country, counting all the toddy I done put in my young belly! . . .

I nurse the sick folks too. Sometimes I dose with blue mass pills, and sometime Dr. Fawcett leave rhubarb and ipecac and calomel and castor oil and such. Two year after the war I git marry and git children of my own and then I turn into the wet nurse. I wet-nursed the white children and black children, like they all the same color. Sometime I have a white one pulling the one side and a black one the other.

I wanted to git the papers for midwifing but, Law, I don't never have no time for larning in slave time. If Marse cotch a paper in you hand he sure whup you. He don't 'low no bright niggers round, he sell 'em quick. He always say, "Book larning don't raise no good sugar cane." The only larning he 'low was when they larn the colored children the Methodist catechism. The only writing a nigger ever get am when he git born or marry or die, then Marse put the name in the big book. . . .

B. A. Botkin, ed. *Lay My Burden Down.* Chicago: University of Chicago Press, 1945. Norman R. Yetman. *Life Under the "Peculiar Institution."* New York: Holt, Rinehart and Winston, 1970.

JOANNA DRAPER
Mississippi

. . . When I is about six year old, they take me into the big house to learn to be a house woman, and they show me how to cook and clean up and take care of babies. That big house wasn't very fine, but it was mighty big and cool, and made out of logs with a big hall, but it didn't have no long gallery like most the houses around there had. . . .

I didn't have to work very hard. Just had to help the cooks and peel the potatoes and pick the guineas and chickens and do things like that. Sometime I had to watch the baby. He was a little boy, and they would bring him into the kitchen for me to watch. I had to git up way before daylight and make the fire in the kitchen fireplace and bring in some fresh water, and go get the milk what been down in the spring all night, and do things like that until breakfast ready. Old Master and Old Mistress come in the big hall to eat in the summer; and I stand behind them and shoo off the flies.

Old Doctor didn't have no spinning and weaving niggers 'cause he say they don't do enough work, and he buy all the cloth he use for everybody's clothes. He can do that 'cause he had lots of money. . . .

One evening 'long come a man and eat supper at the house and stay all night. He was a nice-mannered man, and I like to wait on him. The next morning I hear him ask Old Doctor what is my name, and Old Doctor start in to try to sell me to that man. The man say he can't buy me 'cause Old Doctor say he want a thousand dollars, and then Old Doctor say he will bind me out to him.

I run away from the house and went out to the cabin where my mammy and pappy was, but they tell me to go on back to the big house 'cause maybe I am just scared. But about that time Old Doctor and the man come, and Old Doctor make me go with the man. We go in his buggy a long ways off to the south, and after he stop two or three night at people's houses and put me out to stay with the niggers, he come to his own house. I ask him how far it is back home, and he say about a hundred miles or more, and laugh, and ask me if I know how far that is.

I wants to know if I can go back to my mammy sometime, and he say "Sure, of course you can, some of these times. You don't belong to me, Jo, I's just your boss and not your master."

He live in a big old rottendy house, but he ain't farming none of the land. Just as soon as he git home, he go off again, and sometimes he only come in at night for a little while.

His wife's name was Kate and his name was Mr. John. I was there about a week before I found out they name was Deeson. They had two children, a girl about my size, name Joanna like me, and a little baby boy, name Johnny. One day Mistress Kate tell me I the only nigger they got. I been thinking maybe they had some somewhere on a plantation, but she say they ain't got no plantation and they ain't been at that place very long either.

That little girl Joanna and me kind of take up together, and she was a mighty nice-mannered little girl, too. Her mammy raised her good. Her mammy was mighty sickly all the time, and that's the reason they bind me to do the work. . . .

I sure had a hard row at that house. It was old and rackety, and I had to scrub off the staircase and the floors all the time, and git the breakfast for Mistress Kate and the two children. Then I could have my own breakfast in the kitchen. Mistress Kate always get the supper, though.

Some days she go off with the two children and leave me at the house all day by myself, and I think maybe I run off, but I didn't know where to go. . . .

I stayed at Mr. John's place two more years, and he got so grumpy and his wife got so mean I make up my mind to run off. I bundle up my clothes in a little bundle and hide them, and then I wait until Miss Kate take the children and go off somewhere, and I light out on foot. I had me a piece of that hard money what Master Doctor Alexander had give me one time at Christmas. I had kept it all that time, and nobody knowed I had it, not even Joanna. Old Doctor told me it was fifty dollars, and I thought I could live on it for a while.

I never had been away from the place, not even to another plantation in all the four years I was with the Deesons, and I didn't know which-a-way to go, so I just started west.

I been walking about all evening, it seem like, and I come to a little town with just a few houses. I see a nigger man and ask him where I can git something to eat, and I say I got fifty dollars.

"What you doing with fifty dollars, child? Where you belong at, anyhow?" he ask me, and I tell him I belong to Master John Deeson, but I is running away. I explain that I just bound out to Mr. John, but Dr. Alexander my real master, and then that man tell me the first time I knowed it that I ain't a slave no more!

That man Deeson never did tell me, and his wife never did!

Well, that man asked me about the fifty dollars, and then I found out that it was just fifty cents! . . .

I never will forgive that white man for not telling me I was free, and not helping me to git back to my mammy and pappy! Lots of white people done that. . . .

ELIZABETH SPARKS
Virginia

My mistress' name was Miss Jennie Brown. She died about four years ago, Bless her. She was a good woman. Course I mean she'd slap and beat you once in a while but she weren't no woman for fightin', fussin', and beatin' you all day like some I know. She was too young when de War ended for that. Course no white folks perfect. . . .

I lived at Seaford then and was round fifteen or sixteen when my mistress married. Shep Miller lived at Springdale. I 'member just as well when they gave me to Jennie. We was all in a room helpin' her dress. She was soon to be married, and she turns round and says to us, "Which of you niggers think I'm gonna get when I get married?" We all say, "I don't know." And she looks right at me and point her finger at me like this and sayed, "You!" I was so glad. I had to make her believe I was cryin', but I was glad to go with her. She didn't beat. She was just a young thing. 'Course she take a whack at me sometimes, but that weren't nothin'. Her mother was a mean old thing. She'd beat you with a broom or a leather strap or anything she'd get her hands on.

She used to make my Aunt Caroline knit all day and when she get so tired after dark that she'd get sleepy, she'd make her stand up and knit. She work her so hard that she'd go to sleep standin' up and every time her head nod and her knees sag, the lady'd come down across her head with a switch. That was Miss Jennie's mother. She'd give the cook just so much meal to make bread from and if she burnt it, she'd be scared to death 'cause they'd whip her. I 'member plenty of times the cook ask: "Marsa, please 'scuse dis bread; it's a little too brown." Yes sir! Beat the devil out her if she burn dat bread.

I went with Miss Jennie and worked at house. I didn't have to cook. I got permission to get married. You always had to get permission. White folks would give you away. You jump 'cross a broomstick together and you was married. My husband lived on another plantation. I slept in my mistress' room but I ain't slept in any bed. No, sir! I slept on a carpet, an old rug, before the fireplace. I had to get permission to go to church, everybody did. We could set in the gallery at the white folks' service in the mornin' and in the evenin' the folk held baptize service in the gallery with white folks present. . . .

SLAVERY as a system of labor was most widely used in agriculture, and most people tend to think of all slaves as agricultural workers. In fact, many different kinds of manual labor were done by slaves. Even factories employed slaves. The South was not highly industrialized before the Civil War, of course, but it did have some agricultural processing plants where slaves were either owned outright by industrial entrepreneurs or rented by employers from plantation owners. In the North, free black women commonly worked by taking in boarders, washing, ironing, sewing, or caring for children.

INDUSTRIAL SLAVERY

. . . Slave women and children comprised large proportions of the work forces in most slave-employing textile, hemp, and tobacco factories. Florida's Arcadia Manufacturing Company was but one example of a textile mill run entirely by 35 bondswomen, ranging in age from fifteen to twenty years, and by 6 or 7 young slave males. Young slaves also operated many Kentucky and Missouri hemp factories. . . .

Slave women and children also worked at "light" tasks in most tobacco factories; one prominent tobacco manufacturer, who employed twenty slave women "stemmers," six boys, and a few girls, used for the arduous task of "pressing" the tobacco only ten mature slave males in the entire factory.

Slave women and children sometimes worked at "heavy" industries such as sugar refining and rice milling. . . .

Other heavy industries such as transportation and lumbering used slave women and children to a considerable extent. In 1800, slave women composed one-half of the work force at South Carolina's Santee Canal. Later, women often helped build Louisiana levees. Many lower South railroads owned female slaves, who worked alongside the male slaves. Two slave women, Maria and Amelia, corded wood at Governor John A. Quitman's Mississippi woodyard. The Gulf Coast lumber industry employed thousands of bondswomen.

Iron works and mines also directed slave women and children to lug trams and to push lumps of ore into crushers and furnaces. The Nesbitt Manufacturing Company in South Carolina and the Yeatman Iron Works in Tennessee, for example, owned scores of slave women and children. In Virginia the Oxford Iron Works owned twenty Negro

Robert Starobin. *Industrial Slavery in the Old South.* New York: Oxford University Press, 1970.

boys, twenty-nine women, and six girls, who assisted its sixty-two males. These slave women and children worked mainly either at Oxford's coaling grounds and ore banks or at its furnaces and forges, where ten women, one boy, and one girl joined nineteen prime male slaves.

Slaveowners used women and children in industries in several ways in order to increase the competitiveness of southern products. First, slave women and children cost less to capitalize and to maintain than prime males. John Ewing Colhoun, a South Carolina textile manufacturer, estimated that slave children cost two-thirds as much to maintain as adult slave cotton millers. Another Carolinian estimated that the difference in cost between female and male slave labor was even greater than that between slave and free labor. Evidence from businesses using slave women and children supports the conclusion that they could reduce labor costs substantially.

Second, in certain light industries, such as manufacturing, slave women and children could be as productive as prime males, and sometimes they could perform certain industrial tasks even more efficiently. This was especially true in tobacco, hemp, and cotton manufacturing, where efficiency depended more upon sprightliness and nimbleness than upon strength and endurance. . . .

In addition, some industrialists believed that slave women could do as much work in some heavy occupations as males. "In ditching, particularly in canals . . . a woman can do nearly as much work as a man," concluded a Carolinian. *De Bow's Review* also advocated the use of women ditchers. Fugitive slave Solomon Northrup recalled that bondswomen could chop and pile lumber as capably as bondsmen. One year a rice mill overseer even proposed to use female labor exclusively to thresh the rice.

Third, industrialists used slave women and children in order to utilize surplus slaves fully. "Negro children from ten to fourteen years of age are now a heavy tax upon the rest of the planter's force," editorialized the Jackson *Mississippian*. "Slaves not sufficiently strong to work in the cotton fields can attend to the looms and spindles in the cotton mills," concluded a visitor to a cotton mill where 30 of 128 slaves were children, "and most of the girls in this establishment would not be suited for plantation work." Placing Negroes in cotton mills "render[s] many of our slaves who are generally idle in youth profitable at an early age," observed a textile promoter. "Feeble hands and children can perform this work," concluded a rice miller, "leaving the effective force for improvements or to prepare for another crop." . . .

1820~1865

In the years 1820 to 1865 three fundamentally different labor systems competed for domination in the United States. One was slavery; another wage labor; and a third was farm and artisan labor—that is, a preindustrial system in which manual laborers were self-employed, selling their own products. Perhaps the most significant change during these forty-five years, for women as well as for men, was the victory of the wage-labor system, industrial capitalism, over the other two.

This victory did not mean that by 1865 all working Americans had become wage laborers; women especially remained mostly non-wage laborers until the end of the nineteenth century. But even women, children and other relatives who did not themselves earn wages became increasingly dependent on the men who brought them wages. The family unit decreased in size as production was removed from the home. Women spent most of their time at home performing chores unaided and alone while men left for work and children increasingly went to schools.

Craftsmen in small shops—as, for example, tailors and shoemakers —could not compete with large-scale industrial production, and many became factory workers. Small farmers often could not support themselves and were forced to give up their farms or to supplement their cash income through seasonal labor. Many farmers and artisans, especially if they were recent immigrants, sent their daughters to work in factories. In this period it was rare for married women, and even rarer for mothers, to work outside their homes; when such women did, they were usually in desperate economic situations. At the end of this period approximately 14 percent of women sixteen and over worked for wages, and about 20 percent of the manufacturing employees were women, of whom fully 25 percent were under sixteen years old.

In preindustrial society women's housework was production, highly skilled and varied. The removal of production to factories, and the monopolization of many skills by professions and crafts, reduced the scope of women's work to housework as we know it today. The housewife was a kind of laborer created by industrialism. This transformation of women from home manufacturers into housewives happened gradually, and at different rates in different parts of the country. It was a change almost identical with urbanization. Until 1865 only a minority of women lived in cities, and the majority continued to live on farms. On the farms women's labor still contained many aspects of handicrafts and domestic production.

Indeed, in this period the rural population of the United States was growing in some places while it was shrinking in others because of westward expansion. The long journey west was never undertaken by the very poorest Americans, whether native-born or immigrant. The poor by and large remained in the cities or on eastern farms. Nevertheless, the frontier had a great influence on all Americans. Not only those who went, but even those who stayed were caught up in the reverberations of motion and expansion. Constructing the networks of transportation and communication occupied a large proportion of the country's capital and labor power.

With profit as the motive, another result of this expansion was the near genocide of the Native Americans, the Indians. America's leaders justified their cruel actions with an ideology of religious destiny and racial superiority. Indian resistance to this mass slaughter was unsuccessful. When slavery threatened to follow American expansion westward, there was strong resistance, however; and the controversy over whether slavery could gain new territory heightened the conflicts between the slave and wage-labor systems that led to the Civil War.

While economically the Civil War was in some sense a beginning, politically it was in many ways a culmination, even a temporary end, to a period of political activism. The abolitionist movement, which did so much to end slavery, was one of the more successful of a series of reform movements that flourished in the 1830s and 1840s. These included religious revivals, a popular health movement, labor unions, religious and socialist utopian communities, and a women's rights movement. There was a broad unity of purpose and assumptions and an overlapping of people among these movements. Centered in the Northeast, where industrialism was most advanced, all were motivated by a heightened consciousness of injustice characteristic of people living in a society of rapid economic and social change. Many shared not only opposition to slavery but also a favorable attitude toward women's rights. The popular health movement, for example, combined its attack on the new medical professionals and women's restrictive clothing with a defense of the propriety of women's work as healers and of physical exercise for women. Some utopian communities experimented with sexual and racial equality and alternatives to the nuclear family. The constituency of these social movements was primarily from the prosperous farm, business and educated classes (analogous to the professional classes that formed the social basis for the reform movements of the 1960s). But their ideas had a decided impact on the working class, particularly the antislavery and women's rights sentiments.

On the other hand, the working class, still a minority of the American people, was not well organized and did not have a powerful impact on society. Most agitation was local, as was most industry, so that mass coordinated efforts were difficult. But there were some attempts at working-class organization, and in these attempts, women played an important role, a role disproportionately greater than their participation in the labor force would indicate.

Another factor that retarded the development of the labor movement was immigration. People came seeking a freedom and dignity that they had been denied in the Old World. Before the Civil War, the immigrants were predominantly English, Scottish, Irish, Scots-Irish, German and French-Canadian. Their labor and skills created this country's wealth and unique culture. But each successive wave of immigrants suffered discrimination, at first from the Yankees and later from earlier immigrants. Indeed, the original snobbery of the Yankees plus the traditional ethnocentrism of all peoples turned the natural divisions between peoples of different cultures into hostility and exploitation. Ethnic and racial divisions made it difficult for people to unite around their common interests. On the other hand, many immigrants brought with them traditions of organization and rebellion from their old countries; in this period it was the Irish, English and Germans who stimulated worker militancy.

A particular impediment faced by workingwomen in trying to organize was the ideology of "True Womanhood." This popular myth, expounded through the women's magazines and the media, involved the notion that women's rightful place was at home. Men needed a home in which they were served by a pious, devoted wife as a domestic retreat from the growing horrors of factory life and the cutthroat competition created by capitalism. Although this "ideal" was unattainable for working-class women, their efforts to attain it sometimes made their collective organization as workers more difficult. On the other hand, they also used this ideal of womanhood to help them organize as women and to demand better wages and working conditions.

DISSENT

As in Britain, in the United States cotton textiles led in the industrialization of the country—the more so since the southeastern states of the United States proved well suited to growing cotton. Women were quickly drawn into textile work for a number of reasons: first, because it had been women's work before it was mechanized; second, because women could be hired more cheaply than men; third, because there was a shortage of male labor; and fourth, because there was opposition to enterprise which would draw the male population away from farming.

In the first half of the nineteenth century women dominated in the textile industry. In 1831, for example, 18,539 men and 38,927 women worked in the cotton industry. The cotton industry accounted for such a large proportion of the total industrial sector of the economy that as late as 1850 women accounted for 24 percent of the total number of manufacturing workers. (In the next fifty years the proportion of women dropped to 19 percent.)

The first mill operatives were mainly unmarried daughters of Yankee farmers, and they were often well educated and full of the self-confidence of the Yankee settlers. Most of them worked in the mills only a few years, returning afterward to marriage, the more flexible schedules of domestic work and, occasionally, school teaching. In the context of the general neglect of the history of women's work, these "factory girls" have become relatively famous. It is all the more important to remember, therefore, just how exceptional they were. The conditions that attracted women of their privileged class position into the factories lasted, at best, two decades. After that textile factory workers were drawn from the poorer classes in America, often immigrants.

We would have liked to publish the writings of some of these more typical, poor immigrant women who came to work in the textile mills in the 1840s. But an inevitable part of the lack of privilege of these later factory workers is that they often lacked the skills, time and self-esteem to write about themselves. So we turn to the earlier, more prosperous "factory girls" for a firsthand view of the textile mills. Their class position distorts their view of factory work somewhat. They tended to see it as an adventure, a novel experience that could end whenever they grew tired of it. Furthermore, their recollections were usually written many decades after they had left the mills, when their memories were hazy and a bit rosy. Here we have chosen excerpts from two such descriptions. Harriet Robinson (1825–1911) was the daughter of a poor carpenter, and she was an activist in the mills, a leader in an 1836 strike. She left the mills in the 1840s to marry and become a writer and reformer, working first in the antislavery and later in the woman suffrage movement. Lucy Larcom (1824–1893) worked in the mills for a few years in the 1830s and later graduated from a seminary (the primary institution for those few women who received higher education at the time), and she became a poet and a teacher at Wheaton Seminary. She never expressed sympathy for those agitating for better working conditions, nor was she in favor of woman suffrage later in the century.

Despite their exceptionalness, the experiences of Robinson and Larcom are instructive for several reasons. First, the promises of moral and intellectual opportunity with which they had been enticed into the mills soon proved empty, and like many American industrial workers they experienced *worsening* conditions during the first half of the nineteenth century. Second, the textile workers who were Robinson's and Larcom's contemporaries were the first large groups of women workers to organize and conduct collective struggles against their employers. Third, like most Americans at the time, Robinson and Larcom found their confrontation with the new wage-labor system to be unnerving and oppressive, and their articulateness gives us a sense of how many other women must have felt about the drastic change in their lives that wage labor created.

FACTORY GIRLS

Harriet Robinson:

. . . In 1831 Lowell was little more than a factory village. Several corporations were started, and the cotton mills belonging to them were building. Help was in great demand; and stories were told all over the

Harriet H. Robinson. *Loom and Spindle, or Life Among the Early Mill Girls.* New York: T. Y. Crowell, 1898. Lucy Larcom. *A New England Girlhood.* Boston: Houghton Mifflin, 1889.

country of the new factory town, and the high wages that were offered to all classes of work-people — stories that reached the ears of mechanics' and farmers' sons, and gave new life to lonely and dependent women in distant towns and farmhouses. . . . The stage-coach and the canal boat came every day, always filled with new recruits for this army of useful people. The mechanic and machinist came, each with his home-made chest of tools, and often times his wife and little ones. The widow came with her little flock and her scanty housekeeping goods to open a boarding house or variety store, and so provided a home for her fatherless children. Many farmers' daughters came to earn money to complete their wedding outfit, or buy the bride's share of housekeeping articles.

Women with past histories came to hide their griefs and their identity, and to earn an honest living in 'the sweat of their brow.' Single young men came, full of hope and life, to get money for an education, or to lift the mortgage from the home farm. Troops of young girls came by stages and baggage-wagons, men often being employed to go to other states and to Canada to collect them at so much a head, and to deliver them at the factories. . . .

But the early factory girls were not all country girls. There were others also, who had been taught that 'work is no disgrace.' There were some who came to Lowell solely on account of the social or literary advantages to be found there. They lived in secluded parts of New England, where books were scarce, and there was no cultivated society. They had comfortable homes, and did not perhaps need the *money* they would earn; but they longed to see this new 'City of Spindles', of which they had heard so much from their neighbors and friends, who had gone there to work.

And the fame of the circulating libraries that were soon opened drew them and kept them there, when no other inducement would have been sufficient.

The laws relating to women were such that a husband could claim his wife wherever he found her, and also the children she was trying to shield from his influence; and I have seen more than one poor woman skulk behind her loom or her frame when visitors were approaching the end of the aisle where she worked. Some of these were known under assumed names, to prevent their husbands from trusteeing their wages. It was a very common thing for a male person of a certain kind to do this, thus depriving his wife of *all* her wages, perhaps, month after month. The wages of minor children would be trusteed, unless the children (being fourteen years of age) were given their time. Women's wages were also trusteed for the debts of their husbands, and children's for the debts of their parents. . . .

Lucy Larcom:

. . . The printed regulations forbade us to bring books into the mill, so I made my window-seat into a small library of poetry, pasting its side all over with newspaper clippings. . . .

Some of the girls could not believe that the Bible was meant to be counted among forbidden books. We all thought that the Scriptures had a right to go wherever we went, and that if we needed them anywhere, it was at our work. I evaded the law by carrying some leaves from a torn Testament in my pocket.

The overseer, caring more for law than gospel, confiscated all he found. He had his desk full of Bibles. It sounded oddly to hear him say to the most religious girl in the room, when he took hers away, "I did think you had more conscience than to bring that book here." But we had some close ethical questions to settle in those days. It was a rigid code of morality under which we lived. Nobody complained of it, however, and we were doubtless better off for its strictness, in the end. . . .

One great advantage which came to these many stranger girls through being brought together, away from their own homes, was that it taught them to go out of themselves, and enter into the lives of others. Home-life, when one always stays at home, is necessarily narrowing. That is one reason why so many women are petty and unthoughtful of any except their own family's interests. We have hardly begun to live until we can take in the idea of the whole human family as the one to which we truly belong. To me, it was an incalculable help to find myself among so many working-girls, all of us thrown upon our own resources, but thrown much more upon each others' sympathies. . . .

The girls who toiled together at Lowell were clearing away a few weeds from the overgrown track of independent labor for other women. They practically said, by numbering themselves among factory girls, that in our country no real odium could be attached to any honest toil that any self-respecting woman might undertake.

I regard it as one of the privileges of my youth that I was permitted to grow up among those active, interesting girls, whose lives were not mere echoes of other lives, but had principle and purpose distinctly their own. Their vigor of character was a natural development. . . .

It is the first duty of every woman to recognize the mutual bond of universal womanhood. Let her ask herself whether she would like to hear herself or her sister spoken of as a shop-girl, or a factory-girl, or a servant-girl, if necessity had compelled her for a time to be employed in either of the ways indicated. If she would shrink from it a little, then she is a little inhuman when she puts her unknown human sisters who are so occupied into a class by themselves, feeling herself to be somewhat their superior. She is really the superior person who has accepted her work and is doing it faithfully, whatever it is. This designating others by their casual employments prevents one from making real distinctions, from knowing persons as persons. A false standard is set up in the minds of those who classify and of those who are classified. . . .

I do not believe that any Lowell mill-girl was ever absurd enough to wish to be known as a "factory-lady," although most of them knew that "factory-girl" did not represent a high type of womanhood in the Old World. But they themselves belonged to the New World, not to the Old; and they were making their own traditions, to hand down to their Republican descendants, — one of which was and is that honest work has no need to assert itself or to humble itself in a nation like ours, but simply to take its place as one of the foundation-stones of the Republic.

The young women who worked at Lowell had the advantage of living in a community where character alone commanded respect. They never, at their work or away from it, heard themselves contemptuously spoken of on account of their occupation, except by the ignorant or weak-minded, whose comments they were of course too sensible to heed. . . .

Work, study, and worship were interblended in our life. The church was really the home-centre to many, perhaps to most of us; and it was one of the mill regulations that everybody should go to church somewhere. There must have been an earnest group of ministers at Lowell, since nearly all the girls attended public worship from choice. . . .

FOR INDUSTRY to be profitable, the new labor force had to be broken of their old habits of self-direction in their work. Workers had to be transformed into wage laborers willing and able to accept bosses' orders to work long hours uninterruptedly and without variety, to regard their labor as a commodity which, when sold, rendered their own innate intelligence, inventiveness and craftsmanship worthless.

Such a transformation was difficult. Workers resisted it both actively and passively. Many textile companies devised detailed regulations of conduct, both in and out of the factory, in efforts to control their workers more thoroughly and thereby increase their productivity. The following are examples of these regulations.

RULES AND REGULATIONS

POIGNAUD AND PLANT BOARDING HOUSE
AT LANCASTER

(Decade 1820–30)

Rules and Regulations to be attended to and followed by the Young Persons who come to Board in this House:

Rule first: Each one to enter the house without unnecessary noise or confusion, and hang up their bonnet, shawl, coat, etc., etc., in the entry.

Rule second: Each one to have their place at the table during meals, the two which have worked the greatest length of time in the Factory to sit on each side of the head of the table, so that all new hands will of course take their seats lower down, according to the length of time they have been here.

Rule third: It is expected that order and good manners will be preserved at table during meals—and at all other times either upstairs or down.

Rule fourth: There is no unnecessary dirt to be brought into the house by the Boarders, such as apple cores or peels, or nut shells, etc.

Rule fifth: Each boarder is to take her turn in making the bed and sweeping the chamber in which she sleeps.

Rule sixth: Those who have worked the longest in the Factory are to sleep in the North Chamber and the new hands will sleep in the South Chamber.

Rule seventh: As a lamp will be lighted every night upstairs and placed in a lanthern, it is expected that no boarder will take a light into the chambers.

Rule eighth: The doors will be closed at ten o'clock at night, winter and summer, at which time each boarder will be expected to retire to bed.

Edith Abbott. *Women in Industry.* New York: D. Appleton and Co., 1913.

Rule ninth: Sunday being appointed by our Creator as a Day of Rest and Religious Exercises, it is expected that all boarders will have sufficient discretion as to pay suitable attention to the day, and if they cannot attend to some place of Public Worship they will keep within doors and improve their time in reading, writing, and in other valuable and harmless employment.

THE LOWELL MANUFACTURING COMPANY'S RULES AND REGULATIONS

(DECADE 1830–40)

The overseers are to be punctually in their Rooms at the starting of the Mill, and not to be absent unnecessarily during working hours. They are to see that all those employed in their Rooms are in their places in due season; they may grant leave of absence to those employed under them, when there are spare hands in the Room to supply their places; otherwise they are not to grant leave of absence, except in cases of absolute necessity.

All persons in the employ of the Lowell Manufacturing Company are required to observe the Regulations of the overseer of the Room where they are employed; they are not to be absent from work without his consent, except in cases of sickness, and then they are to send him word of the cause of their absence.

They are to board in one of the Boarding-Houses belonging to the Company, and to conform to the regulations of the House where they board; they are to give information at the Counting-Room, of the place where they board, when they begin; and also give notice whenever they change their boarding place.

The Company will not employ any one who is habitually absent from public worship on the Sabbath.

It is considered a part of the engagement that each person remains twelve months if required; and all persons intending to leave the employment of the Company are to give two weeks' notice of their intention to their Overseer, and their engagement is not considered as fulfilled unless they comply with this Regulation.

The Pay Roll will be made up to the last Saturday of every month, and the payment made to the Carpet Mill the following Saturday, and the Cotton Mill the succeeding Tuesday, when every person will be expected to pay their board.

The Company will not continue to employ any person who shall be wanting in proper respect to the females employed by the Company, or who shall smoke within the Company's premises, or be guilty of inebriety, or other improper conduct.

The Tenants of the Boarding-Houses are not to board or permit any part of their houses to be occupied by any person, except those in the employ of the Company.

They will be considered answerable for any improper conduct in their Houses, and are not to permit their Boarders to have company at unseasonable hours.

The doors must be closed at ten o'clock in the evening, and no person admitted after that time without some reasonable excuse.

The keepers of the Boarding-Houses must give an account of the number, names and employment of the Boarders when required, and report the names of such as are guilty of any improper conduct.

The Buildings, and yards about them, must be kept clean and in good order, and if they are injured otherwise than from ordinary use, all necessary repairs will be made and charged to the occupant.

It is desirable that the families of those who live in the Houses, as well as the Boarders, who have not had the Kine Pox, should be vaccinated; which will be done at the expense of the Company for such as wish it.

Some suitable chamber in the House must be reserved, and appropriated for the use of the sick, so that others may not be under the necessity of sleeping in the same room.

No one will be continued as a Tenant who shall suffer ashes to be put into any place other than the place made to receive them, or shall, by any carelessness in the use of fire, or lights, endanger the Company's property.

These regulations are considered a part of the contract with the persons entering into the employment of the Lowell Manufacturing Company.

BY THE 1840s the myth that textile factory work was an opportunity and the "factory girls" a privileged lot had been dispelled, at least among the workers themselves. Declining profits had led the manufacturers to force increases in their workers' productivity through wage cuts and speed-ups. The employers welcomed and perhaps even encouraged immigration, particularly of Irish families, into New England, because these newcomers provided laborers more desperate for work than the Yankee girls. But the evidence shows that the squeezing of the workers began *before* immigrants were replacing native-born workers on a large scale. The first excerpt is from a paper put out by the Lowell mill women; the second from testimony before the Massachusetts House of Representatives hearings on industrial conditions.

SPEED-UPS

The *Voice of Industry:*
It is a subject of comment and general complaint among the operatives that while they tend three or four looms, where they used to tend but two, making nearly twice the number of yards of cloth, the pay is not increased to them, while the increase to the owners is very great.

It is an ingenious scheme which a few capitalists and politicians have invented to blind the eyes of the people—that, because the operatives receive one eighth more pay in the aggregate for accomplishing one third more labor with the same facilities than they did a few years ago, the price of labor has advanced. The price of weaving a yard of cloth has never been lower in this country than at this time. The price for tending, spinning, carding, never lower, nor the wages of those operatives who work by the week. . . .

Massachusetts House of Representatives hearings on industrial conditions, 1845:
. . . The first petitioner who testified was Eliza R. Hemingway. She had worked 2 years and 9 months in the Lowell factories; 2 years in the Middlesex, and 9 months in the Hamilton Corporations. Her employment is weaving—works by the piece. . . . She complained of the hours for labor being too many, and the time for meals too limited. In the summer season, the work is commenced at 5 o'clock, a.m., and continued til 7 o'clock, p.m., with half an hour for breakfast and three quarters of an hour for dinner. During eight months of the year but half an hour is allowed for dinner. The air in the room she considered not to be wholesome. There were 293 small lamps and 61 large lamps lighted in the room in which she worked, when evening work is required. These lamps are also lighted sometimes in the morning. About 130 females, 11 men, and 12 children (between the ages of 11 and 14) work in the room with her. She thought the children enjoyed about as

Norman Ware. *The Industrial Worker, 1840–1860.* New York: Quadrangle, 1964. John R. Commons et al. *Documentary History of American Industrial Society.* Cleveland: A. H. Clark Co., 1911.

good health as children generally do. The children work but 9 months out of 12. The other 3 months they must attend school. Thinks that there is no day when there are less than six of the females out of the mill from sickness. Has known as many as thirty. She herself is out quite often on account of sickness. . . . She thought there was a general desire among the females to work but ten hours, regardless of pay. . . . She knew of one girl who last winter went into the mill at half past four o'clock, a.m., and worked till half past 7 o'clock, p.m. She did so to make more money. She earned from $25 to $30 per month.

INDUSTRIALIZATION dramatically changed the location and kind of work women did. Sometimes, as in textiles, women simply followed into the factories work that had been traditionally in the female sphere. At other times, women entered new fields because mechanization disrupted the old prejudices about what kinds of work belonged to which sex, and because of the capitalists' desire for cheap labor. The following description of the latter process, in the boot and shoe industry, is an example of how technological change could transform all the social patterns of a traditional craft.

This excerpt is from a classic and monumental work, *The History of Women in Industry in the United States*, by Helen Sumner; published in 1910 by the Bureau of Labor Statistics, it was part of a ten-volume work on women and children as wage earners, the first systematic study done in the United States. Helen Sumner (1876–1933) was a brilliant and committed economist and historian of women workers and the American labor movement. A colleague of labor economist and historian John R. Commons, she wrote and edited major parts of his *History of Industrial Society*, a standard history of the nineteenth-century movement. The fact that she is far less widely recognized than Commons is but one of the many examples of the lack of recognition of women of achievement.

BOOT AND SHOE MAKING

It was division of labor which first brought women into the boot and shoe making industry. The introduction of machinery, indeed, later drove large numbers of them out of the business for a time. Types of machinery were soon evolved, however, which made again profitable a division of labor which could utilize the labor of women, and their restoration to the industry followed.

About 1795 or earlier, side by side with the development of the wholesale trade in boots and shoes, shoemakers or cordwainers, as they were called, began to hire their fellows and to gather them into shops where a rough division of labor was practiced. Soon afterwards they began to send the uppers out to women to be stitched and bound. From that time until the introduction of the sewing machine the binding of shoes manufactured for the wholesale market was practically a woman's industry, carried on at home. Localities differed largely, however, in the extent of the employment of women. In Massachusetts the shoe binders appear to have been exclusively women as early as 1810, but in Philadelphia, which was also a large shoe-manufacturing center, the trade remained in the hands of men until much later. A writer in the Philadelphia Mechanics' Free Press in 1829 spoke of the employment of women in shoe making as "derogatory to their sex."

In general, however, by 1830, and in many localities earlier, the manufacture of shoes was divided into two parts—the work of the men in small shops and the work of women in their homes. By 1837 the shoe binders of Lynn not only bound the edging but did all the inside and lighter kinds of sewing.

There were, however, two more or less roughly marked stages in women's work at shoe binding. In the first stage the family was the industrial unit, the man shoemaker being assisted by his wife and daughters in the part of the work which they could easily perform—the sewing. Even when the shoemaker worked for a "boss," he brought home his materials and turned over the work of binding to the women of the family. Gradually, however, as the business developed, it became customary for the "boss" himself to give out the shoes to be bound directly to the women. The division of labor remained the same, but it

Helen Sumner. *History of Women in Industry in the United States,* Vol. IX of *Report on the Condition of Woman and Child Wage-Earners in the United States.* U.S. Congress, 61st Congress, 2nd Session, Senate Document 645, 1910.

was no longer controlled by the shoemaker, but by the "boss." The women, too, instead of having their work and pay lumped with that of the head of the family—instead of being merely helpers without economic standing—now dealt directly with the employer and definitely entered the industrial field. . . .

The introduction of the sewing machine, however, between 1855 and 1865, caused an almost complete transformation in the boot and shoe making industry. Small "stitching shops" equipped with the new machines were at first opened. In Lynn these shops were sometimes small buildings standing by themselves, but more frequently the manufacturers fitted up rooms in the buildings where the men worked. . . .

The women did not, however, after the introduction of the factory system, succeed in retaining their work as completely as they had done in the textile industries. The machines were heavy and difficult to operate, especially the waxed thread sewing machine which was introduced about 1857, and, as a result, were largely operated by men.

The first result of the introduction of machinery in boot and shoe making was, therefore, a decided falling off in the proportion of women employed. In 1850, in the manufacture of boots and shoes, 31.3 per cent of the employees, in 1860 only 23.2 per cent of the employees, and in 1870 only 14.1 per cent of the employees were women. By 1900, however, the proportion of women had risen to 33.0 per cent, higher than in 1850, when all "female hands," regardless of age, were included. In 1905, moreover, the proportion of women was a little over 33 per cent. . . .

It must be borne in mind, moreover, in considering these figures, that before the introduction of the factory system, which immediately followed that of the sewing machine, the women in the industry were home workers and few of them gave their entire time to binding shoes. A larger number, therefore, were required to accomplish a given amount of work than would have been needed under the factory system, even without the aid of machines.

As for the restoration of women to their former position of importance in the industry, it has been occasioned by three factors—improvements in machinery, which have reduced the amount of muscular strength required; the use of water and steam power, which became general between 1860 and 1870; and the further subdivision of labor. Within recent years women have taken the places of men in operating the lighter machines, while children now perform the work that women were doing heretofore. Subdivision of labor, however, as, for example, the splitting up of the process of "heeling" into "nailing," "shaving," "blacking," and "polishing," has tended continually to introduce less skilled labor—first of women and then of children. . . .

In general, it may be said that the boot and shoe industry is the only one of the more important clothing industries in which an industrial cycle has been completed and the women workers have been definitely transferred from the home to the factory. . . .

IN THE CITIES, the increasing numbers of immigrants made job competition fierce. Unemployment was common. Even if a man found work, many families found they could not live on one person's wages. In many cases there was no "other person" because women, especially the Irish, came to America alone. In this excerpt, Robert Ernst discusses where immigrant women worked in New York City in the 1840s and '50s.

IMMIGRANT WOMEN

In a city of countless boardinghouses, large hotels, and elegant mansions of the elite, servants were in constant demand. Domestic service, in most instances, required few if any previously gained skills and admirably met the needs of transplanted peasant women and girls. Thus, by 1855, nearly one quarter of all the immigrants in the city were household help, "nurses," laundresses, cooks, and waiters. Barred from American households because of ignorance of the English language, Continental Europeans usually turned to their wealthier compatriots already established in New York. A few from the Caribbean and Latin America lived in the homes of the British, Spanish, and French merchants who employed them. Newcomers from the British Isles, on the other hand, were hired by all but the German-speaking families.

Nearly all the domestic servants who came from Great Britain were born in Ireland. Of the ten thousand to twelve thousand estimated to be in New York City in 1846, between seven thousand and eight thousand were said to be Irish, another two thousand Germans, and the rest French, Americans, and a sprinkling of other nationalities. A decade later nearly 80 per cent of the thirty-five thousand foreign-born ser-

Robert Ernst. *Immigrant Life in New York City.* New York: Columbia University Press, 1949.

vants and waiters living on Manhattan were Irish, while the Germans supplied another 15 per cent. Irish servants formed a quarter of the Irish working population, whereas German servants comprised only one tenth of the German workers. This relative paucity of German domestics resulted from the Teutonic practice of migrating in family groups, an impossibility for the thousands of single Irish girls and women who could barely pay their passage or who reached New York only through the philanthropic efforts of others. Once in the Empire City, Irish women were far better off in wealthier private households than as miserable seamstresses living singly in the slums or as laborers' wives forced to sew in order to make ends meet. German families remained together, often using skills such as tailoring which women and children had shared in Europe. Other immigrant women followed the German pattern: domestic service claimed nearly 15 per cent of the Welsh, 16 per cent of the Swiss, 14.5 per cent of the French, and 10.5 per cent of the Scottish working people living in the city. Among workers born in England, the British provinces of North America, and Latin America, about one tenth of each group became servants.

An initial handicap of the Catholic Irish servant girls was the prejudice they encountered in America. Potential employers disliked and even feared their religion, shuddered at "Irish impulsiveness" and turbulence, and were disgusted and morally shocked at the Irish propensity for strong drink. While some Americans preferred to hire natives of specific countries, no other immigrant nationality was proscribed as the Catholic Irish were. In congested cities like New York, the presence of a large Irish population sharpened mutual antagonisms, and discrimination against the children of Erin was flaunted in public. The Irish boiled with indignation upon reading the hated words, "No Irish need apply," or their equivalent, as in these advertisements:

> WANTED—An English or American woman, that understands cooking, and to assist in the work generally if wished; also a girl to do chamber work. None need apply without a recommendation from their last place. *IRISH PEOPLE* need not apply, nor any one that will not rise at 6 o'clock, as the work is light and the wages sure. Inquire at 359 Broadway.

> WOMAN WANTED.—To do general housework . . . English, Scotch, Welsh, German, or any country or color except Irish.

All the more obnoxious to the Irish were indications of a preference for the Negro. As the tradition of servitude and the continuing stigma of inferiority prevented most Negroes from pursuing skilled trades, they followed the only course open to them: common labor and the various service occupations. By 1855 some two thousand colored persons were servants, laundresses, cooks, and waiters—over half of all the gainfully employed Negroes. As waiters and coachmen, they were the chief competitors of the Irish, and they sometimes competed with foreigners in menial occupations as whitewashers, carpet shakers, chimney sweeps, and bootblacks. Colored servants were considered more submissive than the Celts, whose reputation for docility under their English rulers was extremely questionable.

Despite the anti-Irish feeling, the great preponderance of Irish housekeepers, nurses, chambermaids, charwomen, laundresses, cooks, and waiters was evidence of a pressing need for them. Good workers usually had no difficulty in getting jobs. Once hired, Irish women found security in the shelter and food provided with such employment, as well as some chance to save money and raise their social status. In the mid-forties wages ranged from $4.00 to $10.00 and averaged $6.00 per month, in addition to free board, lodging, and time for mending and washing. Chambermaids and houseworkers received $5.00 to $6.00 and slop-women $4.00 monthly. Cooks, ladies' maids, nurses, and waiters were better paid, enjoyed more comfortable living quarters, and earned extra compensation if they cared for children.

Although efficient, honest, and virtuous, Irish servant girls astonished even their compatriots by their self-assurance. Poor and uneducated, they reflected in their deportment a newly won status far above the wretchedness of their lot in the Old Country. In New York they often mistook "forwardness if not impertinence" for independence, asserted the *Irish American,* they dressed "too expensively and showily for their calling" and assumed "unbecoming airs." Some forgot themselves "so far as to *hire the employer,* in place of the employer hiring them."

As did the Irish, but in lesser degree, Catholic immigrants from other lands met with religious discrimination in New York. Advertisements for Protestant governesses, cooks, and maids blackballed many French, Germans, and Swiss. Nevertheless, Continental Europeans profited from the vogue of hiring French servants and particularly from the favoritism of an aristocracy of alien merchants.

The employment of women in the Empire City was not limited to domestic service; women were conspicuous in the needle trades. Until the middle of the century, the large majority of seamstresses were American women: wives and widows of mariners, mechanics, and laborers; most of the milliners were also natives, but a sizable proportion was English and French. Dressmakers doing piecework in their homes received $1.00 to $3.00 for each dress, and privately employed seamstresses earned sixty-two and a half cents, seventy-five cents and $1.00 a day. Less independent were the seamstresses in the ready-made clothing industry, who suffered a degradation probably unequaled in any other skilled trade. The competition of country women swarming into the city depressed wages long before the days of immigrant sweatshops. In 1845 the journeymen dressmakers toiled fourteen to sixteen hours a day for the weekly pittance of $1.25 to $1.50. Apprentices worked for six months without wages and frequently paid their employers $10.00 or $15.00 for the privilege of learning the trade.

In the late forties the earlier trickle of foreign women into the sewing trades quickened into a rising flood. The basis of the sweating system had been laid by American employers and American workers, but by mid-century, immigrants not only competed with native labor but contributed as employers to the exploitation of the operatives. Helping to create their own jobs by their demand for cheap dresses, cloaks, and bonnets, the newcomers gradually assumed a dominant role in the sewing trades. By 1855 two thirds of the New York dressmakers, seamstresses, milliners, shirt and collar makers, embroiderers, lace fringe, tassel, and artificial flower makers were foreign-born. Sixty-nine per cent of these immigrants were Irish and 14 per cent German, although in relation to their respective working populations, only 5 per cent of the Irish, English, Scotch, and French and 2 per cent of the Germans (including German Jews) were dressmakers.

The preponderance of Irish seamstresses was a result, not of choice but of necessity. Single Irish women, unable to find positions as servants found the sewing trades the only occupations open to them. Some had become familiar in Ireland with the rudiments of dressmaking. Others mistakenly saw in easily learned needlework the road to independence and advancement. Married women, finding it impossible for their families to subsist on workmen's wages in a decade of rising living costs, tried their hand at the needle. . . .

PROTESTS

WOMEN'S collective resistance to degrading working conditions began in the 1820s. The first strike, or "turn-out" as the workers then called it, that we know about was in July 1828 in a Paterson, New Jersey, cotton mill, set off when the employers changed the lunch hour from noon to one o'clock. Strikes frequently occurred in protest against such dictatorial changes in working conditions. Traditions of freedom and self-employment that had prevailed in the preindustrial culture affected women, who continually fought for control over their working conditions as much as they fought for more money and shorter hours.

These early strikes show that there is no basis for the assumption that women are innately less militant than men workers. They also show that solidarity between female and male workers was common and effective.

These early strikes usually failed. Most frequently they just faded out, as some strikers returned to work and others left for other jobs. (Because of this pattern, we often have no records of the ultimate settlement of the issues, and many of the following descriptions seem unfinished for that reason.) The general reason for the workers' failure was the lack of permanent organization. Without ongoing organization there was no means of developing treasuries to support striking workers, nor strategic thinking on the part of workers. Instead, strikes developed when workers spontaneously walked out, and this was often when times were bad and employers were in their strongest position. Lack of permanent organization also impeded the development of leadership. It was easy for employers to identify and fire individual leaders without resistance and to prevent the workers from learning leadership skills from each other. Furthermore, most of the strikes were local, and coordination with other plants in other places was difficult. Above all, it is important to bear in mind that male workers were losing their strikes as often and for the same reasons as women workers.

But despite these failures, there were important smaller gains, and workers were testing and gauging their power.

WOMEN'S STRIKES

DOVER, N.H.

In December of the same year (1828), there was a strike of cotton-mill operatives at Dover, N.H., which involved three or four hundred girls and women. This strike, according to one indignant writer in the Mechanics' Free Press, "formed the subject of a squib, probably for half the newspapers from Maine to Georgia. The circumstance of three or four hundred girls or women marching out of their factory in a procession and firing off a lot of gunpowder, and the facetious advertisement of the factory agent for two or three hundred better behaved women made, altogether, a comical story quite worth telling."

Another Philadelphia paper said: "The late strike and grand public march of the female operatives in New Hampshire exhibit the Yankee sex in a new and unexpected light. By and by the governor may have to call out the militia to prevent a gynecocracy." Few papers gave the reasons for the turnout, but it is apparent that trouble came on account of an attempt to enforce several new factory regulations. . . .

Inscriptions and placards and even bits of poetry were directed against employers by these early women strikers. One New York paper particularly emphasized this feature in an account stating that "The aggrieved female 'operatives' paraded the town in the received manner, with flags and inscriptions; but, being soon made sensible of their folly, returned, with a few exceptions, to their work." To which another writer, apparently in sympathy with the working women, retorted, with reference to these employers: "What Spartan mothers will their factory girls make who have been trained to sink all the rights of human nature to qualify them to watch a cotton thread." . . .

That the factory girls themselves had no mind for such submission is apparent. They voiced their defiant protests in no uncertain words. When prose seemed unsatisfactory, they did not hesitate to indulge in poetry. "Equally stirring and equally essential in the properly conducted strike of the day," says one writer, "was the verse." That it lent

John B. Andrews and W. D. P. Bliss. *History of Women in Trade Unions,* Vol. X of *Report on the Condition of Woman and Child Wage-Earners in the United States.* Washington, D.C.: U.S. Government Printing Office, 1911.

itself most readily to the needs of the hour at the time of the Dover strike is apparent from the question: Who among the Dover girls could—

> Ever bear,
> The shocking fate of slaves to share?

A second strike among the cotton-factory girls of Dover occurred during February and March, 1834. It was caused by a reduction of wages and involved 800 women. The New York Transcript asserted that the girls had formed a trade union for mutual support, in spite of the "conditions on which help is hired by the Cocheco Manufacturing Company." This firm on February 28, 1834, advertised for "five hundred females." One condition required applicants to sign an agreement to work for such wages "as the company may see fit to pay and be subject to the fines imposed by the company." Other clauses bound them to accept monthly payments of wages and to forfeit two weeks' pay if they left their employment without first giving a fortnight's notice and securing the permission of an agent of the company.

The most significant requirement, however, was as follows: "We also agree not to be engaged in any combination whereby the work may be impeded or the company's interest in any work injured; if we do, we agree to forfeit to the use of the company the amount of wages that may be due to us at the time." This effort to prevent the spread of trade unionism among the women is the first instance of which we have record where employers forced upon women employees the dreaded "ironclad oath." Its use at this early date indicates that working women had made much greater progress toward organization than has been generally supposed.

To the advertisements of the company announcing employment for "five hundred females" the strikers replied next day as follows:

> GIRLS ON HAND.—There are now five hundred of us in the town of Dover, who are now at work for ourselves, but might possibly answer the wants and wishes of the "Cocheco Manufacturing Company, at Dover, N.H.," excepting that we will not consent to work at the reduced tariff of wages to take place on the 15th of March instant, or even one mill less than the wages lately given. We would just say to our sex in the country that we are not to live here long without plenty of work.

A New York daily trade-union paper, in republishing this manifesto, added:

   We beseech the farmers of our country not to permit their daughters
to go into the mills at all, in any place under the present regulations,
if they value the life and health of their children.

The Dover factory girls on this occasion, probably chastened by
public disapproval of their conduct of five years before, "instead of
forming processions and parading the streets, to the amusement of a
crowd of gaping idlers, confined themselves for the most part within
their respective boarding houses." They did hold in the courthouse,
however, probably on March 1, a meeting composed of between 600
and 700 girls, and unanimously adopted a series of strong resolutions.
In these resolutions they declared they would never consent to work at
the reduced wages, and viewed "with feelings of indignation" the
efforts of their employers to place upon those least able to bear it the
effect of the "unusual pressure of the time."
   They voted to raise a fund to defray the expenses of those who did
not have the means to return to their homes, and appointed a committee of 12 to communicate the result of the meeting to the girls employed in the factories at Great Falls, Newmarket, and Lowell. Finally,
they arranged to have the proceedings of the meeting published in the
Dover Gazette and New Hampshire Globe "and in all other papers
printed in this State whose editors are opposed to the system of slavery
attempted to be established in our manufacturing establishments."

PITTSBURG AND ALLEGHENY, PA.

   In the summer of 1844 the factory girls across the river in Allegheny
quit work rather than submit to a reduction of wages. And again, on
September 15, 1845, the operatives in five cotton mills in Allegheny
struck for a ten-hour day. There were some riotous demonstrations
during the early days of the strike, but on October 20 work was resumed, with the understanding that agitation for the ten-hour system
might continue without interference, and that the employers would
grant the demand when it had been complied with in other sections of
the country.
   All requests of the western workers for improved conditions were
met by the Pittsburg and Allegheny employers with the supposedly
final statement that they were powerless to reduce hours or raise wages
on account of the still less favorable conditions of employment in New
England. But this did not satisfy the factory girls west of the moun-
tains. They began to ask their sisters in New England to join with them
in the interest of the common struggle for shorter hours. As a result of
their agitation the factory girls of Manchester in mass meeting resolved

to cooperate with their sisters at Pittsburg and Allegheny, and concurred in the proposal "to declare their independence of the oppressive manufacturing power" on July 4, 1846, unless the ten-hour system was adopted. Funds were raised and conventions were held to further this purpose.

But the Pittsburg employers promptly closed their factories against any who refused to work under the twelve-hour system, and widely advertised that they would keep them closed or move the machinery out of the State.

Several weeks passed, and then on the last day of the month about 100 operatives agreed to work twelve hours. In the words of the Pittsburg Commercial Journal, "The factory opened, steam was got up, and the machinery started." The reporter's account of what next happened is so vivid that it will bear repeating:

We visited the scene of excitement at about 12 o'clock, M. * * * A dense mass of men, women, and children were collected around the front gate of the factory—facing toward the Allegheny—with the avowed intention of taking summary vengeance on the delinquents who had gone to work, so soon as they should get out for dinner.

Tired of waiting, and their passions constantly becoming more excited—demonstrations toward breaking open the gate were at last made.

An axe was procured, and a woman seizing hold of it commenced hewing away with true Amazonian vehemence and vigor.

The gate was of pine, and would soon have yielded to the energetic exertions of this young woman but for the protection afforded by an iron bar, which we were told secured it on the inside.

She at length desisted, wearied with the labor, and a man took the axe and threw it over the fence into the yard of the factory. * * *

At this juncture, a loud shout on Isabella street announced the occurrence of a new subject for excitement in that quarter. * * *

A portion of the crowd remaining, as if to guard the main gate, the greater number of them immediately proceeded to the new scene of action. The whole street * * * was soon densely thronged. * * *

Suddenly a cry arose that several women and children had been scalded from the engine room, and yells of vengeance were heard on all sides. * * *

As if by common consent, a rush was made to storm the factory. A platoon of women were in front as a sort of forlorn hope, followed by a storming party of men, who kept up a continuous cheer as the whole column moved on to the assault.

The scene at this moment was exciting in the extreme. The girls in front acted for the time as pioneers and commenced tearing away the boards from the fence so as to make a breach, through which their storming columns could enter.

Protected by a hurricane of brickbats, mud, and stones, these warriors made great progress, and in a short time a breach was made which the general in command (whoever he was) pronounced practicable. "Now, men!" "hurra!" "give 'em h—ll!" and yells utterly indescribable by any combination of letters, announced the onset upon this second Molina del Rey.

The sheriff of the county, John Forsyth, esq.; the owners of the mill, clerks, and a detachment of the Allegheny police were inside and they prepared manfully to resist the attack.

Placing themselves opposite the breach they awaited the charge.

One moment of calm preceded the bursting of the storm, and then a general volley of brickbats and bludgeons commenced the grand movement of the day.

The authorities made a gallant stand, but in vain. In a minute they began to waver, and finally broke and retired from the disastrous encounter. * * *

The scene of uproar and confusion inside the yard now baffled description.

Stones and brickbats were flying in every direction and the windows in that part of the building were soon entirely destroyed. * * *

At this juncture it is said a man, who was on the fence, reached and struck a girl with a stick. In an instant the man was surrounded, and although he attempted escape he was very badly bruised and beaten. * * *

The battle was now over. No further resistance was attemped, and the insurgents held undisputed sway over the captured fortress; the works were silenced, the machinery stopped, and "Warsaw was conquered."

The operatives who had been employed abandoned their work.

At this moment a woman raised on the point of a pole a hat, which it was alleged had been captured from Mr. Kennedy, one of the owners, who was present with the sheriff when he attempted to resist the storming party. Loud cheers greeted this trophy of victory. * * *

We left the ground about 3 o'clock, when it appeared that the operatives had completely triumphed. The sheriff had abandoned the ground, as had also the police. The factory appeared to be completely in the power of the operatives, and they had it all their own way. * * *

We offer no comments upon the proceedings of yesterday. Our whole duty is discharged when we state the facts of the case. * * *

Toward the end of August all of the factories except one were in partial operation on the ten-hour system, but with a corresponding reduction of one-sixth in wages. The persistence of the women workers, however, is indicated in an item in the Commercial Journal three days later. "A large number of the female operatives in the Allegheny cotton factories," said this paper, "decline to go to work under the ten-hour system, unless at the same wages as under the twelve hours." But this last point was abandoned later. The adoption of the ten-hour day was regarded as "Victory No. 1" by the girls, who predicted that wages would be raised to the twelve-hour rate "after the next legislature perfects the law and the manufacturers discover that they can afford it."

WOMEN'S ORGANIZING went beyond spontaneous strikes toward the creation of continuous organization. One of the most ambitious efforts to create a union was the Lowell Female Labor Reform Association. Both more and less than a union, the association won support from outside the factories with its aggressive propaganda campaign, although it often could not achieve total support from the operatives themselves.

LABOR REFORM

The date of organization of the Lowell Female Labor Reform Association was January, 1845, and it apparently came into existence as a result of the agitation for shorter hours and higher wages that accompanied the strikes of cotton-mill operatives in the early forties. . . .

In her [Sarah Bagley's] official report to the convention [of the New England Workingmen's Association] she gave the membership of the union at Lowell as between four and five hundred. "But this we consider a small part of the work which has been accomplished," she said. "Since the last meeting of the workingmen's convention at Lowell our numbers have been daily increasing, our meetings generally well attended, and the real zeal of the friends of equal rights and justice has kindled anew. The humble efforts of a few females could not be expected to move the world in a day. But, God be praised! we have moved the minds of the community to think and to speak on the subject. This

John Andrews and W. D. P. Bliss. *History of Women in Trade Unions*, Vol. X of *Report on the Condition of Woman and Child Wage-Earners in the United States.* Washington, D.C.: U.S. Government Printing Office, 1911.

is truly encouraging. For when we can arouse the minds of men and women to a sense of their own individual rights, and cause them to think for themselves, then will they begin to act for themselves!" . . .

The Lowell union had already accomplished much in the work of propaganda. Not satisfied with securing thousands of signatures of factory operatives, who petitioned the legislature for a 10-hour day, prominent members of the union, including Miss Bagley, had gone before the Massachusetts legislative committee early in 1845 and testified as to the conditions in textile mills. This was the first American governmental investigation of labor conditions, and it was due almost solely to the petitions of the working women. They then complained of long hours of work, insufficient time for meals, and bad air, and although they did not at the time win all they asked, these organized working women were more influential than any other group of people in creating a public sentiment that from that time to this has made Massachusetts take the lead in protective legislation. . . .

The Lowell union succeeded in continuing this systematic effort to influence public opinion in favor of the factory girls. By newspaper articles, by "factory tracts," by public speeches, and by personal correspondence the officials kept their work before the public . . .

And in their work of publicity they did not hesitate to call public men to account for assailing or ignoring their movement. For instance, at a meeting of the union on April 1, 1845, they expressed, and later published, resolutions of indignation concerning the action of the committee on hours of labor in the Massachusetts legislature. Miss Bagley sarcastically suggested that in the association's next petition they ask the legislature to extend to the operatives the same protection given to animals and declared their condition would be greatly improved. Members of the union charged that the members of the committee in the legislature had been guilty of the grossest dishonesty in withholding from the legislature all the most important facts in the defense made by the union's delegates, and that they therefore regarded them as "mere corporate machines." . . .

The working women of Lowell extended their propaganda work to other parts of New England. In December, 1845, several members of the Lowell union attended a mass meeting of the factory operatives of Manchester, where "Miss Bagley, of Lowell, presented a constitution for their acceptance, accompanied with some remarks characterized throughout for their candor, truthfulness, and beauty, and evidently made a powerful impression. The constitution was adopted and the necessary officers chosen with energy and dispatch."

Thus the members of the Lowell union were personally extending their influence to other cities. . . .

Beginning at this time, the Lowell Voice of Industry, the leading New England labor weekly of this period, published for several months a "Female department," under the immediate supervision of the Lowell Female Labor Reform Association, and supported by contributions from the operatives of Lowell and other manufacturing towns. A little later the women of the Lowell union purchased the press and type of the Voice of Industry and continued the paper in the interests of labor reform.

The social side of labor unionism was not ignored by the women workers of Lowell. Evidence of this is found in newspaper notices of "gatherings" held from time to time. One of these was on St. Valentine's Day, 1846, at the City Hall. The announcement said: "Eminent and distinguished speakers will be present from abroad," and promised other entertainment, with a band of music, and a "rich treat of fruits and other eatables." The proceeds were to be appropriated to the cause of labor reform, and friends from Boston, Lynn, Woburn, Fitchburg, Worcester, Waltham, Andover, Newton, Manchester, etc., were invited. . . .

Encouraged by these ventures, other similar means of reaching the public ear were provided by the Lowell working women. They established, for example, an "Industrial Reform Lyceum," and secured, for the benefit of all who would hear, the best speakers in the country on subjects dealing with the labor reform movement.

By personal representation the Lowell union extended its influence still farther. It sent delegates to the conventions of the New England Workingmen's Association, and at each session they attracted favorable attention. . . .

After two years of continuous activity, the Lowell union, at the annual meeting for the election of officers in January, 1847, changed its name and constitution. They had long felt the need of something that would make a more definite appeal to the factory operatives. They wanted a form of organization that would "appeal to their self-love as well as to their higher natures." They therefore changed the name of the union to "The Lowell Female Industrial Reform and Mutual Aid Society." They amended the constitution to provide for an initiation fee of 50 cents and weekly dues of not less than 6 cents, which together with fines for nonattendance was to create a sick fund. No member was to be eligible to the benefits of the sick fund until she had paid dues for three months, whereupon she might receive not less than $2 nor more than $5 a week for not longer than four weeks, except upon special order by the board of directors.

In the new preamble they said: "We feel that by our mutual united action we can accomplish much which shall tell for the progress of industrial reform—the elevation and cultivation of mind and morals, the comfort and relief of destitute and friendless females in this busy city." Idealism sought support in a system of benefits. Unionism was becoming more practical. . . .

IN THE 1840s women workers were in the leadership of labor militancy in the United States. In both their efforts at organizing and their critique of the factory system, they were able to mount opposition that was extremely threatening to the factory owners. Thus, for example, the owner-influenced and partially financed paper, *The Lowell Offering*, refused to publish the following letter, which was printed instead as a pamphlet by the Lowell Female Labor Reform Association, a labor organization formed by the Lowell mill workers.

It is significant that this strong attack on "wage slavery" offers among its grievances that the workers have no time for "moral, religious or intellectual culture"; that the workers will make poor mothers; that the nation will be weakened. These grievances reflect traditional values, values of educated, once prosperous Yankees— those who still dominated the work force of the textile factories in the 1840s.

FACTORY LIFE

THE EVILS OF FACTORY LIFE. NUMBER ONE

Among the first which we shall notice, is the tendency it has, at the present time, to destroy all love of order and practice in domestic affairs. It is a common remark, that by the time a young lady has worked in a factory one year, she will lose all relish for the quiet, fireside comforts of life, and the neatness attendant upon order and precision. The truth is, time is wanting, and opportunity, in order to cultivate the mind and form good habits. All is hurry, bustle and

Julianna. "Factory Life As It Is, By An Operative." Lowell, Mass.: Lowell Female Labor Reform Association, 1845. We are indebted to Lise Vogel for this excerpt.

confusion in the street, in the mill, and in the overflowing boarding house. If there chance to be an intelligent mind in that crowd which is striving to lay up treasures of knowledge, how unfavorably it is situated! Crowded into a small room, which contains three bed and six females, all possessing the "without end" tongue of woman, what chance is there for *studying?* and much less so for thinking and reflecting? . . .

Let us look forward into the future, and what does the picture present to our imagination! Methinks I behold the self same females occupying new and responsible stations in society. They are now wives and mothers! But oh! how deficient in everything pertaining to those holy, *sacred* names! Behold what disorder, confusion and disquietude reigns, where quiet, neatness and calm serenity should sanctify and render almost like heaven the home of domestic union and love! Instead of being qualified to rear a family, — to instruct them in the great duties of life — to cultivate and unfold the intellect — to imbue the soul in the true and living principles of right and justice — to teach them the most important of all lessons, the art of being *useful* members in the world, ornaments in society and blessings to all around them, — *they,* themselves, have need to be instructed in the *very first* principles of living well and thinking right. Incarcerated within the walls of a factory, while as yet mere children — drilled there from five till seven o'clock, year after year — thrown into company with all sorts and descriptions of minds, dispositions and intellects, without counsellor or friends to advise — far away from a watchful mother's tender care or father's kind instruction — surrounded on all sides with the vain ostentation of fashion, vanity and light frivolity — beset with temptations without, and the carnal propensities of nature within, what *must,* what *will* be the natural, rational result? What but ignorance, misery, and *premature decay* of both *body* and *intellect?* Our country will be but one great hospital filled with worn out operatives and colored slaves! Those who marry, even, become a curse instead of a help-meet to their husbands, because of having broken the laws of God and their own physical natures, in these modern prisons (alias palaces,) in the gardens of Eden! It has been remarked by some writer that the mother educates the man. Now, if this be a truth, as we believe it is, to a very great extent, what, we would ask, are we to expect, the same system of labor prevailing, will be the mental and intellectual character of the future generations of New England? What but a race weak, sickly, imbecile, both mental and physical? A race fit only for corporation tools and time-serving slaves?

Nobility of America! — producers of all the luxuries and comforts of life! will you not *wake up* on this subject? Will you sit supinely down and let the drones in society fasten the yoke of tyranny, which is already fitted to your necks so cunningly that you do not feel it but slightly, — will you, I say suffer them to rivet that yoke upon you, which has crushed and is crushing its millions in the old world to earth; yea, to starvation and death? Now is the time to answer this all-important question. Shall we not hear the response from every hill and vale, "EQUAL RIGHTS, or death to the corporations"? God grant it, is the fervent prayer of

JULIANNA

Lowell, October, 1845

JOURNEY

MIGRATION WITHIN the United States brought its own kind of anguish for women, in which loneliness was combined with great physical hardship and danger. Many women moving slowly westward in their covered wagons kept diaries in which they spoke more openly about these feelings than perhaps their husbands knew. But it is likely that many of these women were expressing fears which their men shared but which were too deeply conditioned to express.

The following is excerpted from an as yet unpublished manuscript based on many diaries and reminiscences of women on the Oregon Trail.

WOMEN ON THE OREGON TRAIL

Today we started across the dreary plains. Sad are the thoughts that steal over the reflecting mind. I am leaving my home, my early friends and associates never to see them again, exchanging the disinterested solicitude of fond friends for the cold and unsympathetic friendship of strangers. Shall we all reach the "El Dorado" of our hopes or shall one of our number be left and our graves be in the dreary wilderness, our bodies uncoffined and unknown remain there in solitude? Hard indeed that heart be that does not drop a tear as these thoughts roll across the mind.

When Elizabeth Goltra, who wrote this diary entry as she was leaving for Oregon from Kansas in 1853, speaks of the sad thoughts that steal over the reflecting mind, she is very specific and detailed. When she speaks of the destination of the travelers she is abstract and even slightly sarcastic. The entry conveys a kind of skeptical distance from

Amy Kesselman. "Diaries and Reminiscences of Women on the Oregon Trail: A Study in Consciousness." Unpublished essay. The major sources of information in this essay are unpublished manuscripts from the collection of the Oregon Historical Society.

the dreams which activated the westward movement. This tone is echoed in many women's trial diaries. It illustrates what Charles Moore, a pioneer of 1852, commented on in his address to the Oregon Pioneer Association in 1904 when he asserted that "For the average woman there was an utter lack of incentive. It was a forced and cheerless march to the promised home on the frontiers of civilization.

As David Potter suggested in his article "American Women and the American Character," the promised land toward which the pioneers were heading was not a land of opportunity for women.

> . . . for American women, as individuals, opportunity began pretty much where the frontier left off. For opportunity lay in access to independent employment, and the employments of the frontier were not primarily accessible to women.

Most women were embarking on a journey full of risks and uncertainties, not in the hopes of fulfilling their dreams but, as illustrated by the following letter in the *National Intelligencer* in 1843, as accessories to their husbands.

> You of the old states cannot readily conceive the every-day sort of business an 'old settler' makes of selling his improvements, hitching the horses to the big wagon, and with his wife and children, swine and cattle, pots and kettles, and household goods, starting a journey of hundreds of miles to find and make a new home. . . .

> Pull off your coat, roll up your sleeves
> For Jordan is a hard road to travel, I believe.

This song extract, jotted down in the diary of Enoch Conyers, a young man traveling with his relatives, expresses an enthusiasm for the challenges of the trip which is uniformly missing from women's diaries. Instead, we find recurrent anxiety and preoccupation with death. It was women who noticed the graves along the way and consistently reported death and illness on the trains. Sarah Cranstone, a pioneer of 1851, counted every single grave which she passed and recorded them every day. When she doesn't see many graves she explains in her diary that they would probably see more if they weren't traveling on the river bottom. "It makes it seem very gloomy to us to see so many of the emigrants buried on the plains," remarked Cecilia Mc Millen Adams. Mrs. Lodisa Frizzel, en route to California in 1852, remarked when halfway to her destination that the journey "tires the soul." She went on to say:

That this journey is tiresome no one will doubt, that it is perilous, the deaths of many will testify, and the heart has a thousand misgivings, and the mind is tortured with anxiety, and often as I passed the freshly made graves, I have glanced at the side boards of the wagon, not knowing how soon it might serve as the coffin for some one of us; but thanks for the kind care of Providence, we were favored more than some others.

A strong element of the sense of apprehension which women's diaries express is the feeling of helplessness. Women felt themselves to be dependent on chance, Providence, and the wisdom of their leaders. As participants in a venture designed and led by men, they had little or no control over the many factors which might determine whether they lived or died. Women's trail diaries illustrate, in an extreme form, a fact of female experience both yesterday and today: powerlessness and uncertainty interact to breed perennial anxiety.

. . . When Maria Belshaw remarked on passing through an attractive part of the countryside, "It's quite pleasant—still give me the home I left in the state of Indiana," it is not Indiana to which she is referring so much as home and community. What community meant for women was primarily the association with other women; the social life centered around church and visiting, in which women shared experience and wisdom. Women attempted to re-create this sense of community on the trail. "During the day," recalled Mrs. Haun,

We women folk visited from wagon to wagon or congenial friends spent an hour walking ever westward, and talking over our home life 'back in the states' telling of the loved ones left behind; voicing our hopes for the future in the far west and even whispering, a little friendly gossip of pioneer life. High teas were not popular but tatting, knitting, crocheting, exchanging receipts for cooking beans or dried apples or swapping food for the sake of variety kept us in practice of feminine occupations and diversions.

"At night," remembered Mary Warren, "the women would sit around the fire and visit while the men would take the oxen to grass and water. As soon as the fire was big enough to furnish coals all the women would steam up their clay pipes. Everyone smoked then and the tobacco was our own home grown brand."

But while women's reminiscences recall the successful aspects of social life, the diaries more often record the loneliness of women who left close friends behind. In an age without telephones, highways and airplanes, closeness depended on geographical proximity. The relation-

ships which women had developed in the small farming communities
from which they came were terminated by the trip west. The finality of
separation from friends became more of a reality each day on the trail.
In frequent expressions of grief over the friendships they left behind
women communicated a profound sense of loss, loneliness and dis-
orientation.

The following poem fragment was the first diary entry written by
Agnes Stewart:

To Martha

Oh friend, I am gone forever, I cannot see you now
The damp comes to my brow
Thou wert my first and only friend, the hearts best treasure thou;
Yet in the shades of troubled sleep my mind can see you now,
And many a time I shut my eyes and look into the past.
Ah, then I think how different our fates in life were cast,
I think how oft we sat and played
Upon some mossy stone,
How we would act and do when we were big girls grown
And we would always live so near
That I could always come to you,
And you would come to me, and this we would always do
When sickness came in fevered brow and burning through each vein. . . .

WHEN THE TRIP was over, the hardships had just begun. Migrant
women were rarely spoiled or idle; most of them had been accustomed to hard work in the European or eastern towns from which
they had come. But life on the "frontier," as the whites called it, was
more laborious for women because they had to do without even the
simplest conveniences. Here Harriet Taylor Upton, a suffragist born
in 1853 in Portage County, Ohio, recollects her early education in the
oppression of women.

RECOLLECTIONS OF A
PIONEER WOMAN

. . . Men had so much to do outdoors that they couldn't bother with
things in the house, and women were in great despair over the incon-

veniences. One sturdy mother became so enraged because her husband procrastinated in building an oven, saying that she could no longer bake bread and do all her cooking in one big iron kettle, that she fashioned some bricks of mud and built an oven which was such a success that people travelled out of their way to see it in action. . . . When these early housewives got their ovens to going, they would bake fifty mince pies at a time, put them in a cold room, often "the parlor chamber" as the guest room was called, where they would freeze and would bring them out as occasion required, reheating them by the fire. The woman who made the oven of bricks once had it full of pies when the Indians came along in the night and carried them all off. . . .

Grandfather approved of my energy. I used to follow him around as he worked, sometimes stumbling along behind the plow, hoping he would let me drive. Grandmother always made me remove my dirty shoes on the porch after I had been on one of these plowing expeditions. I drove the hay rake occasionally, but was not a real success at it. I grew so excited under the responsibility that I would forget to release the hay at the proper time. Hours I have sat in the barn with him as he thrashed out the wheat with a hand flail. . . . Then the straw would be forked up, the wheat and the chaff scraped together and later put through a machine called a fanning mill, where the chaff was separated from the grain. I was often allowed to turn the wheel which worked the machine. It was easy to do, but it was a dirty job and my grandmother required me to brush myself and comb my hair before I could go inside the house, and even then bits of straw would remain in my hair for days.

I helped to churn and carried water to the men in the field during harvest time, and fed the chickens and rode into the barn from the field on the hay load. I cut and twisted lamp lighters to be used in the winter to save matches, and sewed carpet rags, and enjoyed doing all these things. I have little respect for the person who invented a do-less Heaven.

Perhaps I like the sugar making time the best of all seasons on the farm. My spring vacations were always spent there. . . . I spent most of my waking hours and some of my sleeping ones in the sugar bush, as the sugar camp was then called. My uncles were patient with me and allowed me to follow them in their work all day. When they drove through the woods gathering up the sap from the buckets hung to the

"Random Recollections of Harriet Taylor Upton." Typescript in Schlesinger Library, Cambridge, Mass.

trees and pouring it into casks which were on a sort of sledge with 6-inch boards for runners, I would romp along at their side, falling down at times, drinking out of the full pails at others and riding on the vehicle when I cared to do so. . . .

Just as my grandfather allowed me to run the fanning machine to free the chaff from the wheat, so my grandmother let me reel the yarn she had spun from the spindle to the reeling machine. . . .

Grandmother dried berries, corn, pumpkin; raised her babies, and took into her family anyone unfortunate in the neighborhood. She nursed the sick at their homes when she could leave her own; and when she could not, she brought the well children or the convalescent to her home and cared for them. . . .

After a long hard day, she would gather me in her arms and croon me to sleep, for she could not carry a tune. I thought she was the most beautiful old woman I had ever seen, especially when she wore a cap. Regardless of what she was doing — washing, baking or churning, — she stopped work each morning at ten o'clock, sat down, opened her Bible and read that which her eyes first fell upon. She believed she was led to these verses. Her plain face glowed with love. To be near her was to receive a benediction. She had great sorrows, among them the death of her only daughter, her youngest child, but she never complained. When other women were lamenting about how hard they worked or what troubles they had, she would give a sort of a grunt of disapproval and say, "Oh, shucks!" . . .

CONTROVERSY

THE INCREASE in women's employment and the debate this engenders is always exacerbated by wars. The extraordinary labors of women in the Civil War were for the most part temporary, and after the peace most returned to their prewar occupations and status. This was not the case, however, in the field of nursing. The American Civil War was to American nursing what the Crimean War had been a decade earlier to European nursing: the wartime experiences permanently changed the conventional view of nursing as improper for women to the view that it was a profession not only allowable for women, but one for which they were uniquely suited. This rapid change in ideology, parallel to that of three decades later about clerical work, reveals how practical, really, are the ideologies about what women are suited for. Wherever women are needed economically it is quickly decided that they are biologically or even spiritually destined.

This selection is an example of the debate about women in nursing early in the Civil War from the point of view of the medical profession.

THE NURSING DEBATE

[To the Editor of the *American Medical Times*]

Our women appear to have become almost wild on the subject of hospital nursing. We honor them for their sympathy and humanity. Nevertheless, a man who has had experience with women nurses among male surgical cases, cannot shut his eyes to the fact that they, with the best intentions in the world, are frequently a useless annoyance. Cases are continually occurring in male surgical wards of such a character as

American Medical Times, July 18, 1861, pp. 25–26, 30, quoted in Anne L. Austin, *History of Nursing Source Book*. New York: Putnam, 1957.

require strong arms, and attentions which any reasonable medical man is loath to exact from female nurses. Imagine a delicate refined woman assisting a rough soldier to the close-stool, or supplying him with a bed-pan, or adjusting the knots on a T-bandage employed in retaining a catheter in position, or a dozen offices of a like character which one would hesitate long before asking a female nurse to perform, but which are frequently and continually necessary in a military hospital. Besides this, women, as a rule, have not the physical strength necessary. For example—a man having gunshot wounds of grave severity affecting the lower extremities, with perhaps incontinence of urine, or diarrhoea, would not improbably be attacked with bed-sores if not kept scrupulously clean. Should the soft parts of the back begin to ulcerate, local attention becomes doubly necessary. The patient, under these circumstances, requires often to be lifted up carefully, and bodily, so as not to alter the comparative position of his limbs to his body. To do this properly, at least *four* strong men are required, who, stationed two at the shoulders and two at the hips (one hand from each lower assistant steadying the thigh and leg of that side), can thus raise the man steadily and carefully. A fifth would not be out of place in supporting the feet, while the medical attendant washes the excoriated parts, applies the needed dressings, and throws upon the surface of the bed a clean sheet.

Women, in our humble opinion, are utterly and decidedly unfit for such service. They can be used, however, as the regular administrators of the prescribed medicines, and in delicate, soothing attentions which are always so grateful to the sick, and which at the same time none know so well how to give as do noble, sensible, tenderhearted women.

But as hospital nurses for wounded men, they are by nature, education, and strength totally unfitted, i.e. when we consider *all the duties* surgical nurses are called upon to perform. In conclusion, it may be well to state that a surgeon on duty with troops, by showing proper interest in the men, without allowing himself to be humbugged by them, will gain their affection as well as respect.

                                                                S. G.

THE ENTRANCE of women into the wage-labor force on a large scale was not only a new phenomenon, it also appeared to many as weird, unwomanly, unnatural and unfortunate. The notion that women belonged in homes, doing child care, husband care and home production, was very powerful, and it was by no means limited to the upper classes. Even men of the labor movement, even those who understood that women went to work out of economic necessity, still argued that this need should be met in ways that permitted women to stay home. The trade-union men usually saw themselves without embarrassment as the natural protectors of women, and hence felt inadequate, as if their protective ability had failed, when women took jobs. They also feared for their jobs and worried that women in the labor force would depress wages.

This attitude led to women's exclusion from male-led unionizing activities. One exception was the National Labor Union (NLU), which in the 1860s was admitting women to full membership. The NLU was a federation of trade unionists, reformers and ten-hours-movement agitators. The NLU's head, William H. Sylvis, supported woman suffrage and wrote occasionally for Elizabeth Cady Stanton's and Susan Anthony's feminist newspaper, *Revolution*. Nevertheless, the NLU saw women's participation in the labor movement as an unfortunate necessity; the ultimate solution remained bettering the economic condition of workingmen so that they could afford to support their women at home.

A UNION'S POSITION

. . . The subject of female labor is one that demands our attention and most earnest consideration. There are many reasons why females should not labor outside of the domestic circle. Being forced into the field, the factory, and the workshop, (and they do not go there from choice, but because necessity compels them,) they come in direct competition with men in the great field of labor; and being compelled of necessity, from their defenceless condition, to work for low wages, they exercise a vast influence over the price of labor in almost every department. If they received the same wages that men do for similar work, this objection would in a great measure disappear. But there is another reason, founded upon moral principle and common humanity, far above and beyond this, why they should not be thus employed. Woman was created and intended to be man's companion, not his slave. Endowed as she is with all her loveliness and powers to please, she exercises an almost unlimited influence over the more stern and unbending disposition of man's nature. If there are reasons why man should be

James C. Sylvis, ed. *Life, Speeches, Labors and Essays of William H. Sylvis*. Philadelphia: Claxton, Remsen and Haffelfinger, 1872.

educated, there are many more and stronger reasons why woman should receive the soundest and most practical mental and moral training. She was created to be the presiding deity of the home circle, the instructor of our children, to guide the tottering footsteps of tender infancy in the paths of rectitude and virtue, to smooth down the wrinkles of our perverse nature, to weep over our shortcomings, and make us glad in the days of adversity, to counsel, comfort, and console us in our declining years.

> "Woman's warm heart and gentle hand, in God's eternal plan,
>   Were formed to soften, soothe, refine, exalt, and comfort man."

Who is there among us that does not know and has not felt the powerful influences of a good and noble woman? one in whom, after the busy toil and care of the day are past, we can confide our little secrets and consult upon the great issues of life. These, sir, are my views upon this question. This I believe to be the true and divine mission of woman, this her proper sphere; and those men who would and do turn her from it are the worst enemies of our race, the Shylocks of the age, the robbers of woman's virtue; they make commerce of the blood and tears of helpless women, and merchandise of souls. In the poverty, wretchedness, and utter ruin of their helpless victims, they see nothing but an accumulating pile of gold. In the weeping and wailing of the distressed, they hear nothing but a "metallic ring." To the abolition of this wrong imposed upon the tender sex should be devoted every attribute of our nature, every impulse of our heart, and every energy and ability with which we are endowed. . . .

THE ORGANIZED feminist movement in the United States started in the 1840s. Composed primarily of prosperous Yankee women, the feminists' concern with women's work was at first focused on trying to open higher education and the professions to women. One of the exceptions to this narrowness of concern was Caroline Dall. Despite her own relatively upper-class background, her book *Women's Right to Labor*, written in 1859, argued that prejudices against women's wage labor affected women of all classes. Her bias as a privileged woman is clear in this selection; still, it seems more important that she has transcended that bias to a great extent and seriously explores the interconnections between the situation of wealthy and poor women.

A FEMINIST'S VIEW

. . . I ask for woman, then, free, untrammelled access to all fields of labor; and I ask it, first, on the ground that she needs to be fed, and that the question which is at this moment before the great body of working women is "death or dishonor:" for lust is a better paymaster than the mill-owner or the tailor, and economy never yet shook hands with crime. . . .

If, in my correspondence with employers last winter, one man told me with pride that he gave from eight to fifty cents for the making of pantaloons, including the heaviest doeskins, he *forgot* to tell me what he charged his customers for the same work. Ah! on those bills, so long unpaid, the eight cents sometimes rises to thirty, and the fifty cents *always* to a dollar or a dollar and twenty-five cents.

The most efficient help this class of workwomen could receive would be the thorough adoption of the cash system, and the establishment of a large workshop in the *hands of women* consenting to moderate profits, and superintended by those whose position in society would win respect for labor. When I said, six months ago, that ten Beacon-street women, engaged in honorable work, would do more for this cause than all the female artists, all the speech-making and conventions, in the world, I was entirely in earnest. . . .

I consider the question of intellectual ability settled. The volumes of science, mathematics, general literature, &c., which women have given to the world, without sharing to the full the educational advantages of man, seem to promise that they shall outstrip him here, the moment they have a fair start. But I go farther, and state boldly, that women have, from the beginning, done the hardest and most unwholesome work of the world in all countries, whether civilized or uncivilized; and I am prepared to prove it. I do not mean that rocking the cradle and making bread is as hard work as any, but that women have always been doing man's work, and that all the outcry society makes against work for women is not to protect *women*, but a certain class called *ladies*. . . .

In Ohio, last year, about thirty girls went from farm to farm, hoeing,

Caroline Dall. *Women's Right to Labor*. Boston: Walker, Wise and Co., 1860.

ploughing, and the like, for sixty-two and a half cents a day. At Media, in Pennsylvania, two girls named Miller carry on a farm of three hundred acres; raising hay and grain, hiring labor, but working mostly themselves. These women are not ignorant: they at one time made meteorological observations for an association auxiliary to the Smithsonian Institute. But labor attracts them, as it would many women if they were not oppressed by public opinion.

"In New York," writes a late correspondent of the "Lily," "I saw women performing the most menial offices, — carrying parcels for grocers, and trunks for steamboats. They often sweep the crossings in muddy weather; and I once saw one carrying brick and mortar for a mason."

Several women last winter, and one or two very young girls, gave evidence of bodily strength by skating from Lowell to Lawrence, with a head wind; and one or two made the ten miles in forty minutes. . . .

I have shown you that a very large number of women are compelled to self-support; that the old idea, that all men support all women, is an absurd fiction. . . .

Plenty of employments are open to them; but all are underpaid. They will never be better paid till women of rank begin to work for money, and so create a respect for woman's labor; and women of rank will never do this till American men feel what all American men profess, — a proper respect for Labor, as God's own demand upon every human soul, — and so teach American women to feel it. How often have I heard that every woman willing to work may find employment! The terrible reverses of 1837 taught many men in this country that they were "out of luck:" how absurd, then, this statement with regard to women! . . .

Women want work for all the reasons that men want it. When they see this, and begin to do it faithfully, you will respect their work, and pay them for it. . . .

1865~1890

By defeating the slave system and defending the territorial unity of the United States, union victory in the Civil War strengthened the foundation for a powerful industrial economy. During the war, northern businessmen obtained, sometimes through the use of graft, windfall profits, favorable legislation and governmental financial support. Men frequently called "robber barons"—Carnegie, Harriman, Cooke, Morgan and Rockefeller—seized and exploited the natural resources of the country. Forcing out their competitors, these capitalists used a variety of business devices from pools to trusts to force out their competition and gain control of the major industries; by 1879 Rockefeller controlled 90 percent of the American refining industry.

Industrialization required an infrastructure to move raw materials and finished goods. Massive railroad building was undertaken; between the Civil War and 1893, 150,000 miles of track were laid by underpaid workers. Private railroad companies received outright land grants from federal and local governments and made enormous profits.

New cities like Pittsburgh arose based on industry rather than commerce or access to the sea. In 1860 less than one-quarter of Americans lived in a city or town; by 1890 nearly one-third were urban dwellers. Nevertheless, two-thirds to three-quarters of the country still lived in small settlements or rural communities. Westward expansion continued as families took advantage of homesteading acts. At the same time, the continued mechanization and improvement in farm equipment meant agriculture became increasingly capitalized.

Economic depressions became a constant feature of capitalism. In the 1870s banks and businesses failed, unemployment rose and wage cuts were instituted, and small businessmen and artisans were often forced to forfeit their independent businesses to the corporate giants. Depression affected agriculture as well. In the South, slavery and the plantation system had been replaced by a system of tenancy and share-cropping which left farmers perpetually in debt, with few crops for themselves. In the South and Midwest, droughts, single-crop dependence, market fluctuations, bank foreclosures on mortgages and high rates for railroad shipping storage led to anger among the farmers and small businessmen. They fought the encroaching business interests through organizations like the Grange, the Farmers Alliance and the Agricultural Wheel.

Workers also fought deteriorating conditions and wage cuts. The 1870s and 1880s were years of upheavals, frequent strikes, lockouts, street demonstrations and class violence. Although federal, state and private militias were called in to put down the uprisings, the workers sometimes gained support from local newspapers, sympathetic artisans, merchants and clergy. Even in the depths of the depressions, some workers were able to prevent wage cuts and worsening conditions.

There was a growing feeling among workingpeople that America was no longer the land of opportunity. A labor paper in 1885 commented, "The Golden Age is indeed over—the age of Iron has taken its place. The iron law of necessity has taken the place of the Golden rule." Workers began to organize into national unions to fight these corporate interests.

During this period women continued to enter the ranks of the paid labor force. By 1870 one out of every four non-farm workers was a woman. The Civil War had expanded the occupations open to women, especially in office work, government service and retailing. Yet, in 1870, 70 percent of the women working were still domestics; 10 percent were in industrial employment, and of those nearly four-fifths were working in the garment trades. The average age of these employed women was twenty-three, and they began to work at fifteen. Nearly 80 percent of the women were native-born, although approximately 75 percent of them had foreign-born parents. Nearly 85 percent were single, and most contributed to the support of their families and lived with their parents. Their wages ranged from $4.05 a week in Atlanta to $6.91 in San Francisco, with an average of $5.25 a week. All over the country women's cheap labor was profitable to manufacturers. After Reconstruction a whole new industry developed in the South based on the cheap labor of women and children.

Class divisions especially among women became more and more visible during this period. Differences in dress, manners, speech and consumption patterns became more apparent. While the ideal "lady" was expected to be idle, delicate and asexual, the prosperous classes identified working-class women with rampant sexuality, prostitution and disease. These class divisions, attitudes and mores made it more difficult for working-class and wealthy women to cooperate. The domination of the prosperous women in the feminist movement contributed to the narrowing of the women's rights platform to the exclusive demand for the ballot.

For workingwomen the issue of importance was less the winning of the ballot than the improving of working conditions. They tried continuously to organize themselves. Cigar makers, tailoresses, seamstresses, umbrella sewers, textile workers, printers and laundresses formed local ephemeral groups. Although thirty national unions existed at the time, only two, the printers and the cigar makers, admitted women members. Many trade-union men assumed women's employment to be a temporary aberration or plot of the capitalists to undermine their wages. Keeping women out of the union was a way, they felt, to keep women out of the trade or to limit their participation. Women were important in the Knights of Labor, which had nearly 50,000 women members at its height. There were more men than women in the unions, but the bulk of the working class remained unorganized. Nevertheless, many thousands of women gained experience in labor and community struggles.

INDUSTRIALIZATION– THE PRICE

Women were recruited for factory labor not just by word of mouth or chance. At various times labor agents were sent on a commission basis into the countryside to find young women for the mills and factories. Often whole families would be recruited, or one or two members would leave and the others would hope to join them later.

The first letter is an example of the benevolent arrogance of the do-gooding upper-class lady helping the "hardworking and thrifty" members of the working class, in contrast to the second, which reflects the reality of the family the lady was trying to "help."

The third letter illustrates some of the many forms of working-class resistance to control and exploitation both by employers and labor agents.

[The *Putnam Patriot,* Putnam, Connecticut, October 10th, 1878]

Mr. Cumnock [hiring agent for Dwight]: Dear Sir: — I take the liberty of writing a line to you regarding a French family that has recently gone from this place . . . to your town, and are employed by your corporation. The name is Langevin. Mrs. Langevin is as brave and good a woman as she knows how to be, doing her *best* for the great family of eleven children; and as long-continued sickness and ill luck has reduced the family sorely, they certainly need all the encouragement humaneness can give them. Knowing by experience what shiftlessness and utter lack of sense and judgement is generally found among the class you much-tried manufacturers are compelled to employ, I only write to assure you that this family are really above the average of their class; and if any favor by way of good tenement, work, etc. lies in your gift, to assure such favor will not be thrown away in them. They are Protestants, and therefore the Catholic element is not

Papers of Dwight Manufacturing Company, Chicopee, Mass. Baker Library, Harvard University, Labor file.

disposed to be over friendly to them; and if Mrs. Langevin should ask for a change of tenement it will be because of this. Pardon my freedom in thus addressing you; and let my deep interest in the family be my excuse. I only wished to commend them to your favorable knowledge, from among the multitude of their class from whom so little is to be expected. The Langevin children are members of Rev. Mr. Best's Sunday school, and their mother writes me that they are much interested in it. It is solid Christianity to help those who are disposed to help themselves. Very respectfully, Mrs. E. C. Stone, wife of the Publisher of the *"Patriot."*

Chicopee May 6 79   Mr. Cumnock   Sir my daughter is said to have gone out of the mill without leave and i beleive it is so i am very sorry she disobeyed so much will you be so kind as to see the overseer and ask him to take her back i hope she will behave better in future if he does not want her himself if he will give her bill so she can get another job for we are poor and need her help i hope he will forgive her this time for my sake yours Mary Langevin

Chicopee, September/86
Mr. Cumnock
Dear Sir
I would like to let you know about a few french family living on Cabot St one of them Elizabeth Bonvill [sic] No. 23 she is one I brought from Cornwall and she told me that she had five to work in the mills and when she got here she only had two fit to work the oldest was sixteen and she tried to work herself in the cardroom but could not get along and then she left me and went and got a tenement on cabot St No 23 and Kept house for her two children and two of my boarders she took with her, and now five of the ten I brought from Canada lately she coaxed them away to live withe her and she charges them five dollars per month for the use of their rooms and they have to buy their own food and they owe me for their fare from Canada and four more that she helped to runaway from my house at twelve oclock at night and shiped them to Worcester, she is the cause that I loose so much money . . . she says it is good enough for me I have no right to go after so many people it makes them cut the wages down and I think that when the five she has with her now has enough money she will send them to some other place and I will have to loose all they owe me for their fares . . . she is always complaining that she can't make anything in this mill and they go in and out at any time they like after ten . . .

Mr. Duplessis No 17 Cabot St he has his house filled with boarders and some of them don't work in the mills and they like it better there because they can come in and out when they like after ten. . . .

TWO OF THE more common generalizations about women's work are that women's jobs all move from the home into the factory and that women always displace men with their "cheaper labor." But important exceptions to these beliefs, like many others about women's employment, are found when industry by industry case studies are made, as in this survey of the roles of women in cigar-making.

JOB DISPLACEMENT

The increased employment of women in cigar-making seems to indicate its tendency to develop into a "women's industry" and furnishes an interesting example of the industrial displacement of men by women. The history of the industry makes it of peculiar interest, because originally the women were displaced by the men, and in these later years, they have only come into their own again.

The manufacture of cigars in this country is an industry of nearly a century's growth, but it has not continuously throughout its history employed a large proportion of women. This is, at first, not easy to understand, for it has always been a trade for which women are seemingly better qualified than men. No part of the making of cigars is heavy work, and skill depends upon manual dexterity—upon delicacy and sensitiveness of touch. . . .

The preliminary process of "stripping," which includes "booking," is the preparation of the leaf for the hands of the cigar-maker. The large mid-rib is stripped out, and, if the tobacco is of the quality for making wrappers, the leaves are also "booked"—smoothed tightly across the knee and rolled into a compact pad ready for the cigar-maker's table. Even in the stripping-room there are different grades of work, all unskilled and all practically monopolized by women and girls.

Division of labor has been slow in making its way into cigar factories. The best cigar is still made by a single workman, and the whole

Edith Abbott. "Employment of Women in Industries: Cigarmaking—Its History and Present Tendencies." *Journal of Political Economy* 15 (January 1907) : 1–25.

process demands a high degree of skill. Slightly inferior cigars, however, can be made with "molds" by less skilled workmen.

Packing cigars is called a "trade by itself." Those of like color must be packed together, and only the experienced eye can detect the varying shades of the leaf. Packers are the aristocrats of the trade in most places, and get better pay even than cigar-makers, though it is difficult to see that their work really requires more skill or more training than "making." The packer stands at his work, while the maker seldom leaves his seat.

Originally cigar-making was one of the household industries, and in the early years of the century nearly the whole of the Connecticut tobacco crop was made by the farmers' wives and daughters into cigars known to the trade as "supers," "long mines," and "short sixes." These cigars were sometimes peddled by the women, but more frequently they were bartered at the country stores, where they served as a substitute for currency. All of the groceries and dry goods used by the family during the year were often paid for in this way and represented the exchange value of the "leisure hours" of the farmer's wife. Although these were very inferior cigars, they were sold pretty generally throughout New England. The passing of this early "homestead industry," which existed in Pennsylvania and other tobacco-growing states as well as in Connecticut, was very gradual; for the transition to the factory system did not, in cigar-making, involve the substitution of machine for hand-work, and farmers' wives continued to roll cigars until the imposition of the internal revenue tax—and even after that. Their cigars, however, did not compare favorably with the finer factory-made product, and as Connecticut tobacco grew in favor, it became unprofitable to use it for the cheaper grades of work. Household industry, therefore, furnished a gradually decreasing proportion of the total manufactured product. But, unlike most work that left the home, cigar-making had not finally passed into the factory; for it was to be established as a domestic industry on a much larger scale in the tenements of New York. Two questions are of interest at this point with regard to the history of the employment of women: Did they follow their work from the home to the factory? and, What was their part in the establishment of cigar-making as one of the early tenement industries?

Women undoubtedly worked in the earliest factories. What was possibly the first cigar factory in this country was established at Suffield, Conn., in 1810 and employed only women. In 1832 returns from ten cigar factories in Massachusetts showed 238 women, 48 men, and 9 children employed; but complete statistics for the period are not available. It was estimated that one-third of the persons employed at the trade in Connecticut in 1856 were women, and the census shows that 740 women were employed in 1860. . . .

But if the displacement of the woman cigar-maker is not easy to express statistically, the reason for it is not difficult to find. Cigar-making, as has been pointed out, is a highly skilled trade, and it was early discovered that among our immigrants were men able to make cigars that could compete with those imported from Germany and Spain. These immigrant cigar-makers who proved to have the superior workmanship that was indispensable to the development of the industry, took the places of the American women who had been formerly employed. The Cuban is said to have been the first male cigar-maker employed in this country, and as Spanish tobacco and Spanish-made cigars were in high favor, a large market was found for the Spanish cigars made here by Cuban workmen. Later expert workmen among immigrants from other countries became competitors of the Cuban, and among German immigrants especially were men of exceptional skill and experience in the trade. The woman cigar-maker almost disappeared during this time, and there are men, both cigar-makers and manufacturers, in New York who say that there was "not a woman in the trade," except in the unskilled work of stripping, "back of the seventies"; and a recent report of the commissioner of labor confirms this statement. . . .

The year 1869 begins a new period in the history of the industry. Since then three factors seem to have worked together to bring about a very rapid increase in the employment of women: (1) increased immigration from Bohemia, where women are exclusively employed in cigar factories; (2) the invention of machinery, which has made the skilled workman less necessary; (3) a feeling on the part of employers that women are more docile than men, and that a large proportion of women among the employees would mean fewer strikes.

The immigration of Bohemian women cigar-makers began in 1869, and meant the re-establishment of cigar-making as a household industry—but this time under the domestic rather than the handicraft system. The home-work which occupied the leisure of the Connecticut farmer's thrifty wife is clearly not to be compared with the home-work of the Bohemian immigrant in the New York slums. The New England women were independent producers. They owned their raw material, the homes in which they worked, and the finished product which they disposed of at their own convenience; the tenement women were helplessly dependent upon an employer who furnished the raw material, owned and marketed the product, and frequently charged them exorbitant rentals for the rooms in which they both lived and worked; they were merely hired wage-earners working for a single employer in their own homes instead of in his factory. The explanation of the home-work in both cases is found in the fact that cigar-making is peculiarly adapted for household manufacture, and for this reason it still exists, not only as a domestic industry, but as a lingering survival of handicraft. When the only machine required is a pair of wooden molds, it is possible for the workman to own his own tools and a pair of molds, purchase his tobacco in small quantities, and, by disposing of the product quickly, carry on his trade as his own master and without having any capital.

By 1877, the year of the "great strike" which was meant to abolish it, cigar-making as a tenement industry had become firmly established. It grew rapidly after 1869 and aroused the first determined protest against "unsanitary home-work." Its development was due to Bohemian women who had worked in cigar factories in their own country. It is said that the customary method of Bohemian immigration was for the women to come first, leaving the men at work in the fields. Five or six wives would come over together, work at cigar-making as they did in Bohemia, and send money back for their husbands' passage, and then "the entire united family would take up the manufacture of cigars, emulating the industry of the mother." At this time, too, came the introduction of the team system—a division of labor by which one person prepares the bundles and another rolls them. In Bohemia the men had worked only in the fields, and their wives taught them cigar-making at home after they came over. It was much easier, of course, for these men to learn the relatively unskilled work of "bunch-making" while their wives did the rolling than to learn how to make the whole cigar.

The decade, during which cigar-making established itself as a tenement industry, was also the decade of greatest prosperity in the history of the trade. It was surely a decade of extraordinary exploitation of immigrant labor. Large manufacturers acquired blocks of tenements, for which they charged excessive rentals to their employees, who frequently, too, found themselves obliged to pay high prices for groceries and beer at stores owned by the employer. The expense of maintaining a factory was thus made part of the employees' burden; and the wages of "strippers and bookers" were also saved to the manufacturer, for the tobacco was prepared in the homes by the workers themselves, or more often by their children. The system also proved an effective coercive measure, and the eviction of the tenement strikers by the landlord manufacturers in 1877 was one of the distressing features of the strike. It is difficult to make an exact statement either as to the extent of home-work or as to the number of women employed. It was estimated roughly that a majority of the cigars in New York were the product of tenement-house factories, and so large was the proportion of women at work in them that the newspapers and manufacturers referred to the strike, which was directed largely against the home-work system, as an attack on the employment of women and children. In 1882 a circular issued by the union estimated that between 3,500 and 3,750 persons were employed at cigar-making in tenement houses, and it seems reasonable to say that during the decade from 1870 to 1880 between two and three thousand women had engaged in cigar-making in their own homes.

The increased employment of women as a result of the introduction of machinery comes at a later stage in the history of the industry. So many unsuccessful machines were tried from time to time that it is not easy to fix any exact date as the period when machinery was first considered successful enough to be widely adopted. By 1887, however, several of the large factories had begun to use machines, and in 1888 we find machines with women operators taking the places of skilled cigar-makers who were on a strike in Philadelphia. . . . Statistics obtained in this investigation show that in nine open, or non-union, factories which had more than 4,000 employees, and in all but one of which machinery was used, 73.1 per cent. of the employees were women; while in eight union shops, which used no machinery, and employed only 527 persons, the proportion of women employed was only 36.1 per cent. It is important to note that the machine, the large factory, and the increased employment of women go together. . . .

In discussing further the tendency toward increased employment of women as a means of avoiding or ending strikes, some account may also be given of the relation of the women to the Cigar-Maker's Inter-national Union. The union was organized in 1851; and in 1867 the constitution was altered so that women and negroes, heretofore ex-cluded, became eligible to membership. In 1877 women were employed in large numbers to break the strike of that year. Several hundred girls were taught the trade, and employers went so far as to call the strike "a blessing in disguise," since it "offered a new employment for women and secured workers whose services may be depended on at low wages." In this same year, however, the Cincinnati cigar-makers struck successfully for the removal of all women from the workshops, and in some other cities similar strikes were inaugurated, but failed. In 1879 the president of the union announced that one of its aims would be "the regulation of female labor;" and in 1881 he strongly advised the unions, in view of the fact that the employment of women was constantly increasing, "to extend the right hand of brotherhood to them;" and added: "Better to have them with us than against us. . . . They can effect a vast amount of mischief outside of our ranks as tools in the hands of the employer against us." The president of the New York local in 1886 complained that Bohemian women were doing work "that men were formerly employed to do. They have driven the American workmen from our trade altogether. They work for a price that an American could not work for." In 1894 a president of the international union said: "We are confronted with child- and female labor to an alarming extent;" and in 1901, at a meeting of the American Federation of Labor, the cigar-makers asked for the passage of resolutions expressing opposition to the use of machinery in their trade and to the employment of women and children. The hostility of the union to women is not difficult to understand. The women seemed to be lowering a standard wage that the men, through organization, were trying to uphold. They had, moreover, the workingman's belief in the old "lump of labor" fallacy, and for every woman who was employed they saw "a man without a job." The union has, however, stood squarely for the same wage scale for both men and women, while in England the union maintains a woman's scale that is 25 per cent. lower than the men's. As in other industries, a much smaller proportion of the women than of the men in the trade are members of the union, and the women seldom attend the meetings, and take small part in the proceedings when they do.

ONE OF THE worst forms of exploitation of working-class women in the nineteenth century was the prostitution industry, which was patronized by men of all classes. Its size and prevalence in midcentury America was enormous, as this selection shows. By many it was seen as absolutely necessary, the "sewer" whereby society was purified. Through prostitution, millions of poor women by sacrificing themselves maintained the "purity" of upper-class white women. Prostitution was the other side of the repression of female sexuality so common in Victorian bourgeois society. This ideology of sexuality held that respectable women had no sex drive, did not enjoy sex but surrendered to it for the sake of their husbands and reproduction, but that the sex drive among males was a powerful, albeit dangerous, force that was very difficult to control.

This selection is from the first extensive examination of prostitution in America. The author was the resident physician at the Blackwell's Island Women's Prison in New York City; he used his position there to interview a sample of 2,000 prostitutes who were its inmates.

PROSTITUTION

New York	1 prostitute to every 57 men.
Buffalo	1 " " " 57 "
Louisville	1 " " " 56 "
New Haven	1 " " " 76 "
Norfolk	1 " " " 26 "
Savannah	1 " " " 39 "
and the mean of the whole is	1 " " " 52 "

This mean may be fairly assumed as the proportion existing in all the large cities of the Union, and the farther assumption that the men who visit houses of prostitution form one fourth of the total population will give a basis upon which the total number of the Prostitutes in the United States may be estimated with some accuracy. The calculation can not, of course, be claimed as absolutely correct, as that would be an impossibility, but is submitted as a probability on which the reader can form his own conclusion. . . .

QUESTION. *What was the cause of your becoming a prostitute?* . . .

First in order stands the reply "Inclination," which can only be understood as meaning a voluntary resort to prostitution in order to gratify the sexual passions. Five hundred and thirteen women, more than one fourth of the gross number, give this as their reason. If their representations were borne out by facts, it would make the task of grappling with the vice a most arduous one, and afford very slight grounds to hope for any amelioration; but it is imagined that the circumstances which induced the ruin of most of those who gave the answer will prove that, if a positive inclination to vice was the proximate cause of the fall, it was but the result of other and controlling influences. . . .

But it must be repeated, and most decidedly, that without these or

William Sanger. *A History of Prostitution*. New York: The Medical Publishing Company, 1858.

some other equally stimulating cause, the full force of sexual desire is seldom known to a virtuous woman. . . .

Destitution is assigned as a reason in five hundred and twenty-five cases. In many of these it is unquestionably true that positive, actual want, the apparent and dreaded approach of starvation, was the real cause of degradation. The following instances of this imperative necessity will appeal to the understanding and the heart more forcibly than any arguments that could be used. As in all the selections already made, or that may be made hereafter, these cases are taken indiscriminately from the replies received, and might be indefinitely extended. . . .

M. M., a widow with one child, earned $1.50 per week as a tailoress. J. Y., a servant, was taken sick while in a situation, spent all her money, and could get no employment when she recovered." . . .

M. S., also a servant, received *one dollar a month wages*. A. B. landed in Baltimore from Germany, and was robbed of all her money the very day she reached the shore. M. F., a shirt-maker, earned one dollar a week. E. M. G.: the captain of police in the district where this woman resides says, "This girl struggled hard with the world before she became a prostitute, sleeping in station-houses at night, and living on bread and water during the day." He adds: "In my experience of three years, I have known *over fifty cases* whose history would be similar to hers, and who are now prostitutes." . . .

"Seduced and abandoned." Two hundred and fifty-eight women make this reply. These numbers give but a faint idea of the actual total that should be recorded under the designation, as many who are included in other classes should doubtless have been returned in this. It has already been shown that under the answer "Inclination" are comprised the responses of many who were the victims of seduction before such inclination existed, and there can be no question that among those who assign "Drink, and the desire to drink" as the cause of their becoming prostitutes, may be found many whose first departure from the rules of sobriety was actuated by a desire to drive from their memories all recollections of their seducers' falsehoods. . . .

The probabilities of a decrease in the crime of seduction are very slight, so long as the present public sentiment prevails; while the seducer is allowed to go unpunished, and the full measure of retribution is directed against his victim; while the offender escapes, but the offended is condemned. Unprincipled men, ready to take advantage of woman's trustful nature, abound, and they pursue their diabolical course unmolested. Legal enactments can scarcely ever reach them, although sometimes a poor man without friends or money is indicated and convicted. The remedy must be left to the world at large. When our domestic relations are such that a man known to be guilty of this crime can obtain no admission into the family circle; when the virtuous and respectable members of the community agree that no such man shall be welcomed to their society; when worth and honor assert their supremacy over wealth and boldness, there may be hopes of a reformation, but not till then. . . .

. . . the man whose conduct to his wife is such as to lead her to vicious practices. . . .

C.C. "My husband deserted me and four children. I had no means to live." . . .

J.S. "My husband committed adultery. I caught him with another woman, and then he left me." . . .

A.G. "My husband eloped with another woman. I support the child." . . .

A.B. "My husband accused me of infidelity, which was not true. I only lived with him five months. I was pregnant by him, and after my child was born I went on the town to support it." . . .

C.H. "My husband was a drunkard, and beat me." . . .

P.T. "My husband was intemperate, and turned out to be a thief. He was sent to prison."

. . .

QUESTION. *What trade or calling did you follow before you became a prostitute?*

OCCUPATIONS.	NUMBERS.	OCCUPATIONS.	NUMBERS.
Artist	1	Shoe-binders	16
Nurse in Bellevue Hospital, N.Y.	1	Vest-makers	21
School-teachers	3	Cap-makers	24
Fruit-hawkers	4	Book-folders	27
Paper-box-makers	5	Factory girls	37
Tobacco-packers	7	Housekeepers	39
Attended stores or bars	8	Milliners	41
Attended school	8	Seamstresses	59
Embroiderers	8	Tailoresses	105
Fur-sewers	8	Dress-makers	121
Hat-trimmers	8	Servants	933
Umbrella-makers	8	Lived with parents or friends	499
Flower-makers	9	Total	2000

. . .

Before leaving the question of employment, the effects of different branches of female occupation, as inducing or favoring immorality, must be noticed. Apart from the low rate of wages paid to women, thus causing destitution which forces them to vice, the associations of most of the few trades they are in the habit of pursuing are prejudicial to virtue. The trade of tailoress or seamstress may be cited as a case in point. One mode in which this business is conducted between employer and employed is as follows: The woman leaves either a cash deposit or the guarantee of some responsible person at the store, and receives a certain amount of materials to be made up by a specified time: when she returns the manufactured goods she is paid, and has more work given her to make up. This may seem a very simple course, and so it is, but one feature in it gives rather a sinister aspect. The person who delivers the materials, receives the work, and pronounces on its execution, is almost invariably a man, and upon his decision rests the question whether the operative shall be paid her full wages, or whether any portion of her miserable earnings shall be deducted because the work is not done to his satisfaction. In many cases he wields a power the determinations of which amount to this: "Shall I have any food to-day, or shall I starve?" . . .

As THE nineteenth century progressed, the demand for prostitutes outstripped the supply of "willing women." The "working life" of a prostitute was often short, due to disease, crime and the customers' demands for youth. Increased demand stimulated the growth of the white slave trade—the forced or deceptive entrapment of women into prostitution.

The white slave trade was practicable even without constant armed supervision of the women because women were taught that losing their virginity ruined them forever. Young women who were raped or seduced often feared to return to their homes or families.

The brutalities of the white slave trade made banner headlines and shocked many Americans when they were first made public in the last decades of the nineteenth century. As more and more young women left their families for work in the large cities and a sex life unknown to their parents, the outcry about white slaves and prostitution grew out of proportion to the actual numbers involved in the profession; the result was a number of reform laws against white slavery, such as the Mann Act.

There was a racism in this response since forced prostitution had gone on invisibly when it was not "white," involving black, Asian,

Latin-American or other non-Yankee women. In San Francisco, for example, many thousands of Asian immigrant women were forced into prostitution or brought to this country specifically to houses of prostitution, as this selection shows. This excerpt is from testimony before a California State Senate Committee investigating Chinese immigration.

"WHITE SLAVERY"

San Francisco, April 12, 1876. Rev. Otis Gibson sworn.

Q. What is your profession?

A. A clergyman. . . . I was a missionary to the Chinese of the Methodist Episcopal Church. . . .

Q. Do you know upon what terms the Chinese are imported into this country?

A. They come free. I think all Chinamen come free, except the women. . . .

Q. Is it not a well-settled matter that a great many people are held in slavery here—bought and sold?

A. Only the women. I don't think there is a man so held. The women as a general thing are held as slaves. They are bought or stolen in China and brought here. They have a sort of agreement, to cover up the slavery business, but it is all a sham. That paper makes the girl say that she owes you four hundred dollars or so, passage money and outfit from China, and has nothing to pay. I being the girl, this man comes up and offers to lend me the money to pay you if I will agree to serve him, to prostitute my body at his pleasure, wherever he shall put me, for four, five, or six years. For that promise of mine, made on the paper, he hands him the four hundred dollars, and I pay the debt I owe you according to contract. It is also put in the contract that if I am sick fifteen days no account shall be taken of that, but if I am sick more than that I shall make up double. If I am found to be pregnant within a month, you shall return the money and take me again. If I prove to have epilepsy, leprosy, or am a stone woman, the same thing is done. . . .

Q. Then, so far as the women are concerned, they are in slavery? . . .

The Social, Moral and Political Effect of Chinese Immigration. Testimony taken before a Committee of the Senate of the State of California, April 1876. Sacramento: State Printing Office, 1876.

A. Yes, sir. And even after the term of prostitution service is up, the owners so manage as to have the women in debt more than ever, so that their slavery becomes life-long. There is no release from it.

Q. When these people become sick and helpless, what becomes of them?

A. They are left to die.

Q. No care taken of them?

A. Sometimes, where the women have friends.

Q. Don't the companies take care of them?

A. Not frequently.

Q. Is it not a frequent thing that they are put out on the sidewalk to die, or in some room without water or food?

A. I have heard of such things; I don't know. . . . Sometimes the women take opium to kill themselves. They do not know they have any rights, but think they must keep their contracts, and believe themselves under obligations to serve in prostitution.

Q. What is their treatment? Is it harsh?

A. They have come to the asylum all bruises. They are beaten and punished cruelly if they fail to make money. When they become worn out and unable to make any more money, they are turned out to die.

The Rev. A. W. Loomis, a Presbyterian clergyman, at the head of the Chinese Mission established by his church in San Francisco, says, (Evidence, pp. 55 and 56):

These Chinawomen that you see on the streets here were brought for the accommodation of white people, not for the accommodation of Chinese; and if you pass along the streets where they are to be found, you will see that they are visited not so much by Chinese as by others —sailors and low people. The women are in a condition of servitude. Some of them are inveigled away from home under promise of marriage to men here, and some to be secondary wives, while some are stolen. They are sold here. Many women are taken from the Chinese owners, and are living as wives and as secondary wives. Some have children, and these children are legitimate.

Q. These women engaged in prostitution are nothing more than slaves to them?

A. Yes, sir; and every one would go home to-day if she were free and had her passage paid.

Q. They are not allowed to release themselves from that situation, are they?

A. I think they are under the surveillance of men and women, so that they cannot get away. They would fear being caught and sold again, and carried off to a condition even worse than now.

Q. Are not the laws here used to restrain them from getting away— are they not arrested for crime?

A. Oh, yes. They will trump up a case, have the woman arrested and bring people to swear what they want. In this way they manage to get possession of her again. . . .

Mr. Alfred Clark, for nineteen years past connected with the police force of San Francisco, and for the last eight years Clerk of the Chief of Police, testifies as follows, (Evidence, p. 63): "In regard to the vice of prostitution, I have here a bill of sale of a Chinawoman, and a translation of the same." Witness submits a paper written in Chinese characters, and reads the translation, as follows:

> An agreement to assist the woman Ah Ho, because coming from China to San Francisco she became indebted to her mistress for passage. Ah Ho herself asks Mr. Yee Kwan to advance her six hundred and thirty dollars, for which Ah Ho distinctly agrees to give her body to Mr. Yee for service of prostitution for a term of four years. There shall be no interest on the money. Ah Ho shall receive no wages. At the expiration of four years Ah Ho shall be her own master. Mr. Yee Kwan shall not hinder or trouble her. If Ah Ho runs away before her time is out, her mistress shall find her and return her, and whatever expense is incurred in finding and returning her Ah Ho shall pay. On this day of agreement Ah Ho, with her own hands, has received from Mr. Yee Kwan six hundred and thirty dollars. If Ah Ho shall be sick at any time for more than ten days, she shall make up by an extra month of service for every ten days sickness. Now, this agreement has proof—this paper received by Ah Ho is witness.
>
> TUNG CHEE.
>
> Twelfth year, ninth month, and fourteenth day (about middle of October, eighteen hundred and seventy-three).

AN AGREEMENT TO ASSIST A YOUNG GIRL NAMED LOI YAU.

> Because she became indebted to her mistress for passage, food, etc., and has nothing to pay, she makes her body over to the woman, Sep Sam, to serve as a prostitute to make out the sum of five hundred and three dollars. The money shall draw no interest, and Loi Yau shall serve four and one-half years. On this day of agreement, Loi Yau receives the sum of five hundred and three dollars in her own hands. When the time is out, Loi Yau may be her own master, and no man shall trouble her. If she runs away before the time is out, and any

expense is incurred in catching her, then Loi Yau must pay the expense. If she is sick fifteen days or more, she shall make up one month for every fifteen days. If Sep Sam shall go back to China, then Loi Yau shall serve another party till her time is out; if, in such service, she should be sick one hundred days or more, and cannot be cured, she may return to Sep Sam's place. For a proof of this agreement, this paper.

Dated second, sixth month of the present year.

LOI YAU.

THE "SWEATSHOP" and the "sweating system" were terms which were first used to describe the clothing industry. Later they became synonymous with many low-wage, unsanitary industries where the work took place in tenements. In this excerpt, Louis Levine, the official historian of the early years of the Ladies Garment Workers Union, describes the origins of the sweatshop.

SWEATSHOPS

. . . already before 1880, there appeared in the women's clothing industry the beginnings of the contracting system. By 1882, when the immigration of the Jews from Eastern Europe began to assume perceptible proportions, the distinction between the so-called "inside" and "outside" shop was already established. The "inside" shops were those which were directly connected with the selling department of the business firm. In some of these "inside" shops the garments were cut, made up, bushelled, and examined; in short, the entire manufacturing process was begun and completed under the same roof. In other "inside" shops only the cutting and final examining was done, while the cut garments were sent out to be made up elsewhere, that is in "outside" shops. The owners of the "inside" shops were the large manufacturers and merchants in whose hands the industry was centered. Those who operated the "outside" shops became known as contractors. They "contracted" to make up the cut garments for the owners of the "inside" shops at so much per garment. They were middlemen. Their profit was

Louis Levine. *The Women Garment Workers*. New York: B. W. Huebsch, Inc., 1924.

made by paying the workers less for making the garment than they received themselves.

The three main features of the sweat-shop have been described as insanitary conditions, excessively long hours, and extremely low wages. The shops were generally located in tenement houses. As a rule, one of the rooms of the flat in which the contractor lived was used as a working place. Sometimes work would be carried on all over the place, in the bedroom as well as in the kitchen. Even under the best of conditions this would have made for living and working in grime and dirt. But the conditions were not of the best. In New York City, the Tenth Ward, where the Jewish immigrants congregated, and which was usually referred to as Jew-Town, was said to be the most crowded district in the world. Investigations showed that about one out of every three persons whose living quarters were examined "slept in unventilated rooms without windows." One can imagine what happened when these "homes" were also turned into shops and became home and workshop at the same time.

A writer who made a valiant fight against the evils of the tenement house and of the sweat-shop, gives a graphic description of the district in New York City where the sweat-shops were situated. "Take the Second Avenue Elevated," he writes, "and ride up half a mile through the sweaters' district. Every open window of the big tenements, that stand like a continuous brick wall on both sides of the way, give you a glimpse of one of these shops as the train speeds by. Men and women bending over their machines or ironing clothes at the window, half-naked. . . . The road is like a big gangway through an endless work-room where vast multitudes are forever laboring. Morning, noon, or night, it makes no difference; the scene is always the same." Not only the insides of the tenements were turned into working places. "It is not unusual," reported the New York State factory inspector, "when the weather permits to see the balconies of the fire escapes occupied by from two to four busy workmen. The halls and roofs are also utilized for workshop purposes very frequently." The same factory inspector describes one of the many sweat-shops which he visited. This particular one, which was typical of others, was that "of a cloakmaker, who used one room for his shop, while the other three rooms were supposed to be used for domestic purposes only, his family consisting of his wife and seven children. In the room adjoining the shop, used as the kitchen, there was a red-hot stove, two tables, a clothes rack, and several piles of goods. A woman was making bread on a table upon which there was a baby's stocking, scraps of cloth, several old tin cans, and a small pile of unfinished garments. In the next room was an old woman with a diseased face walking the floor with a crying child in her arms."

In the "outside" shops, the working hours were eighty-four per week. But besides "regular" hours, there was "overtime" in both the "inside" and "outside" shops, and in addition many of the workers "took material home and worked until two and three o'clock in the morning." It was quite common to work fifteen and sixteen hours a day, from five in the morning to nine at night, and in the busy season men frequently worked all night. "If you look into the streets any morning," wrote an investigator of conditions in New York City, "at four o'clock you will see them full of people going to work. They rouse themselves up at three o'clock and are often at their machines at four. The latest is sure to be there at five. The general time is five o'clock all year round in good times, winter and summer, and if the boss will give them gaslight, some will go even earlier than three o'clock." Old-timers in the industry are fond of telling to-day about the over-zealous workers of those days, cloak pressers and operators, who saved time and rent by sleeping on "bundles" in the shop between working. It was a current saying that one could always do a little more work by "borrowing a couple of hours from the following day." No wonder the industry, and especially the cloakmaking trade, early acquired the sad distinction of being the "worst-driven trade in the matter of hours in the season."

There are only fragmentary statistics on wages in the industry for the period under consideration. But from the evidence at hand, it is clear that the coming of the immigrants and the spread of the contracting system tended to keep wages at a low level. The workers in the "inside" shops suffered from the competition of the workers in the contractors' shops. The cloak and sackmakers in the "inside" shops of Boston, mostly women and girls, according to the report of Massachusetts Bureau of Labor for 1884, "had to work very hard to average $6 a week the year round." Many of these women were piece-workers and were paid "15 cents for an entire cloak, raised, however, on protest to 25 cents, and 22 cents for making a short walking coat, running two rows of stitching around the entire edge and sewing on thirty buttons. It makes three and a half hours to make a cloak for 25 cents." In Baltimore, in 1884–1885, women cloakmakers received an average of $1.50 per cloak and earned $3.50 to $5 a week. The Maryland Bureau of Statistics also reported that the price for making a complete lace dress was 50 cents, for making a skirt from 17 to 19 cents. "At these prices," says the report, "the operator can earn $5 a week. Work in this line continues all year round, and the girls work late into the night."

In New York City, where the effects of the sweat-shop system were most keenly felt, wages were from $15 a week in 1883 to $6 and $7 in 1885. The New York State Bureau of Labor Statistics reported that the "very best" workers were "getting $10 a week, while the women employed in the industry were earning from $3 to $6 a week." According to the report, "some even with the aid of their families and working fourteen hours a day could earn only $12 and $15 a week. Others could only make $4 by working ten hours a day." Towards the end of the decade wages in New York City rose a little, the average wage of cloakmakers in 1888 being about $12 a week.

The investigators of the sweat-shop denounced it as a "system of making clothes under filthy and inhuman conditions" and as a "process of grinding the faces of the poor." Some of these investigators were especially aroused by conditions in the cloak trade. "This trade," we read in one of the official reports, "is one of those which have justified the complaints against the hardships and underpay of labor" and against "the shocking conditions under which work is done in a Christian community where we have so much charitable sentiment and a sanitary administration." In explaining these conditions, the investigators generally took the view that the sweat-shop was the result of the inferior standards introduced by the immigrants. Some even declared the sweatshop a special Jewish institution explicable by the "racial" and "national" characteristics of the Jewish workers. An official of the State of Pennsylvania wrote that the Russian Jews "evidently prefer filth to cleanliness," while another investigator of the problem concluded that the "factory system with its discipline and regular hours" was "distasteful to the Jew's individualism" and that the Jewish worker preferred "the sweat-shop with its going and coming."

The bias involved in such explanations is evident. Sweating in the United States existed in the men's clothing trades long before the coming of Jewish and Italian immigrants. It has existed in various industries in other countries. Sidney and Beatrice Webb pointed out many years ago that in England "all the evils of sweating exist where neither Jews nor foreigners have as yet penetrated . . . or where their competition is but little felt." In other words, sweating is primarily an industrial problem, a phase of the general problem of cheap and exploited labor. The Jewish, and later also the Italian, garment workers worked in sweat-shops beacuse they had no other entry into American industry.

INDUSTRIALIZATION– THE CONSEQUENCES

Two of the major problems facing anyone trying to organize among workers are stool pigeons (people who spy on other workers for management) and blacklisting (the keeping of a list of organizers and militants which circulates among employers, who then refuse to hire them).

BLACKLISTING

Malvina Fourtune and her brother Henry Fourtune it was them who started the strike and they go from house to house and tells the people to keep up the strike and any how all the Fourtunes were a nucience to the Corporation since them around the town and Frank White also and Faufite Parenti No 11 Cabot St most live in Cabot St and the Dufriesne related to the Fourtunes they are as bad as them and others that is like them is the Samsons they live on Dwight St and the Greenwoods and Odile Roy they are all of the head strikers and even since these people are in the mills they have made trouble and they have seen living here for many years most of them worked in Chicopee falls in summer and come and work here in winter and make trouble and when I bring some strange they are the first to discourage them and tell them they won't make nothing and the Desilla and Samsons of Cabot St they are all alike and they all think they are going to win the strike this is what I hird from some who newe it well

Papers of Dwight Manufacturing Company, Chicopee, Mass. Baker Library, Harvard University, Miscellaneous folder.

LYMAN MILLS

Holyoke, Mass. June 21st 1882

J. M. Fumnock, Agent.
Dear Sir.

We note the names Victoria Lenroy and Justine Nadeau and will "black list" them.

Yours truly
Theop. Parsons, Agent

ONE OF THE methods of redress used by working-class women was the petition. In this case, a group of workingwomen presented their demands to the Massachusetts legislature to have the state help finance decent homes for them, as a way to improve their working and living conditions. The demands were discussed at a meeting of both working- and middle-class women held in Boston in 1869. This report is from the *Workingman's Advocate*, one of the most influential labor papers of this period.

PETITIONS

A convention of Boston work women was held in that city on the 21st ult. at which some extraordinary developments were made. We append some of the discussions:

OPENING ADDRESS BY MISS PHELPS

Miss Phelps said: the subject of this meeting is to bring out the purpose of the petition just read, and the facts whereon it is based. We do not think the men of Massachusetts know how the women live. We do not think if they did they would allow such a state of things to exist. Some of us who signed the petition have had to work for less than twenty-five cents a day, and we know that many others have had to do the same. True, many get good wages comparatively for women. There

"THE WORKING WOMEN. White Slavery in New England. Twenty Cents a Day. The Right Kind of Talk by the Right Kind of Folks, etc." *Workingman's Advocate* 5 (No. 41), May 8, 1869, 3.

are girls that get from $1 to $1.50 per day, either because they are superior laborers or have had unusual opportunities. But many of these poor girls among whom it has been my fortune to live and work, are not skilled laborers. They are incapable of going into business for themselves, or carrying on for themselves, and incapable of combination; they are uneducated, and have no resource but the system that employs them. There are before me now women who I know to be working at the present time for less than twenty-five cents a day. Some of the work they do at these rates from the charitable institutions of the city. These institutions give out work to the women with the professed object of helping them, at which they can scarcely earn enough to keep them from starving; work at which two persons, with their utmost exertions cannot earn more than forty-five cents a day. These things, I repeat, should be known to the public. They do not know how the daughters of their soldiers fare. I do. They have a little aid, to be sure, from the State, but it is only a little and they have to-day to live in miserable garrets without fire, and during the cold winters, with scanty food and insufficient clothing, they go out daily to labor-along these beautiful streets. Do not you think that they feel the difference between their condition and that of rich, well-dressed ladies who pass them? If they did not they would be less than human. But they work on bravely and uncomplainingly, venturing all things for the hope of the life that is to come. We know that there is wealth enough in this state and in this city to remedy this state of things, and that it only needs to be brought before the people to be done. Our legislators will not let such a state of affairs last. There are lands close to the city of Boston, which can be bought at prices ranging from 50 to 75 an acre, near enough to the city for working women to come to their work there or take it home. And these homes can be made cheaply. It can be done at a less cost than these poor women now occasion in the shape of public charities. For last winter many of them did not get work enough at even ten cents a garment to live upon, and were obliged to ask charity. They get it doled out to them, but at what a loss of self respect, of independence. How much better to have these girls independent, earning their own living, enjoying their own homes than, that they should be compelled to go to station-houses for soup. That is what many of them had to do last winter. The people have wondered how these girls live. Can you imagine how you should live upon 20 cents a day. Rent is one or two dollars at the lowest and there is your clothes and your food. Count it up. Where does it come from? There is often no resource in health but the charities, or in sickness but the hospital. As for the hospitals, the poor girls that have been there have told me that they would almost sooner lie down and die than go again. But we think the women could sustain themselves under the plan we propose, even at the small wages they get. It seems like a good deal to do, but day by day the pennies will count up, and after a time the homes be secured. And then, again, these girls working and living in these garrets and cellars, damp, unwholesome places, are not well. They cannot go into kitchens and do housework as their mothers did. Men often ask me why these working women do not go into housework. One sufficient reason is that there are not houses enough for them all nor any large proportion of them. But if there were them they are not skilled in housework, and mistresses would not have them. Another reason is that their strength is not sufficient. They have not been so brought up and thus . . . labor they have been employed at has so weakened their whole system, bodily and mental, that they cannot do the work. They are said to be improvident and shiftless. I grant it. Who would not be in their condition? Make their condition better and they will not resort to the streets after dark. Make their condition better and you will see them educate themselves for skilled labor and become what our grandmothers were, good wives and good mothers. . . . Give these women little homes and they will not be obliged to take work at such rates. Many of these women sent their husbands, their brothers, their sons to the battlefield. They were alone, listening to every echo, and expecting by every mail news of loved ones deaths. And the torture of that suspense who can tell? It is far, far worse than the strife of the war itself. And then when the little homes we ask for them will save them from starvation, I ask, have not soldiers widowes, have no soldiers daughters, a right to have them. Have they not earned it? I know the State will help them. I know it. We do not want to blame any one. We do not feel that individuals were to blame. It is the fault of the system which makes women homeless. . . .

Often when we go to the shop we have to wait one, two, three hours for work to be given us. We work for half an hour, an hour, two hours and then have to wait again. When I was younger girls were taught full trades. They made pants, coats, overcoats and then they learned to cut. Now one stiches the seam, another makes the button-holes, and another puts the buttons on, and when the poor girl stitches up the seams and finds her work slack she goes from shop to shop, perhaps for weeks, before she can find the same kind of work. . . .

Only help us to earn a home that we can attach ourselves to, that will make us feel that we have a country. It has been said that we can go anywhere and be at home. Women cannot. It is because they have no homes. They have a husband's or a father's home, none of their own. And to those poor working women they have no husband or Brother, only think what a boon a home of their own would be. . . . We ask in this petition that these homes should pass to our female heirs, if we should have any; that then should be kept in the hands of women. We do not want that by trick and chicanery they should pass into the hands of speculators . . . I am met often with the objection that these women can go to California or Nevada. But our mothers live here. We know not these distant places. We cannot get work where we are acquainted; how can we be certain to get it where we are not acquainted? This is the invariable feeling of these girls. Why do they not go into the country and work in a farmhouse? Girls love independence, girls love society, just as much as men do. A woman must have some intellectual society or she goes down. I am no speechmaker—only a worker. . . .

Mrs. Warner said she had learned that the pay of the paper-box makers and tailoresses had been raised that day for fear they would attend this meeting. These paper-box makers get from $2.50 to $3 per week. How can they live on that? Where do they get their dresses? I say to you ladies that every costly dress you wear makes three prostitutes. Some girls in the city of Boston got out of employment last winter. They went to a firm on Winter street, and asked for employment. They were told that they could not be given enough to support them, but if they had gentlemen friends to dress them, they would be hired.

THE NATIONAL LABOR UNION was a national labor federation which existed between 1866 and 1872. It was made up of trade unions, workingmen's and -women's associations and eight-hour leagues. At the 1868 convention, Susan B. Anthony attended as a delegate from the Workingwomen's Association. At the 1869 convention her credentials were rejected because she was not a representative of a "bona-fide" trade-union organization. This was a rather specious argument, since many of the male delegates were not trade unionists either. However, the rejection of Anthony's credentials was also due to her encouragement of women typographers to break the male strikes in order to "learn the trade." Anthony's position was based on her belief that this was the only way women could get a toehold in the skilled trades; she did fail, however, to understand the importance of worker solidarity during strikes.

In the arguments surrounding her ouster, prejudices of both a class and sex nature are clear. The man who defended her the most was Austin Puitt, an Indiana attorney and not a trade unionist. The workingman who opposed her the most, M. R. Walsh, appeared to be against her on antifeminist grounds.

EXPULSION

The committee reported in the case of Miss Anthony, saying that they objected to her being admitted as a delegate, as there was no locality mentioned in the credentials presented by her.

Miss Anthony explained that the omission was the fault of the Secretary of the Workingwomen's Protective Association, of which she is the President.

Mr. Welsh, of Typographical Union, protested against her admission on the ground that she did not represent a bona-fide labor organization, also because during the recent struggle of that Society, she had striven to procure situations for girls from which the men had been discharged, at lower wages than they had received.

A delegate moved to admit the lady as a delegate. . . .

Mr. Walls, of Philadelphia, offered a resolution to the effect that the action of the convention yesterday, in refusing to admit Miss Susan B. Anthony as a delegate, was not based upon any personal objection to the lady, but on the ground that she was not a member of any working organization or trades' union. In support of this Mr. Walls stated that the impression had gone forth to the world that the refusal was based on personal grounds, and he desired to set the matter right. . . .

Mr. Puitt, of Indiana, moved to amend by adding the latter clause "that Miss Susan B. Anthony be now admitted as a member on the floor," and gave the following reasons for so doing: If I understand our constitution and Miss Anthony's relation to us as a member of the Workingwomen's Association she is entitled to a seat here until we change the constitution. (Applause.) As some feeling may exist in relation to the different names that they call each other in the type-

"Proceedings, National Labor Union, August 1869." *Workingman's Advocate* 6 (No. 5) September 4, 1869.

setting business, I wish to state that I know nothing about them. I dislike in a body like this meeting, where we are assembled for a great purpose in common with all the laboring community of the United States, that we should call out the word "rat" because the man is not an highly-educated and intelligent person; and to use any term in that way is an absurdity. We in the West know nothing about these things.

How is it that a man representing but one trade in one of the States comes up here and objects to a lady who has done perhaps more than any one of us, through her paper, for I have been a reader of the *Revolution* for twelve months, and in every instance her whole power as a publisher has been thrown in our behalf.

I know that there are, somehow or other, persons with prejudices, who come from foreign countries where women have no rights. I know that prejudices exist in the United States. I have had them myself, but I thank God I have got on that higher platform, which is more Godlike, where women's rights are recognized. (Applause.)

Let me ask you as men, are you not ready to give to the females of the United States all the rights you ask for yourselves (applause) to give to the colored men throughout the land the same rights, and thus shake off this prejudice? I give to the colored man all the rights I claim myself (applause), and enter upon the grand platform of competition, and I do not care whether he is a "rat" or a mouse. We must help one another more. We must have charity one for another, and do right, come what may. . . .

Mr. M. R. Walsh said: The gentleman who has just taken his seat has convinced me that he is not a workingman or he would know what a "rat" meant. It is not a slur on a man for lack of intelligence or education, but it is because of a want of spirit. What we term a "rat" is the man who comes in like a sneak, and when we are compelled to strikes takes the bread from our mouths. I am interested in the movement of men who are really workingmen and who work on the streets from five in the morning until dark for a mere pittance. If Miss Anthony was a working woman I would be willing to take her hand as soon as any man. We have one here from the St. Crispin's Society. Who objected to her admission? Nobody. She is a bona-fide working woman, and we want her with us. I agree with the last speaker — "Equal rights for all" — but if I am a "rat" or a renegade, I do not expect anything from fair men, and I do not expect to give them anything. It is a fair deal and a fair fight, and it is the union men in this convention that know what strikes are. The lady goes in for taking women away from the wash tub; and in the name of heaven who is going there if they don't? I believe in a woman doing her work, and men marrying them and supporting them. (Applause.) . . .

When I received instructions from the union I represent to make the protest, I wrote to Miss Augusta Lewis — my union is at present supporting and paying the expenses month after month to sustain a female trade union — now I wrote to the president of that union and requested her to give me some information in reference to the matter. I only received the answer but an hour ago in this room, and will read it:

"The Workingwomen's Association was organized immediately before the last session of the Labor Congress. I was the first vice president. Mrs. Stanton was anxious to have a workingwomen's suffrage association. It was left to a vote, and ruled out. The society at one time comprised over one hundred working women, but, as there was nothing practical done to ameliorate their condition, they gradually withdrew. I do not know who introduced the "literary" in the society, but the debates and introduction of "suffrage" were introduced by Mrs. McKinley. After the adoption of constitution and by-laws several members of the Sorosis joined, and were on the committee to nominate officers, which they did, ignoring working women.

"Miss Norton intimated that our resignations would be agreeable, instead of asking the wealthy officers, who did not attend to their duty, to resign, as their absence prevented a quorum as well as Miss John's and my absence did. The workingwomen were by another member asked to resign. Although the society comprises many wealthy ladies, they raised thirty dollars for the laundresses of Troy. As a society, either the want of knowledge or the want of sense renders them, as a workingwoman's association, very inefficient.

"I wish I could assist you in your protest more than I have; I hope it is not too late for the purpose. Trusting you understand the cause of my seeming neglect, and with the wish that you may be successful, I am &c.,

"Augusta Lewis"

"P.S. I sent a word to the delegate from the Workingwomen's Association that she would in all probability not be received. She will go, however." . . .

Miss Anthony then said.

Mr. President and Gentlemen: Some women, I am glad to see, are on the floor already. With reference to this matter of the collar laundry of New York, I have to plead an immense amount of ignorance, as the affair occurred when I was in the west, but I have heard it said that the Workingwomen's Association had a meeting at which the president of the Collar-makers' Union of Troy was to be present, and that the Workingwomen's Association of New York took up a collection of $30 for the Union. I can not vouch for the statement any more than what the treasurer told me the other day, when I inquired how the funds stood, and was informed so much, and that there was the $30 that was collected for the Troy Collar and Laundry Union, and to whom the president had made application, but could not ascertain where to send the money. This is the most I can tell you.

The objection raised to my admission was not that the National Workingmen's Association of New York, which is incorporated by a special law of the Legislature of New York, is not a proper workingmen's or labor organization. That was not the main point at issue last night. The objection was that Susan B. Anthony had been a renegade to the principles and interest of the workingmen of New York, and I suppose they want me to answer these specific charges, that exist according to Miss Lewis' letter.

Miss Anthony then explained her connection with the association. She agreed that it was proper for men and women to be married, and that the former should support the latter; but she worked for a class of women that had no husbands, and who were on the street penniless, homeless and without shelter. Now, I ask you what we are to do with these girls? Shall we tell them to starve in the garrets because the printers, by their own necessities, open their doors and give a slight training to a few girls for a few weeks? Shall I say to the girls, "Do not go in, but starve?" or shall I say, "Go in, and get a little skill into your hands, and fit yourselves to work side by side with men?" I want to ask the Co-operative Union of New York how many girls they have taken to learn the type-setting business? How many women have you ordered each department or establishment to take as apprentices, and to train in the art of type-setting?

Mr. Walsh, of New York, rose and said: We belong to a trade union, and a part of our obligation is first to give preference to a fellow union man. If a girl is a member of our union, we will give her work, having already admitted two women, but we do not go outside of our organization. You might as well ask why we don't send for the colored men or the Chinese to learn the trade. There are too many in it now, and if the lady will allow me to inquire something of her, will she please tell us why she does not pay the girls employed on the *Revolution* the same wages as we receive? (Cries of "That's the idea" and applause.) Why don't she put her paper into the hands of a unionist or a price-paying establishment?

Miss Anthony: I want to say to the gentleman, in the first place, and I want you all to understand it, that I do not employ any type-setters, either men or women. I have no control whatsoever in the hiring or employing of type-setters on my paper. I want to ask this gentleman if the editors of the *Nation* or of any other paper published in the city of New York are to be held responsible for Green & Gray? That is exactly my position. I wish you men and type-setters would give me money to buy type, and I would show you a pattern office. (Applause.) As I said last night, I did not choose to run the risk with a new paper, and am I in duty bound to risk a chance in my paper in order to be recognized as a friend of labor.

With regard to Miss Lewis' dismissal I knew nothing about it until she informed me of it. I heard there was to be some opposition raised to my admittance into this body on Saturday evening last, when I called on one of the delegates appointed to come here by the Working-women's Association. Out of these three only one, myself, came as they could not afford it. The question is whether every single labor organization that knows nothing of trades unions, but is formed for the purpose of establishing the principle of equalizing the rights of laboring women with those of men is to be represented or not. Now, I think men have great wrongs in the world between the existence of labor and capital, but these wrongs as compared to the wrongs of women, in whose faces the doors of the trades and avocations are slammed shut, are not as a grain of sand on the sea shore, and if some of us who advocate the wrongs of down-trodden women do take a position which you do not like you must remember that our clients are in a very suffering condition, and we must act and speak for them.

Now, as to the workingwomen of New York, numbers who first joined the association joined with the idea of deriving pecuniary aid from it but when they found it was organized to establish the great principle of throwing open the trades' doors to them they gradually fell off.

I perfectly agree that women should be married, but, unfortunately, you men do not do your duty. (Laughter and applause.) The real fact of life is that women have to support themselves.

In looking over the columns of the New York *Herald,* the other day, I found that there were 1,200 advertisements from persons seeking employment; 500 of them were women who solicited employment as school teachers, seamstresses, &c.; 200 others were inserted by lady boarding house keepers. Thus you see 700 out of 1,200 were from working women, and that contradicts the rule of society that all women are supported by men. (Applause.)

I grant you, married men, that it is very important that you should earn money enough to support your wives and little ones; but then it is also important for us single individuals to earn money enough to support ourselves honestly.

All women in this country are in the power of men. We ask for a change, and we demand a change. There is no solution to this problem of prostitution but to give them a chance to earn an honest living with men; not merely a pittance, enough to keep body and soul together, but sufficient to enable them to invest in building societies, and have houses and homes of their own, and make them just as independent as anybody in the country.

I thank you for this hearing. I feel it is my duty to stand here and speak for women today, who are as dumb as the four millions of slaves were a few years ago on the plantations. When you are asked not to admit Miss Anthony, I ask you to pardon them, for they know not what they do. . . .

WHEN TRADE-UNION activity did not prove successful, many working-people tried to form producer cooperatives. These cooperatives, some argued, were a way to keep workers "independent of the capitalist employer." Cooperatives were often formed after the failure of a strike to secure the workers' demands.

The Troy Laundry women's union was one of the most militant and strongest unions of women in the country. Nevertheless, when they lost a major strike in 1869 they followed the pattern set by the men of the Molders Union three years earlier and formed a cooperative. Despite support from a New York merchant and the encouragement of the women's rights movement, the cooperative failed several weeks after its formation. Both the failure of the union and the cooperative reflected the relative weakness of the male and female labor movement in this period and the uncertainty that many workingpeople had about the use of trade-union tactics as a way to win their demands.

LAUNDRY WORKERS

Perhaps no organization of women workers has been more effective in the trade-union sense than was the Collar Laundry Union of Troy, N.Y., during this period. Troy then, as now, was the center of the laundry industry. The industry, in addition to the commonly understood laundry processes, includes as well the manufacture of collars, shirts, and waists. The general organization of the trade to-day is known as the Shirt, Waist, and Laundry Workers International Union.

As early as April, 1866 the laundresses of Troy had a prosperous union, which was influential in keeping up the prices in that work. Their spirit may be imagined from their action in contributing $1,000 to the aid of the Troy iron molders, then on strike against a reduction in wages. In 1868, also, they contributed $500 to aid the striking bricklayers of New York.

According to contemporaneous accounts, the work of the Troy laundry women was to stand over the washtub, over the ironing table, with furnaces on either side, the thermometer averaging 100 degrees, for wages averaging from $2 to $3 a week. "At last, said one writer," they formed a trade union whereby through their own exertions and their faithfulness to their organization, they increased their wages to $8 to $14 per week by working on an average from twelve to fourteen hours a day."

In 1868 the thanks of the National Labor Congress was unanimously tendered Miss Kate Mullany, chief directress of the Troy union, for her indefatigable exertions in the interest of working women, and she was made national organizer of women for the National Labor Union, apparently the first appointment of the kind in American labor history.

In May, 1869, the Troy union, composed of about 400 laundresses, made a demand for a further increase of wages. The demand was met with the most bitter opposition of the employers, who not only refused to advance wages, but joined together in a determined effort to break up the organization.

John Andrews and W. D. P. Bliss. *History of Women in Trade Unions*, Vol. X of *Report on the Condition of Woman and Child Wage-Earners in the United States*. Washington, D.C.: U.S. Government Printing Office, 1911.

The Laundry Workers' Union was regarded by many of the men as "the only bona fide female union in the country" at that time, and the trade unions of Troy took up their cause with a will. The molders, who remembered how loyally and liberally the women unionists had stood by them three years before, now voted $500 a week to support the women in their strike.

This strike excited universal interest. A mass meeting brought out 7,000 people and even the merchants and professional people of Troy extended substantial sympathy and support. But the employers crushed the union.

One outcome of the struggle was the establishment of a cooperative "Union Linen Collar and Cuff Manufactory," under the direction of Kate Mullany, president of the Union. The girls found a friend in the New York merchant prince, A. T. Stewart, who offered to take all of their goods and place them immediately upon the market.

THE LAUNDRY COOPERATIVE

THE GIRLS' CO-OPERATIVE COLLAR CO.—A private letter from Kate Mullany, President of the "Laundry Union and Co-operative Collar Co.," of Troy, New York, says:

I write to know what the ladies are doing in the way of taking the stock for our company. We are getting started now. We have enough subscribed to begin with, and we are starting up with a good prospect of getting a quick sale for our goods as soon as we have got them ready for the market. Of course, we depend altogether on the working people of the country, and on the people who are able and willing to help working girls and wish to see them get along.
Yours,   KATE MULLANY,
President Collar Laundry Union

The stock is five dollars per share, and is only an investment, which will directly benefit working girls, not a charity. The interest will be regularly paid, and the stock bought in by the girls themselves as soon as possible. Any person wishing to subscribe for one share or more can address a note to Kate Mullany, President of the Troy Laundry Union.

"The Girls' Co-operative Collar Co." *Revolution* 5 (No. 17) (April 28, 1870), p. 267.

IN THE MIDST of the Civil War, conditions for workingwomen in the major cities had become so terrible that a workingman suggested to the editor of the *New York Sun* that a meeting be held to organize these women. Evidently hundreds of impoverished women appeared, and the "gentlemen" (apparently not trade unionists) who ran the meeting were pressed to find a solution to their dilemmas.

These businessmen and lawyers finally came up with a response. A Working Women's Protective Union was formed in 1868 to serve as a legal assistance and employment agency for women. Its major function was to win back wages for women who had been cheated by their employers. It was clearly not a trade-union organization and only attempted to ameliorate on an individual basis some of the worst conditions for women. The "Union" itself had almost no effect on wages or working conditions.

The beginning of the union's constitution makes its philosophy clear: "Our object is not to molest or annoy employers. We have a higher, holier object in view—the saving of our companions in toil from early graves. We believe that every honorable man and woman will take pleasure in assisting their operatives, when they are assured that the movement will aid to improve their social condition."

Protective unions, like the one in New York, became common in several other cities, including Chicago, Philadelphia, St. Louis, Indianapolis and Boston. The New York protective union opened in 1868 and lasted until 1890.

White slavery in this case does not mean the procuring of prostitutes but refers to workingwomen and wage slavery.

WORKING WOMEN'S PROTECTIVE UNION

. . . Seven years ago an institution arose in our midst, which sprang into being at once in answer to the necessities of the working-women of New York. This class, always large, had been fearfully increased by the war. This new organization was given the name of

THE WORKING-WOMEN'S PROTECTIVE UNION

and its rooms are now to be found at 38 Bleecker Street. Here these ladies—a Superintendant, Mrs. Ferrer; her assistant, Mrs. Seelbach; and financial assistant, Miss Morley—are always to be found, ready to

Emily Verdery [Mrs. Battey]. "Among the White Slaves of New York." *Woodhull and Claflin's Weekly* 1 (No. 19), September 17, 1870, p. 2.

answer any call made upon them for aid and sympathy, or patience in the way of inquiry.

Perhaps no association in our city has done more for humanity in the last seven years than this.

Though it is supported entirely by private contributions, it cannot be called a charity. It is really a beneficial society, organized for the relief of women making honorable employment in trades, at wages proportioned to the cost of living.

During the last seven years this Union has prosecuted to final judgment more than 1,300 cases of fraud against working women, compelling the payment of wages due and withheld to the amount of over $5,000. Most of these claims were for exceedingly small amounts—many for sums less than a single dollar—the average sum involved in the whole being scarcely four dollars.

A larger amount—and often in smaller sums—was, during the same period, secured to working-women through the mediation of the Union and without the necessity of prosecution. It is by no means unreasonable to estimate that the direct and indirect influence of the Union secures to working-women the payment of $10,000 every year, which must otherwise be entirely lost to them. That it has been the means of thus securing to them more than $50,000 cannot, properly, be questioned.

It is not by the amount of these collection, however, that we measure the beneficial effects accomplished. None but those for whom the service is rendered can understand how much of new life and vigor such timely assistance and encouragement impart. The woman, who, without them, must succumb in her great struggle, and cast herself upon society as a useless pauper, or become the victim of an evil worse than pauperism, is thus aided to cross a fearful abyss and plant her feet firmly on solid ground.

During the years 1868 and 1869, the superintendents in charge received 29,102 applications for protection, for advice, and for employment by working-women, and by employers having need for their services.

Of this number 5,548 applicants were furnished with employment; 2,181 were furnished with the assistance required; 579 with useful legal protection; and 20,794 with such advice and information as they desired, of such as could be extended to them.

Nearly $2,500 was collected in small sums and paid over to the working-women who had earned them—sums the payment of which was secured only at the interposition of the Union.

In nearly 200 cases of dispute, the claims of the working-women were carried to court at the expense of the Union, and the several sums involved were ultimately collected by process of law, and paid over without the least deduction for the costs and expenses of legal proceedings.

During the same period, the number of working-women who for the first time enjoyed the benefits provided by the Union was 9,310.

The managers of this admirable institution, with the exception of the lady superintendent and her two assistants are gentlemen. . . .

The very existence of such an association, thus represented, has acted as a check upon employers, and materially increased the pay of women as a class of workers. It has also lessened the hours of labor, but has lacked activity in this respect also. Statistics show that some of the women toilers of New York, the hoop-skirt-factory girls, for instance, labor fourteen hours out of the twenty-four, and, in times of press, eighteen hours a day; while the most favored class of workers, saleswomen, copyists, press-feeders and type-setters work ten hours per day.

The wages, too are at starvation rates, in spite of all that has been done. . . .

ORGANIZED IN 1869, the Knights of Labor by the 1880s had become the first large-scale national labor federation in America. Women were actively organized into the Knights beginning in 1881. At its height, over 113 all-women locals or assemblies (including black and white women) were formed. The list of these local assemblies included every type of work imaginable: housekeepers, rubber workers, lead pencil makers, farmers, cabinet makers, various factory operatives and weavers.

At the 1885 convention, or General Assembly, three women delegates were appointed to serve as a committee on women's work. By 1886 the women were strong enough (this is relative, of course, since there were only 16 women delegates out of 660 present) to recommend that a department of women's work, with a full-time general investigator and organizer, be established.

The post was given to Leonora Barry, a hosiery worker from Amsterdam, New York. Born in Ireland, Leonora Barry was brought to upstate New York as a small child. At the death of her husband, she went to work to support her three children in a local factory. By 1866 she had become the Master Workman (or president) of an assembly of nearly 1,000 women and a delegate to the annual convention.

For the next three and a half years she traveled extensively throughout the country, organizing women's and men's locals, lecturing on women's issues and lobbying for protective labor legislation. Barry's annual reports to the Knights give us a picture of the difficult conditions for workingwomen, the obstacles to organizing from both employers and male trade unionists, the feminist consciousness of the women workers and her own changing perspective on the problems and direction of her organizing.

Throughout their history, the Knights organized women into "separate but equal" locals. Judging from the letters to the Knights' paper, the *Journal of United Labor*, the women appear to be happier in separate locals. Some even requested a separate labor movement only for women. In her 1889 report, however, Barry suggested that there was no longer a need for a women's department because "women should organize as a part of the industrial hive, rather than because they are women."

In 1890 she remarried another Knight, O. R. Lake of St. Louis, Missouri. In a letter (see page 125), Terrence V. Powderly, the leader of the Knights of Labor, used the metaphor of death to describe Barry's marriage and its consequence: her return to the home. The one woman delegate at the 1890 convention refused to replace her and the women's department was dissolved. By then, the Knights were no longer strong nationally, although local assemblies continued to be active throughout the '90s and into the twentieth century.

KNIGHTS OF LABOR

1887

Having no legal authority I have been unable to make as thorough an investigation in many places as I would like, and, after the discharge of Sister Annie Conboy from the silk mill in Auburn, in February last, for having taken me through the mill, I was obliged to refrain from going through establishments where the owners were opposed to our Order lest some of our members be victimized; consequently the

"Report of the General Investigator." *Proceedings of the General Assembly of the Knights of Labor*, 1887. "Report of the General Investigator." *Proceedings of the General Assembly of the Knights of Labor*, 1888. "Report of the General Investigator and Director of Women's Work." *Proceedings of the General Assembly of the Knights of Labor*, 1889. Papers of Terence K. Powderly, Catholic University (Terence V. Powderly to R. Glocking, Esq., Toronto, Ontario, Letterbook 48, April 10, 1890).

facts stated in my report are not all from actual observation but from authority which I have every reason to believe truthful and reliable.

Upon the strength of my observation and experience I would ask of officers and members of this Order that more consideration be given, and more thorough educational measures be adopted on behalf of the working-women of our land, the majority of whom are entirely ignorant of the economic and industrial question which is to them of such vital importance; and they must ever remain so while the selfishness of their brothers in toil is carried to such an extent as I find it to be among those who have sworn to demand equal pay for equal work. Thus far in the history of our Order that part of our platform has been but a mockery of the principles intended.

Went to Auburn, N.Y., Feb. 20. I found the working-women of this city in a deplorable state, there being none of them organized. There were long hours, poor wages and the usual results consequent upon such a condition. Not among male employers alone in this city, but a woman in whose heart we would expect to find a little pity and compassion for the suffering of her own sex. To the contrary, on this occasion, however, I found one who, for cruelty and harshness toward employees, has not an equal on the pages of labor's history—one who owns and conducts an establishment in which is manufactured women's and children's wear. Upon accepting a position in her factory an employee is compelled to purchase a sewing machine from the proprietress, who is agent for the S.M. Co. This must be paid for in weekly payments of 50 cents, provided the operative makes $3. Should she make $4 the weekly payment is 75 cents. At any time before the machine is paid for, through a reduction of the already meager wages, or the enforcement of some petty tyrranical rule—sickness, anger or any cause, the operative leaves her employ, she forfeits the machine and all the money paid upon it, and to the next applicant the machine is resold. She must also purchase the thread for doing the work, as she is an agent for a thread company. It takes four spools of thread at 50 cents a spool to do $5 worth of work, and when $2 is paid for thread, and 50 cents for the machine, the unfortunate victim has $2.50 wherewith to board, clothe and care for herself generally; and it is only experts who can make even this. Many other equally unjust systems are resorted to of which lack of space forbids mention.

I succeeded in organizing two Local Assemblies in this city, one of wood-workers, and one women's Local Assembly, numbering at organization 107 members, which has grown rapidly and is now one of the most flourishing Local Assemblies in the State. Here it was that Sister

Annie Conboy was discharged from the silk mill for having taken me through the mill, although she had received permission from her foreman to take a friend through, yet, when the proprietor found out I was a Knight of Labor she was discharged without a moment's warning. . . .

May 12 returned to complete the work mapped out for me in D.A. 99. Summing the State of Rhode Island up, on the whole, the condition of its wage-workers is truly a pitiful one—its industries being for the most part in the control of soulless corporations, who know not what humanity means—poor pay, long hours, yearly increase of labor on the individual, and usually a decrease of their wages, the employment of children, in some cases, who are mere infants. The following is a fair sample of the contemptible, mean trickery resorted to by some of the kings of the cotton industry. A law in this State prohibits the compulsory labor of women over ten hours per day. Upon one occasion women weavers were asked to work overtime. They refused. The foreman went to the men weavers, asked them to work overtime, saying it would be money in their pockets, a favor to their employer, and would make the women jealous of their larger months' wages. Then they would consent to work overtime, too. This is only one instance of how the wage-workers are made the instruments of injury to one another. The years of cruel oppression and injustice which those people have endured has so sapped the milk of human kindness from their hearts that the same system of selfishness applied to them by their employers they in turn practice toward each other, and to this and no other reason can be traced the falling off in the jurisdiction of D.A. 99, as well as in many others. . . .

1888.

My understanding of the duties implied in my office was that I was to do everything in my power that would in my judgement have a tendency to educate and elevate the workingwomen of America and ameliorate their condition. Therefore, when I spoke to a public audience of American citizens, exposing existing evils and showing how, through the demands of Knighthood, they could be remedied, I felt that I was fulfilling the duties of my office. When I found a body of workingmen who were so blind to what justice demanded of them on behalf of women as to pass unanimously a resolution excluding women from our organization, I felt I was performing a sacred duty toward women by trying to enlighten those men and showing their mistake. When I found an opportunity of laying before other organizations of women the cause of their less fortunate sisters and mold a favorable sentiment, I felt I was doing that which is an actual necessity, as woman is often unconsciously woman's oppressor. . . .

On March 25 to April 1 I represented women in the Knights of Labor at the Women's Congress at Washington, D.C. The good results of that meeting have been widespread. As to all countries represented there by delegates, a more satisfactory knowledge of the aims and objects of Knighthood were obtained than could have been disseminated by any other method; also in a number of cities and towns of our own land. Women who heretofore ignored the cause of workingwomen now work earnestly and faithfully for their welfare. . . .

On July 1 at Rockford, Ill. There are very many industries here employing women—principally the Rockford Watch Factory and Watch-case Factory; but at the time of my visit mostly all were closed for the national holiday, so I was unable to learn any definite details concerning general conditions, except the universal complaint of low wages, women not being allowed to make over $1.25 per day. July 4 was celebrated here under the name of our "Foremothers' Day." It has been celebrated of "Our Forefathers" for so many years that the women of Rockford conceived the idea of resurrecting our good old foremothers for a change. It was a glorious success, notwithstanding the pressure of political effort to make it a failure. Over 3,000 people listened to my address on the need and benefit of organization; also Senator Whiting's masterly address. . . .

Closed a meeting August 27 at Norristown, Pa. A few of both sexes comprise the Local, and even those stand in terror of losing their positions if it were known they were organized, as one firm had offered a reward of $25 for information of a Knight of Labor in their employ. . . .

From September 19 to October 4 I visited the jurisdiction of D.A. 95, in Danbury, Conn. The principle industry is hatmaking; very many married women are employed, owing largely to the idle time men have in this industry. The women do the binding, banding, putting in the tips and sweat-bands, also making tips; wages are fairly good, conditions very good, as this industry is thoroughly organized.

It has been intimated that the Woman's Department was started on sentiment. Well, if so, it has turned out to be one of the most thoroughly practical departments in the Order. Without egotism I can safely say it has done as much effective work in cheering, encouraging, educating and instructing the women of this Order in the short year of its existence as was done by the organization in the whole time of women's connection with it previous to its establishment.

As you will all doubtless remember, I instituted a Beneficial Department for women, of our Order by way of encouragement and that they might have some tangible proof of the benefits of our organization. Owing to the lack of business methods and selfishness of others, and a general apathy with which comfortably-situated women are afflicted, it did not become the universal success I had hoped, but it was firmly and successfully established in many places, principally in Rhode Island, the whole State being thoroughly organized and having one of the strongest, both financially and numerically, women's beneficial departments in the country

I have made many unsuccessful attempts to found a manufactory of women's and children's underwear so that I could have some positive proof to offer against the slop-shop or contract made work. I have been partially successful, as a plant is being established in Elizabeth, N.J., and the girls of the Solidarity Co-operative Shirt Company of New York have commenced the production of these garments, so that now we will have something to offer the public, as being well made and well paid for instead of the garments manufactured by men who sacrifice human happiness, life and immortal souls on the altar of selfish greed and low, sordid, groveling ambition. . . .

1889.

My work has not been confined solely to women and children, but to all of earth's toilers, as I am of the opinion that the time when we could separate the interests of the toiling masses on sex lines is past. If it were possible, I wish that it were not necessary for women to learn any trade but that of domestic duties, as I believe it was intended that man should be the bread-winner. But as that is impossible under present conditions, I believe women should have every opportunity to become proficient in whatever vocation they choose or find themselves best fitted for.

A few words about the Woman's Department. When I took a position at its head I fondly hoped to weld together in organization such a number of women as would be a power for good in the present, and a monument to their honor in the relief it would establish for the women of the future. I was too sanguine, and I am forced to acknowledge that to fulfill my best hopes is a matter of impossibility; and I believe now we should, instead of supporting a Woman's Department, put more women in the field as Lecturers to tell women why they should organize as a part of the industrial hive, rather than because they are women. There can be no separation or distinction of wage-workers on account of sex, and separate departments for their interests is a direct contradiction of this, and also of that part of our declaration which says "we know no sex in the laws of Knighthood." Therefore, I recommend the abolition of the Woman's Department, believing, as I now do, that women should be Knights of Labor without distinction, and should have all the benefits that can be given to men—no more, no less—thereby making it incumbent upon all to work more earnestly for the general good, rather than for sex, Assembly or trade.

IN 1890 Terence Powderly of the Knights of Labor wrote this letter to a union comrade just before Leonora Barry's marriage.

A FATE WORSE THAN DEATH

. . . The request for the services of Sister Barry comes from other localities but she can not comply, in fact, Sister Barry's days are numbered. You will never, in all probability, rest eyes on her again. I know you will unite with me in sorrowing over this, for us, unhappy event, but the fates are against us and soon the name of Sister Barry will exist only in the fond remembrance of the members of our Order and her many friends outside of it. She has not yet been called across the dark river but she will soon be buried in the bosom of a Lake that shall wash away all claim that we may have to her, and the papers will chronicle the event in this way: On April 17th, at St. Louis, Mrs. L. M. Barry of Amsterdam, N.Y. to O. R. Lake of St. Louis, Mo., the Rev. Mr. —— officiating. The bride was dressed in a ——. Brother Glocking, words fail and you will have to describe the bridal outfit yourself. . . .

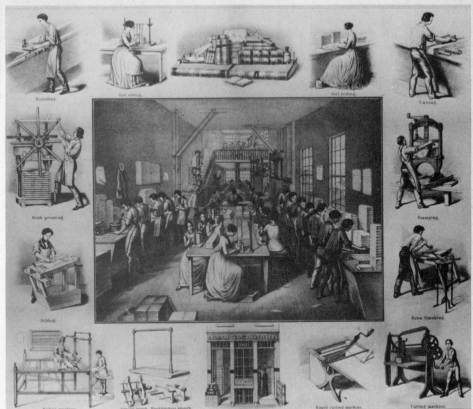

The sexual division of labor in nineteenth-century book manufacturing, from an advertisement.

Women being interviewed in an employment agency operated by the Working Women's Protective Union in New York City in 1879.

Women delegates to the 1886 convention of the Knights of Labor.

Women workers refusing to leave the factory in sympathy with striking garment workers.

A black woman vendor of the nineteenth century.

1890~1920

Between 1890 and 1920 the United States became the most powerful nation in the world. Only slightly more than a century away from being a rebellious colony, the United States was in a position to impose its will not only on its former "mother country," but also on much of Europe and Latin America. At the beginning of this period the United States emerged as a major imperialist power, moving into the Philippines, Central America, the Caribbean and the Far East. By 1920 the victorious intervention of the United States in World War I made both its allies and its enemies financially and politically dependent.

Behind this expansionism into other countries were the economic needs of U.S. capitalism. "Dollar diplomacy" was dedicated above all else to protecting U.S. investments abroad, invading and assuming direct military and political control when patriots in those countries resisted. The lure of foreign investment was great, as American companies intensified their search for cheap raw materials, new markets for their products and, above all, investment opportunities which assured them the high profit that cheap labor made possible.

Domestically, large corporations were exercising enormous influence over almost all aspects of government. Legislation was designed to regulate the corporations, but the commissions set up to control them were often manipulated by the corporations. Despite a great deal of public fear and suspicion of the corporate giants and the powerful magnates who ran them, the tendency toward monopolization was not checked. Corporations like U.S. Steel and Standard Oil had assets and employees greater than those of large state governments. In defending themselves against the growing claims of their workers, such corporations often used state troops against striking workers; when state troops were insufficient, they secured federal troops and court injunctions. Big corporations crushed small businesses and even small banks. Through the Federal Reserve System they established centralized control over the monetary system of the country, ending any hope of popular control over banking and currency as had been demanded by the Populists.

The early twentieth century saw the reform of municipal and state government. Attacking the corruption of big-city political machines, especially those grown strong by exploiting the vulnerability of immigrants, "Progressive" reformers fought for civil service, honesty in government and in some cases increased popular control. While these gains were significant, they also represented great consolidation of local political control in the hands of the educated business and professional classes at the expense of the poor and the working class. In many instances these reforms were used by big business to consolidate its power.

The consequence of unchecked business growth was worsening economic depressions. The depression of 1893, which lasted four years, was the worst yet: hundreds of banks failed, many railroads went into bankruptcy; 3 million people were unemployed, thousands of them tramping the countryside and riding the rails.

Industrial expansion had transformed the working class. One change was massive immigration; between 1900 and 1914 annual immigration figures topped 1 million. The immigrants were no longer mainly from western and northern Europe, but from Russia, eastern and southern Europe. Their appearance, language and religion distinguished them sharply from many earlier Americans. The migration of blacks to the northern and midwestern cities of the United States also increased sharply in the early twentieth century, particularly during World War I. Unfamiliar environments combined with terrible wages, housing and working conditions created ghetto slums. Employers exploited ethnic differences, hiring from diverse groups and placing them in the same shop to make communication more difficult and deliberately turning workers against each other.

The development of mass-production techniques, notably the assembly line, changed the experience for some of the working class. In order to speed up production—that is, to increase production without increasing expenditure on labor—employers developed efficiency engineering as a "science." The "scientific managers" broke down production processes into many small, separable jobs, requiring workers to do one tiny job over and over. The effect was not only to worsen working conditions (the tedium and the required speed were often unbearable), but also to prevent workers from understanding the total production process and thereby exerting any control over it. The employers hoped that by depriving the workers of control and blocking them from taking any initiatives, they would become more passive, resigned and separated from each other.

The employers' hopes were not realized. On the contrary, militant resistance by the workers emerged. Indeed, this period was richer in radical and reform movements than any in U.S. history. In the 1880s and 1890s agrarian discontent was organized into a mass political and economic movement of angry farmers called Populism. The labor movement meanwhile was growing rapidly. The most important trade-union organization at this time was the American Federation of Labor, which was devoted to protecting the interests of skilled workers, the "aristocracy of labor," while neglecting and deliberately excluding the largest parts of the working class: poor immigrant, black and female unskilled workers.

In spite of the A.F.L.'s conservatism, workers organized and fought to improve their working conditions. Employers used court injunctions, informers, blacklists, lockouts and above all intimidation and violence against the burgeoning labor movement. At the Homestead steel strike of 1892, the Pullman strike and boycott of 1893 and the coal field battles of the 1890s and 1900s, workers had to fight armies of federal troops and Pinkertons, bought by employers' money and political power. These conditions created, in 1903, a new kind of labor union: the Industrial Workers of the World, the "Wobblies" or I.W.W., dedicated to organizing *all* workers along industrywide, not craft, lines, including women and even the unemployed. The I.W.W. offered a program for complete political change, including demands for workers' control of industry. Because of its concern for unskilled, mass-production workers, the I.W.W. supplied important leadership in several great strikes in textile and garment factories between 1909 and 1913 in which women were sometimes the majority. Women by the thousands marched at the front of picket lines, bearing up as well as men under clubbings and economic misery. Indeed, even conservative labor leaders acknowledged with surprise the tenacity and leadership ability of these workingwomen.

This widespread working-class militancy created the basis for a powerful socialist movement. The U.S. native socialist tradition combined with European Marxian socialism to build a massive Socialist party. The S.P. brought together radical intellectuals, big-city immigrant workers, western miners, migrant workers and many other socialists.

On the eve of World War I a powerful working-class movement and an overlapping socialist movement made radical change seem likely in the United States. After 1917 the country experienced a rapid shift to the Right, much of it deliberately engineered by worried capitalists and conservatives. The patriotism stimulated by the war was encouraged and whipped into xenophobia and the baiting of pacifists and others who opposed the war because they believed its only purposes were imperialist ones. Later in 1917, the Bolshevik Revolution in Russia brought inspiration to many American Leftists, but also served the ruling class as a basis for maligning domestic radicals as foreign agents or traitors. Many were hounded, arrested, jailed and deported (even if they were citizens, the foreign-born were subject to deportation) on charges such as "criminal syndicalism." In 1919 over 4 million workers struck, when their expectations and demands (heightened after the sacrifices they had made for "their" country during the war) were ignored. In response, employers fought back more violently than ever, haunted by the specter of the Russian Revolution and the realistic fear that the working class could in fact take over.

In this period increasing numbers of women entered the paid labor force; industrial development and urbanization concentrated workers in larger units. Many were recent immigrants, and some of them brought with them the ideas and experiences of European labor and socialist movements. At the same time many educated women were becoming reformers. Radicalized by their contact with working-class women, some joined union organizations and the Socialist party. Through these and other activities workingwomen and reformers came together to work for protective legislation, welfare programs, workers' education and women's trade unions. These political alliances created in the early twentieth century a potential for a mass women's movement greater than in any period other than today. But because not enough women were in the labor force and because those who were lacked some of the conditions necessary for political activism such as birth control, education and independence from men, a mass women's movement was never born.

MIGRANTS AND
IMMIGRANTS

FROM 1916 TO 1918 nearly 500,000 black people left the South for the industrial cities of the North and Midwest. The migration had been in progress for decades but swelled during the years of World War I. In the South, floods and the recurrence of the boll weevil had devastated cotton crops. The passage of Jim Crow segregation laws in the '90s and the increase in lynchings and violence were making life in the South increasingly miserable and dangerous for blacks. In addition, a rising level of black education created expectations which the Southern economy and conditions could not meet.

In the North, World War I had cut off European migration and taken many thousands of white men out of the labor force. Northern factories needed a new labor force. They sent labor agents to the South to encourage the migration of black workers, offering to pay rail fares to the cities. Black newspapers like the *Chicago Defender* also encouraged the migration by painting rosy pictures of work and living conditions in the cities. Advertisements were carried in the papers for northern jobs; the papers were distributed throughout the South and eagerly read.

The result was overwhelming: between 1910 and 1920 the black population of Chicago increased by 65,000 people, or 148.2 percent; in Detroit, by 611.3 percent. Many whole families migrated together; others sent one member to earn enough to bring up the rest of the family. The pattern was not unlike that of many other immigrant people who came to the cities hoping to better their way of life.

This selection is from letters sent to the *Chicago Defender* by black people in the South inquiring about jobs in Chicago.

LETTERS FROM
BLACK MIGRANTS

Jacksonville, Fla., May 22, 1917.

Chicago Defender:

I wish to go North haven got money enuff to come I can do any kind of housework laundress nurse good cook has cook for northern people I am 27 years of age just my self would you kindly inderseed for me a job with some rich white people who would send me a ticket and I pay them back please help me. I am brown skin just meaden size.

Jacksonville, Fla., April 29, 1917.

My dear Sir:

I take grate pleazer in writing you. as I found in your Chicago Defender this morning where you are secure job for men as I realey diden no if you can get a good job for me as am a woman and a widowe with two girls and would like to no if you can get one for me and the girls. We will do any kind of work and I would like to hear from you at once not any of us has any husbands.

Biloxi, Miss., April 27, 1917.

Dear Sir:

I would like to get in touch with you a pece of advise I am unable to under go hard work as I have a fracture ancle but in the mene time I am able to help my selft a great dele. I am a good cook and can give good recmendation can serve in small famly that has light work, if I could get something in that line I could work my daughters a long with me. She is 21 years and I have a husban all so and he is a fireman and want a positions and too small boy need to be in school now if you all see where there is some open for me that I may be able too better my condission anser at once and we will com as we are in a land of starvaten.

From a willen workin woman. I hope that you will healp ne as I want to get out of this land of sufring I no there is som thing that I can do here there is nothing for me to do I may be able to get in some furm where I dont have to stand on my feet all day I dont no just whah but I hope the Lord will find a place now let me here from you all at once.

Emmett J. Scott, collector. "Letters from Negro Migrants, 1916–1918." *Journal of Negro History* 4 (No. 3), July 1919, pp. 296–319.

THE FIRST PART of this excerpt describes the immigration to the United States of Rosa Cristoforo, an Italian orphan formerly employed in the silk mills of Lombardy. She was married against her wishes to Santino, who immigrated to the United States alone. After she joined him, he was so brutal to her that she left him and went alone to Chicago.

ROSA CRISTOFORO COMES
TO THE UNITED STATES

The day came when we had to go and everyone was in the square saying good-bye. I had my Francesco in my arms. I was kissing his lips and kissing his cheeks and kissing his eyes. Maybe I would never see him again! It wasn't fair! He was *my* baby! Why should Mamma Lena keep him? But then Pep was calling and Mamma Lena took Francesco away and Zia Teresa was helping me onto the bus and handing up the bundles.

"But Rosa, don't be so sad!" It was the other Rosa and Zia Maria in the station in Milan, kissing me good-bye and patting my shoulder. "It is wonderful to go to America even if you don't want to go to Santino. You will get smart in America. And in America you will not be so poor." . . .

Day after day in Havre we were leaving the lodging house and standing down on the docks waiting for a ship to take us. But always the ship was full before it came our turn. "O Madonna!" I prayed. "Don't ever let there be room! Don't ever let there be room!"

But here, on the sixth day we came on. We were almost the last ones. There was just one young French girl after us. She was with her mother and her sister, but when the mother and sister tried to follow, that *marinaro* at the gate said, "No more! Come on the next boat!" And that poor family was screaming and crying. But the *marinaro* wouldn't let the girl off and wouldn't let the mother and sister on. He said, "You'll meet in New York. Meet in New York."

All us poor people had to go down through a hole to the bottom of the ship. There was a big dark room down there with rows of wooden shelves all around where we were going to sleep — the Italian, the

Marie Hall Ets, ed. *Rosa, The Life of an Immigrant Woman.* Minneapolis: University of Minnesota Press, 1970.

German, the Polish, the Swede, the French — every kind. And in that
time the third class on the boat was not like now. The girls and women
and the men had to sleep all together in the same room. The men and
girls had to sleep even in the same bed with only those little half-boards
up between to keep us from rolling together. But I was lucky. I had two
girls sleeping next to me. When the dinner bell rang we were all standing in line holding the tin plates we had to buy in Havre, waiting for
soup and bread.

"Oh, I'm so scared!" Emilia kept saying and she kept looking at the
little picture she carried in her blouse. "I'm so scared!"

"Don't be scared, Emilia," I told her. "That young man looks nice
in his picture."

"But I don't know him," she said. "I was only seven years old when
he went away." . . .

On the fourth day a terrible storm came. The sky grew black and the
ocean came over the deck. Sailors started running everywhere, fastening this and fastening that and giving orders. Us poor people had to go
below and that little door to the deck was fastened down. We had no
light and no air and everyone got sick where we were. We were like
rats trapped in a hole, holding onto the posts and onto the iron frames
to keep from rolling around. Why had I worried about Santino? We
were never going to come to America after all! We were going to the
bottom of the sea!

But after three days the ship stopped rolling. That door to the deck
was opened and some sailors came down and carried out two who had
died and others too sick to walk. Me and all my *paesani* climbed out
without help and stood in line at the wash-house, breathing fresh air
and filling our basins with water. Then we were out on the narrow deck
washing ourselves and our clothes — some of us women and girls
standing like a wall around the others so the men couldn't see us.

Another time there was fog — so much fog that we couldn't see the
masts and we couldn't see the ocean. The engine stopped and the sails
were tied down and a horn that shook the whole boat started blowing.
All day and all night that horn was blowing. No one could sleep so no
one went to bed. One man had a concertina and the ones who knew
how to dance were dancing to entertain the others. Me, I was the best
one. There was no one there to scold me and tell me what to do so I
danced with all my *paesani* who knew how. Then I even danced with
some of the Polish and the French. We were like floating on a cloud in
the middle of nowhere and when I was dancing I forgot for a little

while that I was the wife of Santino going to him in America. But on the third day the fog left, the sails came out, the engine started, and the ship was going again.

Sometimes when I was walking on the steerage deck with Giorgio — the little boy of one woman from Bugiarno who was all-the-way sea-sick — I would look back and see the rich people sitting on the higher decks with nice awnings to protect them from the cinders and the sun, and I would listen to their strange languages and their laughing. The rich always knew where they were going and what they were going to do. The rich didn't have to be afraid like us poor.

Then one day we could see land! Me and my *paesani* stood and watched the hills and the land come nearer. Other poor people, dressed in their best clothes and loaded down with bundles, crowded around. *America!* The country where everyone could find work! Where wages were so high no one had to go hungry! Where all men were free and equal and where even the poor could own land! But now we were so near it seemed too much to believe. Everyone stood silent — like in prayer. Big sea gulls landed on the deck and screamed and flew away.
. . .

"There!" said Pep, raising his hand in a greeting. "There it is! *New York!*" . . .

"And there's Castle Garden."

"Castle Garden! Which? Which is Castle Garden?"

Castle Garden! Castle Garden was the gate to the new land. Every-one wanted to see. But the ship was being pulled off to one side — away from the strange round building.

"Don't get scared," said Pep. "We go just to the pier up the river. Then a government boat brings us back."

Doctors had come on the ship and ordered us inside to examine our eyes and our vaccinations. One old man who couldn't talk and two girls with sore eyes were being sent back to the old country. "O Madonna, make them send me back too!" I prayed. "Don't make me go to Santino!" . . .

THE IMMIGRANTS not only faced a new culture but often found them-selves confronting urban living and middle-class values for the first

Mary Heaton Vorse Collection, Archives of Labor History and Urban Affairs, Wayne State University, Detroit, Michigan, Articles and Stories, Di-Fai, Box 19, October 1901. (Mary Heaton Vorse, "Making or Marring, The Experiences of a Hired Girl.")

time. In this selection, Mary Heaton Vorse, a prominent labor jour-
nalist in the early twentieth century, has fictionalized the adjustment
experience of an Irish "greenhorn" or new immigrant.

AN IRISH HIRED GIRL

. . . I come to this cuntry when I was 15 like I said with my cusin Joe
Brennan an his wife he had a job all fixed for him it was down in
Newjersy so I said goodby to them when we landed and went off with
Eliza McCarty she was my second cusin on my mothers side and had
been in this cuntry a long time, I guess she forgot what greenhorns
lookt like for I could see rite of she seemed suprized to see me I dident
have no hat I had a little shawl pined over my dress and big hevy boots
on my feet. I had never been farther than the market town near us my
father was small farmer, the floor of our house was dirt and it was
thached with straw like you see in the old cuntry, the pig an chikens
run in an out like the children dont you know things is like that in
Ireland and I took care of the younger children and gone after peat in
the bogs and hoed potatoes as for cookin I had made stirabout an
boiled potatos an made tea, you mite say there was no housework done
in our house. Mrs. drake I tell you this because that is the sortof thing
most green girls come from I dont no how fokes live in sweeden or in
other cuntries but they dont live like they do in this cuntry I am sure,
why when a green girl comes in a house she dont know what half the
things is four ladys dont reelize this an girls thats been here sumtime
forget how it was with them when they was green.

I was a tall girl for my age and had fat red cheeks and lookt strong
and helthy Eliza took me an bought me a hat she ment to be real kind I
think but she coudnt help showin she felt ashamed of my looks she
made me by shoes with my own money and cotton stockings insted of
my nit wool ones and a shirtwaist my skirt would have to do she said
until I got my wages she told me they needed a kitchen made where she
was workin, it was quite a big house there was no men servants the
gentlemen dident like them on account of there drinkin mostly, I felt
like I was in a dream.

I hadent ever been inside of a big store or seen a city an the noises
an hurry made me feel confused Eliza kepp warning me not to tell how
I was green and making up a story for me. I dont know what kind of
fokes I was workin for as I never seen the lady only wonce she wasent
old and was dressed luvely and she said was it the new kitchen made

well what makes you bother me, if she suits Annie its allright, I dont think she will suit Annie she looks stupid they said I wasent stupid I was justbashfull and dazzed like.

Fokes dont no how strange things is I usto cry an cry most all the night just from homesickness and discuragment. Eliza was chamber made so she coudent help me and the cook dident have time to be bothered with me nobody showed me ennything, I was willin an I am no duller than the next one and I think with a little showin I might have done fine there because it wasent like in some places where the kitchen made has to cook a lot of little things, I was just fritened clear through all the time I was in that place they thought I was sullen I think the cook was good-harted enough to help me if I had told her how I felt but green girls is awfull bashfull and dont know how to speak up for themselvs any more than children.

Eliza seen I wasent goin to do an she told me to give warning before I was fired an I did, my next place was as genral houseworker with a young maried couple she wont keep you Eliza said but perhaps you will learn somethin she and evrybody treated me as if it was a crime to be a greenhorn They had a gas stove and I dident know how lite it but I managed somehow she found me out right of she says to me Nora you dont know how to make a bed, in the week I was in the other place I hadent been up stares accept that wonce when I saw the lady, an she showed me how to make one and that is all the showin I ever got from anybody for 3 months there aint one single sole willing to be bothered with a greenhorn that is what I mean by getting a bad start thats where all those girls come from that dont know nothin and dont care if they dont. I was luckier than lots I had a place I could go to when I was out of work to my aunts. It was in that place I learned what a dum waiter shaft was by puttin the mayonnaise on the dum waiter standin there and thinking it was a cubboard about all I learned in the others was about hot an cold water running and pluming I found I dident know about ennything. . . .

FAITH THAT THE American "way of life" could automatically change the culture and living patterns of immigrants was challenged by mass immigration at the turn of the century. Industrialists and social workers worried that the laissez-faire approach to Americanization was not working and decided to help the process along. Beginning in the 1880s, social workers, militant U.S. nationalists, patriotic organizations and "public-spirited" businessmen joined in various coalitions to "Americanize" the immigrants.

Much of their early efforts were focused on teaching English and transforming immigrants into pliable and willing industrial workers. To accomplish this the Americanizers had to change the living patterns and character structures of immigrants, most of whom came from peasant cultures where the concepts of clocked worktime and formal employer-employee relations did not exist.

At first the public schools were expected to perform this task, but it soon became clear that not even night classes could reach the mass of immigrant adults. So the campaign was moved into the factory itself. One group helping the Americanization effort was the National Safety Council (N.S.C.), an employer-controlled industrial safety organization. The N.S.C. used nurses not only to patch up wounded and sick workers and send them back to work, but also to influence workers' habits in the home and factory. While the living conditions of immigrant workers certainly needed improvement, the employer-initiated changes did not so much help the workers as attempt to obliterate independent cultures.

The following is from the report of an industrial nurse employed by the Clark Thread Company in Newark, New Jersey, in 1916.

AMERICANIZATION

The history of the nurse in industry is recent. The first one so employed of whom any personal information can be obtained was Miss Anna B. Duncan who began her work less than twenty years ago for the Benefit Association of John Wanamaker, New York. . . .

This nurse found that her nursing skill and ability to give instruction and advice gained her the unquestioning confidence of those she visited and that the question of malingering was a very small one, met with only in a few cases, and many of these proving on further study to be a real incapacity or a sincere but mistaken conviction of inability to work. . . .

TEACHING HEALTH, MORALITY AND THRIFT

When most of the workers were English-speaking and either American-born or from European countries whose standards of living are not so different from ours, many problems did not arise which now cause us

Florence S. Wright. "The Visiting Nurse in Industrial Welfare Work." *Fifth Safety Council Proceedings.* Detroit: National Safety Council, 1916.

the most anxiety. With laborers coming from the four quarters of the globe, speaking strange languages and bringing with them their own traditions, superstitions, diseases, religions, it becomes necessary for the employer who is awake to his own needs and to those of the country to do something toward educating these masses in habits of cleanliness, health, morality and thrift, and especially in suitable standards of living and in adapting their lives to changed conditions.

We see an Italian family of six living in three rooms, taking boarders. They do this, not because the man does not earn enough, but to get money to buy a home, and because they were used to being crowded in Italy. They do not know that conditions which did not injure health in the warm, sunny, outdoor life of the homeland become a menace when every one works indoors and when doors, windows and cracks are stopped up to keep out the cold. The father is at home with a "cold." The children are anaemic. The mother wonders why no one is well in this country.

A Polish mother refuses to nurse her baby because she wants to work in the mill and gives it condensed milk because "cow's milk gets bad too quick."

A Lithuanian woman buys sausages, new white bread and coffee as the sole food of her growing family. She had a garden, chickens and a goat in the old country. Here the "store milk" sours and vegetables seem expensive and not necessary to her. They cost nothing at home.

CHILDREN RUN WILD

A Russian father cannot control his boys because they speak a language he does not know and in their new surroundings have become ashamed of the homeland ways.

An American mother loses a baby each summer because she cannot nurse her children. She has no idea of cleanliness, using a long tube nursing bottle in which the milk is often clotted solid and which is never cleaned. . . .

A Slavish woman (tubercular) is sent to a sanitarium. She cries all the time and no one can talk to her. The nurse takes an interpreter and discovers that the woman has given her money to a dozen different countrymen to keep for her. She cannot write and knows nothing of our banks.

MAKING OF AMERICANS

These instances could be related for hours from memory of actual cases and results, accomplished and not accomplished, but is it not proven that these masses of foreigners must be educated in cleanliness, home-making and infant care; in fact, that they must be made into good Americans as fast as possible?

No one can do this who does not reach the homes, and who can reach the homes except the visiting nurse?

She goes out in the morning with a list of names and addresses. (Let us hope she is provided with an automobile, for her work is hard and she will not *need* the exercise of walking.) She finds the Italian family taking boarders. She goes slowly and keeps the family on her list. In time each member will accept her advice without question. The father has his chest examined, is found to be an incipient tuberculosis case, and after a period of rest and education is given outdoor work suited to his strength. The mother is taught to buy and to cook. The children are sent to open-air school. It takes time but in the end the boarders are no longer there, the father is well and doing suitable work, the children are gaining, and the mother is making a home of which the family and the nurse are proud.

Incidentally, the nurse has increased her Italian vocabulary and has six firm friends. Needless to say the unseen employer who sent the nurse also has six loyal friends although he may never know of their existence. . . .

THE HUMAN COST OF INDUSTRY

ONE OF THE worse aspects of working-class life at the turn of the century was housing. In the urban ghettos, street after street was lined with dank, unhealthy tenements that bred despair and exhaustion along with disease.

Appalled by these conditions, middle-class reformers and social workers began to "investigate" the problem of housing in earnest. Revised housing codes were developed in most major cities, but powerful landlords and weak enforcement provisions undermined the laws.

The following testimony is taken from the model, and most important, of these investigations, the 1900 New York State Tenement House Commission hearings. Mr. Moscowitz, the "tenant" being questioned, was an active Jewish investigator and reformer prominent within his community and reform circles in New York.

TENEMENT HOUSE LIFE

Mr. Henry Moscowitz then took the witness chair and was interrogated by the secretary.

THE SECRETARY. Where do you reside?

MR. MOSCOWITZ. 95 Forsyth Street.

THE SECRETARY. Is that a tenement house?

MR. MOSCOWITZ. Yes, sir.

THE SECRETARY. How long have you lived in tenement houses?

MR. MOSCOWITZ. Seventeen years. . . .

Dr. Henry Moscowitz. "Testimony of a Tenant," in *The Tenement House Problem*, ed. Robert W. DeForest and Lawrence Veiller. New York: The Macmillan Company, 1903.

THE SECRETARY. What have you got to say about the air shaft; do you think it is a good thing?

MR. MOSCOWITZ. I think it is decidedly a bad thing. I must confirm the statements made by other witnesses that the air shaft is a breeder of disease, and especially that there can be no fresh air in any building with an air shaft, from my experience, because of the refuse thrown down in the air shaft, the stench is so vile and the air is so foul that the occupants do not employ the windows as a means of getting air. . . .

THE SECRETARY. Are there any other objections to the air shaft?

MR. MOSCOWITZ. It destroys privacy.

THE SECRETARY. How does it do that?

MR. MOSCOWITZ. I know where I lived in a house where there was a family opposite, the windows which are usually diagonal, I heard everything, especially loud noises, and when the windows are not covered one sees into the house. . . .

THE SECRETARY. Do you think that the tenement houses should be restricted in height?

MR. MOSCOWITZ. Decidedly. I think that no tenement house ought to be built over five stories high. It is injurious to the health of the women.

THE SECRETARY. In what way?

MR. MOSCOWITZ. The women complain, and I know this to be a fact, there is a Jewish word "Stiegen," the stairs. Families who live on the third floor complain that they have to go up and down, and I know that many a woman has complained of the side ache to me because of the "stiegen."

THE SECRETARY. Is it true that because of the stairs many of the women in the tenement houses seldom go down into the street and outdoors?

MR. MOSCOWITZ. Decidedly true. I know this for a fact; that they do not visit their neighbors often. Complaints, serious complaints are made, "Why don't you come to visit me?" and they say "We live so high up we seldom come."

THE SECRETARY. Do you know of many families where the mother does not go out oftener than twice a week?

MR. MOSCOWITZ. I do. . . .

THE SECRETARY. Are there any other reasons why you object to tall buildings?

MR. MOSCOWITZ. I think the children are kept in the street a good deal; the parents, especially the mother, very often loses sight of the children, and she has to open the windows and shout down for the little one at play when she wants it in the room, and the parents cannot trace the children; cannot keep track of them. . . .

THE SECRETARY. Have you noticed the practice of people sleeping on the roofs and in the street in the summer-time?

MR. MOSCOWITZ. Yes, sir, I have, because I myself have done so.

THE SECRETARY. Why?

MR. MOSCOWITZ. Because it was too hot to sleep in the room in the summer-time. . . .

The home is very unattractive for the children and they are glad to get out to meet their friends. They want to supply a social need, and they go out and meet other friends and the home has no tie upon them. The father—there is not the authority of the parent that existed in the old country, and I believe because the child is not at home as often as he should be. The tenement house is a decidedly disintegrating influence in the family, and that is seen especially on the East Side to-day.

THE SECRETARY. I have always understood that among the Jewish people the patriarchal form of government was very strong and the authority of the father very strong?

MR. MOSCOWITZ. Yes.

THE SECRETARY. Do you mean to say that this is being weakened by the tenement houses?

MR. MOSCOWITZ. The tenement house is not the only thing, but a very strong influence. . . .

THE SECRETARY. Would you have us infer from your statement that the young men and young women have to meet each other on the street because the home is unattractive?

MR. MOSCOWITZ. Well, they meet each other on the streets, and in club-rooms, and in settlements, but very few I think meet each other there. In dancing academies, in social clubs, in balls and receptions.

THE SECRETARY. And you think this is a bad thing?

MR. MOSCOWITZ. Decidedly a bad thing, because of another point, the tenement house life destroys a certain delicacy of feeling, which is noticeable in one brought up in a good home. That is a decided characteristic of the young men and women living in the tenement houses, that they are too socially dependent.

FINDING A decent place to live was one of the major problems facing workingwomen. This selection is part of a larger study made on the living conditions for women in New York City in 1915. The study was conducted by the YWCA; organized in the 1860s, the "Y" had long been concerned with the problems of women working away from their homes.

SINGLE WOMEN IN THE CITY

THE ORGANIZED HOMES

There are, in New York City, in the Borough of Manhattan, at least fifty-four organized, non-commercial Homes for self-supporting women and girls. . . . Almost every nationality has a Home for its immigrant girls. . . . These fifty-four organized Homes can accommodate 3599 girls. . . .

The question of maintaining order—in fact the whole problem of closing hours, rules, and regulations—is one of the most difficult that the Homes have to meet. . . .

"Show me a rule and I'll break it," this from a quiet, well-poised girl of twenty-five voices, if rather startlingly, the attitude of a great many girls towards the restrictions current in many Homes. The curious fact—curious, that is, at first, but intelligible to one at all familiar with the principles of modern psychology—is that complaints against a 10.30 o'clock closing hour come not always from the little, blonde, gad-about type, as one would expect, but in great part from quiet, well-mannered girls who would never think of being out after 10.30 o'clock. It seems to be the idea of the rule, rather than the rule itself which oppresses. . . .

Of the thirty-one houses reporting on a closing hour, there were seven closing their doors at ten o'clock, seven at ten-thirty, six at eleven, and nine at twelve. Special permission could usually be obtained from the superintendent for a later hour of return if this was not requested too frequently. Only four houses gave keys to the girls, and two kept open all night with a woman night clerk in charge.

"It makes me feel like a baby to be in at a certain hour," remarked one woman of thirty. . . .

Esther Packard. "The Organized Homes." *A Study of Living Conditions of Self-Supporting Women in New York City.* New York: Metropolitan Board of the YWCA, 1915.

"We never let the girls dance here," said the matron of one house, "but on a Wednesday and Saturday night I play a Virginia Reel tune and let them skip. . . ."

Of the fifty-four Homes in New York City only five are entirely self-supporting—that is, the income from board and room rent pays for initial expenses of building and furnishing, (or rent), running expenses, repairs and taxes. . . . A great many places frankly depend on charity, and appeal to the public for help on their heavy subsidy, not even attempting to meet their running expenses or repairs. . . . Two men, high up in the department store world, themselves employing large numbers of girls, said very frankly that a heavily subsidized house, where board could be had at prices far below the ordinary commercial price, tends very directly to reduce wages. When a salesgirl complains that she cannot live upon the $6 or $7 a week wage offered her, the answer is apt to be, "Go to such and such a Home. You can live there for $3.50 a week." As long as the public is willing to take from the shoulders of industry its responsibility to pay living wages, just so long, said these two men, will industry refuse to pay living wages. . . .

A large retail Dry Goods Store gave publicly a sum of $5,000 to a Home for low wage girls. The next year a state commission investigated wages in that store, among others, and when horror was expressed at the number of clerks receiving only $6 and $7 a week, the manager suavely replied, "But you forget! I gave $5,000 only last year to a Home where girls can get room and three meals a day for $4.25 a week. Let my employees go there and live. . . ."

One of the very frequent reasons given by girls for not living in a Home was, "Oh! I don't want to take charity unless I have to. . . ." Occasionally one finds a girl who will conceal, from her working companions, the fact that she lives at a Home, for fear of ridicule. . . .

LIVING CONDITIONS OF GIRLS LIVING IN FURNISHED ROOMS, WITH PRIVATE FAMILIES, AND IN APARTMENTS

There were, in 1910, 345,443 wage-earning women in the Borough of Manhattan. The census of 1900 revealed 19.7% of boarders in Manhattan and the Bronx among the women breadwinners 16 years of age and over (exclusive of servants and waitresses). If the same percentage held true five years ago, there were 68,052 women boarding in Manhattan in 1910.

By using every known means to locate her, the names and addresses and a certain amount of data for 842 girls were secured. . . .

The large number of factory and department store workers and waitresses is due to the kind of firms who were good enough to cooperate in this study by furnishing names of their employes. . . .

Of the 535 who were personally seen, the girls who were living in furnished rooms received a higher wage than those living with private families. . . . The $6 a week girl has not the money to pay $2.50 for her room and from $3.50 to $4.00 for her meals. She must of necessity board with a private family, with relatives or friends, who will "knock off" something on the price. . . .

The study made of the furnished room houses shed much light upon the terrific problems which face girls who are alone in the city. . . . The first thing noted was that the preference was almost invariably given to men. The landlady who prefers girls is an unknown individual. "Men don't stay in their rooms so much," was the general verdict. "They never want to wash out their clothes and hang them on the furniture to dry. They're more quiet and don't complain so much, and are not fussy about little things." The investigators, after a few days of hearing about the sins of womankind, became quite depressed with the sense of belonging to the sex. . . . Where women were taken, the cheap rooms would almost invariably be saved for men. The attempt was made for several days to locate a $1.50 a week room for a girl and, although there were a number of advertisements appearing in the papers, no house was found which would rent these to a girl. . . .

In only twenty-six out of the five hundred houses visited was there a public parlor where the roomers could entertain their friends, and eight of that number were boarding houses. In thirteen houses the private sitting room of the landlady was at the disposal of the guests. This meant, of course, that when the landlady wished to retire early the girl and her friends had to depart. And since the privilege was looked upon as a personal favor, it was granted only if not asked for too frequently. In all the other houses, girls either had to meet their friends on the street or entertain them in their rooms. Seventy-three landladies refused to let girls entertain men in their rooms or men, girls. "Do you think I want the police up here?" one woman asked. The dangers of entertaining men in one's bedroom are too obvious to need comment, but to have no place whatever in which to receive friends has also its dangerous side. . . .

The variety of ways in which landladies try to safeguard the respectability of their houses is interesting in the extreme. The most commonly used device is the rule that one may entertain only "steadies" in one's room. . . . The working girl who numbers among her acquaintances more than one man is looked upon askance. In some houses landladies would look at the investigator suspiciously and ask, "Are you respectable?", and after fervent assurances of respectability would say, "Well, then you can have your men friends in your room if you like. But no goings on, remember!" . . . Another woman asked the investigators if they were "professionals" and after a positive answer replied, "As long as you're professionals it's all right. I let theatre folk entertain men friends in their rooms." . . .

Girls living in furnished room houses in every section of the city had tales to tell of disagreeable experiences endured. "If you entertain a man in your room in the evening, no matter if he's your brother", said one girl, "the next morning the men in the house all smile at you in a knowing manner in the halls and try to pick you up." . . .

If one has never known the loneliness of life in a tiny furnished room, one cannot possibly imagine the cramped conditions under which thousands of girls live. . . .

A tiny room, the window opening on to a staring red brick wall; the furniture, consisting of one straight-backed chair, a chiffonier, a table, and a folding cot, worn and shabby; no closet, but clothes hung on pegs in a corner and covered by a faded curtain—this is what two little waitresses get for $3 a week. When the investigator called the girls were just finishing what they called their "supper"—a bottle of milk, a box of soda crackers and some cheese. "Sometimes we make coffee over the gas jet", they confided, "but if the landlady ever found that out she'd fire us from the house quick." The room was so tiny that considerable manoeuvering had to be done to have it hold three people—the two girls on the cot and the investigator grandly placed in the one and only chair. "There's one thing about this room—you can't get lost in it", said one of the girls with an embarrassed giggle. "May's hours are different from mine; she works in the mornings and evenings, and I from twelve until seven, so we're usually not in here at the same time except at night. And when we are, we take turns at our chair." . . .

Many people doubtless remember the article appearing in the New York Times about a year ago called "The Cry of a Lonely Woman in a Great City." The author, a stenographer of twenty-six, who had tried furnished room life for ten years, was happened upon by chance one evening. She writes:

"You can not have the remotest idea of the wretched loneliness, the utter isolation, and the bitter desolation of a young woman working hard all day and then going 'home' to her tiny furnished room at night.

"You, who have your pleasant, cheerful homes, with hosts of friends, just try to fancy a life like this; work at the office or shop all day, leave your work after the day's labor has been completed, go to a restaurant alone, eat a solitary meal, then back to your little cell, which usually is icy cold except in summer, and where the gas is about one candle power, so that reading or sewing is an impossibility. Furnished room life, to my mind, is the most horrifying, soul destroying existence possible in this world, or the next, I should fancy." . . .

The girl quoted above has tried living at the organized Homes and many of them. She, like dozens of other girls, wanders from organized Home to furnished room and from furnished room to Home, and back again. "I don't know which is worse", she says, "the cramped, and awful loneliness of a hall bedroom, or the humiliating and soul-depressing charity and rules of a Home." . . .

Many girls seek to satisfy their craving for home life by boarding with private families. Almost every tenement has its one or more families who take in girls. Sometimes a sign is placed outside of the house. "Room to let. Apply Mrs. So and So, 4th floor". The informal, friendly, word-of-mouth advertising of the poor is most generally used, however, in securing lodgers. A girl overhears another girl beside her in the laundry or bookbindery factory say that Mrs. B. "takes in" girls, and that evening she goes home with her friend, and the introduction to the new landlady is informally and kindly made.

Usually a girl living with a family, in this way, is treated almost as one of the family group. The landlady looks out for her and guards her as she would her own daughter, mends her clothes, oftentimes does her washing, scolds, and comforts, and pets her as any normal mother would. Mary, for instance, has lived with Mrs. D. for a year, ever since her mother's death. She gets $5 a week as bundle girl in a department store and pays Mrs. D. $3.50 for her room and board. She sleeps in the same bed with the daughter of the house. . . .

Another girl, Ethel O., was living with a young married woman of whom she had heard through friends. She was getting $5 a week in a printing establishment and paying Mrs. R. $2.75 for her board and room. Mr. R. had been out of work for six months, and he and his wife with two small babies, his mother-in-law, and the girl boarder were all living cooped up in three tiny rear rooms on the top floor of a tene-

ment. Ethel and the mother-in-law slept in the same room—a room too
sparsely furnished to be called the "living room". The woman had a
dilapidated old couch for her bed, and Ethel a cot which stood folded
up in a corner during the day time. This room opened on to the "real"
bedroom of the flat where the husband and wife and two children slept.
A bedraggled portiere furnished the partition between.

This dreary description, however, fails completely, for it summons to
mind no picture of the love and sympathy and tender humanness of the
bare little home. There were quarrels and jokes in the crowded kitchen,
laughter and tears, and through it all the sound of children's voices.
Ethel had brought home to the youngest child a cheap little toy, and,
while alternately scolding and petting him, was explaining to the investigator, "You see I'm trying to help what little I can with my $5 a
week. When I first came here I was looking for work and Mrs. R. let
me stay on for three whole weeks without paying a cent. So now that
Mr. R. is down on his luck I feel that I ought to turn to and help
him." . . .

AT THE TURN of the century, taking in boarders was one of the most
common forms of work for women, especially for immigrant women.
Boarding places were needed, since many immigrants left their families behind. In 1910, 5 percent of the country's population, or 4.5
million people, lived with families to whom they were not related. A
1907 survey of working-class families in New York City found that
there were one or more boarders in half the homes surveyed. Taking
in boarders was often the only way of earning money open to women.
The additional rent paid by the boarders, earned by the washing,
cooking and cleaning of the woman, could mean economic survival
for her family. Yet this work was often ignored in the census figures
since it was considered unpaid housework.

MILL TOWN WIVES

Family life in Homestead depends for its support almost entirely upon
the men's earnings; women and children rarely work outside the home

Margaret F. Byington. *Homestead, the Households of a Mill Town.* New York:
Charities, 1910; reprint ed., New York: Arno and The New York Times, 1969.

since the steel plant and machine works cannot use them and there are no other industries in the town. . . .

Among the immigrant families, however, and among all those in which the man's earnings fell within the day labor rate, our budget studies disclosed that another and exceptional source of support was resorted to; namely, payment from lodgers. It is upon the women of the household that this burden falls. In families where the man's wage was normally less than $12 a week, more than half found it necessary to increase their slender income in this way. . . .

Against many of these deaths was the physician's entry "malnutrition due to poor food and overcrowding"; that is, the mother too poor, too busy, and too ignorant to prepare food properly, rooms over-tenanted, and courts too confined to give the fresh air essential for the physical development of children. A priest told me he believed that the taking of lodgers caused the appalling death rate among the babies in his parish. Neither preaching nor pointing out to women personally the folly of the economy had sufficed to check the habit.

Not only is the mother too busy to give much time to her babies, but she also suffers from overwork during pregnancy and from lack of proper care afterward. Housework must be done, boarders must be fed, and most women work until the day of confinement. In accordance with their home customs, almost all of them employ midwives and call a doctor only in an emergency. I was told by a local physician that nearly half of the births in Homestead, the large proportion of them among the Slavic people, were attended by midwives. . . .

The women have few opportunities for relaxation. Sometimes they gossip around the pump or at the butcher's, but washing, ironing, cleaning, sewing and cooking for the boarders leave little time for visiting. The young people perhaps suffer most from the lack of home festivities. A two-room house has no place for games or "parties," or even for courting; there is not even space enough, to say nothing of privacy. So young folks are driven to the streets for their gayety. Almost the only time when the house is really the scene of festivity is when those primal events, birth, and marriage, and death, brings together both the old-time friends and the new neighbors. . . .

The men are inclined to trust all financial matters to their wives. It is the custom in Homestead for the workman to turn over his wages to his wife on pay day and to ask no questions as to what it goes for. He reserves a share for spending money; otherwise his part of the family problem is to earn and hers to spend. When the man was at home and I suggested to him that they keep accounts for this investigation he usually referred the matter genially to the wife, saying, "Oh, she's the one that knows where the money goes. If she wants to help you out she can."

Though the men show in general a frank appreciation of home comforts, they do not always realize all the work behind them. One wife said, "The only time 'the mister' notices anything about the house is when I wash the curtains." But many chance remarks showed that the women realizes the importance of keeping the home attractive. One woman compared her husband, who stayed at home evenings unless they went to "the show" together, with the man next door who was always going off to Pittsburgh "on a lark." Her explanation of the difference was simply, "I always put on a clean dress and do my hair before he comes home, and have the kitchen tidy so he will enjoy staying. But she never tidies up a bit." Her kitchen was spotless, with a bright geranium in the window; that of her neighbor was hot and mussy and the children were noisy. No wonder the husband did not care to stay at home; but in a small house with washing and cooking to do, with babies to look out for, it is often hard for the housekeeper to have time or energy, after the children are home from school and the dinner cooked, to stop and make herself presentable. That so many women do this is a proof of their energy and genuine ability.

Supper time in Homestead will always be associated in my mind with one family whom I knew. When the men began to come from the mill in the evening the mother with a fresh apron on and the two children in clean dresses came out on the front porch. The children sat on the lowest step until the father was in sight, and long before I could recognize him were off down the street, the older one to carry his bucket, the little one to take possession of his hand. After supper he smoked contentedly with a child on each knee and talked with his wife of the day's doings. That hour of rest was bought at the price of a busy day for her; she swept off porch and walk, she washed almost daily to keep the dresses clean, she had dinner all cooked before he came. A woman must be a good manager and have the courage to appear cheerful when tired, if she is to make the evening at home happy.

The thoughtful women are especially conscious that part of the responsibility for keeping the men away from the saloons belongs to them. The heat and thirst due to mill work, combined with the lack of other amusements, make the brightness and festivity of bar-rooms very appealing, and intemperance is consequently a serious evil in the town. The wives feel that they must help to overcome this temptation. One woman told me that she had been brought up to consider it wrong to play cards. She feared, however, that if she refused to have them in the house, her husband who was fond of playing would be tempted to go to the back rooms of the saloons for his entertainment. So, putting aside her scruples, she planned informal gatherings to play in the evenings. To her the drink evil was the more serious. There are many, however, to whom these real homes are not possible. . . .

WHILE THE United States became gradually more urban in the late nineteenth and early twentieth centuries, until 1920 the majority of Americans lived in the countryside or in towns with less than 2,500 inhabitants. Working on a farm was still the most common form of women's work.

One sharp difference between rural and city life was the isolation of women's labor on the farm. In 1914 the Department of Agriculture sent out a mass questionnaire to their crop correspondents' wives asking them how the USDA could better meet the needs of farm house-wives. The following are excerpts from the 2,241 responses received.

DOWN ON THE FARM

TEXAS

The condition of the farm women of the South is most deplorable. Her liege lord is availing himself of labor-saving appliances such as reaper, binder, thresher, riding plow, gas engines, etc., while the woman's labor-saving help consists of her sewing and washing machines. The routine work of the southern farm woman is about as follows: at this time of the year she is up at 5 A.M. preparing the breakfast, often building her own fire; milks the cows, cares for the milk—churns the cream by hand. Puts the house in order, gets the dinner, eats with the family at noon; leaves the house in disorder, goes to the cotton field and picks cotton all the afternoon, often dragging a weight of 60 pounds along the ground. At about sundown she goes to

U.S. Department of Agriculture. *Social and Labor Needs of Farm Women.* Report No. 103. Washington, D.C.: U.S. Government Printing Office, 1914.

the farmhouse, puts the house in order, washes the dishes left over from the noon meal, prepares the supper—most of the time too tired to eat; gets the children to bed, and falls asleep herself—and so it goes on from day to day. Somehow she finds the time to do the washing and ironing, mending, knitting, and darning between times. If she is under 45 years of age, while all this is going on she is either enceinte or she is nursing a baby. The result is she is weak and frail as a rule. There are a few well-to-do farmers in whose homes we find better conditions, but the above description of conditions applies to negroes, to white tenants and to the young farmers who are trying to build their homes. Get statistics of the sale of farm implements and the sales of nostrums for the cure of the ills of women and you will ascertain the relative condition of the farmers and their wives in the South. . . .

COLORADO

. . . As a farmer's wealth increases he buys more land and stock, requiring more help; builds larger houses, which take more labor to keep in order; sends his sons and daughters away to school; hires extra help in the sons' places, and deprives his wife of the help of her daughters. . . .

Serving hot, substantial meals at 6 o'clock A.M., 12 o'clock noon, and 6 o'clock P.M., and clearing up the dishes, I leave the reader to figure out how much time a woman has to leisurely enjoy church, afternoon clubs, or social visiting, even with an automobile on the farm. The remedy for all the trouble is simple. Every wife should flatly refuse to labor for any one outside of the family. That much is a duty, more is an imposition, considered all right by farmers because it has become customary. As I say, the remedy is simple. Each wife can "strike. . . ."

Some may argue that the daughters of the house share the work of the mother, or a hired girl lends her assistance. This may be true in some parts of the country. Most girls in the Rocky Mountain tier of States marry before they are 20. The unmarried daughter in the house is the exception to the rule. Hired girls are scarce for the same reason and do not care to work on farms.

OREGON

The farmer may aid a great deal by sticking to the 10-hour labor system, which will lighten the labor of the woman on the farm. I know a great many farmers who will be in the field by 6 A.M. plowing, and they plow 13 hours. Of course the mother of the family must arise very early in order to prepare breakfast.. The husband doesn't mind the long hours of labor because he thinks when he harvests the crop he will get his pay. The hired man gets paid for his work, but the tired housewife on the farm merely gets her board and clothing, the same as the farmer's work animals.

OKLAHOMA

The main cause of it all in my opinion is because the majority of us are landless people, renters and homeless, therefore, a dissatisfied, discontented and enslaved people. Now, if you really wish to do something to help the farmers' wives you must work to get the Government to lend money direct to the farmers and their wives (not through the bankers or any one else) with which to buy themselves homes. . . .

The Government ought to tax the land held for speculation purposes to the limit and let the use and occupancy of land constitute title to land, and then the renters everywhere could get little homes and be prosperous people. Putting $50,000 in the banks to help the farmers is of no benefit to them, as they can not pay the high rate of interest to the bankers.

The farmer gets only about one-half what the spinner pays for the cotton, and this causes the women and children to kill themselves from exposure and hard work to pay the bills. The banks of this country usually charge from 24 to 40 percent on money. If you borrow $100 March 1, they make your note payable October 1 for $124, with interest from maturity, to avoid the usury law. This causes these women to work and pay all grafts—those I have spoken of are the worse—and our children are going uneducated and dying from exposure and women dying from consumption, where, if we had our just rights, we could live and let live. . . .

TEXAS

Many farm women don't get off their own premises more than a dozen times a year. The fathers get so accustomed to the mothers' staying at home, they seem to forget that they might enjoy a little rest and recreation and really feel that she must stay at home "to keep the ranch going," as I have heard them express it. And the mother gets so accustomed to it, she, too, seems to forget she is human. The more intelligent and broader-minded men become, the more they appreciate woman and understand that she is equal in all things. But the men in the country realize this far less than the men in town. . . .

AT THE END of the nineteenth century there was a "servant problem." The usual definition of it was that the supply of potential servants was shrinking, and that those who took jobs as servants were increasingly "uncooperative." This view took for granted as normal a situation in which poverty and lack of any other alternative forced an entire class of women to accept jobs only just removed from outright slavery.

But the problem, a change, was nevertheless quite real. Women of the working class were increasingly unwilling to accept the conditions of domestic service. The economic basis for this unwillingness was the availability of other jobs, in retailing and in manufacturing, with higher wages and a relative increase in personal freedom; and the crumbling of the patriarchal assumption that respectable women ought to live in families where they could be supervised.

This article by Mary Trueblood reports on a survey done in Massachusetts, inquiring into the causes of the "servant problem." Notice that Trueblood, like all commentators by that time, assumed that the nature of the "problem" was common knowledge.

HOUSEWORK VS. SHOP AND FACTORIES

There is no need to say to any one in this country that housework is the last occupation the intelligent American working girl will seek. . . .

For one trade to be persistently shunned by intelligent workers while the others are overcrowded cannot be an accident, and to find a definite reason for the unpopularity of housework by comparing it with other occupations was the object of the investigation that furnishes the data for this article. In the State of Massachusetts, where this investigation was made, shoe factories, textile mills, department stores and restaurants are the principal industries that attract girls away from housework—hence these were chosen for comparison. . . .

It is an interesting fact that of the five occupations the shops (department stores) contained the highest percent of American-born girls, while of the houseworkers considered not one was born in the United States. Ireland furnished the largest number, while the others came from Canada, England and Scotland. Apparently the choice of work was made with little regard to the healthfulness of it, for in housework

Mary Trueblood. "Housework vs. Shop and Factories." *Independent* 54 (November 13, 1902).

alone was there no deterioration in strength reported. A few years of work in the mills and factories affects the health of fully half the girls. A stitcher in a shoe factory was quite right in saying: "The stitching room will take the bloom out of any girl's cheek." In the textile mills there is a marked contrast between the bright, active girls who are beginning and the dull-faced, lifeless women who have worked a few years. The work in shops and restaurants is wearing, but for the most part the girls seem to have vitality enough to rebound when the day's work is over. The good health of the houseworkers and waitresses is to be accounted for in part by good food. The former have, as a rule, the same food as the family, the latter take their meals in the restaurants where they are employed. . . .

In shops, restaurants and housework there is little lost working time, so that in the long run it is doubtful if more money is to be made in mills and factories than in the other three occupations. . . . The houseworker not only earns more than the shop and restaurant girl, but by reason of living in a family she has the opportunity of doing for herself many things that they must pay for. The girls of all occupations understand perfectly that "housework pays well."

The percent of savings was largest among houseworkers, as was also the amount of money given for the support of others. The shop girls saved least and also gave least. The difference in expense for necessary clothing and in standards of living accounts for this in large measure. . . .

As to working hours, the shop girls fare best of all. The average for those considered was 8.2 hours per day, excepting Saturdays in summer, when it was 4.6. For the waitresses the average was 9.5 hours. Where there was Sunday work there was invariably extra pay. Working hours in mills and factories are limited by law to 58 per week, the arrangement always being such as to give the Saturday half holiday. Houseworkers seldom know the exact number of working hours. The estimates given ranged from 7½ to 15½ hours per day. The average was 11.6, and that for seven days in the week instead of for six. Probably one hour should be deducted for meals, but as much or more should be added for the time when the girls were "on call." Without exception there was one day "off" each week—that is, after having worked as long as a full day for the shop, the houseworker was allowed time out from three until ten P.M.

In vacations also the shop girls have the advantage. Half reported from one to two weeks with pay, the others were allowed the same without pay. The Saturday half holiday in summer takes nothing from their wages. A few restaurant girls were given vacations with pay, but most of them, and also the factory and mill workers, were given any length of time desired without pay. In housework there seemed to be no fixed custom in regard to vacations. Some of the girls mentioned length of service as a condition, as was the case in many restaurants and shops. A few had two weeks' vacation with pay.

The difference in intelligence and education in the five occupations was marked. The shoe factory and shop girls were much better educated than the others. . . . With them a comfortable room and a certain amount of free time for recreation and self-improvement are necessaries of life. The night schools and classes in clubs of various kinds afford for all who wish it an opportunity to continue their education. The wish "to know more" was the one expressed more often than any other among these working girls, and the efforts that some were making to educate younger brothers and sisters were nothing short of heroic. Ten hours of work in the textile mills leaves the girls with little strength or ambition for any sort of exertion in the evening. Houseworkers as a class are prevented by lack of time from making use of the means of improvement offered to other working girls. . . . Truly no amount of money can compensate a self-respecting person for the loss of a reasonable amount of free time and independence. No one who is acquainted with the recreations of other working girls—the evenings at a club, a sewing circle, or a neighborhood party, the trolley rides, wheeling parties and excursions into the country or to the seashore—will wonder to hear them say, "We will never give up our evenings and Sundays." This was invariably the first objection given when they spoke of housework. . . .

"If conditions were right I would rather do housework than anything else, but I would not have a woman say *'my servant,'* referring to me."
". . . if I wish to have my friends in and serve a cup of tea I can do it. . . .'
"I tried housework, but came back to the mill; I will not be at everybody's beck and call."

WOMEN WITH CHILDREN have often worked the night shifts in plants because they have to care for their families during the day. They work all night, come home to spend days with their families, possibly

"Women on the Night Shift." *Life and Labor* 6 (December 1914).

catching a few hours of sleep before returning to their jobs. For these women, their work is truly "never done."

The excerpt was printed in *Life and Labor,* the official newspaper of the Women's Trade Union League. Issued monthly, it contained articles of concern for workingwomen, notices of trade-union meetings, descriptions of different kinds of women's work, strike reports, poems and general news and stories. As in this case, the paper also excerpted government reports and made them readable and interesting to a workingwomen's audience. *Life and Labor* is one of the most valuable sources we have for the history of working-class women.

THE NIGHT SHIFT

One of the worst abuses coming in the train of modern industry is the night work that falls to the lot of women, especially married women with children. The effects on the health of the worker herself from overwork and want of sleep and the necessary neglect of the children telling on their health are all brought out in the pathetic account given of the women night workers in a cordage works in Auburn, N.Y. . . .

The wretched life that a poor woman leads who, because of poverty is induced to take employment in a factory at night, and who is at the same time compelled to do her housework and take care of her children during the day can be gathered from the evidence.

The twine made is used for agricultural machines. The night shift employs more than 130 women, and half as many men. Very few speak English. Poles are predominant, Italians next. *A large proportion of the women are married.*

The night force work from 7 P.M. to midnight, when they have half-an-hour for supper; and from 12:30 A.M. to 5:30 A.M., five nights a week, making fifty hours weekly. No men under 18 nor women under 21 are on the night shift.

The investigators state that men workers are scarce, and the mill cannot get enough men to work at night, but also that *it would be impossible to engage men at the same rates that are paid women and get the same efficiency.*

The management bring forward reasons so hoary with age that it is time they became extinct.

1. If night work were prohibited in this state the company would be compelled to transfer the night work from this plant to plants in other states.

2. If night work of women were prohibited throughout the United States, the company would be compelled to enlarge its buildings and equipment. . . .

It was impossible to strike any average of the wages earned, which are on a piece-work basis. One woman earned $12; the lowest listed group of 11 from $6 to $7, and a group of twenty-three earned such varying sums below $6 that no definite wage could be named.

One of the saddest features in the life of these working women is found in the paradox that the employers do not seem to have been brutal; obeyed the State laws; followed without protests suggestions made by the Commission as to ventilation, the removal of dust from the air of workrooms by a specially installed plant, did not inflict the heaviest work upon women, reported all accidents to the proper authorities, and employed a physician and two matrons to take care of the health and comfort of the women. And yet, what a life it is these married workers lead. . . .

M. R.—I am strong and healthy and I am glad to work and take care of my children. Else what would become of them? Don't stop the night work with troubling the foreman. They might shut down and then (pointing to the little girl) she will have nothing to eat and nothing to wear. I don't want to have to work days, as then my children are alone. The boss had warned the girls that their wages are going to be cut if they talk to the investigators.

Mrs. M. N.—You can't feed and clothe a lot of children on what a man makes any more. (She changed from night to day work because it took all her strength to stay up all day beside. Now working days, she gets up and dresses and cares for all the children before she goes to work. Children were ragged and tattered and sickly.)

N. M.—I would rather work days if I could leave my baby with some one. I burn up my pay envelopes, my pay is so small I am ashamed.

Y. Z.—I want to work nights so I can take care of my children in the day. Why ain't men's pay more so women wouldn't have to work? I spent lots of money on my eyes; the dust makes them so sore. It's hard to work nights, but you got to live. . . .

All the women with families did their own housework; they prepared three meals a day, including breakfast, after a night's work. They also did the washing for the family. They averaged about 4½ hours sleep a day. The time of sleep varied with the individual. Some slept an hour or two in the morning and for a time in the afternoon; others slept at intervals of about an hour each during the day. They all slept in bedrooms which had been occupied during the night by husband and children. When the mother works at night the little ones learn to keep quiet out of doors while she is sleeping in the day time.

"HOME WORK" to working-class people in the early twentieth century did not refer to the assignments children do after school, but to manufacturing labor done in the home. Through a system of subcontracting, batches of work were given to families to complete in their homes. Although one family member was usually the "employee," it actually took an entire family's labor to make enough to survive. Industries which operated on the piecework system (that is, where workers were paid by the item rather than by the hour) were most suited to this kind of labor.

In preindustrial times families had also worked together in their homes. But then they could do the work they wanted. In the industrial period piece-rates were set so low that when there was work, people had to labor long hours at a killing speed; furthermore, the work was usually seasonal and the workers were unemployed for large parts of the year.

The home-work system turned the tenements of the largest cities into factories. For the family there was no longer a home to which they could escape from the monotony and constant pressure of earning a living. Home work, on the other hand, was very profitable for employers, who were saved the overhead costs of a factory. Home workers were a constant source of low-wage competition for those who worked in the manufacturing lofts owned by the employers.

In this selection Mary Van Kleeck investigated the circumstances of Italian artificial flower makers. In New York in 1912, 78 percent of home workers were Italians. Home work was particularly common among Italian families because many Italian husbands forbade their wives to work outside their homes.

HOME WORK

Four large questions are pertinent. Who are the workers making flowers at home? How much do they earn? In what type of family are they found? Is the system good for the workers, the trade, and the community?

Mary Van Kleeck. *Artificial Flower Makers.* New York: Survey Associates, 1913.

These questions were answered for the flower trade by interviewing family after family. . . .

In a tenement on Macdougal Street lives a family of seven—grandmother, father, mother, and four children aged four years, three years, two years and one month respectively. All excepting the father and the two babies make violets. The three-year-old girl picks apart the petals; her sister, aged four years, separates the stems, dipping an end of each into paste spread on a piece of board on the kitchen table and the mother and grandmother slip the petals up the stems.

"We all must work if we want to earn anything," said the mother. They are paid 10 cents for a gross, 144 flowers, and if they work steadily from 8 or 9 o'clock in the morning until 7 or 8 at night, they may make 12 gross, $1.20. In the busy season their combined earnings are usually $7.00 a week. During five months, from April to October, they have no work. They live in three rooms for which they pay $10 a month. The kitchen, which is used as a workroom, is lighted only by a window into an adjoining room. The father is a porter. Both he and his wife were born in Italy but came to New York when they were children. The wife when a child, before she was able to work in a factory, made flowers at home. Later she worked in a candy factory. "That's better than making flowers," she said, "but we can't go out to work after we're married." . . .

When visited, she was working on yellow muslin roses for which she was paid 25 cents a gross. There were five petals of different shapes, and each must be put into its right place. The first one was twisted around the "pep" to make the bud. Then paste was smeared upon another petal which was slipped up the wire stem. Two others were pasted on and then the tube stem slipped over the wire, and the flower hung on a line above the kitchen table to dry. . . .

In another tenement nearby is a young married woman who, working alone at home, can earn the exceptional wage of from $8.00 to $12 in a week. She is a skilled brancher and represents the experienced worker who has learned the trade in the shop, an unusual type among home workers. She had made flowers for fifteen years before her marriage. Her wages from home work usually equal those of her husband, who is a porter in a saloon. Her mother-in-law does the housework and takes care of the eleven-months-old baby, thus leaving the mother free to work without interruption. The flowers given her are made abroad and branched or bunched here. Manufacturers usually do not give out such work unless they are sure that they can trust the worker's skill. In a day she can branch about two gross of the kind upon which she was engaged at the date of our visit. "But it's all according to the work," she said. "Sometimes I can make $1.50 and sometimes $3.00 a day. You can't count home work by the day, for a day is really two days sometimes, because people often work half the night. When the boss asks me how many flowers I can make in a day I say I cannot tell, but I know how many I can do in an hour. Some girls are so foolish. I've heard them praising themselves and telling the boss that they did the work in a day. They're ashamed to say they worked in the night too. But they only hurt themselves, for the boss says if they earn that much in a day he can cut the price." In the summer this woman works on feathers, which her employers give her in order not to lose track of so skilled a home worker during the dull season of the flower trade. . . .

OCCUPATIONAL DISEASES are a common part of every worker's daily existence. Some occupations even have their own particular diseases: "wrist drop" (an inability to hold your hand up straight) was characteristic of painters and was caused by the lead in the paint. The Mad Hatter of *Alice in Wonderland* fame was patterned after the fact that hatters often went mad from the mercury used in the manufacture of felt. Very little attention was paid to these diseases; they were an expected part of working-class life.

As more women became industrial workers, however, there was an increase in the concern about occupational diseases. As the investigations of women's work showed an increasing number of married women in the work force, social workers and some public health officials became worried about the effect of industrial work on the future generations.

Much of the debate centered around the question of whether or not women were subject to diseases more often than men. In part, reformers used the women-as-weaker-sex argument as an argument for wages and hours legislation. Since so many women were integrated into a factory work force, if an employer was forced to lower hours for women employees, he would have to lower hours of work for all his employees in a plant. Some of the outcry, however, was based on questionable medical evidence that women were weaker and more subject to illness. The debate on this subject is far from settled. In fact, much of the data that we have today is based on the investigations done sixty years ago. It has yet to be reevaluated.

INDUSTRIAL HEALTH:
CASE NO. 45, SADIE G.

Sadie is an intelligent, neat, clean girl, who has worked from the time she got her working papers in embroidery factories. She was a stamper and for several years before she was poisoned, earned $10 a week. In her work she was accustomed to use a white powder (chalk or talcum was usual) which was brushed over the perforated designs and thus transferred to the cloth. The design was easily brushed off when made of chalk or of talcum, if the embroiderers were not careful. Her last employer therefore commenced using white lead powder, mixed with rosin, which cheapened the work as the powder could not be rubbed off and necessitate restamping.

None of the girls knew of the change in powder, nor of the danger in its use. The workroom was crowded and hot, the stampers' tables were farthest from the windows and the constant use of the powder caused them to breathe it continually and their hands were always covered with it.

Sadie had been a very strong, healthy girl, good appetite and color; she began to be unable to eat, had terrible colic, but continued to go to work in spite of the fact that she felt miserable. Her hands and feet swelled, she lost the use of one hand, her teeth and gums were blue. When she finally had to stop work, after being treated for months, for stomach trouble, her physician advised her to go to a hospital. There the examination revealed the fact that she had lead poisoning—which was unaccountable as no one knew that her work had involved the use of lead until some one who had been on the job also recalled hearing the manager send a messenger out with money several times to buy a white lead powder.

Sadie was sick in the hospital for six months—(losing $10 per week). She said her employer bought off several of her witnesses, but before the case came to trial two years later several of them also became ill and consequently decided to testify for her. The employer appealed to the girl's feelings and induced her, on the day of the trial, to accept $150. He said that he had had business reverses and consequently would be unable to pay in case she won.

Her lawyer was suing for $10,000. At the present time the girl is 23

"Case No. 45, Sadie G." *Preliminary Report of the New York State Factory Investigating Commission.* Albany, N.Y., 1912.

years old and though she has apparently good health, she is no longer strong and is very susceptible to disease.

THERE WAS no guarantee that a sudden illness or death of a husband would not make a woman responsible for the welfare of her entire family. In fact, industrial accidents resulting in the death of the major wage earners in the family were more common in this period when there was little in the way of even minimal state or federal safety regulations. The maiming or death of industrial workers, especially those employed in heavy industries like steel, railroading and mining, was extremely common. The working widow was a familiar sight in most industrial towns and cities.

Workmen's compensation as we know it today did not exist even minimally until 1911. Under common law, injured workers or their families had to sue the company to get any compensation for an accident. They also had to prove that the company was primarily responsible for the accident, that the worker had not been contributorily negligent or had voluntarily assumed the risk as part of his work. Under these rules, it was uncommon for workers or their families to collect any money for compensation. At best the family might be given a few dollars for the funeral expenses in the case of fatal injuries. Out of anger or protest, widows often refused to accept the pennies offered by the companies. If there was any outside financial support for the family, it came from burial funds or insurance schemes of working-class fraternal organizations.

The following selection is from the most important reform study done at this time on work accidents and the need for workmen's compensation, by Crystal Eastman. Eastman was a feminist lawyer and writer and a founder of the Woman's Party.

THE EFFECT OF INDUSTRIAL FATALITIES UPON THE HOME

A few histories,—not extreme cases,—will best illustrate what industrial fatalities entail in the homes of the workers. . . .

William Brown, crane director at the Pressed Steel Car Company, on

Crystal Eastman. "The Effect of Industrial Fatalities Upon the Home." *Work Accidents and the Law.* New York: Survey Associates, 1915.

October 25, 1906, was struck by a truck attached to a crane. It was at 5:30 A.M. and the lights in the mill were not lighted. The foreman testified at the inquest that the crane man could not see below on account of the darkness, and probably for the same reason Brown did not notice that the truck was so near him. This man was taken to a hospital and lived for a month after the accident. The company paid all but $8.00 of the hospital bill, and gave his widow $150. Brown was a man of forty-five, earning $20 a week. He belonged to the Maccabees, and was insured for $2,000 in that society. There are seven children in the family, the oldest a rather sickly little girl of fourteen. In spite of her home cares, Mrs. Brown has been able to get work to do. She washes curtains and gives a few music lessons at fifty cents a lesson. She was making in these ways from $5.00 to $8.00 a week. Her relatives help her in clothes and food once in a while. Once she has had to ask money from the city for shoes and coal.

Mrs. Joseph Gikovitch, widow of a Slavic miner who was crushed by a fall of slate, was visited ten months after her husband's death. She has left a four-room house and is occupying one room in a basement with her five children (oldest a daughter of thirteen years). The Carnegie Coal Company, by which Gikovitch was employed, gave nothing but Mrs. Gikovitch received $1,000 from a Slavic benefit society to which he had belonged, and $75 from the Miners' Accident Fund, to which he had contributed 50 cents a month. After spending $150 on the funeral, she is apparently trying to save the rest of this money. She keeps a cow and sells milk, and this is apparently her only source of income. As the Slavic investigator put it, "She and the children are living in an evident misery."

WORKING-CLASS POWER

THE LEADERSHIP of the unions making up the American Federation of Labor believed that women should stay at home. For years the A.F.L.'s official newspaper, *The American Federationist,* printed articles condemning the employment of women in industry. In fact, in 1898 and again in 1914, the annual conventions of the A.F.L. nearly passed resolutions against women in the paid work force. Most of the unions in the A.F.L. disallowed women members. One international leader summed up their position: "Keep women out of the trade, and if not, out of the union."

Under pressure from women, the A.F.L. appointed Mary E. Kenny as an organizer in 1892, but when her term expired she was not re-hired or replaced. Between 1903 and 1923, a period of enormous expansion in women's employment, the A.F.L. hired only thirty women organizers, and many of them for very brief periods of time.

The following selection, by the Secretary of the Boston Central Labor Union, an affiliate of the A.F.L., is typical of the antifeminist material that appeared in *The American Federationist.* It is interesting to note that he not only falls back upon arguments about women's natural behavior and the sanctity of the home, but also uses the word "the sex" to refer to women. This term was common among middle- and upper-class writers in the nineteenth century and reflects the extent to which the trade union leadership viewed women in the accepted bourgeois framework.

THE A.F.L. VIEW OF WOMEN WORKERS

The invasion of the crafts by women has been developing for years amid irritation and injury to the workman. The right of the woman to

Edward O'Donnell. "Women as Bread Winners—the Error of the Age." *American Federationist* 4 (No. 8), October 1897.

win honest bread is accorded on all sides, but with craftsmen it is an open question whether this manifestation is of a healthy social growth or not.

The rapid displacement of men by women in the factory and workshop has to be met sooner or later, and the question is forcing itself upon the leaders and thinkers among the labor organizations of the land.

Is it a pleasing indication of progress to see the father, the brother and the son displaced as the bread winner by the mother, sister and daughter?

Is not this evolutionary backslide, which certainly modernizes the present wage system in vogue, a menace to prosperity—a foe to our civilized pretensions? . . .

The growing demand for female labor is not founded upon philanthropy, as those who encourage it would have sentimentalists believe; it does not spring from the milk of human kindness. It is an insidious assault upon the home; it is the knife of the assassin, aimed at the family circle—the divine injunction. It debars the man through financial embarrassment from family responsibility, and physically, mentally and socially excludes the woman equally from nature's dearest impulse. Is this the demand of civilized progress; is it the desire of Christian dogma? . . .

Capital thrives not upon the peaceful, united, contented family circle; rather are its palaces, pleasures and vices fostered and increased upon the disruption, ruin or abolition of the home, because with its decay and ever glaring privation, manhood loses its dignity, its backbone, its aspirations. . . .

To combat these impertinent inclinations, dangerous to the few, the old and well-tried policy of divide and conquer is invoked, and to our own shame, it must be said, one too often renders blind aid to capital in its warfare upon us. The employer in the magnanimity of his generosity will give employment to the daughter, while her two brothers are weary because of their daily tramp in quest of work. The father, who has a fair, steady job, sees not the infamous policy back of the flattering propositions. Somebody else's daughter is called in in the same manner, by and by, and very soon the shop or factory are full of women, while their fathers have the option of working for the same wages or a few cents more, or take their places in the large army of unemployed. . . .

College professors and graduates tell us that this is the natural sequence of industrial development, an integral part of economic claim.

Never was a greater fallacy uttered of more poisonous import. It is false and wholly illogical. The great demand for women and their preference over men does not spring from a desire to elevate humanity; at any rate that is not its trend.

The wholesale employment of women in the various handicrafts must gradually unsex them, as it most assuredly is demoralizing them, or stripping them of that modest demeanor that lends a charm to their kind, while it numerically strengthens the multitudinous army of loafers, paupers, tramps and policemen, for no man who desires honest employment, and can secure it, cares to throw his life away upon such a wretched occupation as the latter.

The employment of women in the mechanical departments is encouraged because of its cheapness and easy manipulation, regardless of the consequent perils; and for no other reason. The generous sentiment enveloping this inducement is of criminal design, since it comes from a thirst to build riches upon the dismemberment of the family or the hearthstone cruelly dishonored. . . .

But somebody will say, would you have women pursue lives of shame rather than work? Certainly not; it is to the alarming introduction of women into the mechanical industries, hitherto enjoyed by the sterner sex, at a wage uncommandable by them, that leads so many into that deplorable pursuit. . . .

WHEN THE Women's Trade Union League tried to organize women into unions, it was acutely aware of the problems which prevented women from joining unions or taking leadership in them. In the first selection, Alice Henry discusses these problems and the ways the W.T.U.L. tried to overcome them. Her analysis is strikingly similar to that of the women's liberation movement of the 1970s.

Alice Henry was an Australian writer who came to the United States in 1906 to work on suffrage; she joined the W.T.U.L. in 1907, edited their paper, *Life and Labor*, between 1910 and 1915 and in the 1920s became the director of their training school for women organizers.

In the second selection, Lillian Matthews explores some of the problems of women in male-dominated union locals and discusses how one women's local decided to overcome male resistance to their issues and problems.

THE TRADE UNION WOMAN

The commonest complaint of all is that women members of a trade union do not attend their meetings. It is indeed a very serious difficulty to cope with, and the reasons for this poor attendance and want of interest in union affairs have to be fairly faced.

At first glance it seems curious that the meetings of a mixed local composed of both men and girls, should have for the girls even less attraction than meetings of their own sex only. But so it is. A business meeting of a local affords none of the lively social intercourse of a gathering for pleasure or even of a class for instruction. The men, mostly the older men, run the meeting and often are the meeting. Their influence may be out of all proportion to their numbers. It is they who decide the place where the local shall meet and the hour at which members shall assemble. The place is therefore often over a saloon, to which many girls naturally and rightly object. Sometimes it is even in a disreputable district. The girls may prefer that the meeting should begin shortly after closing time so that they do not need to go home and return, or have to loiter about for two or three hours. They like meetings to be over early. The men mostly name eight o'clock as the time of beginning, but business very often will not start much before nine. Then, too, the men feel that they have come together to talk, and talk they do while they allow the real business to drag. Of course, the girls are not interested in long discussions on matters they do not understand and in which they have no part and naturally they stay away, and so make matters worse, for the men feel they are doing their best for the interests of the union, resent the women's indifference, and are more sure than ever that women do not make good unionists.

Among the remedies proposed for this unsatisfactory state of affairs is compulsory attendance at a certain number of meetings per year under penalty of a fine or even losing of the card. (A very drastic measure this last and risky, unless the trade has the closed shop.)

Where the conditions of the trade permit it by far the best plan is to have the women organized in separate locals. The meetings of women and girls only draw better attendances, give far more opportunity for all the members to take part in the business, and beyond all question form the finest training ground for the women leaders who in consider-

Alice Henry. "The Woman Organizer." *The Trade Union Woman*. New York: D. Appleton and Co., 1915.

able numbers are needed so badly in the woman's side of the trade-union movement today.

Those trade-union women who advocate mixed locals for every trade which embraces both men and women are of two types. Some are mature, perhaps elderly women, who have been trade unionists all their lives, who have grown up in the same locals with men, who have in the long years passed through and left behind their period of probation and training, and to whose presence and active coöperation the men have become accustomed. These women are able to express their views in public, can put or discuss a motion or take the chair as readily as their brothers. The other type is represented by those individual women or girls in whom exceptional ability takes the place of experience, and who appreciate the educational advantages of working along with experienced trade-union leaders. I have in my mind at this moment one girl over whose face comes all the rapture of the keen student as she explains how much she has learnt from working with men in their meetings. She ardently advocates mixed locals for all. For the born captain the plea is sound. Always she is quick enough to profit by the men's experience, by their ways of managing conferences and balancing advantages and losses. . . .

But with the average girl today the plan does not work. The mixed local does not, as a general rule, offer the best training-class for new girl recruits, in which they may obtain their training in collective bargaining or cooperative effort. . . . Many of the discussions that go on are quite above the girls' heads. And even when a young girl has something to say and wishes to say it, want of practice and timidity often keep her silent. It is to be regretted, too, that some trade-union men are far from realizing either the girls' ends in their daily work or their difficulties in meetings, and lecture, reprove or bully, where they ought to listen and persuade.

The girls, as a rule, are not only happier in their own women's local, but they have the interest of running the meetings themselves. They choose their own hall and fix their own time of meeting. Their officers are of their own selecting and taken from among themselves. The rank and file, too, get the splendid training that is conferred when persons actually and not merely nominally work together for a common end. Their introduction to the great problems of labor is through their practical understanding and handling of those problems as they encounter them in the everyday difficulties of the shop and the factory and as dealt with when they come up before the union meeting or have to be settled in bargaining with an employer.

WOMEN IN TRADE UNIONS

Women are less apt to be aggressive in their manner of making demands than are men and the men have criticised their more patient methods of working gradually toward a desired result. The women hold that their way of handling difficulties results in less friction and gains them a readier hearing in the long run. For the same reason women favor the industrial form of organization. Jurisdictional disputes do not sap their time and strength. Thus the laundry workers employed in garment factories belong to the union of garment workers and all women who work in binderies are included in one union instead of being divided according to occupation as is common elsewhere.

While it is true that men were first in the field of organized action and have frequently been the instigators of organization among women, they have not dictated the terms of the demands the women saw fit to make. The attitude of the men when they first encouraged women to form unions was actuated not so much by the desire to better conditions for women as by the spirit of self-protection from the effect that women's competition threatened to have in causing wages to fall. This is marked in the earlier days of the movement when we find numerous complaints such as this, "While women have not been benefited to any considerable extent through the throwing open to her, of late years, of avenues of employment hitherto monopolized by men, the earnings of men have been reduced." This hostile attitude broke out into open contention between the men and women in several instances, notably among the garment workers and the laundry workers. The men cutters discovering that the women would hold out for their own points were not satisfied to remain in the same union with them and were allowed to withdraw, but the women have since persistently refused to readmit the men. In the first days of organization the men in the laundry workers union attempted to submit a wage schedule which called for an increased wage for the branches at which men were employed but left the women on the old basis. The men knew that the employers would doubtless grant the larger wage to a part of the workers but that trouble might ensue if all the workers demanded more. The women refused any support to the measure and held out until the demand for a higher wage was extended to every branch.

Lillian Matthews. *Women in the Trade Unions in San Francisco.* University of California Publications in Economics, Vol. 3, No. 1. Berkeley, June 19, 1913.

AT THE TURN of the century the American working class was a mixture of scores of different nationalities. In many shops there was no common language. Each national group brought to the workplace cultural attitudes and stereotypes of other nationalities which made organizing difficult. Employers exploited these differences, often deliberately hiring from a mixture of nationalities to make unity less likely.

In this selection Mary Van Kleeck explores some of the problems in the flower-making industry where Italian women predominated but Jewish workers played a leading role in the struggle for unionization. The Italian women often came from peasant cultures where patriarchal power was strong. Many of the young Jewish immigrants, by contrast, had been industrial workers of some sort in the ghettos of eastern Europe, many of them participants in radical labor movements in their homelands. They tended to be more urbane than their Italian counterparts, and correspondingly they often fell into arrogance toward their fellow and sister workers.

ETHNIC DIFFERENCES AMONG WOMEN WORKERS

Many exceptions must be made to any characterization of national traits. Nevertheless, the difference is marked between the attitude of the Italian flower maker toward her work and that of her fellow worker, a Jewish girl from Russia or Austria or Germany. Briefly stated, it may be said that when the Italian girl exhibits an interest in her trade it is an interest in craftsmanship or in her own wages rather than in general trade conditions. The Jewish girl, on the contrary, has a distinct sense of her social responsibility and often displays an eager zest for discussion of labor problems. These traits naturally make a marked impression on an investigator. The Italian girl will receive her visitor with courteous hospitality and will proudly show her some artificial flowers which she has made, often insisting on presenting one or two as a gift. She will answer all questions graciously but briefly, considering work in the flower trade as only one of many interesting topics of conversation. It is vital to her not as a general industrial problem but as a means of supplying money for the needs of her family, to whose welfare she is traditionally inclined to subordinate her individual desires. The Jewish girl, on the other hand, will probably plunge at once into a

Mary Van Kleeck. *Artificial Flower Makers.* New York: Survey, 1913.

discussion of her trade, its advantages and disadvantages, wages, hours of work, and instances of shabby treatment in the shops, or of unsanitary conditions in the workrooms. Her attitude is likely to be that of an agitator. Nevertheless, she has the foundation of that admirable trait, "public spirit," and a sense of relationships to a community larger than the family or the personal group of which she happens to be a member. It follows that the Italian girl is more willing than the Jewish girl to accept conditions as she finds them. The owner of a large flower factory says that he prefers to employ Italians because they "are more tractable."

These differences in point of view prevent a sense of fellowship among them: their common interests as workers in the same occupation have never been realized or expressed in any representative group organization in the artificial flower trade. The attempt on the part of the Jewish girls to organize a trade union has failed so signally that not until several months after the investigation began did we find any girls who had ever heard of such an effort. Finally two were found who had been members. They were interviewed at different times and the visitor thus records their reports of the organization:

I. The Flower Makers' Union was organized about 1907, but broke up in six months or so. There were about 200 members including girls and men cutters, colorers, etc. They met every Friday evening in a hall on 2nd Street near Avenue A. The dues were 5 cents a week. The girl interviewed said it was hard to persuade girls to join. They were not interested. One girl said, "I'm going to get married soon," and another, "I got a fellow. Vy should I join?" When asked the aims of the union, the girl informant said, "We started to kick about wages. But when I asked my boss for a raise, he said, 'For vy should I gif you a raise? Didn't I teach you the trade?'" However, even this girl is not interested in starting the union again, as she has a fairly good position with steady work all year, and does not now feel a personal need for its support.

II. The second girl said that the union was started chiefly by girls in the Broadway flower factory in which she happened to be employed. She was the secretary. Most of the members were Jewish girls, who had just come from Europe and could not speak English, and the discussions were carried on and the minutes kept in Yiddish. They met in a hall on 2nd Street. They had several mass meetings, but these were very poorly attended, with one exception, when several forewomen came, and there were English and Italian speakers. In 1909 or 1910 an attempt was made to unite the milliners, wire makers, and flower makers into one union so that they could control the trade, but it was not successful. Since then the Flower Makers' Union has been replaced by the Educational League of Flower Makers, which meets every Saturday evening. Yiddish only is spoken at its meetings. It was thought that more girls would join, if it were not called a union, but this girl left, saying that she would not return unless they frankly called themselves a union.

The old union had saved up $100 in its treasury, which in 1910 they turned over to help the shirtwaist strikers. After the success of that strike in winning members for the shirtwaist union, some of the flower makers thought of organizing their union again. But many girls, "especially the Americans," are not interested in joining, "because they don't expect to stay in the trade. They think only of themselves," said this girl. "Perhaps some day they will have daughters working at this same trade, and they could help them if they would form a union." The Italian girls, she says, have no interest in unions. This Russian Jewish girl's comment was, "If they were more civilized, they wouldn't take such low pay. But they go without hats and gloves and umbrellas." . . .

The following letter was sent to members of the committee on labor and industries of the legislature while this bill [limiting women's work to fifty-four hours a week] was pending. It was the result of a unanimous vote of an Italian girls' club, and was written by a committee appointed by the club after a discussion of factory laws in New York state. Only the signature and some of the spelling have been changed. Otherwise it stands as it was written by the girls themselves without other aid.

ITALIAN GIRLS' INDUSTRIAL LEAGUE
28 Macdougal Street.

New York March 7th, 1912.

To Whom it May Concern:

We, the members of the Italian Girls' Industrial League, have come to the conclusion that the girls of this state are working too many hours a week and we think that the 54 hour bill ought to be passed and not only passed but inforced. Now in our club we represent all different lines of industry. We have the flower trade, we have the hair trade, the embroiderers, the book binders, the cloak makers, childrens' dresses, shirt waist makers, dress makers, sales ladies, candy makers & a good many other trades & also a brush maker. We also know of girls that work in candy factories that go to work at 7 in the morning and work through until seven in the evening, with only ½ hour for lunch & only get 7 cents for the extra hour & in the flowers the girls have to work so

hard & when they are busy they have to work overtime & also take work home. They do not care whether a girl is sick or not, she has to work, but when they are slack they do not care whether a girl needs work or not, she is laid off. We could tell you so much of other trades but it would take up too much space. We think it would be a very good idea if some of you gentlemen would go & visit some of the different factories and see for their selves, & I do not think they would be very long in passing that bill. We do also want to speak about the canneries up state. We think it an outrage that those people have to work such long hours not only for the girls and women but for those innocent little children who have to work so hard when they ought to be at play.
from

MRS. MARIA GONZAGA, President.

SEEMINGLY SPONTANEOUS outbursts of workers are usually the result of years of built-up frustration. Often it is the act of one person or a group of persons which sparks a walkout leading to a strike. In this selection Agnes Nestor gives us a picture of both the conditions in the shops and how the glove-making shop in which she was working became unionized. Nestor later became the vice-president of the International Glove Workers Union and president of the Chicago Women's Trade Union League.

BIRTH OF A RANK-AND-FILE ORGANIZER

Our machines were on long tables in large rooms, and we operators sat on both sides of the tables. At last I was where I had longed to be, and here I worked for ten years. I was earning fairly good pay for those times, and I was happy. We would mark out the quantity of our work and keep account of our earnings. I still have that little book in which I kept my accounts. It is interesting to see how I gradually increased my weekly pay.

To drown the monotony of work, we used to sing. This was allowed

Agnes Nestor. "I Become a Striker." *Woman's Labor Leader*. Rockford, Ill.: Bellevue Books, 1954.

because the foreman could see that the rhythm kept us going at high speed. We sang *A Bicycle Built for Two* and other popular songs.

Before we began to sing we used to talk very loudly so as to be heard above the roar of the machines. We knew we must not stop our work just to hear what someone was saying; to stop work even for a minute meant a reduction in pay.

We did want to do a little talking, though. In order not to lose time by it, we worked out a plan. We all chipped in and bought a dollar alarm clock which we hung on the wall. We figured that we could do a dozen pairs of gloves in an hour. That meant five minutes for a pair. As we worked we could watch the clock to see if we were on schedule. If we saw ourselves falling behind, we could rush to catch up with our own time. No one was watching us or pushing us for production. It was our strategem for getting the most out of the piecework system. We wanted to earn as much as we possibly could.

But, though we all seemed happy at first, gradually it dawned dimly within us that we were not beating the piecework system; it was beating us. There were always "pacemakers," a few girls who could work faster than the rest, and they were the ones to get the new work before the price was set.* Their rate of work had to be the rate for all of us, if we were to earn a decent wage. It kept us tensed to continual hurry.

Also, there were some unjust practices, outgrowths from another era, which nettled us because they whittled away at our weekly pay. We were charged fifty cents a week for the power furnished our machines. At first we were tolerant of the charge and called it "our machine rent." But after a time that check-off of fifty cents from our weekly pay made us indignant.

We were obliged, besides, to buy our own needles. If you broke one, you were charged for a new one to replace it. We had, also, to buy our own machine oil. It was expensive; and to make matters worse, we had to go to certain out-of-the-way places to obtain it.

But this was not all. Every time a new foreman came in, he demonstrated his authority by inaugurating a new set of petty rules which seemed designed merely to irritate us. One such rule was that no girl must leave her own sewing room at noon to eat lunch with a girl in another room. My sister Mary had now come into the factory, and we were in the habit of grouping at lunch time with friends from other departments. But even two sisters from different departments were not permitted to eat lunch together. Mary was in a different department at

---

* The price changed at random and often varied from day to day [ed.].

the time, and this regulation seemed too ridiculous to be borne. Consequently, whenever the foreman had left the room at noon, we went where we pleased to eat our lunch. Sometimes he spied on us and ordered us "Back where you belong!"

In the face of all this, any new method which the company sought to put into effect and disturb our work routine seemed to inflame the deep indignation already burning inside us. Thus, when a procedure was suggested for subdividing our work, so that each operator would do a smaller part of each glove, and thus perhaps increase the overall production — but also increase the monotony of the work, and perhaps also decrease our rate of pay — we began to think of fighting back.

The management evidently heard the rumblings of a threatened revolt. Our department was the "glove-closers." A representative of the company sent for a group from another department, the "banders," asking them to give this new method of subdividing the work a trial and promising an adjustment if the workers' earnings were found to be reduced. The group agreed to try out the new method; but when they got back to their department and told the banders about it, the banders revolted, refused to work the new way on trial, and walked out.

We of our department felt that we should be loyal to the girls who had walked out, and we told the foreman that if the company tried to put new girls in the places of the banders, we would walk out, too!

We had taken a bold step. Almost with spontaneity we had acted in support of one another. Now we all felt tremulous, vulnerable, exposed. With no regular organization, without even a qualified spokesman, how long would such unified action last? If anyone ever needed the protection of a firm organization, I for one at that moment felt keenly that we certainly did.

The glove-cutters, all men, had a union which had existed for about a year. The girl who sat next to me told me about it. She had a boy friend in this union, but she was always careful not to let anyone hear her talk about it because in those days unions were taboo. She said that the cutters — all men — had talked of trying to get the girls to join the union and had wanted to approach our plant to suggest it, but that some of the members had said, "You'll never get those girls to join a union. They'll stand for anything up there!"

The banders had been smart. They had walked out on Saturday. One of their number decided to get publicity about their grievances and she gave the newspapers the full story about their strike.

The Chicago Federation of Labor was having a meeting that day, and the glove-cutters from our shop had special delegates there. A labor reporter went to these delegates asking for details about the walk-out of the banders. It was the first the delegates had heard of the matter. But, learning that the banders of their own factory had struck, they decided to try to get all the girls to join the union.

On Monday the president of the union tried to arrange a meeting with our group. But it was too late. During the week end, the boss had decided to abandon the new system. Workers had been sent word to come back and everything would be all right, that they could work as before. We felt that now we had a certain power and were delighted over what seemed to us a moral victory. Monday morning found us back at work.

All was not settled, however. On Monday the glove-cutters' union rented a hall within a block of the factory. As we came out from work that afternoon, members of the glove-cutters' union met us telling us to go to a union meeting at this hall.

Israel Solon was one of these men. Sometimes, if a girl hesitated about going to the hall, he would urge:

"Don't be afraid of the boss; protect yourself! Go to the union meeting!"

I was only too anxious to go and did not care who saw me. It seemed legitimate to protect one's self from unjust rules. I went without hesitation.

The meeting was a great success; workers packed the hall, and many non-members signed for membership. The work of organizing continued for three evenings, until most of the shop had been persuaded to join.

Toward the end of the week, there was a disturbance in the cutting department. It leaked through to us that a cutter had been discharged and that the cutters were organizing a protest strike. We were young and inexperienced in union procedure; and, as I look back now, I see that because of that lack of experience, and because we were newly organized and therefore anxious to use our new organization, we did a rash thing. We started a strike movement in protest at the discharge of the cutter and also for the redress of our own grievances. We even celebrated the event with a birthday party for one of our girls and had a feast with lemon cream pie at lunch time. During the feast we formulated our plan. We decided it would be cowardly to walk out at noon. We would wait until the whistle blew for us to resume work, and then, as the power started up on the machines, we would begin our exodus.

Somehow the foreman got wind of our plan. We were forming a line when reinforcements from the foremen's division scattered around the room ordering us to go back to our places. We began to chant: "We are not going to pay rent for our machines!" We repeated it over and over, for that was our chief grievance. . . .

We walked out. We did not use the near-by stairs but walked through the next room in order that the girls there might see us leaving. The girls there were busily at work quite unconscious of our strike movement. I knew that our cause was lost unless we got those girls to join us. When we got out to the street, I told my companions that all was lost unless we could get those others to walk out too. We lined up across the street shouting "Come on out!" and calling out the names of some of the girls. We kept this up until a few did obey us. Gradually others followed until the shop was almost emptied. Then we paraded to the hall on Leavitt Street for the meeting with the union leaders.

At the meeting we were called upon to state our demands. We gave them: no more machine rent; no paying for needles; free machine oil; union shop; raises for the cutters who were paid the lowest wages. . . .

Evidently the union officers thought I was a ringleader, for when the committee was appointed to represent our group, my name was called. When Mary heard it, she said:

"Why did they put Agnes on? She can't talk!"

This seems amusing to me now; also to certain of my friends who were present at that meeting, for they assure me that I have been talking ever since. . . .

We joined the picket line again and held meetings every day and evening in the hall the cutters had rented. How important we felt! Speakers sent to our evening meetings were furnished by the Chicago Federation of Labor Organization Committee headed by John Fitzpatrick. One evening they sent Sophie Becker of the Boot and Shoe Workers Union, the only woman on the organization committee. I am afraid that I was a great hero-worshipper in those days! I was so thrilled with her speech that as she left the hall I leaned over just to touch her. Then I leaned back satisfied because I had got that close to her.

All this was happening at the same time that streetcar conductors were being discharged because it became known that they were forming a union. Some of the conductors, as they passed our picket line, would throw us handsful of buttons which read:

ORGANIZE. I'M WITH YOU!

We wore those buttons on our coats, and when we boarded the cars we would watch the expression on each conductor's face to find out whether or not he had joined the union. . . .

The second week of our strike began. About the middle of the week, we girls on the picket line each received a letter from the company urging us to come back to work and promising that if we reported upon receipt of the letter our old places would be restored to us, that there would be no more machine rent or "power charge," as they called it, that needles would be furnished at cost, that machine oil would be furnished free, and that the cutters would receive a dollar a week raise. But no mention was made of our demand for a union shop.

We talked it all over with misgivings, lest some of the girls be misled by these promises. Without a company recognition of our union, we might all be lured back to work, the more progressive and outspoken of us discharged one by one, and all the old practices put back in force, perhaps even more tightly than ever. Such things had happened before. Our safety and our future, we knew, lay in our union. We decided not to return to work just yet. Meanwhile we doubled our picket line, determined that none of our group should falter.

We had hoped to get all the girls in the factory into our union, but we had had trouble with the girls of the kid glove department. Only a few of these "aristocrats" had ventured to walk out with us. The rest had remained aloof. Like the gloves they made, the kid glove makers felt that they were superior to the rest of us and used to refer haughtily to the rest of us as the "horsehide girls."

During one of the last days of our strike, one of these kid glove girls passed along our picket line on her way to work. We told her that she wasn't going in; we formed a circle around her and took her to the streetcar a block away and waited to see that she went home. We stood waiting for the car beside a long water trough where teamsters watered their horses. One girl who was holding tightly to the kid glove maker threatened, "Before I let go of you, I will duck you in that water trough." It was only an idle threat; of course she did not intend doing it.

Newspapermen were on hand trying to get stories about the strike. Luke Grant, a veteran labor reporter, was watching as we put the girl on the streetcar.

Next morning a front-page story appeared headlined, "STRIKERS DUCK GIRL IN WATER TROUGH." Other newspapers carried the same fiction and played it up for several days, some even with cartoons of the fictitious event. . . .

Perhaps because of this newspaper publicity — and Luke Grant always insisted that his story won the day for us — or perhaps because it

looked as though we girls would refuse forever to return to work unless
all our demands were met, the management agreed to our union shop
and to the redress of all our grievances. We went back to work the
following Monday with, as we said, "flying colors." Our union shop,
we felt, was our most important gain.

THE ASSUMPTION was often made that working women only liked to
read romantic and fanciful stories or escape literature. The following
letter to *Life and Labor*, the paper of the Women's Trade Union
League, suggests otherwise. The editors began to serialize the story
of Jean Valjean, from Victor Hugo's *Les Miserables*, as the letter
writer requested.

A LETTER OF PROTEST

At our League meetings every time we are asked to write to you and
tell you what we think of Life and Labor, and that is why I write to you
today. I am a Jewish girl, and I like Life and Labor; but the girls in our
factory are not interested in Life and Labor, and I will tell you why.
They do not know much—they have not much learning; they cannot do
much thinking after the day's work, and no one can do any thinking
"speeding up" at a machine, and only when they see something written
by someone they know, like Pauline Newman, will they take the trouble
to read it. What they need is stories, but stories that will stir them.

I do not know if I can tell you in English, but I will try, to tell you
why I think the stories of Life and Labor do not mean much to the
Jewish girls. You see, they are all *pleasant stories*, and we Jewish
people have suffered too much to like just "pleasant stories." We want
stories that tell of struggle, and that tell of people who want justice—
passionately. You see, with the people in your pleasant stories we have
no fellowship. They do not seem real.

Last night I was with some of our factory girls, and they begged me
for a story and I told them the story of Jean Valjean, and they all
listened eagerly, and when I finished they said, "So long, so long have
men and women struggled for justice and it is not here yet. We, too,

"Letter from a New Yorker." *Life and Labor* 1 (December 1911).

must struggle," and so they went on with more courage in their hearts for the struggle, and then I thought why not have Life and Labor give us the story of Jean Valjean, so that we may all take new heart and new courage.

A New New Yorker.

STRIKES AND THE TRADITION OF STRUGGLE

"RIOTS" AS A form of protest have been used repeatedly by poor people to obtain economic or political goals. While rioters are usually viewed as an unorganized mindless rabble by the established press (as in this selection) and the disconcerted upper classes, riots more often than not had an internal logic and organized objective.

One of the functions of the riot often was not to loot but rather to mete out justice and punishment. In 1902 Jewish immigrant women in New York organized a boycott of the kosher meat butchers. The boycott began on the Lower East Side of New York City and then spread to Brooklyn, Newark and Boston. Organized by Orthodox Jewish women and led by a woman butcher, the boycotters were protesting a steep rise in the price of meat and the betrayal of a promised boycott of the meat trust by retail butchers. Rather than looting, the women punished the butchers by closing their shops, destroying the meat by dousing it with kerosene. They demanded the setting of reasonable prices by a rabbi.

KOSHER MEAT BOYCOTTS

BROOKLYN MOB LOOTS BUTCHER SHOPS

Rioters, Led by Women, Wreck a Dozen Stores Dance Around Bonfires of Oil-Drenched Meat Piled in the Street—Fierce Fight with the Police.

A mob of 1,000 people, with women in the lead, marched through the Jewish quarter of Williamsburg last evening, and wrecked half a dozen

"Brooklyn Mob Loots Butcher Shops." *New York Times*, May 23, 1902.
"Butchers Appeal to Police for Protection." *New York Times*, May 26, 1902.

butcher shops. Men and women who were seen coming out of the shops with meat and chickens in their hands were attacked. In the throng of women leaders of the mob there were many who carried bottles of kerosene oil. . . .

During the march the crowd attacked the butcher stores, carried the meat they found there into the street, poured oil upon the heap, and set fire to it, while the men and women yelled their approval and danced about the bonfire.

The start of the butcher shop wrecking was made in Manhattan Avenue. At 46 there was a shop kept by a man named Klimins. He stood in front of his shop last evening when the mob marched toward his place. A shower of stones smashed every window in the store. In two minutes the mob leaders were inside of the store and were threatening to set the building on fire. All the meat which could be found was confiscated and destroyed with kerosene oil.

The next butcher's shop wrecked was that of a man named Knoll, at 46 Moore Street. A few policemen on patrol tried to disperse the crowd, but failed, and word was sent to the . . . Station for the reserves. The women then began their work of destruction quickly and urged the men on to greater efforts. The mob ran through the street, howling in their peculiar Russian and Polish dialects, wrecking with stones and other missiles, every butcher's shop in their path.

Several of the women leaders of the mob laughed at the fear of the men in doing damage. They took bottles of kerosene and scattered the oil in store after store, afterward setting fire to it with a match. In every instance the small fires started by the mob were extinguished by the proprietors, who were on watch expecting that some damage would be done to their place.

When the reserves of the . . . Station met the crowd there was a fierce encounter. The women threw bottles, stones and whatever they could place their hands on at the policemen. Women shook their fists in the faces of policemen and tore off their shields and buttons from their coats. There was a charge on the mob and night sticks were used freely. . . .

All that the police could do was to arrest four women who were charged with being ringleaders of the mob. Two policemen were badly injured about the face and hands, and it was some time before the crowd was dispersed. . . .

BUTCHERS APPEAL TO POLICE FOR PROTECTION

Practically all of the kosher butchers on the east side served notice yesterday on the Captains of the various police precincts that they intended to open their shops today and asked that the police protect them against any attacks that may be made by the women rioters who have been attacking the shops for selling meat, and the customers for buying meat, when a boycott was on against the prevailing high prices.

The Anti-Beef Trust Association during the past two weeks raised a fund of more than $500 to bail out those who are arrested on the charge of inciting riot. . . . A conference was also held late Saturday night between the Anti-Trust Association committee of fifty and some of the butchers in an endeavor to patch up existing differences, the rabbis to decide which shops would be permitted to resume business. At a late hour last night the Anti-Trust Association committee of fifty was trying to decide whether to accept the proposal of the butchers or not.

During the day, however, a circular, printed in both Yiddish and English, was distributed, showing that the matter is by no means settled. The circular, signed by four of the association leaders, representing the committee of fifty, is as follows:

"Women, victory is near. Order and persistence will win the struggle against the butchers. Do not buy any meat. All the organizations fighting against the Jewish meat trust have now united under the name of the Allied Conference for Cheap Kosher Meat. Brave and honest men are now aiding the women. The conference has decided to help those butchers who will sell cheap kosher meat under the supervision of the rabbis and the conference. The trust must be downed. For the present do not by (sic) any meat. Patience will win the battle. Seek the sympathy for your cause of old and young. Respectfully, Dr. D. Blaustein, the Rev. I. Zinster, the Rev. P. Joches, Mrs. Shatzburg, and the committee of fifty. . . ."

"It is conservatively estimated that 50,000 Jewish families have been abstaining from the use of meat for over two weeks. The people feel very justly that they are being ground down, not only by the Beef Trust of the country, but also by the Jewish Beef Trust of the City, which has now as its ally the Retail Butchers' Association. The people realize the seriousness of the situation and are ready to fight the trust for months if necessary. . . ."

THE SHIRTWAIST strikes of New York and Philadelphia during the
winter of 1909–1910 were the first large-scale women's strikes: 80 percent of the twenty to thirty thousand workers who participated were
women. The strikes were long and bitter, with mass arrests and police
brutality against picketers. Striking received massive support from
outsiders, mainly women organized by the Women's Trade Union
League and the Socialist Party. The WTUL was especially crucial to
the strike in its work organizing relief stations, providing bail and
other legal services, arranging publicity and fund-raising.

The workers were defeated in their key demand—union recognition.
Some of the worst problems in the strikes, and one of the main reasons
for their failure, was the arrogant role of the male union leaders, who,
halfway through the strike refused to back up the women workers in
their determination to hold out for all their demands. Many reformers
who had supported the strike also withdrew their support when the
union leadership did, leaving the strikers alone. Another problem was
a leadership dominated by Russian Jews, who were often contemptu-
ous of the Italians and native-born Americans for what they believed
was a lesser militancy.

Despite defeat on the union recognition demand, the strikes won
important gains for workingwomen and created a firm basis for the
continuing struggle for unionization. The strikes were training
grounds for many women who went on to become organizers and
served as powerful proof that women could organize and fight effectively. In this selection Helen Marot of the WTUL evaluates both the
problems and the achievements of the New York strike.

THE SHIRTWAIST STRIKE

. . . The shirtwaist-makers' "general strike" as it is called, followed
an eleven years' attempt to organize the trade. The union had been
unable during this time to affect to any appreciable extent the conditions of work. In its efforts during 1908–9 to maintain the union in
the various shops and to prevent the discharge of members who were
active union workers, it lost heavily. The effort resolved itself in 1909
into the establishment of the right to organize. The strike in the Triangle Waist Company turned on this issue. . . .

The company had undertaken to organize its employes into a club,

Helen Marot. "A Woman's Strike—An Appreciation of the Shirtwaist Makers of
New York." *Proceedings of the Academy of Political Science of the City of New York*,
Volume 1, Number 4, October 1910.

with benefits attached. The good faith of the company as well as the working-out of the benefit was questioned by the workers. The scheme failed and the workers joined the waist-makers' union. One day without warning a few weeks later one hundred and fifty of the employes were dropped, the explanation being given by the employers that there was no work. The following day the company advertised for workers. In telling the story later they said that they had received an unexpected order, but admitted their refusal to re-employ the workers discharged the day previous. The union then declared a strike, or acknowledged a lockout, and picketing began.

The strike or lockout occurred out of the busy season, with a large supply at hand of workers unorganized and unemployed. Practical trade unionists believed that the manufacturers felt certain of success on account of their ability to draw to an unlimited extent from an unorganized labor market and to employ a guard sufficiently strong to prevent the strikers from reaching the workers with their appeals to join them. But the ninety girls and sixty men strikers were not practical; they were Russian Jews who saw in the lockout an attempt at oppression. . . . The men strikers were intimidated and lost heart, but the women carried on the picketing, suffering arrest and abuse from the police and the guards employed by the manufacturers. At the end of the third week they appealed to the women's trade union league to protect them, if they could, against false arrest. . . .

A brief inspection by the league of the action of the pickets, the police, the strike breakers and the workers in the factory showed that the pickets had been intimidated, that the attitude of the police was aggressive and that the guards employed by the firm were insolent. The league acted as complainant at police headquarters and cross-examined the arrested strikers; it served as witness for the strikers in the magistrates' court and became convinced of official prejudice in the police department against the strikers and a strong partisan attitude in favor of the manufacturers. The activity and interest of women, some of whom were plainly women of leisure, was curiously disconcerting to the manufacturers and every effort was used to divert them. At last a young woman prominent in public affairs in New York and a member of the league, was arrested while acting as volunteer picket. Here at last was "copy" for the press.

During the five weeks of the strike, previous to the publicity, the forty thousand waist makers employed in the several hundred shops in New York were with a few exceptions here and there unconscious of the struggle of their fellow workers in the Triangle. There was no means of communication among them, as the labor press reached comparatively few. . . .

The arrests of sympathizers aroused sufficient public interest for the press to continue the story for ten days, including in the reports the treatment of the strikers. This furnished the union its opportunity. It knew the temper of the workers and pushed the story still further through shop propaganda. After three weeks of newspaper publicity and shop propaganda the reports came back to the union that the workers were aroused. It was alarming to the friends of the union to see the confidence of the union officers before issuing the call to strike. Trade unionists reminded the officers that the history of general strikes in unorganized trades was the history of failure. They invariably answered with a smile of assurance, "Wait and see."

The call was issued Monday night, November 22nd, at a great mass meeting in Cooper Union addressed by the president of the American Federation of Labor. "I did not go to bed Monday night"; said the secretary of the union, "our Executive Board was in session from midnight until six a. m. I left the meeting and went out to Broadway near Bleecker street. I shall never again see such a sight. Out of every shirtwaist factory, in answer to the call, the workers poured and the halls which had been engaged for them were quickly filled." In some of these halls the girls were buoyant, confident; in others there were girls who were frightened at what they had done. . . .

As nearly as can be estimated, thirty thousand workers answered the call, or seventy-five per cent of the trade. Of these six thousand were Russian men; two thousand Italian women; possibly one thousand American women and about twenty or twenty-one thousand Russian Jewish girls. The Italians throughout the strike were a constantly appearing and disappearing factor but the part played by the American girls was clearly defined.

The American girls who struck came out in sympathy for the "foreigners" who struck for a principle, but the former were not in sympathy with the principle; they did not want a union; they imagined that the conditions in the factories where the Russian and Italian girls worked were worse than their own. They are in the habit of thinking that the employers treat foreign girls with less consideration, and they are sorry for them. In striking they were self-conscious philanthropists. They were honestly disinterested and as genuinely sympathetic as were the women of leisure who later took an active part in helping the strike. They acknowledged no interests in common with the others, but if necessary they were prepared to sacrifice a week or two of work. Unfortunately the sacrifice required of them was greater than they had counted on. The "foreigners" regarded them as just fellow workers and insisted on their joining the union, in spite of their constant protestation, "We have no grievance; we only struck in sympathy." But the Russians failed to be grateful, took for granted a common cause and demanded that all shirtwaist makers, regardless of race or creed, continue the strike until they were recognized by the employers as a part of the union. This difference in attitude and understanding was a heavy strain on the generosity of the American girls. It is believed, however, that the latter would have been equal to what their fellow workers expected, if their meetings had been left to the guidance of American men and women who understood their prejudices. But the Russian men trusted no one entirely to impart the enthusiasm necessary for the cause. It was the daily, almost hourly, tutelage which the Russian men insisted on the American girls' accepting, rather than the prolongation of the strike beyond the time they had expected, that sent the American girls back as "scabs." There were several signs that the two or three weeks' experience as strikers was having its effect on them, and that with proper care this difficult group of workers might have been organized. For instance, "scab" had become an opprobrious term to them during their short strike period, and on returning to work they accepted the epithet from their fellow workers with great reluctance and even protestation. Their sense of superiority also had received a severe shock; they could never again be quite so confident that they did not in the nature of things belong to the labor group. . . .

The feature of the strike which was as noteworthy as the response of thirty thousand unorganized workers, was the unyielding and uncompromising temper of the strikers. This was due not to the influence of nationality, but to the dominant sex. The same temper displayed in the shirtwaist strike is found in other strikes of women, until we have now a trade-union truism, that "women make the best strikers." . . . Working women have been less ready than men to make the initial sacrifice that trade-union membership calls for, but when they reach the point of striking they give themselves as fully and as instinctively to the cause as they give themselves in their personal relationships. It is important, therefore, in following the action of the shirtwaist makers, to remember that eighty per cent were women, and women without trade-union experience.

When the shirtwaist strikers were gathered in separate groups, according to their factories, in almost every available hall on the East Side, the great majority of them received their first instruction in the principles of unionism and learned the necessity of organization in their own trade. The quick response of women to the new doctrine gave to the meetings a spirit of revival. Like new converts they accepted the new doctrine in its entirety and insisted to the last on the "closed shop." But it was not only the enthusiasm of the new converts which made them refuse to accept anything short of the closed shop. In embracing the idea of solidarity they realized their own weakness as individual bargainers. "How long," the one-week or two-weeks-old union girls said, "do you think we could keep what the employer says he will give us without the union? Just as soon as the busy season is over it would be the same as before." . . .

Important as were the specific demands, they were lightly regarded in comparison with the issue of a union shop.

Nothing can illustrate this better than the strikers' treatment of the arbitration proposal which was the outcome of a conference between their representatives and the employers. In December word came to the union secretary that the manufacturers would probably consider arbitration if the union was ready to submit its differences to a board. The officers made reply in the affirmative and communicated their action at once to the strikers. Many of the strikers had no idea what arbitration meant, but as it became clear to them they asked, some of them menacingly, "Do you mean to arbitrate the recognition of the union?" It took courage to answer these inexperienced unionists and uncompromising girls that arbitration would include the question of the union as well as other matters. The proposition was met with a storm of opposition. When the strikers at last discovered that all their representatives counseled arbitration, with great reluctance they gave way, but at no time was the body of strikers in favor of it. A few days later, when the arbitrators who represented them reported that the manufacturers on their side refused to arbitrate the question of the union, they resumed their strike with an apparent feeling of security and relief. Again later they showed the same uncompromising attitude when their representatives in the conference reported back that the manufacturers would concede important points in regard to wage and factory conditions, but would not recognize the union. The recommendations of the conference were rejected without reservation by the whole body.

The strikers at this time lost some of their sympathizers. . . .

It was after the new year that the endurance of the girls was put to the test. During the thirteen weeks benefits were paid out averaging less than $2 for each striker. Many of them refused to accept benefits, so that the married men could be paid more. The complaints of hardships came almost without exception from the men. Occasionally it was discovered that a girl was having one meal a day and even at times none at all.

In spite of being underfed and often thinly clad, the girls took upon themselves the duty of picketing, believing that the men would be more severely handled. Picketing is a physical and nervous strain under the best conditions, but it is the spirit of martyrdom that sends young girls of their own volition, often insufficiently clad and fed, to patrol the streets in mid-winter with the temperature low and with snow on the ground, some days freezing and some days melting. After two or three hours of such exposure, often ill from cold, they returned to headquarters, which were held for the majority in rooms dark and unheated, to await further orders.

It takes uncommon courage to endure such physical exposure, but these striking girls underwent as well the nervous strain of imminent arrest, the harsh treatment of the police, insults, threats and even actual assaults from the rough men who stood around the factory doors. During the thirteen weeks over six hundred girls were arrested; thirteen were sentenced to five days in the workhouse and several were detained a week or ten days in the Tombs.

The pickets, with strangely few exceptions, during the first few weeks showed remarkable self-control. They had been cautioned from the first hour of the strike to insist on their legal rights as pickets, but to give no excuse for arrest. Like all other instructions, they accepted this literally. They desired to be good soldiers and every nerve was strained to obey orders. But for many the provocations were too great and retaliation began after the fifth week. It occurred around the factories where the strikers were losing, where peace methods were failing and where the passivity of the pickets was taunted as cowardice. . . .

Before the strike every shop was "open" and in most of them there was not a union worker. In thirteen short weeks three hundred and twelve shops had been converted into "closed" or full union contract shops.

But the significance of the strike is not in the actual gain to the shirtwaist makers of three hundred union shops, for there was great weakness in the ranks of the opposition. Trade-union gains, moreover, are measured by what an organization can hold rather than by what it can immediately gain. The shirt-waist makers' strike was characteristic of all strikes in which women play an active part. It was marked by complete self-surrender to a cause, emotional endurance, fearlessness and entire willingness to face danger and suffering. The strike at times seemed to be an expression of the woman's movement rather than the labor movement. This phase was emphasized by the wide expression of sympathy which it drew from women outside the ranks of labor.

It was fortunate for strike purposes but otherwise unfortunate that the press, in publishing accounts of the strike, treated the active public expression of interest of a large body of women sympathizers with sensational snobbery. It was a matter of wide public comment that women of wealth should contribute sums of money to the strike, that they should admit factory girls to exclusive club rooms, and should hold mass meetings in their behalf. If, as was charged, any of the women who entered the strike did so from sensational or personal motives, they were disarmed when they came into contact with the strikers. Their earnestness of purpose, their complete abandon to their cause, their simple acceptance of outside interest and sympathy as though their cause were the cause of all, was a bid for kinship that broke down all barriers. Women who came to act as witnesses of the arrests around the factories ended by picketing side by side with the strikers. These volunteer pickets accepted, moreover, whatever rough treatment was offered, and when arrested, asked for no favors that were not given the strikers themselves.

The strike brought about adjustments in values as well as in relationships. Before the strike was over federations of professional women and women of leisure were endorsing organization for working women, and individually these women were acknowledging the truth of such observations as that made by one of the strikers on her return from a visit to a private school where she had been invited to tell about the strike. Her story of the strike led to questions in regard to trade unions. On her return her comment was, "Oh they are lovely girls, they are so kind— but I didn't believe any girls could be so ignorant." . . .

In 1912 Lawrence, Massachusetts, became the site of one of the most militant and massive strikes in American history. Located in the center of the New England textile industry, Lawrence was a woolen center employing 30,000 workers. The strike was important for several reasons: first, it proved that unskilled workers of many different nationalities could be brought into a single organization; second, it developed the tactics of mass picketing; third, in an industry in which 50 percent of the workers were women, it showed that women could offer militance and leadership even when working alongside men.

The strike not only won the most militant demands of the workers, but also set off a wave of strikes throughout the New England textile region which engulfed nearly 25,000 workers. It was not a permanent victory, however. During the next year, employers launched a campaign to defeat the organization, using spies and immigrant scabs from Quebec, blacklisting the militants of the strike, and propagandizing against the union through a "god and country" campaign with the help of a right-wing priest. Ultimately the employers began to close down some of their mills.

The description of the Lawrence strike is from the autobiography of Elizabeth Gurley Flynn, who was sent there by the International Workers of the World, a revolutionary industrial union in opposition to the conservative, craft-unionist A.F.L. The second selection is a letter from the President of the Boston Women's Trade Union League to the President of the National W.T.U.L. about how the W.T.U.L. was lured into inactivity by its affiliation with the A.F.L. The letter offers one example of the general contradictions in the league's role.

THE LAWRENCE TEXTILE STRIKE

The strike broke with dramatic suddenness on January 11, 1912, the first payday of the year. A law reducing the hours of women and children under 18, from 56 hours a week to 54 had been passed by the Massachusetts legislature. It affected the majority of the employees. The employers had strongly resisted the passage of this law. Now they cut the pay proportionately in the first pay envelope. Wages were *already* at the starvation point. The highest paid weavers received $10.50 weekly. Spinners, carders, spoolers and others averaged $6 to $7 weekly. Whole families worked in the mills to eke out a bare existence. Pregnant women worked at the machines until a few hours before their babies were born. Sometimes a baby came right there in the mill, between the looms. The small pittance taken from the workers by the rich corporations, which were protected by a high tariff from foreign competition, was the spark that ignited the general strike. "Better to starve fighting than to starve working!" became their battle-cry. It

Elizabeth Gurley Flynn. "The Lawrence Textile Strike." *The Rebel Girl*. New York: International Publishers, 1973.

spread from mill to mill. In a few hours of that cold, snowy day in January, 14,000 workers poured out of the mills. In a few days the mills were empty and still—and remained so for nearly three months.

It was estimated that there were at least 25 different nationalities in Lawrence. The largest groups among the strikers were: Italians, 7,000; Germans, 6,000; French Canadians, 5,000; all English speaking, 5,000; Poles, 2,500; Lithuanians, 2,000; Franco-Belgians, 1,100; Syrians, 1,000—with a sprinkling of Russians, Jews, Greeks, Letts and Turks. The local IWW became the organizing core of the strike. They were overwhelmed by the magnitude of the job they had on their hands and sent a telegram for help to Ettor in New York City. He and his friend, Arturo Giovannitti, responded to the call on the promise of Haywood, James P. Thompson, myself and others to come as soon as possible, which we did. Ettor and Giovannitti . . . organized mass meetings in various localities of the different language groups and had them elect a strike committee of men and women which represented every mill, every department and every nationality. They held meetings of all the strikers together on the Lawrence Common (New England's term for park or square), so that the workers could realize their oneness and strength. . . . There were 1,400 state militiamen in Lawrence, which was like an armed camp. Clashes occurred daily between the strikers and the police and state troopers.

The period of activity for Ettor and Giovannitti was cut short by their arrest on January 30, 1912. A tragedy on the picket line gave the authorities the excuse to get rid of Ettor and Giovannitti. In a fracas between police and pickets, a woman striker, Anna La Pizza, was killed. The two strike leaders, along with a striker, Joseph Caruso, were lodged in the county jail. Caruso, who had been on the picket line, was charged with murder, and the strike leaders were charged with being accessory to murder because of their speeches advocating picketing. It was the same theory of constructive conspiracy which had sent speakers at the Haymarket protest meeting in Chicago to their deaths on the gallows 25 years before. . . .

The militiamen were mostly native-born "white-collar" workers and professionals from other parts of the state who openly showed their contempt for the foreign-born strikers. Colonel Sweetzer, their commander, banned a mass funeral for Anna La Pizza. He ordered the militia *not* to salute the American flag when it was carried by strikers. His orders were "Shoot to kill. We are not looking for peace now." Many acts of brutal violence were committed by these arrogant youths on horseback, such as riding into crowds and clubbing the people on foot. When they marched afoot, they carried rifles with long bayonets. On the same day Ettor and Giovannitti were arrested, an 18 year-old Syrian boy striker, John Rami, was bayonetted through the lung, from the back, and died. In the course of the strike several persons were injured with bayonets. The orders were to strike the women on the arms and breasts and the men on the head. This was actually reported in a Boston paper. . . .

When Haywood came to Lawrence in February 1912 to assume the leadership of the textile strike it created a national sensation. . . . Haywood had been tried for murder five years before, due to his labor activities. . . . But the more he was attacked the more the strikers loved "Big Bill." The strike committee elected him its chairman in place of Ettor. . . .

Haywood introduced special meetings of women and children. It was amazing how this native-born American, who had worked primarily among English-speaking men, quickly adapted his way of speaking to the foreign-born, to the women and to the children. They all understood his down-to-earth language, which was a lesson to all of us. I was then 21 years old and I learned how to speak to workers from Bill Haywood in Lawrence, to use short words and short sentences, to repeat the same thought in different words if I saw that the audience did not understand. I learned never to reach for a three-syllable word if one or two would do. This is not vulgarizing. Words are tools and not everybody has access to a whole tool chest. The foreign-born usually learned English from their children who finished school after the lower grades. Many workers began to learn English during these strike meetings. . . . I have met many American workers who are highly intelligent, better thinkers by far than the average Congressman, but they are handicapped by their meager vocabularies from communicating their thoughts to others in speech and are even more limited in writing. . . .

Wherever Bill Haywood went, the workers followed him with glad greetings. They roared with laughter and applause when he said: "The AFL organizes like this!"—separating his fingers, as far apart as they would go, and naming them—"Weavers, loom-fixers, dyers, spinners." Then he would say: "The IWW organizes like this!"—tightly clenching his big fist, shaking it at the bosses. . . .

We held special meetings for the women at which Haywood and I spoke. The women worked in the mills for lower pay and in addition had all the housework and care of the children. The old-world attitude of man as the "lord and master" was strong. At the end of the day's work—or, now, of strike duty—the man went home and sat at ease while his wife did all the work preparing the meal, cleaning the house, etc. There was considerable male opposition to women going to meetings and marching on the picket line. We resolutely set out to combat these notions. The women wanted to picket. They were strikers as well as wives and were valiant fighters. We knew that to leave them at home alone, isolated from the strike activity, a prey to worry, affected by the complaints of tradespeople, landlords, priests and ministers, was dangerous to the strike. We brought several Socialist women in as speakers, and a girl organizer, Pearl McGill, who had helped organize the button workers of Muscatine, Iowa. The AFL revoked her credentials for coming to Lawrence. We did not attack their religious ideas in any way, but we said boldly that priests and ministers should stick to their religion and not interfere in a workers' struggle for better conditions, unless they wanted to help. We pointed out that if the workers had more money they would spend it in Lawrence—even put more in the church collections. The women laughed and told it to the priests and ministers the next Sunday.

We talked especially to the women about the high cost of living here—how they had been fooled when they first came here when they figured the dollars in their home money. They thought they were rich till they had to pay rent, buy groceries, clothes and shoes. Then they knew they were poor. We pointed out that the mill owners did not live in Lawrence. They did not spend their money in the local stores. All that the businessmen received came from the workers. If the workers get more, they will get more. The women conveyed these ideas to the small shopkeepers with emphasis and we heard no more protest from them about the strike after that. . . .

The IWW was held up to scorn by John Golden, head of the United Textile Workers of America, because "it had only 287 members there" when the strike began. He had made no attempt to organize and defend the foreign workers against the wage cut of January 11, 1912. In fact, he had ordered the skilled workers to stay at work. . . . But Golden had not been able to hold the highly skilled weavers and loom-fixers in the mills. . . . They could not work alone even if they had wanted to, and they did not want to do so.

We talked to the strikers about One Big Union, regardless of skill or lack of it, foreign-born or native-born, color, religion or sex. We showed how all differences are used by the bosses to keep workers divided and pitted against each other. . . . This was more than a union. It was a crusade for a united people—for "Bread and Roses." . . .

Our concepts as to how socialism would come about, were syndicalist to the core. There would be a general strike, the workers would lock out the bosses, take possession of the industries and declare the abolition of the capitalist system. It sounded very simple. Our attitude toward the state was sort of Thoreau-like—the right to ignore the state, civil disobedience to a bosses' state. For instance, Bill Haywood threatened to burn the books of the strike committee rather than turn them over to an investigation committee. He was arrested for contempt of court. However much or little the workers absorbed our syndicalist philosophy, they cheered Bill's defiance to the skies. . . .

We spoke of their power, as workers, as the producers of all wealth, as the creators of profit. Here they could see it in Lawrence. Down tools, fold arms, stop the machinery, and production is dead—profits no longer flow. We ridiculed the police and militia in this situation. "Can they weave cloth with soldiers' bayonets or policemen's clubs?" we asked. "No," replied the confident workers. "Did they dig coal with bayonets in the miners' strikes or make steel or run trains with bayonets?" Again the crowds roared "No." We talked Marxism as we understood it—the class struggle, the exploitation of labor, the use of the state and armed forces of government against the workers. It was all there in Lawrence before our eyes. We did not need to go far for the lessons. . . .

The children's meetings, at which Haywood and I spoke, showed us mainly that there were two groups of workers' children in Lawrence, those who went to school and those who worked in the mills. The efforts of the church and schools were directed to driving a wedge between the school children and their striking parents. Often children in such towns become ashamed of their foreign-born foreign-speaking parents, their old-country ways, their accents, their foreign newspapers, and even their strike and mass picketing. The up-to-date, well-dressed native-born teachers set a pattern. The working-class women were shabbily dressed, though they made the finest of woolen fabrics. . . . Some teachers called the strikers lazy, said they should go back to work or "back where they came from." We attempted to counteract all this at our children's meetings. . . . The parents were pathetically grateful to us as their children began to show real respect for them and their struggles. . . .

Suffering increased among the strikers. They had no financial reserves. They needed fuel and food. Their houses, dilapidated wood-frame barracks, were hard to heat. Committees of strikers went to nearby cities to appeal for support. Labor unions, Socialist locals, and workers in Boston, Manchester, Nashua, Haverhill and other places responded generously. Eleven soup kitchens were opened. The workers of Lowell, a nearby textile town, led a cow garlanded with leaves, to the strikers of Lawrence. I felt sorry for her with her festive appearance and her mild eyes. But she had to be slaughtered to feed hungry children. Her head was mounted and hung up in the Franco-Belgian Hall. . . .

A proposal was made by some of the strikers that we adopt a method used successfully in Europe—to send the children out of Lawrence to be cared for in other cities. The parents accepted the idea and the children were wild to go. On February 17, 1912, the first group of 150 children were taken to New York City. A small group also left for Barre, Vermont. A New York committee, headed by Mrs. Margaret Sanger, then a trained nurse and chairman of the Women's Committee of the Socialist Party, came to Lawrence to escort them. . . . Five thousand people met them at Grand Central Station.

On February 24, 1912, a group of 40 strikers' children were to go from Lawrence to Philadelphia. . . . At the railroad station in Lawrence, where the children were assembled accompanied by their fathers and mothers, just as they were ready to board the train they were surrounded by police. Troopers surrounded the station outside to keep others out. Children were clubbed and torn away from their parents and a wild scene of brutal disorder took place. Thirty-five frantic women and children were arrested, thrown screaming and fighting into patrol wagons. They were beaten into submission and taken to the police station. There the women were charged with "neglect" and improper guardianship and ten frightened children were taken to the Lawrence Poor Farm. The police station was besieged by enraged strikers. Members of the Philadelphia committee were arrested and fined. It was a day without parallel in American labor history. A reign of terror prevailed in Lawrence, which literally shook America. . . . Famous newspaper reporters and writers flocked to Lawrence. . . .

At the insistent demand of Socialist Congressman Victor Berger of Milwaukee the House Rules Committee held a hearing in Washington, D.C. in March 1912. . . . More than 50 striker witnesses came from Lawrence to tell their stories and show their pay envelopes. The cause of the strike, extent of their poverty, the conditions of their lives, the violence of the authorities, were all revealed by them to the American people in this Congressional hearing. . . . There was no more interference with the children leaving Lawrence after that. . . .

On March 1, 1912, the American Woolen Company announced a 7.5

per cent increase in 33 cities. On March 6, 125,000 workers in cotton
and woolen mills of six states were raised 5 to 7 per cent. On March 14,
the Lawrence strike was settled with the American Woolen Company,
the Atlantic Mill and other main mills. Twenty thousand workers assembled on the Common to hear the report of their committee. It was
the first time in six weeks they were allowed to use the Common.
Haywood presided at the meeting and introduced the delegates of all
the nationalities. The demands which they had won secured an increase
in wages from five to 20 per cent; increased compensation for overtime; the reduction of the premium period from four weeks to two
weeks and no discrimination against any worker who had taken part in
the strike. . . . The Arbitration Committee promised to help get Ettor
and Giovannitti speedily released. The workers pledged to strike again
if they were not freed. They had wrested millions from their employers.
Yet their leaders, Ettor and Giovannitti, were still in danger of death,
so they did not go back to work happy.

THE WOMEN'S TRADE UNION LEAGUE AT LAWRENCE

My dear Mrs. Robins:
    In its relation to the strike of the Lawrence Textile Workers, the
Boston Women's Trade Union League has been confronted with an
unprecedented situation, yet liable to recur at any moment in any part
of the country and fraught with deep significance to our work of the
organizing women. . . .
    John Golden, president of the U.T.W., visited Lawrence and upon
his return, counselled the League to stay out of Lawrence temporarily.
He stated that he had had a great deal of past experience with both the
organization of the I.W.W. and with the leadership of Ettor in particular. The League waited two weeks. Many of the members were intensely
restless because of their inactivity and yet they believed that their
affiliation with the A. F. of L. forbade their supporting a group whose
aims and methods fundamentally differed. In the meantime the Lawrence strike revealed itself increasingly as a magnificent uprising of the
oppressed, unskilled foreign workers. . . . By the fourth week in January, the Women's Trade Union League determined that it must in

National Women's Trade Union League Manuscripts, National Archives, Library of
Congress, Headquarters Records, June 1911–May 1913 (Sue Ainslie Clark to Mrs. Ray-
mond Robins, January 1912).

some way aid the fight of the workers. After consultation with Mr. Golden, as the U.T.W. president, the Executive Committee voted to cooperate with the C.L.U. of Lawrence in establishing relief headquarters.

They therefore opened the station about the first of February. The two organizations solicited funds from unions and the public, procured assistants from among the workers and interested groups, and distributed relief in the form of provisions, clothing, rent and medicine and medical care. Owing to the division of the A. F. of L. group from the main group of strikers, the League was never in the forefront of the battle. Its appeal for funds was thus somewhat limited as were its funds.

. . . In the meantime, Mr. Golden with his assistants was striving to bring about a settlement on A. F. of L. principles. Groups of each craft were brought together and demands formulated to present to the mill-owners.

. . . Not long after this, the owners made their first concessions, raises from 5% to 25%, according to the previous pay, the lowest paid workers to receive the largest advance. A few thousand workers had already returned to the mills. The four locals of the U.T.W.—three of them formed during the strike—representing from 1500 to 2000 workers, voted to accept the terms offered. On March 5th accordingly, Mr. Golden took charge of the relief headquarters of the joint committee of the W.T.U.L. and the Lawrence C.L.U., assumed the burden of the deficit of $1300, and from that time on refused relief to any but those who were willing to return to work. From the standpoint of the U.T.W., the strike was over. The W.T.U.L., having no further voice in the running of the relief station and not concurring in the policy pursued, withdrew officially.

. . . Since that time the strike has been ultimately settled. The Committee of Ten, representing the Strike Committee of 60, representing the 15,000 operatives still out, finally obtained a complete and detailed statement from the mill-owners granting increases ranging from 5% to 25%—the lowest paid workers receiving the highest increase.

Moreover, the pay of some hundreds of thousands of operatives in New England has been increased through the influence of the Lawrence strike.

Certain members of the Boston League believe that its course was the only one open to it since it was affiliated with the A. F. of L. and aimed to propagate the principles of craft unionism endorsed by that organization. Certain others believe that we might have cooperated with the Strike Committee from the first, as individuals, though they realize the restraints imposed by the A. F. of L. affiliation. Still others think that our part has been a disgraceful one in this great struggle. Others regard the success of the Lawrence strike, through the I.W.W. methods, as an object lesson by which the League—and the A. F. of L.—must profit in order to play a vital part in the rapidly moving evolution of the labor movement today.

To me, many of those in power in the A. F. of L. today seem to be selfish, reactionary and remote from the struggle for bread and liberty of the unskilled workers. The danger confronted by the A. F. of L. is that immemorially confronted by organizations in church and government when creed and consideration of safety obscure the original spirit and aim. Are we, the Women's Trade Union League, to ally ourselves inflexibly with the "standpatters" of the Labor Movement or are we to hold ourselves ready to aid the "insurgents," those who are freely fighting the fight of the exploited, the oppressed and the weak among the workers? . . .

> Very sincerely,
> (signed) Sue Ainslie Clark

THE TRADITION of working-class struggles incorporates defeats as well as victories. Through speeches and songs, workers have preserved even the bitterest memories that they might be transformed into renewed dedication. One such tragic memory was that of the Triangle Shirtwaist Company fire in which 146 women (some estimates say 143, some 147) died on March 25, 1911. The fire was not an unforeseeable accident, but the direct result of criminal negligence on the part of the company. Triangle was an exceptionally antiunion firm, notorious for its terrible working conditions. The fire started in the loft of the Triangle Factory. The women and girls could not escape because the company had locked the doors to the stairs from the outside to prevent employees' stealing or escape; the fire ladders could not reach that high; there were no fire extinguishers and there was only one fire escape which would have taken three hours to empty the building (the women were all dead within twenty minutes). Most of the bodies were never identified but were buried in numbered coffins.

In the first selection below, Rose Schneiderman, a Women's Trade Union League organizer, is speaking at a meeting two months after the fire called to demand a fire prevention bureau, more factory inspectors, and compensation for the families. The meeting, held at the Metropolitan Opera House, attracted many upper- and middle-class reformers, and by the time Schneiderman rose to speak she was irritated and exhausted by all the platitudes that had been mouthed by those who did not share the experience of working-class people.

THE TRIANGLE FIRE

I would be a traitor to these poor burned bodies if I came here to talk good fellowship. We have tried you good people of the public and we have found you wanting. The old Inquisition had its rack and its thumbscrews and its instruments of torture with iron teeth. We know what these things are today: the iron teeth are our necessities, the thumbscrews the high-powered and swift machinery close to which we must work, and the rack is here in the "fire-proof" structures that will destroy us the minute they catch on fire.

This is not the first time girls have been burned alive in the city. Each week I must learn of the untimely death of one of my sister workers. Every year thousands of us are maimed. The life of men and women is so cheap and property is so sacred. There are so many of us for one job it matters little if 143 of us are burned to death.

We tried you, citizens; we are trying you now, and you have a couple of dollars for the sorrowing mothers and daughters and sisters by way of a charity gift. But every time the workers come out in the only way they know to protest against conditions which are unbearable, the strong hand of the law is allowed to press down heavily upon us.

Public officials have only words of warning to us—warning that we must be intensely orderly and must be intensely peaceable, and they

Rose Schneiderman. "Triangle Memorial Speech." In *All for One*. Rose Schneiderman and Lucy Goldthwaite. New York: Paul S. Erikson, Inc., 1967.

have the workhouse just back of all their warnings. The strong hand of the law beats us back when we rise into the conditions that make life bearable.

I can't talk fellowship to you who are gathered here. Too much blood has been spilled. I know from my experience it is up to the working people to save themselves. The only way they can save themselves is by a strong working-class movement.

AFTER WORLD WAR I both employers and male employees assumed that women would happily relinquish the new jobs and skills they had acquired in replacing men who joined the armed forces, and return to full-time, unpaid housework. This was not the case. In many occupations, women resisted being laid off so that men could be hired, particularly since for many women it was not a question of returning to housewifery but to other jobs, more tedious and more poorly paid.

One of many groups of women who contested layoffs was streetcar conductors. This report from a Women's Bureau publication summarizes the struggles women waged in three cities—Cleveland, Detroit and Kansas City.

WOMEN STREETCAR CONDUCTORS FIGHT LAYOFFS

Conspicuous among the occupations which were opened to women at the time of our entry into the war was the work of conductor on street and elevated railways and subways. While women had been employed as ticket agents by various companies for many years, the woman streetcar conductor was a complete innovation, and about her employment in this capacity have centered much discussion and several bitter controversies. . . .

Having once been accepted as a successful participant in transportation work, there were two factors which were to influence the future employment of women in these occupations. First, Were the men employees going to accept women as fellow workers? Second, Was it

"Controversies Regarding the Right of Women to Work as Conductors." *Women Street Car Conductors and Ticket Agents.* Washington, D.C.: U.S. Government Printing Office, 1921.

going to prove possible to provide such legal regulation as might be necessary for the protection of these women workers and at the same time allow for the unusual difficulties with which a transportation company is faced in arranging the working hours of its employees?

The first question was soon answered in one way for the women conductors in Detroit and Cleveland, and in the opposite way in Kansas City. The history of the situation in Detroit and Cleveland, as it affected the employment of women, is extremely significant. The issue was a clear-cut one, between the men on the one hand who wished to maintain the work of street car conductors as strictly men's work, and on the other hand the women who had proved that they could do the work well, and who were not ready to accept their exclusion from an occupation where the pay was good, and the hours and working conditions no more unsatisfactory than in many other occupations considered to come within the sphere of women's activities.

Women were put on as conductors during the latter part of August, 1918, in Cleveland, when the street railway company of that city claimed that it could not secure a sufficient number of men for this work. The men objected to the employment of women and threatened to strike if it continued. But a compromise was finally effected and the matter submitted to Department of Labor investigators, who were to decide whether the women should be retained during the investigation and whether there was a sufficient shortage of men to require the continued employment of women. The decision to retain the women during the investigation was made almost immediately, but after the investigation it was decided that while there was still a scarcity of male labor it was not sufficient to justify the continued employment of women. This decision was rendered by the investigators in spite of their statement that "It is true the company will have to lower its standards somewhat, owing to the extraction of the best men from civil life into the military service of the country." It was recommended that the women be discharged from the service by November 1. The women protested against this and brought the matter before the War Labor Board. They claimed that it was illegal for the company and the men employees to make the original agreement to submit to arbitration the question of whether the women should be kept, as the company had engaged the women to work during good behavior and to be discharged only for incompetency, insubordination, or other unsatisfactory service. The company expressed itself as completely satisfied with the work of the women, who claimed that the contracts between them and the company were still valid, and that they had not been consulted in any of the negotiations or investigations relative to their dismissal. They also claimed that the agreement to arbitrate was a disregard of their right to be employed and to hold employment as long as their work was satisfactory, and was an abridgement of their constitutional right to work.

The men claimed that the question of the employment of women was a matter between the company and the union. The union had an agreement with the company that no women should be employed, therefore the women had been engaged in disregard of this contract and were not parties to the discussion. . . . On December 2, the union formally demanded that the women be discharged, and threatened to go on strike immediately if this were not done. The strike began on December 3 and the War Labor Board was hurriedly appealed to by the mayor of Cleveland, and immediately handed down a decision that the company should hereafter employ no more women, and that within the next 30 days all women should be replaced by competent men. This decision was not mandatory and the men refused to abide by it. The strike was finally settled by the following agreement between the union and the company:

> It is hereby agreed by and between the undersigned that on and after this date there will be no more women employed as conductors; that the Cleveland Railway Co. will remove and displace the women that are now in its service as rapidly as possible.

This agreement was made by the officers of the union and the company without including the women at any stage of the negotiations. Vigorous protests by various women's organizations as well as by the women conductors themselves followed this settlement, as it seemed to be a very dangerous precedent to deny women the right to work in any occupation for no other reason than that their dismissal was demanded by the men, and without even giving the women a hearing so that they might present their case.

As a result of many protests the War Labor Board held another hearing which was unfortunately delayed until after all of the women employed as conductors had been dismissed according to the agreement made between the company and the union.

The final award of the War Labor Board in this case was handed down on March 17, 1919, and was to the effect that the contract between the company and the union prohibited the employment of women, but that the employment of women having been permitted because of a necessity caused by a shortage of male labor these women were entitled by the terms of the contract under which they were engaged to continue in this service until their employment should cease, either by voluntary withdrawal or by discharge for cause or for other sufficient reason. The board directed, therefore, that the 64 women conductors who had been discharged by the company pursuant to its agreement with the union should be reinstated. The company, however, decided to abide by its original agreement with the union, and would not accept the recommendations of the War Labor Board. In a communication to that board the president of the company wrote:

> If your honorable board can prevail upon Division 268 of the Amalgamated Association of Street Railway Employees of America to agree to the reinstatement of the women conductors, I shall be very glad to order their reinstatement.

A similar situation arose in Detroit in September, 1918. Women were taken on as street car conductors, with the consent of the union whose contract with the company contained the following clause:

"It is understood that no objection shall be made to the employment of women or of colored men if necessity arises."

The arrangement between the Detroit United Railway and its employees provided that the company should make its contract of employment with the local union of the Amalgamated Association of Street and Electric Railway Employees of America, and should agree to employ as permanent employees only members of the union. Under this arrangement the company accepted for its employment any person who seemed fit, and after 48 hours' test the applicant was sent to the proper officer of the union to receive what is called a permit, and then after 90 days of service, if the company found him competent and no reasonable objection to him was presented by the union, he was admitted to the union.

According to this arrangement the women who were employed after September, 1918, were given permit cards, but when, after the 90 day period, they asked for admission into the union, they were refused, and on December 6, after the signing of the armistice, the union demanded the immediate dismissal of the women and refused to give permit cards to 15 women who had been in training and were ready to go on as regular conductors.

This case was argued before the War Labor Board in January, 1919, and was slightly different from the Cleveland case because of the clause in the contract between the union and the company which permitted the employment of women "if necessity arises." There were, therefore, two questions to be decided: Whether a necessity still existed which would justify the company in continuing to engage women to work as conductors, and whether the women already working as conductors should be dismissed, as was demanded by the union.

The first question required a judicial interpretation of the existence and extent of the "necessity" which, according to the terms of the contract, would justify the company in employing women. Although the women claimed that a number of the men employees who were being engaged as conductors were under age, or not sufficiently acquainted with the English language to discharge their duties properly, the board ruled that there was a sufficient supply of available male labor, if the company used diligence to find it, and therefore that the necessity to employ women no longer existed.

The second question was a more fundamental one, involving as it did the right of a group of men to demand the discharge of women who had been engaged in good faith, had performed their work in a satisfactory manner, and who had fulfilled all of the terms of their contract. In its decision on this subject the board stated:

The further issue arises whether we should say to the company, under the contract and circumstances, that it is its duty to discharge the women now in its employ. We find no such express limitation upon the employment of women in the contract. And we find that without such express provision equity and fair dealing toward the women who have prepared themselves for this employment * * * require us to hold that no such implication arises from the wording used and that the union must be content with the continued employment of the women now with the company * * * until in natural course, by voluntary withdrawal, by discharge, or for other causes they cease their connection with the company. * * * The order, therefore, will be that the company may retain in its employ those women now engaged in its service and may receive into its service the 15 already mentioned who prepared themselves for duty as conductors, and that the union shall issue the proper permits to them for such employment, but that no more women shall be employed.

The women were therefore retained although the union never issued the permits, and the Detroit case, so far as it provided that the women already employed should not be dismissed, was a victory for the women, who by this decision could hold on to their jobs until they were ready to give them up. From the point of view of enlarged industrial opportunity for women, however, the result in each city was a decided setback for women, as the unions so effectively controlled the situation that through their contracts with the companies they were able to shut out the women from this field of work.

A very different situation obtained in Kansas City, where women were first employed in June, 1918. The company had wished to employ women in 1917, according to a statement made by the general manager of the company, but had not done so because of the opposition of the union. In May, 1918, however, this opposition was withdrawn, and shortly after this 10 women were put on as conductors. In August, 1918, when there were 125 women employed, there was a controversy between the union and the Kansas City Street Railway Co. regarding wages, the status of women employees, a revision of schedules, and the constitution of the working day. From the women's viewpoint the most significant thing about this controversy, which was submitted to the War Labor Board, was that under the subject "status of women employees" the union was not demanding that the women be dismissed, but that their guaranteed minimum pay be raised to equal the guaranteed minimum for the men. The decision of the War Labor Board recognized this demand and directed that "women employees shall receive equal pay with men for the same work, and the guaranteed minimum for women shall be increased from $60 to $75 per month, as now obtains in the case of men." The women's guaranty was accordingly raised to the same rate as the men's, but the entire award of the board was not put into effect, and in February, 1919, there was a strike called to oblige the company to accept the full award of the board. But a very small number of the women joined in the strike with the men.

Although an interesting and important example of the possibility of cooperation between the men and women working in the same occupation, the Kansas City situation is not reflected in the general policy of the union, for as recently as May 13, 1920, W.D.M., international president of the Amalgamated Association of Street and Electric Railway Employees of America, stated in a letter to the Women's Bureau:

> The dispute that was raised by our organization was against women as conductors on surface and trolley cars. Our organization took the position that it was no fit place for a woman to work and has decided against them.

It would appear, then, that if women are to maintain their place as street car conductors they must do so against the organized opposition of the men who are engaged in this work.

WOMEN'S CONSCIOUSNESS AND CLASS CONFLICT

IN THIS PERIOD for the first time American working-class activity began to take the form of organizations challenging the capitalist system. Most of this effort entirely ignored workingwomen, for a series of reasons: because women could not vote and were not generally considered full citizens; because most people thought women's entry into the wage-labor force an aberration caused by special difficulties, hopefully to be set right by increasing men's wages so they could support their families alone; and because of a widespread conviction among working-class, as among bourgeois, men that women were not capable of good political judgment and action.

Two organizations stand out as exceptions to this rule: the Socialist Party and the I.W.W., International Workers of the World. The former was the larger and more successful at involving working-class women. One of its major contributions to a feminist analysis of women's labor was its appreciation of the significance of women's unpaid labor in their homes.

THE LOWEST PAID WORKERS

. . . Never before has a voice been raised in favor of the lowest paid worker, the average housewife. She works the longest hours and gets the lowest remuneration. The average toiler's work is done when the sun is down, but the housewife's work is never done. The greatest injustice towards her, however, lies in the fact that not only is she not compensated for her work, but, on the contrary, is considered a burden on the shoulders of poor man, who has to support her.

In spite of the fact that she is the real maintainer of the race, our great economists have proclaimed her labor nonproductive, just be-

Theresa Malkiel. "The Lowest Paid Workers." *Socialist Woman*, Vol. II, No. 16, September 1908.

cause it never had a market value. They say: "Oh, she is supported by a man." People claim that the average girl does not bother about improving her lot, because she expects to find a man who will support her. If we would only take the trouble to look deeper into the question, these assertions would refute themselves.

It is true that the man has to bring home enough money to maintain the rest of the family, but this does not mean that he supports the woman, who often does a greater amount of work than he himself, any more than the employer, who gave him the money to bring home, supports him.

The man who is himself nothing but a wage slave, loses sight of this fact, and no sooner does he come home, than he becomes monarch of his small domain. He hands out the miserable pittance to the wife, as if he was conferring the greatest favor upon her, very often reminding her how hard he has to slave for her, while she stays at home and receives the ready-earned money. So long and so persistently has he assumed the air of benefactor, that she herself has come to consider him in that light.

The best that can be had for the little money in her possession is always reserved for him, while the children come next and she herself last of all, with the result that she often goes without proper food, and still oftener without a necessary addition to her scanty wardrobe.

Should she dare to complain of her bitter lot, she would inevitably hear the rebuke: "Don't I slave all my life for you?" Does he slave for her?

MARGARET SANGER, the woman whose name is most associated with the birth control movement in this country, began her work as a member of the Socialist Party. She wrote on birth control, venereal disease and other women's health problems for the *New York Call*, a Socialist paper, until her articles were censored for being "obscene" by the Post Office.

In the early years of her work, before World War I, she saw birth control within a socialist perspective, as a means of self-determination particularly important to working-class women. Her strategies for working-class advancement were not always sound, as for example she believed that if the working class as a whole could reduce its numbers, it would improve its economic position. But her heart was with the poor. After the war, Sanger led the birth control movement in an increasingly conservative direction, sloughing off both its feminist and its class content.

These selections are from letters sent to her by women asking for birth control information.

BIRTH CONTROL

Please tell me what to do to keep from having any more babies. I am only twenty-six years old and the mother of five children the oldest eight years and the others six, four and two, and I have four living. The last time I had a six month's miscarriage and I have been weak ever since. It happened this past August. My husband is gone to try to find work and I have to support my children myself. I have to work so hard until I feel like it would kill me to give birth to another. I am nervous. My back and side give me a lot of trouble. I am not able to give my children the attention that I desire. I take in washing to support my children, I suffered this last time from the time I got that way until I lost it and am yet weak in my back. Please! for my sake tell me what to do to keep from having another. I don't want another child. Five is enough for me.

I don't care to bear any more children for the man I got he is most all the time drunk and not working and gone for days and nights and leave me alone most of the time. I'm sewing for support me and my baby that is two years old and one dead born so I know you don't blame me for not wanting any more children and he is always talking about leaving me he might as well for what he is doing but I am worried that I may get in wrong.

I was married when I was seventeen and seven months. After nine months married I had a miscarriage eight months. After fourteen months I had a baby boy and he is living and is now seven years old. After three years I had another boy. He was born with consumption in the bones and would shake his head one side and another, but doctors did not know what that was. Now I have them nervous spells myself. All through my marriage life I have been working in factories. I took my children to the day nursery. Two months before the birth of my last

Margaret Sanger. *Motherhood in Bondage.* New York: Brentano's, 1928.

child my husband deserted me with my children. He had left home eleven times before that but always came back, but that night his mother gave him money to go out of town. I was then married five years to him. After four years I could not get no trace of him I got the divorce. I had to work hard to keep my furniture and pay the rent as I did not want to go boarding. Now as I was twenty-six and as I had no one to depend on I married again. He is a good young man of twenty-five and he is not a lazy gambler like the other, but even with that I fear having any more children as they will not be healthy. We were married a few months ago and neither of us had any money and he is only a laborer and makes twenty-five dollars a week, so you see I have struggled with the first husband and I wish I will not struggle with this one, so please if you can help me.

MIDDLE-CLASS FEMINISTS often expressed concern for the conditions under which working-class women had to toil. Unfortunately, they often failed to notice these conditions when they impinged on their own lives.

A NINE-HOUR DAY
FOR DOMESTIC SERVANTS

. . . A friend called on me not long since, requesting my signature to a petition which urged the merchants to place seats behind the counters for the use of female clerks.

"The girls," she said, "have to stand on their feet ten hours a day and it makes my heart ache to see their tired faces."

"Mrs. Jones," said I, "how many hours a day does your maid stand upon her feet?"

"Why, I don't know," she gasped; "five or six, I suppose."

"At what time does she rise?"

"At six."

"And at what hour does she finish at night?"

Inez Goodman. "A Nine-Hour Day for Domestic Servants." *The Independent*, Vol. 54 (February 13, 1902).

"Oh, about eight, I think, generally."

"That makes fourteen hours. What time does she have during the day to sit down?"

"Why, she always has time to rest in the afternoon."

"How long?"

"I think about an hour, sometimes more."

"Does she have this hour on wash and ironing days?"

"No–o, I suppose not, but she can often sit down at her work."

"At what work? Washing? Ironing? Sweeping? Making beds? Cooking? Washing dishes?"

"Of course not, but she can sit while preparing vegetables and eating her meals." I assented to this.

"Perhaps she sits for two hours at her meals and preparing vegetables, and four days in the week she has an hour in the afternoon. According to that, your maid is on her feet at least eleven hours a day with a score of stair climbings included. It seems to me that her case is more pitiable than that of the store clerk."

My caller rose with red cheeks and flashing eyes. "My maid always has Sunday after dinner," she said.

"Yes, but the clerk has all day Sunday. Please don't go until I have signed that petition. No one would be more thankful than I to see the clerks have a chance to sit." . . .

_____

WORKING-CLASS women were conscious of the disdain that many of the more prosperous had for them. Without defensiveness or avoidance, many working "girls," as they called themselves, tried to analyze and fight the disrespectful attitudes they encountered. The following is an excerpt from an 1891 article in the monthly journal, *Far and Near,* of the Working Girls Clubs, a network of social and educational clubs begun by a coalition of workingwomen with some educated women reformers. Begun in the 1880s, the clubs began to die out in the late 1890s when workingwomen increasingly turned toward unionization to meet both their economic and social needs.

WHY DO PEOPLE LOOK DOWN ON WORKING GIRLS?

Why do people look down on Working Girls? This is the question that we girls ask each other over and over again. It is not a hard question, but it has never yet been answered to our satisfaction.

Is it because we lack natural ability? . . . Go into the places where we work and see the delicate and difficult work that we are doing—work that requires the help of eye and hand and brain, and, when you have gone the rounds, if you should give us your candid opinion, would not that opinion be that working girls are not deficient in natural ability? . . .

Is it because we lack education? That we do lack education, we admit. We have the brains. Give us the time and opportunity to use them. We are hungering and thirsting for knowledge. . . .

Is it because we lack virtue? Are working girls, as a class, virtuous? Years ago, a man who know whereof he affirmed, wrote: "Not even the famed Hebrew maiden as she stood on the giddy turret, more sacredly guarded her honor than does many a half-starved sewing woman in the streets of New York." . . . It is true, there are exceptions, but has not the immoral working girl her rivals among a class of women who should be her teachers in all pure and noble living?

Is it because we work? What an absurd idea! People "look down" on us because we work? Why, the lawyer and the doctor and the clergyman and the professor and the merchant all work, and work hard, too, and every one looks *up* to them. "Of course," says a bright, young lady, "we expect men to work and support their families, but ladies do not work." Don't they? We have lady artists and musicians, lady doctors, lawyers and lecturers, trained nurses and teachers. If it isn't *work* that they are doing, what is it? "But," says the same young lady, "have you never discovered that there is a difference between brain work and manual labor?" Yes, we have discovered it, to our sorrow. The teacher considers herself superior to the sewing girl, and the sewing girl thinks herself above the mill girl, and the mill girl thinks the girl who does general housework a little beneath her, and Miss Flora McFlimsy, "who toils not, neither does she spin," thinks

Lucy A. Warner. "Why Do People Look Down on Working Girls?" *Far and Near* 1 (No. 3), January 1891. We are indebted to Sarah Eisenstein for this selection.

herself superior to them all. Is one kind of work more honorable than another? . . .

My friend, have you ever considered that 'brain work' enters into every department of manual labor? An intelligent girl will do better work anywhere than an ignorant one. Isn't it a work of art to make a dress? It is just as necessary that a cook should mix her bread with 'brains' as it is that an artist should mix her colors with the same materials.

Dear sister workers, we who work in shop and store and factory, and in countless homes all over the United States, if it is because we work that people look down on us, then let us pray that the Lord will change their opinion, and go quietly about our business, for, among the 'nobility of labor' there is an illustrious company, at whose head stands the Carpenter of Nazareth, by Whom labor was forever glorified.

LUCY A. WARNER,
(Help Each Other Club.)

THE WOMAN SUFFRAGE movement was dominated by educated, prosperous women. But beginning in the 1910's, Wage Earners' Suffrage Leagues were organized as part of the suffrage strategy to reach working-class people. The following speech was given at a 1912 mass meeting criticizing the antisuffrage legislators.

SENATORS VS. WORKING WOMEN

Mollie Schepps, Shirt Waist Maker, answers the New York Senator who says:

"Now there is nobody to whom I yield in respect and admiration and devotion to the sex."

We want man's admiration, but we do not think that is all there is to live for. Since economic conditions force us to fight our battle side by side with man in the industrial field we do not see why we should not have the same privileges in the political field in order to better the conditions under which we must work. . . . We demand a voice as to how politics shall be conducted. Yes, we want man's admiration, but

Manuscripts of Leonora O'Reilly, Schlesinger Library, Harvard University. (*Senators vs. Working Women*, pamphlet, Wage Earners' Suffrage League of New York.)

not the kind that looks well on paper or sounds good when you say it. (Applause.) What we want men to do is to practice, to stop talking of the great comforts that they have provided for us; we know in most of the cases we are the providers; we also want them to know that in these days they will have to try to win our admiration. . . .

Don't you gentlemen worry, our minds are already made up as to what we are going to do with our vote when we get it. Another reason is given against woman suffrage; it is said that equal say will enable the women to get equal pay, and equal pay is dangerous. Why? Because it would keep the women from getting married. Well, then, if long, miserable hours and starvation wages are the only means man can find to encourage marriage it is a very poor compliment to themselves. In the name of a purer marriage we must have equal voice in making the laws for we have found out from experience that it is not only men who have to get married.

There are a few facts from the shirtwaist strike I would like to call to your attention. . . . When the bosses hired thugs to break our ranks and create riots, the police arrested the girls; when the girls were brought before the judge, he showed his *devotion* by sending a sixteen-year-old girl, Rose Perr, to the workhouse for six days. And for what crime, on what evidence? Simply that a thug accused her of violating the law while picketing. The word of the thug was taken in preference every time to the innocent girl's. Again when we sent a committee to Mayor McClellan to speak for protection for 30,000 women on strike in the shirt-waist industry, and to protest against the brutality of the police, what answer did the Mayor give the committee? This. He could not be bothered with any striking shirt-waist makers. Had that same committee represented 30,000 men, men who would have a vote at the next election, you can bet that the committee would have received a different answer, for it would mean 30,000 votes at the next election. This is the kind of respect, admiration and devotion we receive from our admirers the politicians when we fight for a better condition and a decent wage.

One year later, when we had the terrible disaster of the Triangle Shirt-waist factory, where our bodies were burned by the wholesale and many jumped from the tenth floor and smashed their poor bodies rather than be roasted. Then again those very same gentlemen, that a year ago tried to break our ranks when we fought for a safer place to work in, shed tears over the bodies on the sidewalk crushed to pieces. . . . we can not, and must not, wait until our sisters that live in comforts get the votes for us. We know that they have everything that their heart desires in order to make life worth while. That is no reason why they should not have the ballot, but working women must use the ballot in order to bring about conditions where all may be able to live and grow because they work. The ballot used as we mean to use it will abolish the burning and crushing of our bodies for the profit of a very few.

Doing the wash, New York City, 1919.

Sweated labor: an immigrant family
makes artificial flowers at home,
New York City, c. 1909–1912.
Photograph by Lewis Hine for the
National Child Labor Committee.

Lower East Side women discussing
the price of meat during riots over
the high price of meat, 1910.

Typists, 1907.

Americanization: A public health
nurse from the Henry Street Settlement advises an immigrant mother.

Mayday, 1916: women
garment workers
demonstrating with a
banner reading
"Purity" in Italian.

Family labor in a
canning factory,
Baltimore, Maryland,
during World War I.

The tenement community.

1920~1940

America's post–World War I position as the industrial power of the world brought new problems to U.S. capitalism. The war had created a demand for increased production, but when it ended the United States was faced with problems of overproduction. In order to maintain profits, industry needed to stimulate consumption. There is a myth that the 1920s was a carefree decade of prosperity and indulgence; but this mood, if it was true at all, characterized only a superficial stratum of the society. Most Americans had hard times in the 1920s. Employers began a concerted effort to roll back the gains of organized labor, and succeeded in some respects. Political repression and economic squeeze reduced union membership. Jobs were not plentiful. For example, the proportion of women over fourteen holding jobs increased by only 1 percent, compared to very rapid increase in preceding decades. At the same time that employers wanted to keep labor costs down, they also needed to boost consumption, and to do this created a giant advertising industry in the 1920s. The major target of the advertising industry was women. By manufacturing and then advertising an increased array of home-consumer and beauty goods, capitalists hoped to stimulate the demand they needed to increase production.

Beginning in 1929 with a sudden stock market crash, the most severe economic disaster in U.S. history followed, bringing misery to the majority of the population. Children starved, men killed themselves, thousands were homeless and the local charity institutions that existed were quickly overwhelmed. People protested and demanded action. The unemployed, veterans, old people and sharecroppers demonstrated; people formed self-help groups to steal fuel, restore electricity when companies turned it off, move evicted tenants back into their homes.

This pressure stimulated fear that the capitalist system itself might collapse, and even the conservative government of Herbert Hoover had to respond with relief programs. After the election in 1932 of Franklin Roosevelt, the government tried to cope with the situation with a relatively ambitious array of reform measures. The government created jobs; Congress passed protective legislation for men as well as women workers; a combination of legislation and administrative regulation corrected some of the worst abuses of the sweatshop system, and prohibited home work in most industries. Social security, unemployment compensation and workmen's disability compensation were offered. While many workers gained substantially from these reforms, many other workers—especially women in traditional women's jobs, such as domestic service and part-time work, and many men in jobs such as agricultural labor—were entirely omitted from coverage.

Roosevelt tried to fight the depression not only with reforms but also by stimulating a spirit of optimism. Trying to sell the reform program under the title "New Deal," the administration did succeed in creating excitement and inducing much of the Left opposition that began under Hoover's administration to support Roosevelt's leadership. In fact, the New Deal did not end the depression; indeed, the government was unable to end it before World War II finally brought production and employment back up to predepression levels, raising in many people's minds the fear that the capitalist system needed war in order to achieve economic stability.

Probably the most important and lasting impact of the New Deal upon the working class was government endorsement of unionism. This was both a great victory and a source of great weakness in the future. The National Labor Relations Act guaranteed workers in certain industries the right to unionize, even to have government-supervised elections, and required employers to bargain with union representatives for wage rates and working conditions. In gaining official recognition, the big unions also became in many ways a part of the establishment, gaining an interest in operating through the proper channels, in not challenging the system that was guaranteeing them stable control over millions of workers.

For a time the New Deal seemed to support an explosion of union-organizing energy. In 1935 a new national union federation—the Congress of Industrial Organization (C.I.O.)—split off from the A.F.L. as a result of workers' discontent with the latter's conservatism. During the depression the A.F.L. had failed to combat layoffs and wage cuts, refused to organize unskilled workers and continued to defend the privileges of the minority of skilled workers in their craft unions. The C.I.O. organizing drives organized millions of workers on an industrial basis in industries such as rubber, steel, automobiles, electricity and packing houses. From 1936 to 1940 organized labor tripled in size. Once the immediate struggle with employers was over, however, and World War II allowed the government to institute greater controls, the C.I.O. leadership accelerated its tendency to squash rank-and-file militancy and to cooperate in planning for labor stability with employers and government.

Despite the C.I.O. gains, most of the U.S. labor force remained unorganized, and still is. The C.I.O. made few efforts to organize fields of women's work, clerical or service industries. Women relatives of workers were sometimes encouraged to form auxiliaries, while women workers were neglected. In male-dominated industries the unions endorsed contracts with unequal pay between men and women and separate female seniority lists.

During the 1930s the Left worked not only for a program of economic improvement but also to build confidence in the potential of a strong workers' movement. Many people, both working class and middle class, were attracted to the Communist party (C.P.), which had emerged as the main, viable force out of the splintering of the Socialist party in the 1920s.

In reunifying many socialists the Communist party gained great influence; and the existence of the Soviet Union as a powerful socialist state, showing that capitalism was *not* the only economic system that could produce prosperity and gain industrial strength, gave creditability to the Communists' arguments. Ultimately its strong identification with the U.S.S.R. hurt the Communist party, for this enabled its opposition to slander it as alien, and led it to base U.S. policy decisions on false parallels with the U.S.S.R. In fact, its radicalism was minimal during this period (in comparison, for example, to socialist leadership before World War I), and Communist leaders were often indistinguishable from other union bureaucrats and supporters of the New Deal, urging class cooperation and support of Roosevelt.

While there was no distinct women's movement and little public feminist consciousness in the 1930s, many women were active both in the labor movement and in the Left. Women of all classes tended to work alongside men, and often accepted positions behind men— as in auxiliaries. But some sensed the untapped power of angry working-class women and tried to organize women workers, consumers' boycotts and political education programs. For women and for other disadvantaged groups, especially blacks, the 1930s was an important period: full of high expectations, the experiencing of the possibilities and power of a mass movement, painful frustration and a great deal of learning from experience.

HOMEMAKING

MECHANIZATION HAD transferred the production of most goods to the factory by the early twentieth century. Most people could no longer afford to buy handcrafted things, nor could they afford the time to make them themselves. This transformation affected men earlier and in larger numbers than women. In the early nineteenth century men who were industrial wage earners still had wives who made household goods by hand. But the same process of mechanization that brought men from small farms and shops into factories gradually transformed work in the home as well.

Industrial growth under capitalism required expanding markets; and after the initial construction of the machines for mass production, the chief area for the expansion of markets was in private consumption items. Between 1920 and 1940 the advertising industry developed rapidly, inventing powerful techniques of manipulation to make specific groups buy specific items. By the end of the 1920s, two-thirds of the national income was spent in retail stores. Shopping became part of a housewife's work, replacing home preparation. Women needed different skills and a different character structure to be good shoppers and spenders than they had needed as producers of their own goods. They became the objects, and victims, of sophisticated ad campaigns, which used women's fears and insecurities, already intensified by the disintegration of traditional roles, to make them seek fulfillment through purchases. In turn, women who bought most of their necessities were more suspectible to having their values and self-esteem defined by external pressures than women whose work made them independent of the market. The decline of home production also dissolved the bases for cooperative work (as, for example, such institutions as the "change-work" described in Part I). Housewifery became more isolated, and isolated people are also more susceptible to external manipulation than people in close communities.

Industrialization also transformed personal relationships. In preindustrial society women often assisted their husbands at farming or a craft. Children rendered similar assistance. This pattern made family unity an economic necessity and reinforced the supremacy of the father. Industrialization took most husbands and fathers out of their houses and deprived them of ownership of the tools of their trades. The dependents of male wage earners now relied on them simply for money; the man of the household no longer had skills to teach his wife and children, and his authority was reduced to a cash dependency. Meanwhile, mechanized production put a greater variety of jobs within the reach of women. These changes produced, in the nineteenth and early twentieth centuries, a rebellion both of women and later of children against patriarchal authority. With the family no longer an economically essential unit, women could remain unmarried or leave their husbands, and children could leave home. For example, the divorce rate grew enormously after 1870, and it was higher among industrial workers and wage earners generally than among those whose livelihood still came from subsistence farming or crafts.

These changes occurred unevenly throughout different classes and in different regions of America. They happened first in the great industrial cities and last in the rural areas. Somewhere in between was Muncie, Indiana, the subject of the study, *Middletown*, by Robert and Helen Lynd. Muncie was a representative town because, while not in the forefront of American industrialization, it had experienced rapid changes in the decades just before this study was done, in the mid-1920s. Its population had shot up from 6,000 in 1885 to 35,000. In 1920, 2 percent of its people were foreign-born and 6 percent black. In 1923 it had three industrial plants employing over 1,000 workers each, and eight other plants had from 300 to 1,000 employees each.

The Lynds' work is of methodological as well as substantive interest. They used statistical data both about people's practices and their opinions in a manner that transcends the usual limits of quantified research, which tends to show, at best, static and shallow pictures of social situation. The Lynds have managed to show us a town in process, a rapid process, of change. The factors they chose to focus on illuminate the larger economic changes in the whole society: the decline in traditional notions of sexual division of labor, so that men are "helping with the housework" more; the impact of the advertising industry on women particularly; the decline in servants and home production and their replacement by bought commodities. The following excerpt illustrates some of these changes.

CHANGES IN HOUSEWORK

. . . The providing of clothing for individual members of the family is traditionally an activity of the home, but since the nineties it has tended to be less a hand-skill activity of the wife in the home and more a part of the husband's money-earning. One of the housewives interviewed lived in 1890 on a farm just south of town, where wool was clipped from sheep and practically all the family clothing spun by the women of the family. The common practice a generation ago, however, was to buy "goods" and make the garments at home. As late as 1910 there was practically no advertising of women's dresses in the local newspapers, and goods by the yard were prominently featured. Today the demand for piece goods is, according to the head of the piece goods department of Middletown's largest department store, "only a fraction of that in 1890." This store conducted a sale in 1924 at which two bolts of the featured material were sold, "but in 1890 we'd have sold ten bolts the first day." . . .

At no point can one approach the home life of Middletown without becoming aware of the shift taking place in the traditional activities of male and female. This is especially marked in the complex of activities known as "housework," which have always been almost exclusively performed by the wife, with more or less help from her daughters. In the growing number of working class families in which the wife helps to earn the family living, the husband is beginning to share directly in housework. Even in families of the business class the manual activities of the wife in making a home are being more and more replaced by goods and services produced or performed by other agencies in return for a money price, thus throwing ever greater emphasis upon the money-getting activities of the husband. This is simply another instance of the shuffling about of "men's ways" and "women's ways" observable among all peoples, for "it is partly a matter of accident as to how culture is adjusted to the two parts of the group."

As noted . . . , the rhythm of the day's activities varies according to whether a family is of the working or business class, most of the former starting the day at six or earlier and the latter somewhat later. . . . Of the ninety-one working class wives who gave data on the amount of time their mothers spent on housework as compared with themselves, sixty-six (nearly three-fourths) said that their mothers

Robert and Helen Lynd. *Middletown.* New York: Harcourt Brace, 1929 and 1956.

spent more time, ten approximately the same, and fifteen less time. Of the thirty-seven wives of the business group interviewed who gave similar data, seventeen said that their mothers spent more time, eight about the same, and twelve less time.

The fact that the difference between the women of this business group and their mothers is less marked than that between the working class women and their mothers is traceable in part to the decrease in the amount of paid help in the homes of the business class. It is apparently about half as frequent for Middletown housewives to hire full-time servant girls to do their housework today as in 1890. The thirty-nine wives of the business group answering on this point reported almost precisely half as many full-time servants as their mothers in 1890, and this ratio is supported by Federal Census figures. . . .

"Every one has the same problem today," said one thoughtful mother. "It is easy to get good girls by the hour but very difficult to get any one good to stay all the time. Then, too, the best type of girl, with whom I feel safe to leave the children, wants to eat with the family." The result is a fortification of the tendency to spend time on the children and transfer other things to service agencies outside the home. A common substitute for a full-time servant today is the woman who "comes in" one or two days a week. A single day's labor of this sort today costs approximately what the housewife's mother paid for a week's work.

Smaller houses, easier to "keep up," labor-saving devices, canned goods, baker's bread, less heavy meals, and ready-made clothing are among the places where the lack of servants is being compensated for and time saved today. Working class housewives repeatedly speak, also, of the use of running water, the shift from wood to coal fires, and the use of linoleum on floors as time-savers. Wives of the business class stress certain non-material changes as well. "I am not as particular as my mother," said many of these housewives, or, "I sometimes leave my supper dishes until morning, which my mother would never have thought of doing. She used to do a much more elaborate fall and spring cleaning, which lasted a week or two. I consider time for reading and clubs and my children more important than such careful housework and I just don't do it." These women, on the other hand, mention numerous factors making their work harder than their mothers'. "The constant soot and cinders in this soft-coal city and the hard, alkaline water make up for all you save by new conveniences." A number feel that while the actual physical labor of housework is less and one is less particular about many details, rising standards in other respects use up the saved time. "People are more particular about diet today. They care more about having things nicely served and dressing for dinner. So many things our mothers didn't know about we feel that we ought to do for our children."

Most important among these various factors affecting women's work is the increased use of labor-saving devices. . . .

It is in part by compelling advertising couched in terms of certain of women's greatest values that use of these material tools is being so widely diffused:

"Isn't Bobby more important than his clothes?" demands an advertisement of the "Power Laundries" in a Middletown paper.

The advertisement of an electrical company reads, "This is the test of a successful mother—she puts first things first. She does not give to sweeping the time that belongs to her children. . . . Men are judged successful according to their power to delegate work. Similarly the wise woman delegates to electricity all that electricity can do. She cannot delegate the one task most important. Human lives are in her keeping; their future is molded by her hands and heart."

Another laundry advertisement beckons: "Time for sale! Will you buy? Where can you buy back a single yesterday? Nowhere, of course. Yet, right in your city, you can purchase tomorrows. Time for youth and beauty! Time for club work, for church and community activities. Time for books and plays and concerts. Time for home and children." . . .

The rapid and uncontrolled spread of such new devices as labor-saving machinery under a system of free competition makes the housekeeping of Middletown present a crazy-quilt appearance. A single home may be operated in the twentieth century when it comes to ownership of automobile and vacuum cleaner, while its lack of a bathtub may throw it back into another era and its lack of sewer connection and custom of pumping drinking-water from a well in the same back yard with the family "privy" put it on a par with life in the Middle Ages. Side by side in the same block one observes families using in one case a broom, in another a carpet sweeper, and in a third a vacuum cleaner for an identical use, or such widely varying methods of getting clothes clean as using a scrub board, a hand washing machine, an electric machine, having a woman come to the house to wash, sending the clothes out to a woman, or sending them to a laundry for any one of six kinds of laundry service. . . .

New cultural demands pressing upon this earlier compact home and family are altering its form: geographical vicinage and permanence of abode apparently play a weaker part in family life; there are fewer children and other dependents in the home to hold husband and wife together; activities adapted to the age, sex, and temperament of its members are replacing many whole-family activities; with the growth of these extra-home activities involving money expenditure comes an increased emphasis upon the money nexus between members of the family; the impetus toward higher education, sending an increasing proportion of boys into lines of work not shared by their fathers, is likewise tending to widen the gap between the generations in standards of living and habits of thought; such new tools as the telephone and the automobile, while helping to keep members of the family in touch with each other, are also serving to make separate activities easier. . . .

FOR MANY RURAL WOMEN, however, housework was not altered or lightened by mechanization. Indeed, the depression of the 1930s made their lot worse, for it left them struggling to feed and raise their children with little or no income and often without the support of an employed man. One group hardest hit by the depression in America was sharecroppers, white and black. Here Margaret Jarman Hagood, in a study published in 1939, describes housekeeping conditions among southern white tenant farm women.

HOUSEWORK FOR THE SOUTHERN FARM WOMAN

. . . The house, which is the locus of this . . . work, may be described in terms of a few modal traits. Such a composite house is an unpainted, one-story, weatherboard structure of four rooms. It is without electricity, running water, radio, or phonograph, but does have a sewing machine and inadequate screens. There are a few scattered flowers in the front yard, but no grass. The porch steps and floor are badly in need of repair. Cracks under the doors let in icy drafts in

Margaret Jarman Hagood. *Mothers of the South.* Chapel Hill: University of North Carolina Press, 1939; reprint ed., New York: Greenwood, 1969.

winter. The front sitting-bedroom has curtains and, for decoration, calendars on the wall and photographs on the mantel. . . .

Only eight of the homes had electricity—in an area considered progressive in rural electrification—and not a single one had running water. The extra work required to fill and clean kerosene lamps, draw and carry water, empty chambers and slop jars is hard to imagine—as one mother put it bluntly, "Town folks just don't know." Where there was electricity, it was used for lights, radio, and ironing, but in only two cases for power appliances, such as washing machines and refrigerators. In two homes where electricity was quite new, all members of the family were very enthusiastic over it and vowed they would go without anything else to pay the three-dollar-a-month minimum charge. The water supply was most often a well, although quite a few families were without even this and had to carry all water used from a spring or neighbor's well sometimes as far as a half mile away. . . .

"Broomsage" brooms are the only kind in many of the homes and some women prefer them. There were no floor mops visible, although the condition of the unpainted floors usually testified to frequent scrubbings. There was linoleum in several kitchens and bedrooms and a very few small rugs; but floor coverings of any kind were most infrequent. A kitchen visit was interrupted several times when the mother left to chase a pig out of the next room where he came in through an unscreened door to root a ragged matting carpet. The lightening of housekeeping caused by the scarcity of possessions to be kept straight and by the smallness of the establishment seems to be outbalanced by the lack of modern aids. The old-fashioned back-breaking ways of doing things prevail and "straightening" must be done continually because practically all of the belongings have to remain "out."

Even more time consuming is cooking. Factors increasing the time differential between tenant farm and urban cooking are wood stoves with fires to be built and kept going, correspondingly old-fashioned implements, larger size of families to be fed, bigger appetites of outdoor workers, the preparing of raw materials from scratch rather than using expensive, bought, semi-prepared foods, and dietary preferences which demand hot bread at every meal, home baked pies and cakes, and vegetables cooked for many hours. One mother cooks for nine on a small, high-legged, wood stove; another who cooks for twelve cuts her own wood as well as builds her fires; another cooks ninety biscuits twice a day and uses a barrel of flour every two weeks; another cooks for two field hands besides her own family; many have dogs to feed— sometimes as many as a half dozen; and only a few have anything so modern as a pressure cooker. The hours of meals spread cooking and dishwashing over almost the entire span of working hours. "Before light" breakfasts and "after dark" suppers, twelve o'clock dinners, packing school lunches, and feeding the children again when they return in the afternoon are the customary pattern. . . .

The year's canning ranged from none at all in a fourth of the families to over five hundred quarts in several, with "we put up a right smart, but not enough to last through the winter," as the mode. . . .

It is generally conceded that of all the housekeeping tasks, washing is the heaviest and hardest. Here were the only instances in which the mothers had any hired help: in two cases where a colored woman came in once a week to assist with the washing for a few hours, in two cases where it was sent out to a washerwoman, and in one case where the overalls and sheets were sent to a laundry. The scarcity of clothing and linens makes weekly washing the rule, with deviations all on the side of greater frequency. Here again the job is bigger and harder than in town, so much so that a mother is very likely to have help from her husband or children—at least in cutting wood, making a fire under the pot in the yard, and drawing water. Women almost always mention the overalls; scrubbing clean a pair that has been worn a week for farm work requires so much effort that it can not be taken for granted, even though it is routine. The other critical point in washing is baby diapers. If the baby only wets them, they are often simply dried without being washed. When hung before the fire from the mantel or on chairs, the odor is suffused throughout the room. The soiled diapers must be washed, though, and this was designated as the most distasteful task oftener than any other.

The usual amount of sewing done is the mother's own clothes, her baby's, and some for her daughters. Some do none at all, and one makes all her family's wearing apparel except overalls, even shirts for her two-hundred-and-fifty-pound husband. Quite a few mentioned a decrease in sewing since children's clothes can be bought more cheaply now. . . .

Children usually help in many of the housekeeping tasks described, but during the first ten or fifteen years of marriage, it is probably safe to estimate that as much time must be given to the training of children as is saved by their work. And even when several children are old enough to give considerable help, the mother must still keep the responsibility for planning, directing, and articulating the work of each to keep things running smoothly. Another adult woman in the family, mother, mother-in-law, spinster, or widowed sister or daughter affords the greatest help, of course.

At any rate the work is sufficient to keep the women going all day. Few reported ever resting during the daytime—one who is trying to prevent another miscarriage, another who considers herself frail, another since she has had pneumonia. The wish for rest was freely admitted by several to be one reason for giving a cordial welcome. "I like *any* kind of company because it gives me an excuse to stop and rest," said one who insisted upon leaving her work and entertaining the visitor in the front bedroom. . . .

WOMAN'S PLACE/ WORK PLACE

NOT ALL women's jobs were those which moved with women from home into the factory. Some positions were defined as men's work until inventions and changes in the economic structure of business called for a different kind of work force. This selection is excerpted from a longer essay which traces the feminization of the clerical work force.

WOMAN'S PLACE IS AT THE TYPEWRITER

In the last few decades of the nineteenth century, American corporations underwent a period of rapid growth and consolidation. As business operations became more complex, there was a large increase in correspondence, record-keeping and office work in general. This expansion of record-keeping and the proliferation of communications both within and between firms created a demand for an expanded clerical labor force. In 1880 there were 504,454 office workers who constituted three percent of the labor force; by 1890 there were 750,150 office workers. The number of office workers has been increasing ever since. In order to fill the need for clerical workers, employers turned to the large pool of educated female labor. . . . In 1880, 13,029 women graduated from high school in the United States, as compared to only 10,605 men. The figures for 1900 show an even greater disparity: 56,808 female high school graduates and 38,075 male. . . . Excluded from most of the professions, these women were readily available for the clerical jobs that started to proliferate at the end of the nineteenth century. . . .

Margery Davies. "Woman's Place Is at the Typewriter: The Feminization of the Clerical Labor Force." *Radical America* 3 (July–August 1974), No. 4.

Prior to the Civil War there were no women employed in substantial numbers in any offices, although there were a few women scattered here and there who worked as bookkeepers or as copyists in lawyers' offices. During the Civil War, however, the reduction of the male labor force due to the draft moved General Francis Elias Spinner, the U.S. Treasurer, to introduce female clerical workers into government offices. At first women were given the job of trimming paper money in the Treasury Department, but they gradually moved into other areas of clerical work. The experiment proved successful and was continued after the end of the war. Commenting upon this innovation in 1869, Spinner declared "upon his word" that it had been a complete success: "Some of the females [are] doing more and better work for $900 per annum than many male clerks who were paid double that amount." . . .

Although women started to work in government offices during the Civil War, it was not until the 1880's that women began to pour into the clerical work force. In 1880, the proportion of women in the clerical labor force was 4 percent; in 1890 it had jumped to 21 percent. By 1920, women made up half of the clerical workers: 50 percent of all low-level office workers (including stenographers, typists, secretaries, shipping and receiving clerks, office machine operators, and clerical and kindred workers not elsewhere classified) were women. In 1960, 72 percent of them were. This tremendous increase in the number of women office workers has changed the composition of the female labor force. While in 1870 less than 0.05 percent of the women in the labor force were office workers, by 1890 1.1 percent of them were. In 1960, 29.1 percent of all women in the labor force were office workers. . . .

A second factor which eased women's entrance into the office was the invention of the typewriter. By the 1890's the typewriter had gained widespread acceptance as a practical office machine. . . .

It seems fairly clear that it was not until businesses began to expand very rapidly that employers saw the usefulness of a mechanical writing machine. Changes in the structure of capitalist enterprises brought about changes in technology: no one was interested in making the typewriter a workable or manufacturable machine until the utility of having such a machine became clear. But the typewriter no doubt also gave rise to changes in office procedure. Writing was faster on a typewriter. The increase in correspondence and record-keeping was caused in part by the existence of the machine. . . .

The typewriter also facilitated the entrance of women into the clerical labor force. Typing was "sex-neutral" because it was a new occupation. Since typing had not been identified as a masculine job, women who were employed as typists did not encounter the criticism that they were taking over "men's work." In fact, it did not take long for typing to become "women's work": in 1890, 63.8 percent of the 33,418 clerical workers classified as stenographers and typists were women; by 1900, that proportion had risen to 76.7 percent. . . .

Clerical work attracted women because it paid better than did most other jobs that women could get. In northeastern American cities at the end of the nineteenth century clerical wages were relatively high: domestic servants were paid $2 to $5 a week; factory operatives, $1.50 to $8 a week; department store salesgirls, $1.50 to $8 a week; whereas typists and stenographers could get $6 to $15 a week. Also, clerical work enjoyed a relatively high status. A woman from a middle-income home with a high school education was much more likely to look for clerical work than for work as a house servant or as a factory girl making paper boxes, pickles or shoes. . . .

However, despite the fact that women were pouring into offices at the end of the nineteenth century, they still met with disapproval. An engraving of 1875 shows a shocked male government official opening the door on an office that has been "taken over by the ladies." The women are preening themselves before a mirror, fixing each other's hair, reading *Harper's Bazaar*, spilling ink on the floor—in short, doing everything but working. The engraving makes women working in an office seem ludicrous: women are seen as frivolous creatures incapable of doing an honest day's work. . . . A decent girl was risking her morality if she invaded the male preserve of the office. . . . The office was a dangerous place for a woman of virtue. Even in 1900, some people counseled women to leave the office and return to their homes, where they rightfully belonged. . . . In 1900, the *Ladies' Home Journal* warned women that they could not stand the physical strain of working in a fast-paced business office, that business girls and women were apt to suffer a nervous collapse.

But by 1916 the *Journal* was comparing the faithful female secretary to some heavenly body who "radiated the office with sunshine and sympathetic interest." It had not taken very long for the ideology to shift and for people to accept the presence of women in offices. Bok had argued in 1900 that women, by virtue of their "nature," were unsuited to the office. But only a few years later, the *Journal* came close to arguing that the "natural" temperament of women made them good stenographers. And by 1935, *Fortune* had concocted a full-fledged historical justification for the assertion that "woman's place was at the typewriter." . . .

The image of the secretary as the competent mother-wife who sees to her employer's every need and desire was a description which most fitted a personal secretary. Here certain "feminine" characteristics ascribed to the job of personal secretary—sympathy, adaptability, courtesy—made women seem the natural candidate for the job.

Not all clerical workers were personal secretaries. For the large proportion of clerical workers who were stenographers, typists, file clerks and the like, another ideological strain developed, emphasizing the supposed greater dexterity of women. These workers were seldom assigned to one particular boss, but instead constituted a pool from which any executive could draw as he wished. In the case of these low-level clerical workers, personal characteristics such as sympathy and courtesy seemed less important. . . . People started to argue that women seemed to be especially suited as typists and switchboard operators because they were tolerant of routine, careful, and manually dextrous. . . . Differentiating office workers by sex is not the same as dividing them into groups distinguished, say, by eye color. The sexual division of labor in the office—where men hold the majority of managerial positions and women fill the majority of low-level clerical jobs—is a division which is strengthened by the positions which men and women hold outside the office. . . . Patriarchal relations between men and women . . . were carried over into the office. These patriarchal social relations meshed very conveniently with office bureaucracies, where the means by which the workers were told what to do was often an extremely personalized one. For although the number of clerical workers was large, they were often divided into small enough groups so that five or six typists, stenographers or file clerks would be directly accountable to one supervisor. And if that supervisor was a man (as was generally the case in the early twentieth century) and those clerical workers were women, it is easy to see how patriarchal patterns of male-female relations would reinforce the office hierarchy.

The segmentation of the office work force by sex thus promoted a situation where a docile mass of clerical workers would follow without rebellion the directives of a relatively small group of managers. The ideology that women, by virtue of their "feminine docility," were naturally suited to fill the low-level clerical jobs, can be seen as an important buttress of the stability of the hierarchical office structure.

ORIGINALLY telephone operators, like telegraph operators, were male. Emma McNutt became the first female telephone operator in 1878, and when she died in 1926 there were 200,000 women employed by the telephone company. Like the Lowell mill owners a century earlier, the telephone company tried to attract "well-bred" women, providing them with libraries, reading clubs, flower and vegetable gardens and a women's athletic club. Special premiums were given to operators who recommended applicants who stayed on the job for more than three months.

PILGRIM'S PROGRESS IN A TELEPHONE EXCHANGE

"The doctor and nurse are out to lunch now and you had better come back at 2 o'clock to be examined," the stylish young lady with the earrings was saying to me.

I was not applying for admission to a hospital as the above might imply, but merely for a job as a telephone operator with the Chicago Telephone Company. Meekly I complied with the young lady's suggestion and made my exit.

I had been applying all the morning and had successfully passed through the preliminary stages of giving my life history, with reservations, on a large manila card and of answering oral questions propounded in privacy as to whether I lived with my husband and did he object to my working. And now there was only one stage left—having a physical examination. . . .

The actual examination lasted about ten minutes. But at last I was being told to report the next morning to begin my course in the training school. So far I had acquired this much knowledge about my future occupation, that I was to receive $15 a week for the first three months, with a fifty cent increase at the end of that time, and that the hours in the training school were from 9 to 5.

I suppose the sensation of going back to school again, of being seated alphabetically and of being subjected to the discipline of a teacher no older than myself, and of considerably less experience, affected some of my married comrades as it affected me. It was a shock to have a lesson suddenly interrupted by teacher's stern voice saying,

"Pilgrim's Progress in a Telephone Exchange." By a Pilgrim. *Life and Labor,* Part 1, January 1921; Part 2, February 1921.

"Miss Green, are you chewing gum?" And when Miss Green with a guilty expression nodded her head, to have teacher continue in sepulchral tones, "Come up in front then and put it in the waste basket." I felt as if I had been suddenly projected back into a past which I had almost forgotten.

Our training that first day consisted principally of a continuation of the previous day's inquisition. Our physical status having been ascertained, the contents of our brains were now examined by a psychologist who subjected our mental processes to a series of Binet tests. There were many more registration cards of various shapes and colors to be filled out before we were recorded in all the sets of files which were a part of the system of the Company.

There were interims of fifteen minutes in the morning and fifteen minutes in the afternoon when we were sent off single file to the recreation room to rest. The recreation room was the crowning feature in the affluence of the Company's equipment. It was beautifully upholstered in cretonnes, and with wicker furniture—comfy chairs and couches to stretch out on, reading lamps and the usual collection of innocuous magazines. There was a piano, a victrola and a couple of telephones with which to amuse ourselves. Opening off from the restrooms were the lavatories, gleaming white and spotlessly clean, with a goodly supply of the coveted mirrors which young girls usually miss so painfully in most of their places of employment.

At noon we had three quarters of an hour for lunch. We must troop in single file through the hallways to punch our time cards before as well as after lunch, besides in the morning when we arrived and at night when we went home. . . .

Another day in the recreation room I made the acquaintance of one of my own creed, the first I had met in all my various adventures. . . .

"How do you think you'll like being a telephone operator?" I asked.

"Oh, I don't mind it, only there's an awful lot to learn. And all this," waving her hand about the room, "makes me feel like a charity person. If working people's wages was higher they could afford things like this for themselves. But they give us free lunches and things on purpose so as to keep our wages down."

"But most of the girls think it's swell," I argued. "Look at teacher, she's always saying that there's nobody like the Telephone Company to work for and we'll never want to work for anybody else."

"Sure, they think it's swell," retorted my friend. "That's just what the Company wants 'em to think. Keeps 'em nice an' satisfied so's they won't want to do anything for themselves. If you treat slaves well enough they won't want to ever be anything better'n slaves."

"Say, where'd you get that stuff?" I asked, amazed at the intelligence and rebellious spirit of such a timid appearing soul.

"Well, my uncle's a Socialist and my husband's a trade union man," she admitted. "And I go to lectures an' things quite a bit myself."

"D'ye think the girls here could ever get organized?" I pursued.

She shook her head. "They don't care about much else but fellas and clothes, and the Company knows just how much it can pinch 'em without makin' 'em feel any pain."

It was time to go back to the classroom then, but the discovery of one daughter of the working class who recognized and resented the serfdom of her comrades was indeed encouraging.

Meanwhile our school hours were filled with the intricacies of learning how to be good telephone operators. The classrooms were equipped with a couple of dummy switchboards on which we demonstrated each lesson as it was being learned. My disillusionments increased day by day. My first discovery was that it takes two operators to complete a call for a subscriber. Heretofore I had vented my wrath on but one, the unfortunate damsel who said "Number, please," when I took my receiver off the hook. The two switchboards were called the "A" board and the "B" board. But we were all to be "A" operators and so were doomed from the beginning to bear the brunt of the public ire. The "B" operator, it seemed, never talked directly with the subscriber, but it was just as often her fault that mistakes occurred. . . .

In between times we had lessons in enunciation. The classroom sounded at times like an operatic rehearsal as we attempted to learn how to sing out phrases in a patented method. The teacher was the villain demanding things in stentorian tones. We were all candidates for heroine, attempting to reply sweetly with the proper inflections.

Teacher: "Oper-r-rator, you cut me off."

Student (in singsong tones): "I *beg* your *pardon*. With what number were you talking, please?"

Teacher: "Operator, you rang my bell!"

Student: "There is no one on the line now. Will you excuse it, pleaz?"

Teacher: "Say, operator, what's your name?"

Student: "I cannot give you my name. My number is 959."

Lessons like this evolved finally into contests between the two halves of the class. Those who didn't emphasize the words in the proper places were forced to sit down. But finally there came a day when those of us who had survived the three weeks of grilling were told to come the next morning ready to go out to our exchanges. We had been formally graduated three days before with a lecture on speed, accuracy and loyalty to the company and a contest with some fifty other girls who were in the class ahead of us. We were at last full fledged operators. The teacher had dismissed us that night, telling us she expected to see us all supervisors in the not too distant future. It was rather exciting, and despite a certain amount of apprehension and a little regret at having to part from one another, we looked forward to the next day with the suspense of the girl graduate turned out into the world of work. . . .

I had no intention of getting nervous, though I could imagine that for one who was receiving her first taste of the working world it was indeed a time to be feeling shaky.

On the second floor where the switchboards were located there arose a dull roar like that of locusts on a sunburnt prairie, a sense of many voices without any one being distinguishable. Only the backs of the operators were towards me as I was escorted to the desks of the clerical workers, but I could see their hands working swiftly, pulling cords out of the holes, jabbing others in. Serving the Thing that signaled them with little flashing lights, making them hurry, hurry. . . .

It wasn't much like the school had been. One day we had had all police and fire calls. Another day would be devoted to long distance calls. But now none of these complicated things happened. I began to think it wasn't so bad after all, just answering plain calls. Then suddenly a half dozen things happened at once. Someone *did* want a toll call and I had to stop to make out a slip. And meanwhile I could see that receivers were being lifted up and down impatiently, from the little lights that flashed off and on. Feverishly I hurried to answer them.

"Operator, *are* you ringing my number?" asked one crossly. And I hastened to reply with the only answer I was allowed to give: "I will *ring* them again."

And then, "Operator, you cut me off."

More complications. Needless to say I hadn't cut her off. Whose fault it was I didn't know. But in the eyes of an impatient public I was the responsible person.

"I beg your pardon. With what number were you talking, please?" I said in my most polite sing-song, though I felt anything but polite. . . .

It paid to be stupid in school, I reflected and wondered if the girls who stayed four and five weeks had a method in their madness. Same pay, shorter hours and a schedule with so many variations that it did not become tiresome. Here it was one changeless monotony of sitting on a stool, necessarily on the alert every minute. . . .

During the afternoon when the calls did not come so thick and fast I tried to puzzle the thing out. In one of the laundries where I had worked I had been paid $15.00 a week for tying up packages. I could have done that without any schooling at all, and it didn't matter how poorly I was clothed or how uncouth was my language. But the Telephone Company demanded a comparatively high standard of living from its employes, both of education and of culture, and yet it paid the same wages for a highly skilled sort of work which required self-control, patience and a certain amount of refinement. Not but what in a different social order hand work ought to be paid on an equal basis with brain work. But here under a competitive system were skilled workers who were not being recognized as any more valuable than unskilled workers. Perhaps it was because there seemed to be so many girls available for telephone work that wages could be kept so low and hours so long. A task which is such a severe mental strain should certainly not last longer than six hours in any one day and there should be enough extra girls employed so that Saturday afternoon and Sunday shifts could be less frequent.

But the strangest thing of all was that these girls were such slaves to the sugar coating of the Company's policy that they could not or would not make any open complaint. When they found something better they quit and then they said what they liked. But the free lunches, the free medical service, the almost ideal working conditions, as far as physical comfort went, the theater tickets and groceries at reduced prices—well, it just wouldn't be decent to kick while you were receiving these things at someone else's hands. Some of these things, of course, any employer ought to furnish, and as for the rest, well, those of us who retain any sense of independence and self respect would prefer to have our salaries large enough so that we could pay for our own lunches and medical service. . . .

I don't know. But I sometimes wonder if the time is on the way when telephone operators in Chicago will want the independence that their New England sisters won for themselves. Against that day let the Telephone Company be on its guard!

THE DEPRESSION

UNEMPLOYMENT and the depression deeply affected family structure. Some men, like the Mr. Raparka in this excerpt, found their position destroyed in the occupational world and their authority challenged in the home. They sometimes left their families when they were unable to adjust to newly defined roles. Others made the transition to working in the home in spite of pressures from neighbors not to assume "women's work."

FAMILY LIFE

The impact of unemployment did not destroy the Raparka family, but the adjustments made necessary did lead to a complete reorganization of the structure of family relationships. When Mr. Raparka lost his job in the fall of 1933 he dominated the family. Two years later it was Mrs. Raparka who was the center of authority. . . .

Mr. Raparka as the chief breadwinner dominated this situation. His rule was stern and strict. He was not above putting down any dissension from his decisions, either on the part of the children or his wife, by force. On one occasion ten years previously his wife had left him for five days when he knocked her downstairs during an argument. The children received frequent whippings which only he was permitted to administer. All requests for money were made to him. He never told his wife how much he earned or how much he saved. She knew only that on payday she would receive her weekly allowance for household expenses, that he gave her and the children money for clothes and extras when he agreed that their requests were reasonable. . . .

Apparently the evenings at home involved a mutual sharing of indi-

Wight Bakke. *Citizens Without Work.* New Haven, Conn.: Yale University Press, 1940.

vidual activities and interests. All members were regular at religious service and church activities. The weekly family party at the movies was the chief form of recreation. All were interested and nearly equally concerned about the welfare of the baby and shared a pride in every sign of his development. Polish was spoken in the home, and even when schoolmates were present the shame at the parents' language handicap, so frequent in the children of immigrants, did not appear on the surface. The children spoke freely to their parents in Polish. The division of labor within the home provided for a sharing of duties between mother and daughter only, but father and sons were proud of the immaculate and well-kept home and contributed occasionally small items of home decoration from their earnings.

How thoroughly this institutional structure depended on the father continuing his function as the chief breadwinner, however, became evident within two weeks after he lost his job. Earnings of $15 a week had provided no margin of safety, no savings. At best the plane of living had been supported in a hand-to-mouth fashion. The unemployment coincided with the need for new clothes for school. The food for the baby could not wait. A change from fresh to canned milk resulted in convulsions which alarmed the whole family. Mrs. Raparka's pains in the back, present since the birth of the child, suddenly became worse. Her husband, with no money to pay for a doctor, refused to call one either for the mother or child for two weeks. This decision was resented by the whole family. Finally he borrowed money from an aunt without telling his wife. She discovered the loan when the aunt, having suffered an accident, asked for the money back to meet her own expenses. He cashed his insurance policy to pay the aunt, again without telling his wife. He had exhausted his available resources and one day pawned his overcoat. Hunting for work in an early snowstorm, he caught a cold which rapidly developed into a serious illness.

At this point Mrs. Raparka took the initiative. She went to the Catholic Social Service Bureau and asked for help. She received medical attention for her husband and milk for her baby. From this moment the shift in family organization began. When Mr. Raparka regained his feet in about ten days he was furious at this move. He sullenly told his wife to mind her own business when she suggested that he go to the Department of Public Charities where the Catholic society had suggested there might be additional aid. He undertook a desperate search for work and finished a two weeks' job hunt a thoroughly beaten man. The change wrought in him by this experience is evidenced by the fact

that for the first time in his life he submitted to his wife's insistence
that he help with scrubbing the floors and doing the washing (though
he still refused to hang out clothes, in which activity "he would be
seen"). The notes of our visitor who arrived several times while he was
engaged in domestic duties indicates his sullen resentment at this
change in status. The notes also indicate that the wife was gaining a
new position of authority in her supervision of her husband's efforts.
On several occasions she insisted he do over again what he had not
done well. His response to this request made in the presence of the
visitor was to grab his coat from the hook and flee from the house,
slamming the door behind him. At this juncture Mrs. Raparka would
remark, "He'll be back. He say he look for work. But then why not
find? He no look. He can help here." Then she would go into a long
criticism of her husband. She could not understand why he couldn't
find work; he always had before. He must be getting lazy. Maybe if she
made him work at home he would find a job in self-defense.

We do not know the course this readjustment would have taken had
it not been for two facts. The first was that Mrs. Raparka decided to
look for a job herself. After a futile search of ten days, she learned that
jobs cannot be had for the asking. The stories her husband told of "No
Help Wanted" signs, company police who wouldn't even let one apply,
blunt refusals, and vague promises were true. She declared she was
filled with shame at making her husband work at home.

At about the same time Mr. Raparka got a job on C.W.A. (Civilian
Works Administration), and later under F.E.R.A. (Federal Emergency
Relief Administration), for the same wages he had formerly received
as a molder's helper—$15 a week. Once more the normal pattern of
family affairs was on the way to being reestablished. It was noticed,
however, that children and wife did not recognize his authority with
the same passive submission as before. Possibly an adolescent assertion
of independence was overdue. In any case the two older children argued frequently with their father when his decisions crossed their own
desires. Mrs. Raparka also insisted that he turn over his work relief
wages to her in full. This he refused to do, but his refusal had to be
repeatedly made. Nor did he close the issue once and for all as he
would have done a year before. He was less belligerent in the enforcement of his authority, and the renewal of the former pattern of relationships appears to have been the result of restored habits rather than
of any dogmatic assertion of his own position as head of the family.
This situation continued until the fall of 1934. The elder son, now

graduated from trade school, obtained work as a mechanic and was soon earning $25 a week. The importance of this change lies in two facts. In the first place, since the F.E.R.A. wages were based on a budgetary deficiency estimate, added family resources of $25 a week automatically cut Mr. Raparka off work relief. Once more he became "unemployed," and a noncontributor to the support of the family. His status, dependent on his economic contribution, was once more under attack. In the second place, the earnings of the children in foreign-American families are customarily handed over to the mother. The son followed this procedure. Mrs. Raparka now had in her possession $10 a week more than the family resources had amounted to for some time, and *she* controlled the purse strings. It was her husband's turn now to ask her for money for his personal needs. She did not give him an allowance. Each request was judged on its own merits. She now decided how much would go for current expenses and how much would go to pay back bills, what clothes she and the children would have, whether the dentist would be consulted, and whether the daughter could go to the high-school ball. To this shift in roles the husband could offer no objection outside of sullen resentment, since his privilege in the control of expenditures depended on his provision of the income. He was not even called on to share in such decisions. The mother and the older son talked over the matter and shared that responsibility. When the daughter graduated from high school two years later and began earning, she also was taken into the family councils. When the younger son finished the eighth grade, the mother and older son disagreed as to whether he should go to trade school or to Hillhouse [college preparatory high school]. The son, in true paternal fashion, insisted that his younger brother should have the opportunity he had missed. But the mother eventually carried the day, by the use of identical arguments the father had used to send the elder son to trade school.

The consolidation of the mother's position was aided for a four-month period during which the father took a job on a farm as laborer for $20 a month and his keep. This occurred in the summer of 1935. With him absent from home, the organization of family life around the mother's authority proceeded without interruption even from Mr. Raparka's sullen dissent. When he returned to the family circle it was as a beneficiary not as a partner. One day while our visitor was present he went out saying he thought he could commit suicide. Mrs. Raparka remarked, "He won't, you know. But if he did, maybe I could get widow's aid and my boy, he could get married."

In the summer of 1938, Mr. Raparka asked for money to go to New York in search of a job. He has not been heard of since. But his departure caused little change in the routine or structure of family life. He long since had ceased to be an integral part of the major business of family activities. . . .

SINCE WORLD WAR I the number of women entering the labor force has been steadily increasing. In 1920 women were 20 percent of all workers, by 1930 they were 22 percent and by 1940, 25 percent. As the numbers increased, so did the percentage of married women; by 1940, 17 percent of all women who worked were married. But many people were opposed to married women's work. As this article explains, this attitude was even more prevalent during the depression.

SHALL MARRIED WOMEN WORK?

. . . The Gallup poll found, in 1936, that 82 percent of the people were opposed to married women's working. In 1939 Gallup found that 78 percent were opposed. The Vox Pop poll in 1939 likewise showed that the majority were opposed to the idea. In 1936 *Fortune* made a survey of public opinion and found that 85 percent of the men and 79 percent of the women interviewed thought married women should not work outside the home. None of these polls tested the *degree* of opposition. It would seem that it was mild because so far few laws have been passed against the employment of married women in spite of the many attempts.

LEGISLATIVE ACTION

Within the last few years, bills have been introduced in the legislatures of twenty-six states against married women workers. Only one of these passed. This was in Louisiana, and it was later repealed. Six other states have either joint resolutions or governors' orders restricting married women's right to work. Three other states have made a general

Ruth Shallcross. *Shall Married Women Work?* For the National Federation of Business and Professional Women's Clubs, Public Affairs Pamphlet No. 40, New York.

practice of prohibiting married women from working in public employment. . . .

EXTENT OF DISCRIMINATION

The National Federation of Business and Professional Women's Clubs made a survey early in 1940 of local employment policies. This was part of a general study which assembled all materials relating to the employment of married women. The survey shows that married women are most likely to find bars against them if they seek jobs as school teachers, or as office workers in public utilities or large manufacturing concerns. Only a very small number of department stores refuse jobs to married women. However, in 1939, the *Department Store Economist* reported that the sentiment against married women "is growing stronger." Opposition, it was found, came from customers, labor organizations, women's clubs, and miscellaneous groups of the unemployed. Despite this opposition, "nearly all stores are either doubtful whether it would be a wise plan to announce publicly a policy against hiring or retaining married women, or believe it would not be helpful to public relations." This attitude may reflect the fact that married women's employment has been advantageous to department stores because the necessary part-time arrangements suited both parties well. Single women usually want full-time employment, but many married women prefer to work only a few hours each day. . . .

KINDS OF BARS

The bars against married women are of different kinds—all of which exist for some school teachers. They may take the form of refusal to hire married women (the most frequent), of dismissal upon marriage, delay in granting promotion, or actual demotion, and either permanent or temporary dismissal when pregnant. Discrimination is often difficult to detect; a married woman may assume that her marriage is the cause of her inability to hold a job, or to get a new one, when the real reason may lie in her lack of ability, personality, or training.

The National Education Association has from time to time made surveys of employment policies in local communities with respect to married women teachers. Its material is more complete than any other. Its survey, made in 1931, revealed that 77 percent of the cities reporting made a practice of not employing married women as new teachers and 63 percent dismissed women teachers upon marriage. Tenure acts protect married teachers from being dismissed in some states. But although tenure acts may protect teachers who marry after being em-

ployed, they do not assure a new teacher that marriage will not be a bar
to getting a job. The National Education Association reported in 1939
that teachers in at least thirteen states are legally protected by court
decisions from being dismissed for being married. Kentucky seems to
be the only state where the contract of marriage is deemed "the very
basis of the whole fabric of society" and hence is not an obstacle to
employment. . . .

Studies show that men have been affected by unemployment to a
much greater extent than have women, because unemployment has
been most acute in the heavy industries (steel, oil, mining, etc.) where
men are mostly employed. . . . The administrative and clerical jobs
connected with these industries, which are partially filled by women,
have not been eliminated to anything like the same degree as production jobs.

Consumer and service industries (textiles, food, beauty parlors, telephone service, to name only a few), where women are mostly to be
found, were not affected so seriously as heavy industries by the depression. The government's recovery measures, based on artificially increasing purchasing power, chiefly stimulated the consumer and service industries, thus opening up relatively more opportunities for
women than for men. As a result, women have fared better than men in
getting new jobs. . . .

State and federal employment offices also give evidence of the relative ease with which women have obtained jobs compared with men
and indicate that men have been unemployed for longer periods of time
than have women. One study of a community of 14,000 people in the
West makes this point specific. Women's work in the town increased
during the early years of the depression in the needle trades and textiles as well as in the service occupations, while men's work in glass
declined sharply. Another study in a steel town showed much the same
thing. Few of the people who oppose married women's employment
seem to realize that a coal miner or steel worker cannot very well fill the
jobs of nursemaids, cleaning women, or the factory and clerical occupations now filled by women. Unhappily, men accustomed to work in
the heavy industries have not been able to fill the jobs in consumer and
service industries. Retraining of these men has been practically negli-
gible, and could not have been done in time to benefit them immediately. Expenditures for defense are now once more increasing opportunities in the heavy industries, so we may expect to see a fundamental
change in the situation in coming months. . . .

THE NATIONAL RECOVERY ACT (NRA) enacted in 1933 gave some workers the right to organize and bargain collectively with representatives of their own choice. NRA also established, but rarely enforced, minimum-wage codes; in many industries these codes assigned women lower wages than men. But domestic workers were not covered by the codes. The following is an example of the letters written to the government protesting this exclusion.

THE LIMITATIONS OF THE NRA

108 Post Road
Mamaroneck, N.Y.
March 9th 1934

President Franklin D. Roosevelt
Washington, D.C.
My dear Mr. President,

When you delivered your message to Congress in January, I was eager to hear you and under almost unsurmoutable difficulties I did, but was sadly disappointed to find that the large and unprotected class of Domestics were not thought of. I keenly felt for my kind who you spoke of the robbery of the Banker but never mentioned the robbery of the Housewives.

Today as never before we are being robbed, for now it is in three ways, through our stomachs, our strength and health through long hours and last our pocketbooks, which we are called upon to do three and sometimes four Domestics work by one person for less than half of what they formerly paid one. And it is a case of try and do it or starve.

When you mention a code for Domestics, they arrogantly tell you it will and can never be done.

I wonder why it is that the same God made us made the rest of mankind and yet when it comes to hours and wages there is such a difference.

I have appealed to President Green, Miss [Frances] Perkins, Father Coughlin and asked them if they would not intercede for us, but up to present time to no avail. I also wrote to Senator Wagner and he turned it over to the Chairman of the Committee you appointed on Crime, and

Serena Ashford to President Roosevelt, 3-9-34. NRA Files, Library of Congress, Washington, D.C. We are indebted to Maurine Greenwald for this letter.

he, the poor little fellow, didn't know that there was a racket going on, as it had not been reported to his office.

I would like to take him for a few days on some of the jobs I have been on and he would know it quick.

Now Mr. President, as you are the top of this Great American Body and possess more authority than any other President ever has, will you not use some of it for our cause and see that these intolerable conditions are changed.

Trusting that you will not become blind and deaf to our cause, I am.

> Sincerely yours
> Serena Elizabeth Ashford
> (Cook)

NEW DEAL relief programs like the Works Project Administration (WPA), the Public Works Administration (PWA), and the Civilian Conservation Corps (CCC) were administered through the states. Especially in the Southern states, black families got little or no relief because neither black men nor black women got their share of the work and welfare benefits. In desperation people wrote to government officials about their plight.

> Savannah, Ga.
> Jan. 13. 1939
>
> Rec'd. 1/19/39

To the Presandent:

I am ritin of these few line to let you know the way they are doin in Savannah here between the white woman an the colord woman take all of the colard woman out of the sewing room and sent them on the fahm an in the worst field in all . . . to dig up skelton an dead body now Mr. Presendent I dont think it is rite for the people of Georgia to threat colored woman worst as they would threat mans the colored woman if they want to work they must go to the fahm or say we haven nothen for Fall for we are not goin to put no Negro in no sewing room there place

WPA files, Howard University, Washington, D.C., MSS W89 Box 11. (Unsigned to President Roosevelt, January 13, 1939; Workers Council for Col., Raleigh, North Carolina, to Harry Hopkins, October 12, 1937.)

is on the fahms cold an rain the colard woman haft to go no shelter for
they to go out of the rain and till the trucks come from town for them
sometime we get good an wet in the rain before a truck can get from
town to get us. . . . these white men threat at these poor colord woman
an have all the white woman in the house an we are in the wood cutting
down three and digging them up by the roots with grub hoe an pick ax
these thing ant fare if they are have fahm why dont white woman an the
fahm too an have colord woman the sewing room too now if you want
men to go to war the Negro mens haft go side by side with the white
man an now the white man an now the colord woman can goin a sewing
room like the white woman now some must be done with these hard tast
Georgia white people. . . . Please for God sake send some one to see
about us in Georgia we are under a hard tast master here haft to here
from you soon for I am cold haven a piece of wood or cold in my home
me an my one child I had to keep her out of school for haven clothes
sufison to put on please look at this an fix some place for we as colord
woman to have some way to work beside out in the bitter cold on frost
too cold an wet.

From one who is out in the cold an rain an no where to go.

(Unsigned)

Raleigh, N.C.
Oct. 12, 1937

Mr. Harry L. Hopkins
Head Administrator of U.S. W.P.A.
Washington, D.C.

Dear Sir:

We the Workers Council of Colored People in Raleigh, N.C. do wish
to state some facts to you about how the colored women, (mostly heads
of the families) have been treated by W.P.A. heads here. Also wish
you to make investigation about it at once for its pure injustice to us,
the way it has been done.

We are blamed for private service scarcity of servants and farmers
not being able to get workers etc is not our fault.

We can say truly that all women with families and dependent husbands. Cannot get along on such poor wages because wages will not or
is not sufficient etc. responsibilities. Some and most of these women
have never in their lives worked on farms and some left farms 20 & 25
years ago. We are sure that prices paid are the whole cause & such long
work days beginning 6 to 6:30 A.M. till 7:30 & 8:30 P.M. this we

know is whole cause of this scarcity. We answer want adds & meet white people that want such help, prices paid not even the rent let lone food and up keep, (rent here is high and one better gett enough to pay it or he's put out sure). Mr. Hopkins, colored women have been turned out in streets to starve & children go to rack, for these prices paid are not enough for a poor willing working mother to care for her children, there by much more distress & trouble is in for as one question is this; Does the government provide money for white people only a certain class of colored people to get help. As you know we all donot like to work in tobacco for good reasons, We are settled women mostly & different troubles that prevent us from riding in open trucks, standing up 20 odd miles twice a day, stand & work all all day long, we're given no notice but to quit work here and work no where not regarding nothing. We also wish you to investigate why that so many teachers unemployed & elegible to teach have not been employed by the Adult Education here, that these teachers can have classes as they once had & help the illiterate colored people. One time it was many grown & old people going to the classes learning & proud of the opportunities etc. Mr. Hopkins colored women have been turned out of different jobs projects to make us take other jobs we mentioned and white women were hired & sent for & given places that colored women was made to leave or quit.

Let us say that if we cannot work on W.P.A. Projects & be compel to take these poor paying jobs; that food, clothes & rent money be provided for us at once because we are suffering. We the Workers Council understood that no colored women cannot be hired this winter on any of the W.P.A. projects. We wish you to tell us why.

We shall be glad to have a reply from you at your earliest convenience.

Respt.
Workers Council for Col.   Raleigh, N.C.
Reply to: Mrs. Mary O Kelly Abright
8 N. Swain St., Raleigh, N.C.

WOMEN IN THE UNION MOVEMENT

AN EQUAL RIGHTS Amendment (ERA) to the Constitution was first proposed in 1923 by the National Women's party. The amendment read: "Men and women shall have equal rights throughout the United States and every place subject to its jurisdiction." Endorsed by one part of the former suffrage movement and opposed by the other, the amendment became a focal point of division for several decades.

The feminist members of the National Women's party argued that women could achieve freedom only if they were treated as individuals, not as members of a sex. They sought to obliterate sex as a fundamental classification within the law, which had served to set women apart and deny them equal access to jobs, property, credit and so on.

The League of Women Voters (heirs of the National American Women's Suffrage Association) and social reformers opposed the amendment because they thought it would wipe out years of progress and restore intolerable factory conditions by eliminating protective legislation. Fundamentally they believed that women did differ biologically and psychologically from men and should be treated as a special group requiring protection against unprincipled employers.

The controversy about the ERA took place along class lines. Working women, the Women's Bureau and traditional trade unionists believed that professional and business women supported the ERA at the expense of their working-class sisters. The trade-union women believed at that time that the protective labor legislation they had fought for was important and helpful to women workers. They were not opposed to equal rights, but they thought the danger to protective legislation was too great to let the amendment go through.

WORKING WOMEN RESPOND TO THE EQUAL RIGHTS AMENDMENT

WHAT DO WORKING WOMEN SAY?
The Woman's Party Amendment Would Endanger Labor Laws Now Affecting 4,000,000 of Them

BY ELISABETH CHRISTMAN
Secretary International Glove Workers Union, and
Secretary-Treasurer National Women's Trade Union League of America

Would you say that, in order to give women in Ohio the right to be taxi-drivers or open a shoe-shining parlor, you ought to take away the 48-hour law for women in Massachusetts and the hour laws of 42 other states?

Would you say that in order to give the right to jury service to women in twenty states, you ought to throw into court the mother's pension laws of 39 states?

Would you go so far as to say that you would be justified in even taking the risk of such consequences to the millions of wage earning women and mothers, for the sake of a few prospective women taxi-drivers, bootblacks, and jurors?

Especially when you could get what you want without taking such risk?

Where the Risk Lies

Yet it is just exactly those risks—and many more—that the National Woman's Party proposes to take in its constitutional amendment which reads:

"Men and women shall have equal rights throughout the United States and every place subject to its jurisdiction."

The risk is due to the fact, first, that this is an amendment to the United States Constitution and would invalidate automatically all laws in conflict with it, **without automatically replacing** most of them.

Files of the National Women's Trade Union League, Tamiment Library, New York University. ("What Do Working Women Say," leaflet by Elisabeth Christman.)

It is due, second, to the fact that blanket provisions in law, whether in the constitution or in statutes, require court interpretation in each case, and the term "rights" and "equal rights" are subject to diverse construction.

Legal Rights vs. Economic Rights

And, last but not least, the risk is due to the fact that legal rights and other rights are not by any means identical. Legal equality is not necessarily the same as economic equality. It may actually defeat economic equality.

For instance, a state may give the wife a right to sue her husband for non-support. The husband has not the same right to sue her. The proposed amendment would probably, lawyers say, give this man and this woman equal rights by taking away, automatically, the woman's right to sue.

Having thus achieved **legal equality**, however, the wife, whose best years have been spent caring for her home and children, now finds herself confronted with the necessity of earning her living and also of contributing to the support of her children. Untrained for business or industry, her life's experience totally different from her husband's, she is now faced with identical responsibilities and a handicap which only a superhuman could overcome.

Legal equality it may be.

Economic equality it is not.

Reality vs. Theory

Or consider the woman in industry. She is working, say, in a state with an 8-hour law for women, passed because women had been working much longer hours. The man-employing industries of that state, however, are probably on an 8-hour schedule established by their unions. The 8-hour law and the 8-hour trade agreement both limit the worker's freedom of contract. But the **law** would probably be destroyed by the so-called "equal rights" amendment, because the **legal** rights of women are restricted thereunder but not the **legal** rights of men. In other words, to give the women legal equality with the men, the amendment would take away the 8-hour day from the women but not from the men.

This may be legal equality.

Economic equality, decidedly not.

The Sensible Course

The risk involved in the National Woman's Party amendment is, moreover, a wholly gratuitous risk. The amendment is altogether unnecessary, because the things it purports to do can all be done, right now, exactly as most of them would have to be done in any case by Acts of Congress and the states, which already have the power the amendment would confer.

Not only **can** those things all be done, but they are actually being done—86 new laws or amendments to laws in 30 states since the federal woman suffrage amendment was passed.

Why take a gratuitous risk?

[Reprinted by permission of the Women's News Service, Inc.]

In 1920 only 7 percent of women workers were organized into trade unions as compared to 25 percent of men workers. The American Federation of Labor discriminated against women both in a blatant and a subtle manner. Five international unions explicitly excluded women in their by-laws. Year after year women union members tried unsuccessfully to amend the A.F.L. constitution to secure women the opportunity for union membership on the same terms as men.

THE A.F.L. AND WOMEN

Although there are some eleven million women in industry in the United States, only a small proportion, perhaps 250,000, are in the trade unions. The common attitude of most union leaders is that women cannot be organized. Actually, the problem is a different one: how to fit women into the trade unions. The admission of women involves new policies, new responsibilities, and new difficulties. Rather than face them and make the necessary adjustments, union officials have preferred to "let the women alone."

The life of a union official is hard. The work is discouraging and exhausting. The reward for a man is a higher office, with increasing responsibility. He becomes manager of his local union or joint board. He becomes a national officer. There are no such opportunities for

Ann Washington Craton. "Working the Women Workers." *Nation* 124 (March 23, 1927).

women. Women have successfully held minor offices in their local unions. They have been efficient business agents and organizers. Rarely have they held offices of importance. A few women have been international officers, but no woman has ever been on the Executive Council of the American Federation of Labor. Most of the few women who have attained prominence in the trade-union movement have discreetly tried to play the union game as men play it. They have realized that their prestige and position were at stake. On the theory that a poor union is better than no union they have steadily refused to embarrass labor officials by a vigorous protest at the discriminations and inequalities to which women have been subjected in the unions. As a result they have been unable to achieve any outstanding leadership among the rank and file of trade-union women.

When women come into the unions they are, generally speaking, controlled by men officials, particularly when the women in the trade, both organized and unorganized, outnumber the men. I remember one prominent international officer who said, referring to a woman's local which had made remarkable strides under the leadership of women officers: "These women need to be protected. They have a membership now which is ample to pay a good salary to a man official whom we shall appoint. From now on we are going to have iron control over this local." Another official bitterly condemned workers' education classes in his union. The attendance had been largely made up of women. "They have all become lefts," said he indignantly. "That is what education for women does. Now see the trouble they are making us."

The struggles of promising rank-and-file girls for recognition have met not only lack of cooperation but often direct sabotage from their trade-union brothers. The case of Sophie comes to mind. Her life had been full of hardships and deprivations. Insufficient and improper food, too little sleep, exposure to all sorts of weather on the picket line in strikes, work in airless and overheated factories ruined her health. She developed bronchitis and throat trouble, while she wore herself out mentally and spiritually over the injustices and inequalities she experienced in the union. Sophie had been an active trade unionist for ten years, faithfully supporting the machine and loyal to the administration. She was an invaluable lieutenant. A man who had worked as faithfully for his organization would have been taken care of. But Sophie, who had never been allowed to hold a paid job as organizer on the regular staff, had to borrow money and accumulate debts for the vacation she had to take. Instead of returning to her own city, Sophie decided she would work in other clothing centers to obtain first-hand knowledge about the activities of women trade unionists. In Chicago she had been a fast and experienced pocket-maker, earning $50 to $60 a week in the season. To her dismay, in New York union shops, this proved to be a man's job. No woman could be a pocket-maker. No woman had ever been allowed to work at such a well-paid operation, although her international union loudly proclaimed that it stood for "Equal Work, Equal Pay, and Equal Opportunities" for women workers. Sophie could have found work in open or scab shops, where women pocket-makers were preferred to men, as they were paid less wages. She refused this compromise and finally took a job as a corset-worker at $18 a week, an unorganized trade which she had learned as a girl of fourteen. At night the men union officials unhesitatingly called upon her to hold shop-meetings with groups of girls from union shops, who had been forced to accept a severe cut in wages as a concession to the boss, to protect the wages of the men. These angry girls were refusing to pay dues. Sophie, herself bitterly resentful, had to face her furious sister workers and urge them to support their union and not to work in scab shops. . . .

Women coming into the trade-union movement have an optimism and freshness that men officials are likely to resent. They upset the traditional routine. A prominent woman was engaged to direct an organization campaign involving thousands of women. Definite action was imperative in a month, when a wage agreement expired. In twenty-four hours she had appalled the men officials, who had formerly drifted along complacently and casually, with a membership large enough to pay their salaries and with no opposition to reelection. The campaign to them had been merely a gesture to the membership. They had not intended to ask for a wage increase for their women members. It had been tacitly understood between the employers and the union officials that the men's wage increases should be granted.

Miss S., the new organizer, was a shrewd politician. She was determined to maneuver herself and her policies into such a position that her work would not be wasted. She started with a veritable office revolution. Nothing was sacred. She moved the furniture and threw out all the old, broken chairs that had been piled in corners for years. She appropriated an office for herself, a small room long regarded as the exclusive property of a clique that played pinochle. She installed a desk and a telephone. She had an electrician arrange proper lighting for night work. She even had the water cooler moved; it had blocked the hallway, contrary to all fire laws, for a year. Miss S. now turned her energies to the organization campaign. Tons of union literature had to be distributed through the shops. Instead of playing cards, the loungers were forced to fold circulars and lick stamps. Girls from the open shops as well as from the union shops flocked to the office. The men officials were terrified. They were forced into a position where they had to make demands for the women. The employers were furious. Miss S. was triumphant. She now went aggressively around the shops and, as a result, she began to be arrested almost daily. The first time it happened a crowd of excited girls rushed into the office, demanding bail and a lawyer. The men took the situation cheerfully. A group began to play cards. It was Tomasso, the Italian business agent, who mildly voiced the sentiments of all. "Let her stay in jail," said he, persuasively, to the girls. "She's all right. Let her stay until we can have a nice, quiet little executive-board meeting without her. Then we will get her out. Ladies should stay at home. If ladies won't stay at home, let them stay in jail." . . .

In Newark, New Jersey, last summer, a campaign was initiated to try out the American Federation of Labor's Tentative Plan to Organize Women which had been adopted at the 1925 convention. It was the first move on the part of the federation to face the problem of the unorganized women. The plan provided that the various unions in a given locality should make a joint intensive drive to organize women under their jurisdiction. Each union was to supply its own organizers and its own technique and the particular literature necessary for its special trade problems. The impetus given by such systematic and thorough work progressing simultaneously in different industries would create a trade-union consciousness among women workers and have a tremendous educational value in the entire community.

A legislative agent of the federation—Edward F. McGrady—sent from Washington as an "observer," was in charge of the drive. But neither he nor the unions involved cared whether it was successful, and consequently it was a failure. Another woman and myself, both experienced in organization work, made an effort to take part in the Newark campaign. The legislative agent agreed to consider us as organizers and made an appointment to discuss the campaign with us. He took us to lunch at his favorite restaurant in the theatrical district of New York. We selected a modest lunch, appalled at the high prices, while he consumed a most elaborate one. It was apparent that he had repented of his rashness in interviewing us, for now he would not have us. He used all the old arguments to discourage us: women could not be organized; women did not want to be organized; women had been organized, at great trouble and expense, and their unions had not lasted. We countered on every point.

By this time, he was smoking expensive cigars. "You say you want to work with women; I know a good place for you—go to work for the Y. W. C. A."

"We want to work with women in the Newark campaign," we answered promptly.

He was much annoyed, but he made another effort: "Why don't you forget all this business and leave the labor movement to men? It's too rough for women. Why don't you get married?"

"Perhaps we are married," we answered cheerfully; "we still want to organize women into trade unions in Newark."

"You are hopeless," he said angrily. He fled from us in a taxi. His parting words were no more encouragong: "If you want to organize women, you'll have to wait until the federation gets around to it. We think the time isn't ripe yet. It will not be for another twenty-five or fifty years. The trouble with you two is that you are ahead of your time. . . .

"WHAT IS IT That We Want Brother Levin?" was written in the early 1920s, shortly after the formation of the Women's Local 275 of the Amalgamated Clothing Workers of America. Its author Sarah Rozner came to this country from Hungary in 1908 and began to work immediately in clothing shops. In Hungary she had only completed four years of school and it wasn't until she later attended Brookwood Labor School that her English became polished. Sarah Rozner was the first business agent from this local and among the first female business agents in tailoring in Chicago. (A business agent is a full-time union officer, elected or appointed, who handles the union's financial, administrative or labor relations work.) In 1959 when she retired from her union work she established a leadership training scholarship for women, especially Chicanas and blacks, with the Los Angeles local.

PROTEST TO A SHOP STEWARD

Local 275, A.C.W. of A.

What is it that we want Br. Levin?

What do you think will become of our local, What is the need of it, does it serve a necessary function, or is it a hinderance to our organization?

The committee is here to discuss this matter soriously with you. We have promast you before you have gone on your tripp not to couse any disturbance in the organization while you be away, but we have told you that we will wait ontill your return and now we are here for honest a goodness business.

What we want!

Br. Levin you need not get frightent at our demands! Although you may not approve of it as a whole at the first glance. But we are confidant that after you have given it concidirable thought you will no doubt aggry with our demnds fully. We are convincet that you will. You may wonder why we feel so sure about it, we believe honestle that if you would have not approved of our existance, that we would not have been here, for after all it was you that helpt us almost entirly to bring this local into existance in 1920.

We want what ever is duly coming to us!

We feel that our local was created for the purpose of bringing our women coat makers into its folds so that it will annable them to be in closer tuch with the organization, to femiluarise themself with the different activities in the organization, to participate more fully in the organization. For if you, Br. Levin wouldn't have thought of the need of its functions and activities you would'tof helpt us in bringing it to life. Now that you are largely responsiple for its creation, we expect you to help us in making it a real success. In return we assure you that the organization as whole will benfit by it.

We want the women coat makers in our local not for the pupose of building a large treasure, and surely not for political reasons. As a matter of fact for no selfish motives on our part. Our primary interst in bringing them into our folds is not prymarely for the purpose of immideately plcing women on paid jobs, not because we are not entitled

Sarah Rozner. "What Is It That We Want Brother Levin?" We are grateful to Sherna Gluck of the Feminist Research Project, Box 597, Venice, Calif. 90291, for bringing this selection to our attention.

to it, for their is no earthly reason why we shouldn't have it, but that does not happen to be our entire aim at present at least.

Our pupose, our aim and aspirations are for the real purpose of making our organization more firm, more inteligent and more progressive. We believe that our purpose is a good one and we feel that our aims and aspirations will meet with your approval as well as all sane thinking memmbers and officials in our organization. Moreover we believe that such activities as outlined by us for the benefits of women worker members will even travle considirably further than our own organization. The A. F. of L. at its last convention has given this matter considirable thought of working out ways and means of bringing the women into the folds of organized labor.

Br. Levin we want to assure you that we are not interested in creating a sex issue in our organition, if anything we want to do away with it as much as posible. The sex issue does not make for greater prog in our organization whereever it is prevelat. We have a life example of it in our easterm organiztion. We members are not in sympathy with their actions towards our women members, for the symple reason that the organiztion as a whole suffers byit. We want the same posibilities in promoting our members in industry as well as in the organization. We care not for special privilages, we want to be looket upon as part and parsel of our organization. As a worker of the "Discriminated Class", I take the privelege, an opportunity offered by the Chicago Wommen's Local, 275, in answering questions propounded by them. I say a *worker* and not a woman. For to me the sex question does not exist. To me it is a question of one group of workers undermining another. Although, in this instance, we cannot deny that the women workers are discriminated against.

It is true that the leaders in our organization tell this class of "Discriminated Workers", to elect their own officials. They have the full right to choose whom ever they please. But remember! the present exploiting capitalist calss gives us the same privelege. You workers! take for instance a business agent who goes in to make a price on a garment. He agrees with the manufacturer for so much and so much for the garment. Now let us see, how does our union representitive distribute the amount? Well, we will say that pocket makers, head operators and pressers should receive at least at the rate of $45.00 per week. Eighteen Dollars a week, accorded to women workers for the so called minor operations of finishing, button hole making and so forth is considered sufficient by our business agents.

Now let us see what our officials are doing to promote greater activities among women members. To my knowledge, as a member of the A. C. W. of A. since 1914, the fraternal spirit has not been exercised. I know of a number of highly intelligent women who were discouraged from being active in the organization. Let us take as a specific case the late strike conducted against the International and J. L. Tailors. We all agree that the women did splendid work but when it came to acknowledging same all doors close. Not mentioning any names, a prominent official who has given a rather detailed account of their activities enjoyed the spirit shown by our Chicago fighting women members, but when it came to acknowledging same in our official organ he apoligized for not having mentioned some men who perhaps have not been on the picket line once. We want the immideate removel of such representatives that oppenly denounce women members and not only treatens to do away withem but actually does so at his convinient moments. We are able to annumirate cassess at hand. . . .

What have you to say about it Br. Levin and what can we expect from you?

DURING THE 1920s there was extensive migration of the textile industry from the North to the South. The attraction of the South for Northern capital was the numerous, cheaper and unorganized "native" workers. Southerners were considered by employers to be unorganizable because they had not been influenced by "foreign" socialist ideas as had the immigrant workers of the North.

Despite the move to the South, by 1924 there was a depression in the textile industry. Overproduction in a shrinking market, competition from abroad, new synthetic fibers, all contributed to this decline.

As a result of this depression, conditions in the Southern textile mills, which had always been bad, grew worse. Sixty-hour weeks, wage cuts and speed-ups were common.

In response to those conditions, the so-called unorganizable workers began to organize. During the spring and summer of 1929 sporadic strikes spread through the mill towns of Tennessee and North Carolina. The strikes were often protracted and violent. In Gastonia, North Carolina, a woman textile worker, Ella May Wiggins, was killed. Most of the demands of the workers were not met at the conclusion of the strike, but the struggle did succeed in reducing working hours and preventing future wage cuts. The Gastonia strike and

others in the Southern textile towns were the forerunners of the great
struggles of the '30s which led to the founding of the C.I.O.

Ella May Wiggins was an important organizer in the Gastonia mills.
She joined the union, she recalled, when four of her nine children
became sick with whooping cough:

> Four of them died with whooping cough, all at once. I was
> working nights and nobody to do for them, only Myrtle. She's
> eleven and a sight of help. I asked the super to put me on day
> shift so's I could tend 'em, but he refused. I don't know why. So
> I had to quit my job and then there wasn't any money for medi-
> cine, so they just died. I never could do anything for my children.
> Not even keep 'em alive, it seems. That's why I'm for the
> union. So's I can do better for them.

Ella May Wiggins was also a songwriter. Like many other Appa-
lachian women, such as Aunt Molly Jackson, Sarah Gunning and
Florence Reece, she used her songs to organize and inspire her fellow
workers. On her way to a union meeting during the Gastonia strike,
Ella May Wiggins was shot down by hired company thugs. Workers
came out in droves to her funeral, which became an important political event. Here is one of her songs.

MILL MOTHER'S LAMENT

We leave our home in the morning,
We kiss our children good-bye,
While we slave for the bosses,
Our children scream and cry.

And when we draw our money,
Our grocery bills to pay,
Not a cent to spend for clothing,
Not a cent to lay away.

And on that very evening
Our little son will say:
"I need some shoes, mother,
And so does sister May."

Ella May Wiggins. "Mill Mother's Lament." In Margaret Larkin, "Ella May's
Songs." *The Nation* 129 (No. 3353), October 9, 1929.

How it grieves the heart of a mother,
You every one must know;
But we can't buy for our children,
Our wages are too low.

It is for our little children,
That seem to us so dear,
But for us, nor them, dear workers,
The bosses do not care.

But understand, all workers,
Our union they do fear,
Let's stand together, workers,
And have a union here.

THE STRIKE referred to in this excerpt was the militant teamsters'
strike of 1934 in Minneapolis. All trucking in the city was halted except for ice, milk and beer drivers, who were organized and operated
with special union permits. Thirty-five thousand building trades
workers declared a sympathy strike, and many unemployed workers
joined in the struggle. The American Federation of Labor was against
the strike and tried to sabotage the workers, who were trying to
negotiate an industrial union. This militant strike and others like the
San Francisco General Strike (1934) and the Toledo Auto Lite Strike
(1934) paved the way for the formation of the Congress of Industrial
Organizations in 1935.

    As in the case of many union struggles of this period the help of
the women's auxiliaries in time of crisis was welcomed. The women
performed many tasks: secretarial work, mimeographing, running a
huge strike kitchen, keeping the union men supplied with coffee,
nursing the wounded and occasionally departing from their traditional female roles and driving the trucks and leading the marches.

    The author of this excerpt, Meridel Le Sueur, is an extraordinary
writer, poet, reporter and novelist. She was born in Iowa in 1900. Although her origins are middle class (her mother was a feminist and
her father an itinerant preacher), she allied herself with the workers
and Indian movements and made their struggles an active part of her
life. She is little known today outside the Midwest, although her writings reflect a strong sensual feminism.

JOINING THE AUXILIARY

Minneapolis, 1934.

I have never been in a strike before. It is like looking at something that is happening for the first time and there are no thoughts and no words yet accrued to it. If you come from the middle class, words are likely to mean more than an event. You are likely to think about a thing, and the happening will be the size of a pin point and the words around the happening very large, distorting it queerly. It's a case of "Remembrance of things past." When you are in the event, you are likely to have a distinctly individualistic attitude, to be only partly there, and to care more for the happening afterwards than when it is happening. That is why it is hard for a person like myself and others to be in a strike. . . .

For two days I heard of the strike. I went by their headquarters, I walked by on the opposite side of the street and saw the dark old building that had been a garage and lean, dark young faces leaning from the upstairs windows. I had to go down there often. I looked in. I saw the huge black interior and live coals of living men moving restlessly and orderly, their eyes gleaming from their sweaty faces.

I saw cars leaving filled with grimy men, pickets going to the line, engines roaring out. I stayed close to the door, watching. I didn't go in. I was afraid they would put me out. After all, I could remain a spectator. A man wearing a polo hat kept going around with a large camera taking pictures.

I am putting down exactly how I felt, because I believe others of my class feel the same as I did. I believe it stands for an important psychic change that must take place in all. I saw many artists, writers, professionals, even business men and women standing across the street, too, and I saw in their faces the same longings, the same fears.

The truth is I was afraid. Not of the physical danger at all, but an awful fright of mixing, of losing myself, of being unknown and lost. I felt inferior. I felt no one would know me there, that all I had been trained to excel in would go unnoticed. I can't describe what I felt, but perhaps it will come near it to say that I felt I excelled in competing with others and I knew instantly that these people were NOT com-

Meridel Le Sueur. "I Was Marching." In *Proletarian Literature in the United States,* ed. Granville Hicks et al. New York: International Publishers, 1935.

peting at all, that they were acting in a strange, powerful trance of movement *together*. . . .

In these terrible happenings you cannot be neutral now. No one can be neutral in the face of bullets.

The next day, with sweat breaking out on my body, I walked past the three guards at the door. They said, "Let the women in. We need women." And I knew it was no joke. . . .

There seemed to be a current, running down the wooden stairs, towards the front of the building, into the street, that was massed with people, and back again. I followed the current up the old stairs packed closely with hot men and women. As I was going up I could look down and see the lower floor, the cars drawing up to await picket call, the hospital roped off on one side.

Upstairs men sat bolt upright in chairs asleep, their bodies flung in attitudes of peculiar violence of fatigue. A woman nursed her baby. Two young girls slept together on a cot, dressed in overalls. The voice of the loudspeaker filled the room. The immense heat pressed down from the flat ceiling. I stood up against the wall for an hour. No one paid any attention to me. The commissary was in back and the women came out sometimes and sat down, fanning themselves with their aprons and listening to the news over the loudspeaker. A huge man seemed hung on a tiny folding chair. Occasionally some one tiptoed over and brushed the flies off his face. His great head fell over and the sweat poured regularly from his forehead like a spring. I wondered why they took such care of him. They all looked at him tenderly as he slept. I learned later he was a leader on the picket line and had the scalps of more cops to his name than any other. . . .

I kept feeling they would put me out. No one paid any attention. . . .

"Do you need any help?" I said eagerly. "Boy," she said, "some of us have been pouring coffee since two o'clock this morning, steady, without no let-up." She started to go. She didn't pay any special attention to me as an individual. She didn't seem to be thinking of me, she didn't seem to see me. I watched her go. I felt rebuffed, hurt. Then I saw instantly she didn't see me because she saw only what she was doing. I ran after her.

I found the kitchen organized like a factory. Nobody asks my name. I am given a large butcher's apron. I realize I have never before worked anonymously. At first I feel strange and then I feel good. The forewoman sets me to washing tin cups. There are not enough cups. We have to wash fast and rinse them and set them up quickly for buttermilk and coffee as the line thickens and the men wait. A little shortish man who is a professional dishwasher is supervising. I feel I won't be able to wash tin cups, but when no one pays any attention except to see that there are enough cups I feel better.

The line grows heavy. The men are coming in from the picket line. Each woman has one thing to do. There is no confusion. I soon learn I am not supposed to help pour the buttermilk. I am not supposed to serve sandwiches. I am supposed to wash tin cups. I suddenly look around and realize all these women are from factories. I know they have learned this organization and specialization in the factory. I look at the round shoulders of the woman cutting bread next to me and I feel I know her. The cups are brought back, washed and put on the counter again. The sweat pours down our faces, but you forget about it.

Then I am changed and put to pouring coffee. At first I look at the men's faces and then I don't look any more. It seems I am pouring coffee for the same tense, dirty sweating face, the same body, the same blue shirt and overalls. Hours go by, the heat is terrific. I am not tired. I am not hot. I am pouring coffee. I am swung into the most intense and natural organization I have ever felt. I know everything that is going on. These things become of great matter to me. . . .

For a long time, about one o'clock, it seemed like something was about to happen. Women seemed to be pouring into headquarters to be near their men. . . .

I could hear the men talking about the arbitration board, the truce that was supposed to be maintained while the board sat with the Governor. They listened to every word over the loudspeaker. A terrible communal excitement ran through the hall like a fire through a forest. I could hardly breathe. I seemed to have no body at all except the body of this excitement. I felt that what had happened before had not been a real movement, these false words and actions had taken place on the periphery. The real action was about to show, the real intention.

We kept on pouring thousands of cups of coffee, feeding thousands of men. . . .

The voice of the announcer was excited. "The men are massed at the market," he said. "Something is going to happen." . . .

The action seemed reversed. The cars were coming back. The announcer cried, "This is murder." Cars were coming in. I don't know how we got to the stairs. Everyone seemed to be converging at a menaced point. I saw below the crowd stirring, uncoiling. I saw them taking men out of cars and putting them on the hospital cots, on the floor. At first I felt frightened, the close black area of the barn, the blood, the heavy movement, the sense of myself lost, gone. But I couldn't have turned away now. A woman clung to my hand. I was pressed against the body of another. If you are to understand anything you must understand it in the muscular event, in actions we have not been trained for. Something broke all my surfaces in something that was beyond horror and I was dabbing alcohol on the gaping wounds that buckshot makes, hanging open like crying mouths. Buckshot wounds splay in the body and then swell like a blow. Ness, who died, had thirty-eight slugs in his body, in the chest and in the back.

The picket cars keep coming in. Some men have walked back from the market, holding their own blood in. They move in a great explosion, and the newness of the movement makes it seem like something under ether, moving terrifically towards a culmination.

From all over the city workers are coming. They gather outside in two great half-circles, cut in two to let the ambulances in. A traffic cop is still directing traffic at the corner and the crowd cannot stand to see him. "We'll give you just two seconds to beat it," they tell him. He goes away quickly. A striker takes over the street.

Men, women, and children are massing outside, a living circle close packed for protection. From the tall office building business men are looking down on the black swarm thickening, coagulating into what action they cannot tell.

We have living blood on our skirts.

That night at eight o'clock a mass-meeting was called of all labor. It was to be in a parking lot two blocks from headquarters. All the women gather at the front of the building with collection cans, ready to march to the meeting. I have not been home. It never occurs to me to leave. The twilight is eerie and the men are saying that the chief of police is going to attack the meeting and raid headquarters. The smell of blood hangs in the hot, still air. Rumors strike at the taut nerves. The dusk looks ghastly with what might be in the next half hour.

"If you have any children," a woman said to me, "you better not go." I looked at the desperate women's faces, the broken feet, the torn and hanging pelvis, the worn and lovely bodies of women who persist under such desperate labors. I shivered, though it was 96 and the sun had been down a good hour. . . .

The parking lot was already full of people when we got there and men swarmed the adjoining roofs. An elegant café stood across the street with water sprinkling from its roof and splendidly dressed men and women stood on the steps as if looking at a show.

The platform was the bullet riddled truck of the afternoon's fray. We had been told to stand close to this platform, so we did, making the center of a wide massed circle that stretched as far as we could see. . . .

I see that there is a bright clot of women drawn close to a bullet riddled truck. I am one of them, yet I don't feel myself at all. It is curious, I feel most alive and yet for the first time in my life I do not feel myself as separate. I realize then that all my previous feelings have been based on feeling myself separate and distinct from others and now I sense sharply faces, bodies, closeness, and my own fear is not my own alone, nor my hope.

The strikers keep moving up cars. We keep moving back together to let cars pass and form between us and a brick building that flanks the parking lot. They are connecting the loudspeaker, testing it. Yes, they are moving up lots of cars, through the crowd and lining them closely side by side. There must be ten thousand people now, heat rising from them. They are standing silent, watching the platform, watching the cars being brought up. The silence seems terrific like a great form moving of itself. This is real movement issuing from the close reality of mass feeling. This is the first real rhythmic movement I have ever seen. My heart hammers terrifically. My hands are swollen and hot. No one is producing this movement. It is a movement upon which all are moving softly, rhythmically, terribly.

No matter how many times I looked at what was happening I hardly knew what I saw. I looked and I saw time and time again that there were men standing close to us, around us, and then suddenly I knew that there was a living chain of men standing shoulder to shoulder, forming a circle around the group of women. They stood shoulder to shoulder slightly moving like a thick vine from the pressure behind, but standing tightly woven like a living wall, moving gently. . . .

The last car drove in slowly, the crowd letting them through without command or instruction. "A little closer," someone said. "Be sure they are close." Men sprang up to direct whatever action was needed and then subsided again and no one had noticed who it was. They stepped forward to direct a needed action and then fell anonymously back again.

We all watched carefully the placing of the cars. Sometimes we looked at each other. I didn't understand that look. I felt uneasy. It was as if something escaped me. And then suddenly, on my very body, I knew what they were doing, as if it had been communicated to me from a thousand eyes, a thousand silent throats, as if it had been shouted in the loudest voice.

THEY WERE BUILDING A BARRICADE.

Two men died from that day's shooting. Men lined up to give one of
them a blood transfusion, but he died. Black Friday men called the
murderous day. Night and day workers held their children up to see
the body of Ness who died. Tuesday, the day of the funeral, one thousand more militia were massed downtown.

It was still over ninety in the shade. I went to the funeral parlors and
thousands of men and women were massed there waiting in the terrific
sun. One block of women and children were standing two hours waiting. I went over and stood near them. I didn't know whether I could
march. I didn't like marching in parades. Besides, I felt they might not
want me.

I stood aside not knowing if I would march. I couldn't see how they
would ever organize it anyway. No one seemed to be doing much.

At three-forty some command went down the ranks. I said foolishly
at the last minute, "I don't belong to the auxiliary—could I march?"
Three women drew me in. "We want all to march," they said gently.
"Come with us."

The giant mass uncoiled like a serpent and straightened out ahead
and to my amazement on a lift of road I could see six blocks of massed
men, four abreast, with bare heads, moving straight on and as they
moved, uncoiled the mass behind and pulled it after them. I felt myself
walking, accelerating my speed with the others as the line stretched,
pulled taut, then held its rhythm. . . .

I was marching with a million hands, movements, faces, and my own
movement was repeating again and again, making a new movement
from these many gestures, the walking, falling back, the open mouth
crying, the nostrils stretched apart, the raised hand, the blow falling,
and the outstretched hand drawing me in. . . .

THIS EXCERPT is from a collection of oral histories of Congress of Industrial Organizations (C.I.O.) organizers. Some, like Stella Nowicki,
felt that the union alone could not create the necessary social change
and turned to political parties and community organizations as well.
Many like Nowicki joined the Communist party.

Being a woman C.I.O. organizer was unusual in itself, and Stella
Nowicki is an exceptional woman. Brought up on a farm, during the

depression she ran away from home because there was not enough food to feed the family. She came to Chicago and lived with a Communist family, the Marshes. At first she did housework, and later Herb Marsh helped her get a job in meat packing, first at Armour and later at Swift.

RANK AND FILE ORGANIZING

. . . The company didn't give a damn.

The meat would be so hot and steamy your fingers almost blistered but you just stayed on. In 1933–34 we worked six hour shifts at 37½ cents an hour. We would have to work at a high rate of speed. It was summer. It would be so hot that women used to pass out. The ladies' room was on the floor below and I would help carry these women down almost vertical stairs into the washroom.

We started talking union. The thing that precipitated it is that on the floor below they used to make hotdogs and one of the women, in putting the meat into the chopper, got her fingers caught. There were no safety guards. Her fingers got into the hotdogs and they were chopped off. It was just horrible.

Three of us "colonizers" had a meeting during our break and decided this was the time to have a stoppage and we did. (Colonizers were people sent by the YCL [Young Communist League] or CP [Communist Party] into points of industrial concentration that the CP had designated. These included mass basic industries: steel, mining, packing, and railroad. The colonizers were like red missionaries. They were expected to do everything possible to keep jobs and organize for many years.) All six floors went on strike. We said, "Sit, stop." And we had a sit-down. We just stopped working right inside the building, protesting the speed and the unsafe conditions. We thought that people's fingers shouldn't go into the machine, that it was an outrage. The women got interested in the union.

We got the company to put in safety devices. Soon after the work stoppage the supervisors were looking for the leaders because people were talking up the action. They found out who was involved and we were all fired. I was blacklisted.

I got a job doing housework again and it was just horrible. Here I was taking care of this family with a little spoiled brat and I had to

Alice and Staughton Lynd, eds. *Rank and File, Personal Histories by Working Class Organizers.* Boston: Beacon Press, 1973.

pick up after them—only Thursday afternoon off and every other Sunday—and all for four dollars a week of which I sent two dollars home. I just couldn't stand it. I would rather go back and work in a factory, any day or night.

A friend of mine who had been laid off told me that she got called to go back to work. Meanwhile she had a job in an office and she didn't want to go back to the stockyards, so she asked me if I wanted to go in her place. She had used the name Helen Ellis. I went down to the stockyards and it was the same department, exactly the same job on the same floor where I had been fired. But it was the afternoon and Mrs. McCann wasn't there. Her assistant was there. Her assistant said, "Can you do this work," I said, "Oh yes, I can. I've done it." She told me that I would start work the following afternoon.

I came home and talked with Herb and Jane. We decided that I would have to go to the beauty shop. I got my hair cut really short and hennaed (similar to tinting today). I thinned my eyebrows and penciled them, wore a lot of lipstick and painted my nails. Because I hadn't been working, I had a suntan. I wore sandals and I had my toenails painted, which I would never have done before. I came in looking sharp and not like a country girl, so I passed right through and I was hired as Helen Ellis on the same job, the same forelady!

After several days the forelady, Mary, who was also Polish, came around and said, "OK, Helen, I know you're Stella. I won't say anything but just keep quiet" if I wanted to keep the job. I answered her in Polish that I knew that the job wouldn't last long and I thanked her. She knew I was pro-union and I guess she was too, so I kept the job as Helen Ellis until I got laid off. (Later on I was blacklisted under the name Ellis.) . . .

Swift's was in a different class than Armour's. Everyone who worked in Swift's was thought to be a higher class worker—they got more money. Swift's had a group bonus system called the Bedaux system. After you produced so much then each person in the gang got that much more money. It's diabolical. One worker slits the throat of another. They keep going so that the group production is great enough that they can all get a bonus.

Swift and Company had a strong entrenched company union with a paternalistic system to keep people sort of quiescent and controlled. The company actually selected the representatives from the different departments. They called it an "Independent Employees Organization." Anybody who spoke up about it was a troublemaker and they got rid of him.

I went to Swift's to get a job. The personnel director said they weren't hiring but what were my qualifications, where did I work last. I told her Independent Casing. "Well, why aren't you there now?" I told her that I got a scholarship to go to the University of Wisconsin through the Y that previous summer. And she said, "Well that's my Alma Mater!" So she hired me for the casing department.

Later I got sent to the sliced bacon department which is the elite department. It was the cleanest job and you made the most money. They had this visitors' ramp where people went by and would look down. We were freezing our asses off in this cooler of about forty degrees. I wore two pairs of wool socks and a couple of wool sweaters under my uniform and a cap. We'd have to go every two or three hours into the washroom to thaw out and spill out. . . .

The women themselves had gotten together and they would turn out a hundred and forty-four packages an hour of bacon. We were making $15 a week at 37½ cents an hour, but if we each produced 144 packages an hour we got $7 more in our pay. We made 50 per cent more than anybody else but we produced 90 per cent more than the set group rate. A new girl would come in and the oldtimers would train her. They would help her out so that gradually by the end of a certain period of time she was doing the 144. But they would never let anyone go beyond that 144 packages. They maintained that limit and they did it without a union. One smart-aleck girl came in there once and she was going to show them and go beyond that number because she wanted to earn more money: all the bacon that she got from the girls further up the line was messed up and scrappy and she'd have to straighten it up to put it in the package. She couldn't make a hundred packages an hour. (We took a loss just to show her.)

The checker would come around with the stop watch. You learned to wrap a package of bacon using a lot of extra motions because it was a time study thing. When he wasn't there we eliminated all those motions and did it simply. This was done everywhere—sausage, wrap and tie, bacon, everywhere. (It's all done by machine now.) There is always a faster way to do something, a simpler way where you save energy and time. The older women, in terms of experience, would show the new women. It was a tremendous relationship of solidarity. But they weren't about to join the union. They weren't about to put out a buck a month in union dues.

At first the women were afraid. It took quite a bit of courage to join. They were concerned about their jobs. Many of them were sole bread-winners. Also the Catholic Church said that the CIO was red: you join the CIO and you are joining a red organization. To talk about the CIO then was like talking about socialism to some people today. Even to talk union, you talked about it in whispers. You had to trust the person and know the person very well because he could be a stool pigeon. . . .

When I was at the University of Wisconsin, John Lewis made his speech that he was breaking away the coal miners union from the AFL and they were going to set up the CIO. We set up an organizing committee for the stockyards. There were seventeen of us that met, three women and fourteen men. One of them was an Irishman by the name of McCarthy who became the acting chairman of the Packing-house Workers Organizing Committee. We met behind a tavern on Honore Street. The organizing of these seventeen people was on Communist Party initiative and we worked through contacts in the IWO, the International Workers Order. In this group of seventeen there were some Poles and some Slovaks who were indigenous to the community. . . .

We couldn't get the sliced bacon department at Swift's into the union because of the money they were earning. What could the union do that they weren't getting already, and they *were* organized! So I told them that it was the case that they had the money, but what about the conditions—it was colder than hell. What happens if you get sick? What happens if the foreman says that he doesn't like you and he wants somebody else to have your job? I said that the union could protect them on these real problems. But they wouldn't join. I think that I only got one or two out of that great big department.

They were all white, mostly Polish. There was one black woman who worked on scrap bacon way in the back so that no one would see her when visitors came through. The company could always say that they had one black woman in this fancy department. I raised this matter of discrimination but it didn't go over too well with white women.

One day the woman who worked in the coldest spot got sick. She didn't come to work. We found out that she had become paralyzed. The door from the cutting cooler opened as the men came back and forth. It was below freezing there and every time the door opened she would get this tremendous cold blast on her side. The whole right side of her body was paralyzed and she died. Within a week we organized that whole department. She was a young woman, probably around forty, and she died because of the freezing conditions in which we all had to work. It was easier on the company to have it this cold. There was less spoilage. But they didn't give a damn about the workers. We showed that we could handle bacon and that it didn't have to be that cold.

The National Labor Relations Act had been passed, giving workers the right to organize. But this was not easy because people were laid off. I was laid off, for instance, in the gut shanty and they tried to break my seniority. We had departmental seniority and I would be shifted all around. Besides casing and sliced bacon, I got to work in wrap and tie (hams), soap, glue, fresh sausage, pork, ham, almost every department. By being shifted around I became acquainted with many more women. I kept the names and addresses of all the women because I knew that some day I would need them. When we started organizing I knew women all over the whole plant. I would call them and get information as to pro-labor union sentiment, problems and issues, and so forth. We would print it up in the CIO news—the *Swift Flashes* we called it.

The same woman who had hired me at Swift's approached me and asked me if I'd like to work in personnel—they tried to buy me off. They offered me better-paying jobs. . . .

You had to *earn* the respect of your fellow workers or you couldn't talk to them about new ideas or unions, etc. You always had to be a good worker.

Women often did much harder work than men. For instance, in wrap and tie department—where hams were handled, wrapped in paper and tied—it is heavy lifting a twenty-pound ham. Then you'd have to put those great big hams on a slip hook and hang them up so that they could be smoked in the smoke shed. In the sausage department women used to link sausages by hand; but the men would measure the meat and work with a pedal to shoot the sausage into the casings.

The women worked much harder and much faster but they got less pay. We were paid ten cents an hour less than men. There were jobs that men had done that women took over and they'd still get the lesser pay. I worked in a cooler cutting the fat from the lean with the guard on my thumb and the sharp knife. Work with a knife is a butcher's job, but they had a pay differential. (The union corrected this inequity later.) There was also a differential between the southern rates and the northern rates.

Women had an awfully tough time in the union because the men brought their prejudices there. The fellows couldn't believe that women in the union were there for the union's sake. They thought that they were there to get a guy or something else. Some thought that we were frivolous. I would be approached by men for dates and they would ask me why I was in the union, so I would tell them that I was for socialism and I thought that this was the only way of bringing it about.

Some of my brothers, who believed in equality and that women should have rights, didn't crank the mimeograph, didn't type. I did the shit work, until all hours, as did the few other women who didn't have family obligations. And then when the union came around giving out jobs with pay, the guys got them. I and the other women didn't. It was the men who got the organizing jobs. Men who worked in plants got paid for their time loss—women didn't. I never did. But we were a dedicated group. We worked in coolers and from there I would go to the union hall and get out leaflets, write material for shop papers, turn in dues, etc., get home and make supper, get back. These guys had wives to do this but there was nobody to do mine. Sometimes I'd be up until eleven, twelve, or one o'clock and then have to get up early and be punched in by quarter to seven and be working on the job by seven. . . .

For a long time I fought dishonesty within my local. There were some guys who would pocket the dues money. I would debate them on the union floor. Many times I was the only female there.

The women felt the union was a man's thing because once they got through the day's work they had another job. When they got home they had to take care of their one to fifteen children and the meals and the house and all the rest, and the men went to the tavern and to the meetings and to the racetrack and so forth. The fellows were competing for positions and the women didn't feel that that was their role. They were brainwashed into thinking that this union was for men.

The union didn't encourage women to come to meetings. They didn't actually want to take up the problems that the women had. I did what I could to get the women to come to the meetings but very few came—only when there was a strike. I tried to make the meetings more interesting than just a bunch of guys talking all evening.

We organized women's groups, young women's groups. They liked to dance and I loved to dance so we went dancing together and I talked to them about the union. The women were interested after a while when they saw that the union could actually win things for them, bread and butter things.

We talked about nurseries. In World War II we finally did get some because women were needed in greater quantities than ever before in the factories. But the unions had so many things they had to work for—the shorter work day, improved conditions—so many things that they couldn't worry about these things in relation to women.

Later on, during the war, there was one department where I got the women but couldn't get the guys in. They hung out in the tavern and so

I went there and started talking with them. I didn't like beer, but I'd drink ginger ale and told them to show me how to play pool. I learned to play pool and I got the men into the union. I did what they did. I went into the taverns. I became a bowler and I joined the league. The only thing I didn't do is rejoin the Catholic Church. . . .

An Arkansas sharecropper scrubbing.

Cannery workers, Dania, Florida, 1937.

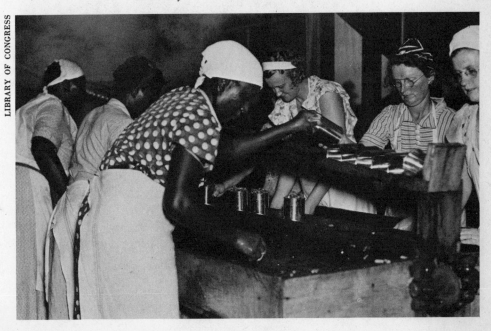

A Mexican-American
grandmother migrant
worker who followed
the crops from Arizona
to California, 1938.
Photograph by
Dorothea Lange.

Emancipation changed
very little, June 8, 1928.

Federal employee, Washington, D.C., 1942. Photograph by Gordon Parks.

Mexican-American workers headed for a picket line, Corcoran, California, 1933.

Picketers outside a Georgia textile mill, May 1941.

Packing-house workers jitterbug
during meat strike.

Sit-down strike at Woolworth's,
1937.

1940~1955

World War II had profound effects on the U.S. economy, one of which was to pull the United States out of the depression and solve, temporarily, the problem of unemployment. U.S. companies also profited handsomely from the war.

Unions during the war developed significantly for several reasons: a larger work force, dues checkoffs that permitted employers to deduct union dues from employee paychecks, and maintenance of membership clauses prohibiting withdrawal from a union before the contract was up. These changes assured unions of steady dues-paying members, regardless of how dissatisfied they might be with union leadership. Despite the increase in numbers and control, unions lost some of their prewar power when (with the single exception of the United Mine Workers) they took a no-strike pledge for the duration of the war. Furthermore, workers were pressured by unions, management and government to make sacrifices because of the war and accept less beneficial working conditions: the average work week was forty-eight hours, time-and-a-half for overtime was suspended and piece work (being paid on the basis of the number of items produced) was reinstated. In spite of patriotic propaganda, workers called unauthorized strikes and wildcats by the thousands to protest their working conditions.

While the war had a repressive effect on workers in general, one ethnic group was singled out for political persecution. 130,000 people of Japanese origin were summarily rounded up on the West Coast and incarcerated in concentration camps. Although the excuse given was their potential disloyalty, racism, hysterical patriotism and the desire of a few for their valuable property were more likely the real causes.

One of the greatest of the war's impacts was on women. The proportion of women working increased from 25 percent to 36 percent, a rise greater than that of the preceding four decades. Wages rose, the number of wives holding jobs doubled and unionization of women quadrupled. Employers' attitudes toward hiring women remained skeptical, but since women were the only available labor force reserve, they were hired.

The war gave women access to skilled, higher-paying industrial jobs for the first time. Many women taking these jobs had always worked, but had been previously restricted to lower-paying, unskilled, service jobs. Women responded to these new opportunities with skill, ingenuity, patriotism and resourcefulness, as they became switchwomen, precision toolmakers, overhead crane operators, lumberjacks, drill press operators and stevedores, demonstrating that women could fill any job, no matter how difficult or arduous. War plants paid wages often 40 percent higher than in the traditional women's industries. Twenty-nine thousand women joined the Women's Land Army, helping to replace the farmers who had been shipped overseas. Three hundred thousand enlisted in the military services, although none were trained in the use of weapons. All the women's services were volunteer, and the requirements for admission were higher than those for the men's Selective Service.

Not only were more women working, but different kinds of women were drawn into the labor force. Despite employer resistance, many black women found jobs in the manufacturing sector for the first time. The proportion of married women in the female labor force increased greatly; as the fighting ceased, wives for the first time composed the majority of women workers. Previous bans on the employment of married women were discarded, and the average age of employed women increased.

Although the war made rapid changes in women's economic status, it did not make a lasting or profound difference in the public attitude toward women who worked nor did it redefine the sex roles. During the war women continued to receive less pay than men (65 percent less in manufacturing), to be denied opportunities for training and advancement and to work in separate job categories. The perpetuation of these conditions represented a tacit agreement between labor unions and managements. Unions fought for equal pay when women took jobs left by men, usually out of concern for preserving a high wage for the returning veterans; but they rarely fought the separate seniority lists of distinctly female job classifications. Often, collective-bargaining contracts created separate job classifications, and granted women union membership and seniority only for the duration of the war.

Paying women less wages for equal work became even more profitable for many companies. The government encouraged companies to hire women with grants, special tax reductions and other incentives for installing women's rest rooms, lighter fixtures and conveyors to slide parts from one machine to another. In many cases, whole new factories were built with the government footing most of the bills. Yet industrialists argued that women should receive lower wages because they had to make special adjustments for them.

In 1945 the United States was the only major country involved in the war not devastated by it. The tenuous wartime alliance with the Soviet Union was broken, ushering in the era of the Cold War. Military spending on massive defense networks was used to prevent domestic depression and to defend the world against the alleged menace of international Communism directed from Moscow. Using the Cold War rhetoric, the world was divided into two hostile camps, "free" and socialist. The United States government fought Communism on the economic level, through massive U.S. aid to Europe, and on the military level, through troop interventions such as in Korea. U.S. capital began increasingly to dominate the economies and often the political life of many countries without overt takeovers. The international tensions that stemmed from these developments made nuclear destruction a major and persistent fear.

At home, corporate profits soared to all-time highs, 250 percent higher than the prewar level, while prices rose 45 percent and wages were frozen at 15 percent above the 1941 level. Workers, who had endured no-strike pledges, speed-ups and long hours, refused to continue to pay for the profit-making and responded to the inflation with the biggest strike wave in U.S. history between 1945 and 1947. Strikes, usually led by rank-and-file members, hit almost every major industry. Government and corporate interests countered with a full-scale war against what they believed to be domestic "communism" in this strike wave—a tactic designed to weaken the Left and labor movement and to develop support for a Cold War foreign policy. During the McCarthy period, loyalty tests were instituted, Communists in the unions were required to register with the government and Communists and Communist sympathizers were jailed, harassed and kept from employment. In the height of the hysteria, Ethel and Julius Rosenberg were executed on poorly proven charges of giving away the atom bomb secret to the Russians. This was the only case in U.S. history of an execution in peacetime for espionage.

As the majority of the unions cooperated with these moves, repression was directed against the organized Left in the unions. The Communist party had already been losing its rank-and-file support due to its lack of militancy on the shop floor and was thus unable to gain worker support to fight the political persecution.

In a further attempt to break labor's power, the Taft-Hartley law was passed in 1947, allowing injunctions against strikes, giving courts the power to fine alleged violators, establishing a sixty-day cooling-off period during which strikes could not be declared, outlawing mass picketing, denying trade unions the right to contribute to political campaigns, abolishing the closed shop, prohibiting secondary boycotts and authorizing employer interference in attempts of employees to join unions.

In addition to this retrenchment and repression of organized labor, educators, social workers, psychologists and journalists tried to convince women that their place was in the home rearing children and not in the paid labor force. Their public relations arguments rationalized taking away jobs from women and giving them to men, even bumping of women with seniority off their jobs. Behind these efforts were important economic considerations. On the one hand, the system could not provide full employment; on the other hand, continued industrial profits required, with the diminution of military spending, an expansion in the consumption of household durable goods. An emphasis on "homemaking" encouraged women to buy. To increase private consumption, families were encouraged to leave the cities for the suburbs by low-cost Federal Housing Administration loans and miles of commuter highways subsidized by the government.

But the inflationary spiral (meat prices rose 122 percent between 1945 and 1947) created an economic pinch for almost everyone and made an adequate standard of living possible only if both the husband and wife worked. Thus many women displaced in the heavy industries did not in fact return to the kitchens, but found work in the "traditional" women's jobs still available to them. Despite the feminine and suburban mystiques, many millions of women continued to work out of economic necessity.

WAR WORK

THE WAR Manpower Commission undertook campaigns to encourage women to take jobs in 1943. Newspaper ads, radio spots, even ten-minute films for local movie theaters were used. The following is a sample of an outdoor billboard.

MOTHERS IN OVERALLS

"What Job is mine on the Victory Line?"
If you've sewed on buttons, or made buttonholes, on a machine,
you can learn to do spot welding on airplane parts.
If you've used an electric mixer in your kitchen,
you can learn to run a drill press.
If you've followed recipes exactly in making cakes,
you can learn to load shell.

AT THE BEGINNING of the war, black people found it difficult to obtain jobs and housing despite the increased demand for laborpower. In January 1941, A. Philip Randolph, the head of the Brotherhood of Sleeping Car Porters, proposed a March on Washington to demand that the government take remedial action. To head off the demon-

Eve Lapin. *Mothers in Overalls*. New York: Workers Library Publ., 1943.

stration, President Roosevelt promised Randolph that the government would act against discrimination. Thus in June 1941 the
President issued Executive Order 8802 banning discrimination in defense industries or in government "because of race, creed, color, or
national origin." A Fair Employment Practices Commission was
set up to carry out the order. This government intervention plus increased labor shortages brought more blacks into the labor force.
Black women entered steel foundries, munition and aircraft plants,
the Army, canneries and hospitals. The number of blacks in civilian
jobs increased by a million between April 1940 and April 1944; 6,000
of this increase were women. The most significant change for black
women in these war years was a movement from the farms to the
factories; the proportion of black women on farms halved in four
years. Some upgrading took place, but most blacks remained in unskilled jobs. For many black women the war nevertheless provided
a first opportunity to demonstrate ability in factory work.

The following excerpt describes the situation in St. Louis, and is
reasonably typical of the problems faced by black women in other
industrial centers.

BLACK WOMEN
IN WAR PRODUCTION

In July 1942, the Curtiss-Wright Company and the U. S. Cartridge
Company announced that they would accept Negro applicants for
training for skilled and semiskilled operators. By August the Curtiss-
Wright Company had approximately 500 Negro workers in a segregated building on a variety of skilled jobs including welders, riveters,
assemblers and inspectors.

Simultaneously, the U. S. Cartridge Company provided a segregated
plant identical with other production units and employed a complete
force of Negro production workers. . . .

At peak production the company employed a total of 4,500 Negroes,
many of whom held jobs as machine operators, millwrights, inspectors,
and adjusters.

If this form of segregation in industry can be looked upon with
favor, it might be said that these firms made a reasonable effort to use
the available Negro labor supply. However, other large industries attempted to restrict the number of Negroes to the population ratio of

Richard R. Jefferson. "Negro Employment in St. Louis War Production." *Opportunity* 22 (No. 3), July–September 1944.

one to ten. Further, they made little or no effort to upgrade Negroes according to seniority or skills. This flat refusal to comply with the spirit and letter of the Executive Order has precipitated a very unsatisfactory situation and has caused numerous strikes and work stoppages among dissatisfied Negro workers. The prejudices of white workers in the area is usually blamed for the failure to upgrade Negroes. In at least 100 important war production plants no Negro workers have been employed.

The employment of Negro women in St. Louis industries presents a more discouraging picture as might be expected. Stronger resistance to their use except as maids and cleaners, or in segregated workshops, has been encountered in almost every instance. With the exception of the Curtiss-Wright Company which employs about 200 women as riveters, assemblers, and inspectors, and the U. S. Cartridge Company which used almost 1,000 women as operators and inspectors, few plants in the area have attempted to use them. The lack of separate toilet facilities and the prejudices of white women workers are the main barriers to the wider use of Negro women, according to officials of many of 200 plants that refuse to employ them.

Perhaps the one bright spot in this picture is the development in the garment industry, although the policy of segregation has been followed even in this field despite our efforts to eliminate it. Since 1930 the Urban League of St. Louis has worked to secure employment opportunities for Negro women in some of the numerous textile plants. In the Spring of 1941 the Acme Manufacturing Company opened an all-Negro plant employing 28 operators, a packer and a foreman. . . .

Until March, 1943, no other manufacturer would consider the employment of Negro women. With depleted labor reserves and mounting war orders, several plants were forced to look elsewhere for workers and the Portnoy Garment Company was one of the first to consider the use of Negroes. While not willing to integrate Negroes in the plant, the Portnoy Company agreed to open an all-Negro plant if a suitable building could be obtained and qualified workers were available. Because of the exclusion of Negroes from the trade, there were few if any experienced operators except those employed by the Acme Co. However, the St. Louis and East St. Louis N.Y.A. projects had given training to approximately 300 girls and a few had been trained at the Washington Technical School. From these groups, it was possible to recruit a sufficient number of operators to open the new plant on May 10, 1943. By the end of the year 60 women were employed and by May 1, 1944 the

factory had 90 workers and was planning an expansion to accommodate an additional 40 operators. . . .

Negro workers in the St. Louis area have not accepted the discrimination against them without protest. Through mass meetings and petitions they have expressed their disapproval of the situation even after
they secured employment. No less than a half dozen all-Negro strikes
have occurred in protest to discriminatory hiring or working policies.
In June, 1943, Negroes employed in the segregated plan of the U. S.
Cartridge Company struck because the company would not upgrade
qualified Negroes to jobs as foremen. The company finally agreed to
comply with their demands. A few weeks later the workers in the segregated Curtiss-Wright staged a sit-down strike protesting the lack of
adequate cooling equipment. In August, 1943, 600 Negro workers in
the General Steel Castings plant in Madison, Illinois, struck because of
a number of grievances including differentials in pay rates and discrimination against Negro women workers. After several weeks of negotiations in which the Urban League took an active part, 61 of the 62
grievance cases were satisfactorily adjusted.

In November, 1943 and March, 1944, 380 Negro employees of the
Monsanto Chemical Company staged a series of work stoppages, one of
which lasted 10 days. Long-standing grievances against both the company and the union were responsible for the difficulties, but the refusal
to upgrade Negro workers was the major complaint. The League was
instrumental in placing their grievances before company and union
officials and an acceptable settlement was finally negotiated. Minor
incidents involving the introduction and integration of Negro workers
in the industries in this area have been too frequent to enumerate, and
they have served to further confuse a very tense and unsettled war
production center. . . .

AUGUSTA CLAWSON was a federal government worker who went to
work in a shipyard in Oregon in order to write up her experiences
and encourage other women to enlist in war production. Her employers were not aware of her patriotic purpose.

Until World War II women were not accepted in shipbuilding, even
as office secretaries, and the lone telephone operators were kept under

lock and key. By January 1944 women were 9.5 percent of all the workers in the industry. The problems of physical, administrative and psychological adjustment in an industry totally unprepared for women workers were formidable.

SHIPYARD DIARY
OF A WOMAN WELDER

Back to work and more welding. I "dis-improved" as rapidly after lunch as I had improved during the morning. One girl stopped to ask, "How you doin'?" and watched me critically. "Here, let me show you, you're holding it too far away." So she took over, but she couldn't maintain the arc at all. She got up disgusted, said, "I can't do it—my hand shakes so since I been sick," and I took over again. But she was right. I held it closer and welded on and on and on. . . .

The redheaded mother of seven was terribly upset. Her boy got his papers yesterday, and she hadn't slept all night. First thing this morning she had to take her test and was as jittery as could be. I wonder if this is the sort of thing that people glibly call "the emotional instability of women" without investigating first to find its cause! A mother has a right to be at less than her calmest when her eldest son is leaving to join the Army. But this woman, in the midst of all her worry, had room for concern about me. She came running up. "Say, my eldest boy leaves tomorrow. You can come and live with us if you like." I hesitated, reflecting that it would be difficult to record my daily impressions without risking her suspicion that I might have an ulterior motive for taking this job. So I temporized. "You're a brick to suggest it, but you can't spare a room for me when you still have six children in the house." She looked puzzled. "A room?" she said. "Why, I don't know—maybe I could fix you up a room." Then she shrugged her bewilderment away. "No, I mean just come and live with us." That's what I call hospitality. . . .

We were called to another safety lecture—good sound advice on Eye Safety. . . . Only Chile has a higher accident rate than the United States. Last year the shipyard had fairly heavy absenteeism, but this year they hope to build an extra ship on the decrease in absenteeism. He cautioned us about creating hazards by wearing the wrong kind of

Augusta Clawson. *Shipyard Diary of a Woman Welder*. New York: Penguin, 1944.

clothing, and told us not to wear watches or rings. After it was over, Missouri was bothered about her wedding ring. It hadn't been off in fourteen years. She was willing to take it off, but only if necessary.

The lecturer brought up the rumor that arc welding causes sterility among women. He said that this was untrue, and quoted an authoritative source to prove its falsity. . . . Actually, welders had *more* children than other people. "No, thanks," said the first girl; "I don't like that either!"

The Big Swede is a real pal. She had not forgotten the patch for my overall trouser leg. She had cut a piece from an old pair of her husband's, scrubbed it to get the oil out, and brought it to me with a needle stuck in the center and a coil of black thread ready for action. "Here," she said, "I knew you wouldn't have things handy in a hotel room. Now you mend that hole before you catch your foot in it and fall." . . .

I, who hates heights, climbed stair after stair after stair till I thought I must be close to the sun. I stopped on the top deck. I, who hate confined spaces, went through narrow corridors, stumbling my way over rubber-coated leads—dozens of them, scores of them, even hundreds of them. I went into a room about four feet by ten where two shipfitters, a shipfitter's helper, a chipper, and I all worked. I welded in the poop deck lying on the floor while another welder spattered sparks from the ceiling and chippers like giant woodpeckers shattered our eardrums. I, who've taken welding, and have sat at a bench welding flat and vertical plates, was told to weld braces along a baseboard below a door opening. On these a heavy steel door was braced while it was hung to a fine degree of accuracy. I welded more braces along the side, and along the top. I did overhead welding, horizontal, flat, vertical. I welded around curved hinges which were placed so close to the side wall that I had to bend my rod in a curve to get it in. I made some good welds and some frightful ones. But now a door in the poop deck of an oil tanker is hanging, four feet by six of solid steel, by *my* welds. Pretty exciting! . . .

Poor Texas had to work all afternoon in double bottom. She said she couldn't stand; she couldn't even sit up straight. She rested somewhat on a narrow pipe and did production. She was not very happy about it. It's funny the way we all dodge production. There isn't such a great difference between the techniques of tacking and doing production welding, but there is in the responsibility. When we tack we know a production welder will weld over the tack, and any gaps will be filled by him (or her). But when we do production we know ours is the final responsibility. . . .

I talked with Joanne, a very attractive brunette who had previously been a waitress in Atlantic City. She came West when her husband came on for a job. She, like the other waitresses, preferred welding because you "don't have to take so much from the public." . . .

I had a good taste of summer today, and I am convinced that it is going to take backbone for welders to stick to their jobs through the summer months. It is harder on them than on any of the other workers—their leathers are so hot and heavy, they get more of the fumes, and their hoods become instruments of torture. There were times today when I'd have to stop in the middle of a tack and push my hood back just to get a breath of fresh air. It grows unbearably hot under the hood, my glasses fog and blur my vision, and the only thing to do is to stop.

For almost an hour I tacked on in spite of the fact that there was no blower in the room. Then I took Texas's advice and decided "no blower, no welder." . . . My work was in the poop deck where the last crew had put brackets in place *upside down*. The burner had to burn off six of them completely. For me, this meant climbing halfway up the wall and tacking them in place with horizontal, vertical, and overhead tacks. One's position is often so precarious at such an angle that it is hard to maintain a steady arc. Add to this that often I could not stand straight nor kneel. The result was that trying to hold a position halfway between would start some contrary nerve quivering so that my hand would carry out the "jiggle" and affect the weld. Yet the job confirmed my strong conviction—I have stated it before—what exhausts the woman welder is not the work, nor the heat, nor the demands upon physical strength. It is the apprehension that arises from inadequate skill and consequent lack of confidence; and this *can* be overcome by the right kind of training. I've mastered tacking now, so that no kind bothers me. I know I can do it if my machine is correctly set, and I have learned enough of the vagaries of machines to be able to set them. And so, in spite of the discomforts of climbing, heavy equipment, and heat, I enjoyed the work today because I *could do it*. . . .

The drinking fountains are a godsend in such weather as this. The water is always cold. Often I hesitate to leave work long enough for a drink, since if a tack is needed the shipfitters have to stop work until it is done. But I think we are all getting to be more sensible about realizing that once in a while we have to stop, even if work waits for a moment. So midway in the morning I told my men, "Guess I have to have a drink," and off I went. All the time that I was tacking, three or four shipfitters would be sitting down waiting for me to finish. Several weeks ago this would have given me a hurried feeling; I'd have rushed the work, done it less well, and been more tired. I've learned now to work a steady pace and to ignore the fact that anyone is waiting. It relieves the strain and the work really gets done faster. There is a lot in this game in learning to relax *on* the job as well as *between* jobs. . . .

DESPITE THE MANY mothers working during World War II, the ideology that held mothers primarily responsible for their young children remained unchanged. Paul McNutt, head of the War Manpower Commission, stated that "the first responsibility of women with young children, in war as in peace, is to give suitable care in their own homes to their own children."

Day care was not an important public issue before World War II because mothers had never worked outside their homes in such significant numbers. The day care that was established during the war was far from adequate. About half the employed mothers had their children cared for by relatives in the household. For many others there was no child care help available, and child neglect verged on a national scandal. Children left alone at home while their mothers worked were killed and injured in accidents; questionable foster homes sprung up; "door key kids" (youngsters with keys tied around their necks so that they could get into the house when school was out) became commonplace; and increased juvenile delinquency was blamed on mothers' neglect.

Day care was provided during the war as temporary, emergency measures for mothers unable to make private arrangements. Most of the centers were located in areas of heavy war industry. Their primary purpose was to bring mothers into war production, not to liberate women or educate children. Many of the centers provided inadequate care, which made mothers fearful of leaving their children and gave day care a bad reputation.

Other services, such as shopping, precooked meals and shoe repair, were provided for women workers by private enterprise at a profit. But the fact that these services existed gave women a vision of what was possible when government policy encourages women entering the labor force, and demonstrated that when services were provided women were as effective on their jobs as men.

CHILD CARE

Day nurseries to care for children of employed mothers were first established by welfare groups in several large cities. The first such nursery in the United States opened in 1854 at Nursery and Child's Hospital, New York City. Employed mothers who had been patients in this hospital left their children under the care of nurses. Similar day nurseries were opened in 1858 in Troy, N.Y., and in 1863 in Philadelphia. By 1897, it was estimated that 175 nurseries had been established in various cities, located mainly in settlement houses. The day nurseries were chiefly custodial and provided little of educational value for the young child. . . .

The marked increase in the employment of married women in the postwar years, as well as during World War II, has been a major influence in the recognition that nursery schools and day-care centers for working mothers' children are a part of the established pattern of the economic life of the mid-twentieth century. The federally sponsored Work Projects Administration and Lanham Act programs provided a more widespread experience with such services than formerly had been available. This acquainted mother and the public with their advantages.

In the World War I period such nursery schools and day-care services as existed for working mothers were on a local basis. . . . A considerable part of the extensive entry of women into the World War I labor force was felt to be temporary, and in fact the percent of increase from 1910 to 1920 in the employment of women was smaller than in any other decade. Furthermore, the proportion of married women who were in gainful work remained about the same through the decades 1910 to 1930, and the marked increase did not show up until 1940. . . . Employed mothers undoubtedly depended with great frequency on relatives or neighbors for care of their children, though there is no measure by which the extent of this can be compared with the experience in later periods.

When the economic depression of the 1930's impelled the Government to make plans to increase employment, nursery schools were among the types of educational work organized. They were specifically authorized by the Federal Emergency Relief Administration in October

Employed Mothers and Child Care. Washington, D.C.: U.S. Government Printing Office, 1953 (Women's Bureau, No. 246).

1933. They enabled many children to attend nursery schools whose families otherwise could not have given them this experience, even though the primary objective had been to give useful work to unemployed persons and though these services had to be fitted in among other work projects.

In 1934–35, the Works Progress Administration reported some 1,900 nursery schools in which 75,000 children were enrolled. Early in 1938 the Administrator estimated that more than 200,000 children of low-income families had benefited from these schools. As the country moved toward greater prosperity, fewer families were eligible to send children to the WPA schools, but the value of nursery schools had been so fully shown that public demand for them continued.

During World War II women were drawn into the labor force more extensively than at any previous time in this country's history. . . . From June 1940 to June 1942 more than two million women were added to the labor force. The demand for workers continued to increase, and by June 1943 more than another three million women were added, and still the peak in woman employment was not reached. Before the war, single women were only 27 percent of the woman population and almost half of them already were in the labor force. Married women constituted the country's greatest labor reserve. The proportion of married women in the labor force increased from 15 percent in the prewar period to 23 percent in the war period while among single women the increase was from 46 to 55 percent. More than three million married women entered the labor force from 1940 to 1944. Many of these were mothers, though figures as to the exact number are not available.

Many communities were seriously concerned over the situation as to care of working mothers' children, which became increasingly acute. These children were not eligible to attend the still-existing WPA nurseries, which were open only to those whose parents had very limited income. Private nurseries existed chiefly in the larger cities, while many of the working mothers were in communities that had mushroomed with new war-production plants. Even where private nurseries existed their capacity was limited, and of course their fees had to cover costs at least. There were practically no facilities for the care of school-age children after school. Increased juvenile delinquency in some communities and high absenteeism in some war-manufacturing plants often were attributed to the lack of adequate child-care services. . . .

Comments from employed mothers, officials of war industries, and others interested in the problems of child-care for working mothers pointed up the possibility that the WPA nurseries, if a change in admission requirements were effected, could become the nucleus around which a Federal child-care program for employed mothers could be established. After a year and a half of effort, supplemented by organized work of many State agencies, a vigorous program was at length under way by mid-1943. It operated for about two and a half emergency years, until Federal funds ceased to be available in February 1946. . . .

In July 1942 a sum of $400,000 was granted to the Office of Education and the Children's Bureau from the President's emergency fund. . . . Grants totaling $163,143 were made to States, enabling them to employ specialized personnel to work with communities expanded by war industries to set up school programs for working mothers' children. At the same time grants were made to public welfare agencies in 28 States to set up day-care centers and other services for working mothers' children. . . . The program financed from the President's emergency fund was discontinued June 30, 1943, because of legal restrictions on use of this fund. . . .

In June 1941, Congress passed Public Law 137 (the Lanham Act) assigning responsibility to the Federal Works Agency "to provide for the acquisition and equipment of public works (community facilities) made necessary by the defense program." The language contained no specific provision that child-care facilities would come within the meaning of public works.

The liberalization of this law, sought by the Federal Works Agency, was granted in August 1942 by the Committee on Buildings and Grounds, whose members recognized the imperative need and specified that child-care centers were public works within the meaning of the act. . . . The number of child-care centers receiving financial assistance from the Federal Government varied from month to month. The first regular report, August 1943, showed 49,197 children enrolled in 1,726 centers operating with an average daily attendance of 36,923. Enrollments, attendance, and number of units in operation continued to increase, with few exceptions every month until the peak in July 1944, when 3,102 units were in operation servicing 129,357 children, with an average daily attendance of 109,202. About 60 percent of the children served throughout the program were of preschool age. . . .

It is difficult to establish the total number of different children cared for during the life of the Lanham Act program, since there was considerable turnover throughout the period as families moved from one area to another, changed employment, or withdrew their children from centers for various reasons. However, it has been estimated that roughly 550,000 to 600,000 different children received care at one time or another during the period of time Lanham Act funds were dispensed for these purposes. . . . After the war, the number of centers decreased gradually, then more rapidly. Federal funds finally were discontinued at the end of February 1946. Communities continued programs with local funds for periods varying in length. After the withdrawal of Federal funds, State funds were made available in California, New York, Washington, the District of Columbia, and to a limited extent in Massachusetts. Meanwhile, the Public Housing Administration had provided in many housing projects facilities for nursery schools and recreation centers, without charge for space in schools or other community agencies that would operate services. . . .

The increasing employment of women was accelerated after Korean hostilities began, and the subject of care of working mothers' children again came to the fore. The Defense Housing and Community Facilities and Services Act of September 1951 (Public Law 139, 82d Cong.) authorizes loans or grants to public or nonprofit agencies to provide community facilities or services, the definition including day-care centers. However, when funds were provided, the use of money for this purpose was specifically excluded. . . .

WORKERS' SERVICES

SHOPPING

To correct conditions such as Mrs. War Worker often faces, local industries are cooperating in many places to provide night shopping hours for industrial workers. In one case a grocery store, meat market, and barber and beauty shop have been established at the plant. At another factory the local department store brings out a display of articles for selection and order placement at the plant during the lunch and off hours. Banking services also are available at this plant on pay days for deposit of checks.

In many cities, stores are readjusting shopping hours for the benefit of war workers. Some stores are staying open one or two nights a week. Various other methods have been adopted in an effort to solve the problem.

Kathryn Blood. *Community Services for Women War Workers.* Washington, D.C.: U.S. Government Printing Office, February 1944 (Women's Bureau, No. 5).

In Philadelphia some butchers hold back part of their meat supply until 6 P.M. to accommodate housewives who must do their shopping late. St. Louis volunteers collect last-minute information on the "best buys" at stores and markets, and get it to the warplant workers before they leave their jobs, eliminating unnecessary shopping.

Several plants in New York and New Jersey have plans worked out by management and unions that are helping to solve the food problem. A representative from a grocery store comes to the plant every morning, takes food orders from the women workers, and brings the food at the end of the shift. A plant manufacturing electrical equipment has arranged with a local department store to open a branch in the plant. The items sold are selected to cover essentials, and a special extension service has been set up which will help workers solve their shopping problems without having to miss work.

When women war workers in the Niagara Frontier Area were not getting a fair shopping break, the Labor-Management Council decided to do something about it. Mrs. Stay-At-Home was buying up all the bargains; Mrs. War Worker found the stocks depleted. The council, composed of representatives of management, of the AFL, the CIO, and the International Association of Machinists from 28 war plants in this area, and representing more than 200,000 potential shoppers, sought the cooperation of the merchants in the Buffalo area. Merchants promised to keep back a certain part of their bargains until evening for women war workers.

In an attempt to ease the shopping problem for its thousands of employees who work in the Pentagon, world's largest office building, in Arlington, Va., just across the Potomac from Washington, the War Department has set up various shopping facilities within the building. Among the most popular of these services is a shoe-repair shop, which reports a flourishing business. Many hundreds of pairs of shoes a week are rejuvenated here. Employees may also order articles from the Washington stores through personal shoppers stationed in the building.

In four big war plants, the personnel workers accept lists of wanted articles culled from the advertisements in a nearby city's newspapers. Department-store representatives call at the plants with samples, from which the employees may order. Deliveries are made to the workers at the plants.

Even the most ideal shopping conditions, however, will not solve the food problem. Consider the case of Jean Smith, who is all too typical. She works in a west coast aircraft factory and likes her job. But she's not getting enough to eat. In order to make the 8 A.M. shift she must leave her home at 6 o'clock, which means that she very often eats no breakfast. (In another west coast plant it was found that of 293 workers interviewed 84 percent of the women factory workers were eating poor breakfasts and 40 percent of the men had insufficent breakfasts.) The company provides a good hot lunch, but dinner is a problem. Mrs. Smith, tired, hot, and dirty after a day in the plant, must either stand in line at some restaurant or shop for food when she finishes work. Then the chances are that the butcher and the grocer are out of nearly everything. As a result she is suffering from malnutrition.

It is for people like Mrs. Smith that a Detroit food company has begun a prepared-food service for carry-out orders in its 21 stores. The carry-out line thus far worked out includes such items as macaroni and cheese, spaghetti, chile con carne, codfish balls, chicken à la king, chicken pies, potato salad, and creamed spinach.

Mrs. Dorothy Roosevelt, specialist on women's problems in war industries for the War Production Board in the Detroit area, in urging that such a program be set up on a mass basis said, "Through such a set-up we figure we could save a woman three hours a day—a minimum for shopping and preparing and cooking food."

Since the early days of the war the Women's Bureau has recommended that community kitchens be established where women war workers might purchase hot, nutritious food at prices within the means of working people, which they could take home.

"British restaurants" are serving daily over ten million nourishing meals in some 2,000 restaurants and canteens. These meals are priced at about 23 cents. . . .

HOUSING

In recruiting women, one large firm told them among other things that there was a nice housing project near the plant. The recruiters failed to add that the nice housing project was already filled. Needless to say, such tactics worked havoc with the morale of the company's new employees. Fortunately for war production such false promises are rare.

Women looking for rooms face problems just as difficult, for all too often only men are wanted by the renters. Landladies report that women are "more bother," "more trouble around the house," "always under foot," "always using the one bathroom in the house to do personal laundry," "women want to wash and iron and cook, and they think the telephone is their private property."

In a small North Carolina town a survey showed that only six percent of the housing listed was available to women. . . .

In one city a Mrs. A. turned her small grocery store and most of her house, which is attached, into a dormitory and several large sleeping rooms. At first she had men roomers, but she changed to women roomers after a girl who was unable to find lodgings came to her one night and pleaded for a place to stay. She is now furnishing accommodations for industrial women who work at an airfield and the two shipyards. . . .

THE FEMININE MYSTIQUE

By THE LATE forties the women's journals were flooded with articles which examined the tensions between being a workingwoman and being a real woman (that is, mother and housewife).

Most but not all of this material was in the so-called women's magazines, aimed primarily at middle-class women, yet much of it found its way into the journals read by working-class women. In this article from *Good Housekeeping* a young woman describes her decision not to work. While *Good Housekeeping* was predominantly a magazine for the middle-class woman, it was also read by working-class women, especially those who moved to the suburbs and owned homes.

This article illustrates some of the tensions surrounding a woman's decision not to work and her ambivalence about the decision.

WHY I QUIT WORKING

Just over a year ago, I was suffering from that feeling of guilt and despondency familiar to most working mothers who have small children. During the hours I spent in the office, an accusing voice charged continuously, "You should be home with the children." I couldn't have agreed more, which only created an additional tension: the frustrated anger of one who knows what is right but sees no way of doing it. Children need clothes as well as attention; they must be nourished with food as well as love. . . .

One day in 1950, I finally worked out a compromise: a way to be at home with the children and still do some work for which I'd be paid. . . .

A year has passed, and I've had time to judge the advantages and

Jennifer Colton. "Why I Quit Working." *Good Housekeeping*, September 1951.

disadvantages of leaving my office job. How they will total up ten years from now, I don't know. But here is my balance sheet of the results to date.

LOST

The great alibi: work. My job, and the demands it made on me, were my always accepted excuses for everything and anything: for spoiled children, neglected husband, mediocre food; for being late, tired, pre-occupied, conversationally limited, bored, and boring.

The weekly check. And with that went many extravagances and self-indulgences. I no longer had the pleasure of giving showy gifts (the huge doll, the monogrammed pajamas) and the luxury of saying "My treat." . . .

The special camaraderie and the common language. The warm but impersonal and unprying relationship among working people is one of the most rewarding things about having a job. . . .

One pretty fallacy. For some reason, most working mothers seem to think they could retire with perfect ease; that they could readily adjust themselves to their new role. I don't think so. When you start to devote all your time to homemaking, you run into a whole *new* set of problems. The transition from part-time to full-time mother is difficult to make.

One baseless vanity. I realize now (and still blush over it) that during my working days I felt that my ability to earn was an additional flower in my wreath of accomplishments. Unconsciously—and sometimes consciously—I thought how nice it was for my husband to have a wife who could *also* bring in money. But one day I realized that my office job was only a substitution for the real job I'd been "hired" for: that of being purely a wife and mother.

The sense of personal achievement. A working woman is someone in her own right, doing work that disinterested parties consider valuable enough to pay for. The satisfactions of housekeeeping are many, but they are not quite the same.

The discipline of an office. The demands made on you by business are much easier to fulfill than the demands you make on yourself. Self-discipline is hard to achieve.

Praise for a good piece of work. No one can expect her husband to tell her how beautifully clean she keeps the house or how well she makes the beds. . . .

FOUND

A role. At first I found it hard to believe that being a woman is something in itself. . . . Later, when I understood the role better, it took on unexpected glamour. Though I still wince a little at the phrase "wife and mother," I feel quite sure that these words soon will sound as satisfying to me as "actress" or "buyer" or "secretary" or "president."

New friends and a wider conversational range. It was sad to drift apart from my office colleagues, but their hours and, alas, their interests were now different from mine. So I began to make friends with people whose problems, hours, and responsibilities were the same as mine. I gratefully record that my friendship with them is even deeper than it was with business associates. . . . As for conversation, I had been brought up on the satirical tales of the housewife who bored her husband with tiresome narratives about the grocer and the broken stove. Maybe it was true in those days. But not any more. I've had to exercise my mind to keep up with these new friends of mine. . . .

Normalcy. The psychiatrists say there is no such thing, but that's what it *feels* like. My relationship with my children is sounder, for instance. I have fewer illusions about them. I have found I can get bored with them. Exhausted by them. Irritated to the point of sharp words. At first I was shocked, and then I realized that when I worked and we had so little time together, we had all played our "Sunday best." . . . Now I'm not so interesting to them as I was. I'm not so attentive and full of fun, because I'm myself. I scold, I snap, I listen when I have time. I laugh, I praise, I read to them when I have time. In fact, I'm giving a pretty good representation of a human being, and as the children are going to spend most of their lives trying to get along with human beings, they might as well learn right now that people's behavior is variable.

The luxury of free time. This is one of the crown jewels of retirement. The morning or afternoon that occasionally stretches before me, happily blank, to be filled with a visit to a museum or a movie, a chat with a friend, an unscheduled visit to the zoo with the children, the production of the elaborate dish I'd always meant to try, or simply doing nothing, is a great boon.

Leisure. The pleasure of dawdling over a second cup of coffee in the morning can be understood only by those who have, sometime in their lives, gulped the first cup, seized gloves and bag, and rushed out of the house to go to work.

Handwork. This may seem trivial, but making things at home is one of the pleasures the businesswoman is usually deprived of. Homemade cookies, presents, dresses, parties, and relationships can be worth their weight in gold.

Intimacy. The discovery of unusual and unexpected facets in the imaginations of children, which rarely reveal themselves in brief, tense sessions, is very rewarding.

Improved Appearance. Shinier hair, nicer hands, better manicures, are the products of those chance twenty-minute free periods that turn up in the busiest days of women who don't go to business. . . .

Proof positive. If I hadn't retired, I would have remained forever in that thicket of self-delusion called thwarted potentials. It was almost too easy: the shrug, the brave little smile, and the words "Of course, I've always *wanted* to write (or paint or run for Congress), but since I'm *working*, I never have time." . . .

Relaxation. Slowly, I'm learning to forget the meaning of the word tension. While I was working, I was tense from the moment I woke up in the morning until I fell into bed at night. . . .

THE FEMININE mystique was a propaganda campaign aimed at women of all classes, purveyed by all the media. Furthermore, there was nothing subtle about it. It not only argued that women ought to stay home, but predicted failure if they ventured outside their appropriate sphere.

I DENIED MY SEX

From the first moment I can remember I wanted to be a boy. With three roughneck brothers, and a father who was football coach at the high school, I suppose it was natural. Besides, my mother had died in giving birth to me and, as a child, I shuddered at the whispered tales of her childbed agony. As I grew up, there was never any woman in our house to talk to, so I never learned to appreciate my own sex. . . .

"Don't call me a girl!" I'd scream. "I'm just as good as my brothers! Just as strong and tough!" . . .

So Dad began to pretend he had four sons—Michael, John, Harry,

"I Denied My Sex." *True Romance,* April 1954.

and "Al." He let me take all the bumps and bruises that came my way. . . .

One night at dinner Harry said to Dad, "I can lick any kid in this block except Al. And personally I think it's about time she began washing her face and doing girl-things."

"Oh, shut up!" I yelled. "I'll never do that sissy stuff!"

Mike and Johnny laughed, but Dad said thoughtfully, "Harry has a point. It won't be long now before you'll have to settle down and be a girl whether you like it or not." . . .

I listened with anger and resentment welling up inside of me. "It isn't fair!" I stormed finally. "I didn't ask to be a girl!" . . .

That summer Butch [a boyfriend] and I went to dances, or to the movies, or just sat in the old swing on our front porch talking. But there was no thought of love in my mind. Even after we started going steady. Everyone admired Butch and trusted him, and I was proud to be his girl—that was all.

Outwardly I was changing, though, becoming less and less of a tomboy and looking and acting more like a girl. I found myself trying hard to win nice compliments from Butch on my appearance. But inwardly, I hid my real feelings from myself. And then strange things kept happening between Butch and me.

There were those tennis games, for instance. I used to try so hard to beat him, and when I couldn't, it filled me with a fury Butch couldn't understand.

"But, honey," he'd say, "I should think you'd want me to win. After all, I'm the man in this outfit."

I'd turn on him almost hysterically. "I'm as good as any boy. I've beaten every other boy I've known at tennis."

Why I didn't know. I just *had* to. Butch might not like me if I couldn't keep up with him. Fear struck me.

It struck me again that first night he kissed me. When I felt his arms tighten around me and his lips searching for mine, my body responded with such fire and excitement that I was filled with terror. I pushed away from him furiously. "Don't!" I cried. "Don't ever do that again."

His face was white and angry. "Are you trying to make me feel like a heel just because I kiss my girl good night. What's the matter, Alice?"

"And don't call me Alice!"

"I *will* call you Alice. 'Al' is a boy's name." He turned and left me. I could hear the angry sound of his heels clicking against the pavement. . . .

Then after graduation Butch was called into the service and became an aviation pilot. He looked handsomer than ever in his Army Air Force uniform the few times I saw him on leave. I admired him, but secretly I was consumed with envy. Even when he was sent into the danger zone in Korea, and I knew I would spend years of anxiety and loneliness during his absence, I resented the adventures and opportunities for glory he'd have. . . .

I dreamed of being the first woman to climb Mount Everest, of breaking the men's speed record of flying, of being a champion on the Olympics pole vaulting team. But these were only dreams. I decided finally to be a newspaper reporter. I'd go dashing out to murders, fires, and exciting events.

Because the editor of the local newspaper was a friend of Dad's I got a job all right—pasting typed notices of sports events on a large wall calendar. I was never so bored.

Then Butch came home a Major! Covered with medals! The war was over! But not my private civil war! . . .

He seemed changed, older somehow, willing to settle down. Sometimes there was a sad, tired expression in his eyes as if he had seen too much, and never wanted to see anything more beyond our humdrum little town.

For the first time, I was disappointed in him. Besides, after our first joyful reunion, he had little time for me. I sat and kicked my heels while he spent evenings and Sundays making business calls and going to club meetings. I had sat out the war waiting for him, and now it was the insurance business!

"Every contact I make is important," he had to explain. "I'm not making much money now, but there's a chance to build a good, steady future. Just be patient. After all, in your little job you can work nine to five and forget it afterward. I can't."

My little job! Again that masculine superiority! All right, I decided, I was going to go out and get the toughest job in town! I'd show him.

An idea had been brewing in my mind for some time, and as soon as I was twenty-one, I acted on it. Without saying a word to anyone, I marched down to the Police Department and had a long conference with Captain Clarke, Director of the Policewoman's Bureau. . . .

I gave notice at the newspaper office and went through the preliminaries of physical examinations and signing papers at Police Head-quarters. Afraid there might be some slip-up, I kept it all a secret.

But at the most unexpected moment I had to reveal my plans. Butch had a free evening and we drove to the Look Out Point above Sylvan Lake and parked. It was one of those heavenly nights when the moon is clear and close and all the stars have a personal intimacy as if they're shining just for you.

Suddenly Butch pulled me to him with a little aching cry. He held me so tightly that I could hardly breathe. He kissed my eyes and my hair and finally my mouth. One strong gentle hand caressed me.

My first instinctive reaction was one of complete surrender. I wanted to be loved, to forget myself and be possessed by him.

And then, suddenly, something exploded in my mind. I was con-sumed by the same unreasoning terror I had experienced the first time he had kissed me with passion. I struggled away from him and he released me almost instantly.

"Darling, don't be frightened. We've known each other such a long time. I don't feel ashamed or guilty because I love you like this. I want to marry you as soon as possible. Why do you suppose I've been working so hard?"

"Marriage!" I blurted. "But I don't want to get married!"

He sat stiffly and stared at me as if he could not believe what he had heard. "But why not?"

"I've got a job to do. . . ."

"I'm going to be a policewoman!" I announced grandly.

"A—what?" He laughed. "Have you lost your mind? Do you have any idea what you're getting into?"

"Sure I have. It's a real he-man job. That's why I'm doing it." . . .

"So that's what's behind it. Competition again! Why do you always have to start the battle of the sexes? Couldn't we be a team with you doing your part and me doing mine?"

"By that I suppose you mean I should give up all my opportunities and get stuck in a tiny apartment cooking your cabbage and washing diapers while you spend all your spare time making good contacts," I jeered.

Butch lost his temper then.

"No!" He said furiously. "I don't expect *you* to do that, but I would expect my wife to."

"What do you mean by that?"

"I mean you'll have to make a choice. Either you want me, or a career as a policewoman. You can't have both."

"You're a selfish, domineering—*male!*" I cried. "You can have any kind of job you want, and still get married! Why can't I? It isn't fair!"

"I can't help that. Which do you choose? I'm ready to get married now and settle down."

"Well, I'm not! I'm going to be a policewoman!" I said angrily. All the years of suppressed resentment and anger at Butch for beating me at everything had finally come to a head. . . .

"Okay! This is it!" he said finally through clenched teeth as he started the car. He drove me home in icy silence. His profile in the moonlight was hard and unrelenting. . . .

I went into training as a policewoman. It was rugged. I spent long hours at the rifle range learning to shoot. I would have to carry a revolver in my handbag at all times, as a policewoman is on twenty-four hour duty. To be honest, the gun frightened me and I hoped I'd never have to use it. I took gymnastics and judo until I was almost muscle bound. I studied law and first aid. . . .

As a rookie, I was first assigned to direct traffic at a school crossing. . . . It was a busy corner, a shopping center where mothers parked baby carriages outside the stores while they bought groceries and gossiped.

And while I was worrying about an accident, a baby was kidnapped practically under my nose!

I didn't realize what had happened until the mother started screaming. I knew her by sight. I had often helped her cross the street with her baby carriage, packages, and two other small children. Skipper, the baby, was a blue-eyed boy with sandy hair who looked like Butch must have looked as a baby . . . showing the dimples in his fat cheeks and holding out his arms lovingly to strangers. Everyone adored him.

The police did not find Skipper. The newspapers published a story and his picture, offering a reward for any information about him. The story began: "In broad daylight at one of our busiest corners and under the very eyes of rookie Policewoman O'Hara, six-months-old Daniel, son of Mr. and Mrs. Howard Slocum, was snatched in one of the most daring kidnappings—"

It stung! I decided I would find Skipper if it took the rest of my life. . . .

"Was it terrible, having a baby?" I asked this particular time.

"Terrible?" she replied, as if trying to remember something from a dim past. "Oh, it was no picnic! I nearly died. But that's the price a mother pays for the privilege of having a baby. I think Nature must make mothers suffer so their children will be more precious to them. I'd take the pain again any time to have Skipper back. . . .

"Poor Howard, he's close to a breakdown," she sobbed, "but men can never know the closeness to babies that mothers do. Poor men! They miss so much."

"Poor *men!*" I exclaimed. "I always thought they were so lucky."

"Oh, they go around showing off their muscles and playing lord and master, but they can't have babies. I doubt if they would if they could. It takes real courage to have a baby. Fathers just become slaves working to support their wives and children."

"I never thought of it in that way," I said slowly, mulling her words over and over in my mind. . . .

[After much searching, Alice finally locates the couple who have kidnapped Skipper.]

"Skipper!" I cried out excitedly. "Where did you get him, Mrs. Gorell?"

"I don't know what you're talking about," she said, backing away from me. "His name is Bill, after my husband. He's our baby." . . .

As I moved toward the crib, she pounced on me with maniacal strength, a knife gleaming in her hand. I felt it slashing my left shoulder and arm again and again. I stared in horror at my gashed sweater which was rapidly turning crimson. As we struggled, Skipper cried louder and louder. The sound seemed to drive Mrs. Gorell into a frenzy. She kicked and stabbed wildly. But finally, with the help of my judo lessons I threw her to the floor where she lay limply.

In my pain I hardly knew what I was doing. There was only one thought in my mind—to get Skipper out of here and back to his mother. I picked him up with my good arm and started out of the room. The door was blocked by a burly man in shirt sleeves. . . .

"I'm a policewoman. You're—you're under arrest," I stammered weakly. It sounded ridiculous even to my ears.

The man actually laughed. "Put that baby down! You're not making any arrest, youngster." . . .

But Skipper put his arms around my neck and hid his face against me, crying. It did something to me. . . . Skipper, who went lovingly to any stranger, was afraid of this man and was clinging to me for protection!

My rigid limbs came to life. My bag suddenly sailed through the air and struck Mr. Gorell in the face. A shot rang out and I felt the hot singe of a bullet grazing my head, but the revolver clattered to the floor. As Mr. Gorell bent over, I tripped him expertly and sent him sprawling.

I ran, faster than I ever knew I could, zigzagging through the basement to the rear exit. I heard Mr. Gorell shouting and cursing at me, but somehow I found myself in the alleyway and then out in the street. Then I knew I couldn't go any farther. I was shaking violently all over and my knees were buckling. Skipper was slipping down out of my good arm. That's when I saw the two policemen hurrying toward me with an excited Sally showing them the way.

Thank God, I thought, a man! Someone to take charge and know what to do. I dumped the baby into the first officer's surprised arms just as blackness closed all around me.

When I came to, I was lying in a hospital bed. Harry and Dad were looking down at me, grinning with relief. My shoulder and arm were bandaged.

"What happened?" I asked. "Is the baby all right?"

"The baby's okay," Dad said.

"Did I conk out?" I asked.

"Yeah, just like a girl. When you should have been dragging in the kidnappers," Harry answered gruffly, "you fainted."

"I was wounded! Dying from loss of blood!"

"Just scratched! You took one look at your own blood and fainted." . . .

"You might have been killed!" Harry growled. "What do you carry a gun for, I'd like to know, if you're not going to use it to defend yourself? What do you think it is—a lipstick?" . . .

"All right, I bungled everything! So I'm not meant to be a tough cop," I sobbed. "I'm a girl and I don't care. I want Butch." . . .

My words tumbled over each other in my eagerness to explain to Butch. "Mrs. Slocum nearly died having Skipper and she was ready to do anything to get him back. And poor Mrs. Gorell would have murdered anyone to keep Skipper. Butch, you should have seen the tender expression in her eyes when she cuddled him. They weren't afraid. They were real women! But all this time I've been afraid. I resented being a girl. I fought against it—denied it. Why, it's a privilege!"

"I never *could* see what you had against being a girl," Butch admitted. "I always thought it must be pretty nice to let the men do the fighting and grubbing for you."

"I give up, Butch. I'm not tough enough to take it. I never want to see another fight!"

THE FEMININE REALITY

In 1944–1945 field agents of the Women's Bureau conducted a study of more than 13,000 women employed in ten war-manufacturing areas: Springfield and Holyoke, Massachusetts; Baltimore; Erie County (the Buffalo area); Dayton and Springfield, Ohio; Detroit; Willow Run, Michigan; Kenosha, Wisconsin; Wichita, Kansas; Mobile, Alabama; Seattle and Tacoma, Washington; and San Francisco and Oakland. Women from all industries and occupations, except household employees, were interviewed about their reasons for working, whether they wanted to continue to work after the war, their responsibility for family support, their personal characteristics, work histories and salaries. The following excerpt is from this study.

Most historians have implied that women left the work force without a whimper. The Union grievance files tell another story. For the most part, although women wanted to keep their wartime jobs, they expected to be laid off at the end of the war. What they did not expect, and what made them angry, was that they were not rehired in accordance with their seniority when the plant was reconverted to postwar production. Most of the grievances show that the unions, at least on the lower levels, collaborated to keep the women out of well-paid work, while at the top levels the unions remained noncommittal.

Besides filing individual grievances, women protested collectively. Several conferences were called by a wide range of organizations from the YWCA to ad hoc union committees and government agencies to discuss discrimination in reemployment. At the Ford Highland Park Motor Plant, for example, in December 1945, 200 women picketed over discriminatory practices.

In most of the cases, the local union voted to give women their back pay, but then failed to carry out the mandate.

POSTWAR PLANS
OF WOMEN WORKERS

That very large numbers of wartime women workers intend to work after the war is evidenced by their statements to interviewers. On the average, about 75 percent of the wartime-employed women in the 10 areas expected to be part of the postwar labor force. . . .

These prospective postwar women workers did not, for the most part, contemplate out-migration from their areas of wartime employment. Over 90 percent of them, in most areas, looked forward to continued employment after the war in the same areas where they had worked during the war period. . . .

In each area, the number of wartime-employed women who intended to work in the same area after the war greatly exceeded the number of women employed in the area in 1940. In the Detroit area, for example, for every 100 women who were working in 1940, excluding household employees, 155 women will want postwar jobs. About two and one-half times as many women wanted to continue working in the Mobile area as were employed in 1940. . . .

The highest percentage of prospective postwar workers in most areas came from the group of women who had been employed before Pearl Harbor, rather than from those who had been in school or engaged in their own housework at that time. On the average over four-fifths of the women who had been employed both before Pearl Harbor and in the war period intended to keep on working after the war. Among the war-employed women who had not been in the labor force the week before Pearl Harbor, over three-fourths of the former students expected to continue working, while over half of those formerly engaged in their own housework had such plans. . . .

Very large proportions of the in-migrant women workers planned to continue work in the areas where they had been employed during the war. Although in comparison to resident women employed in the war period smaller proportions of the in-migrants planned to remain in the labor force, the bulk of the in-migrants who did expect to work wanted to do so in the same area where they had been employed during the war. Consequently in the areas where in-migrants were important dur-

Women Workers in Ten War Production Areas and Their Postwar Employment Plans. Washington, D.C.: U.S. Government Printing Office, 1946 (Women's Bureau, Bulletin 209).

ing the war, they also constituted a substantial proportion of the women who intended to work in the area after the war. In four of the seven areas where in-migrants were important, in-migrants constituted between 32 and 44 percent of the total group of women who planned to continue work; and in the other three areas where in-migrants were important, they represented between 10 and 26 percent of the women who planned to continue.

The nature of postwar employment problems is influenced not only by the number of wartime workers who expect to remain in the labor force but also by their expressed desires for work in particular industries and occupations. Postwar job openings as cafeteria bus girls, for example, are not apt to prove attractive to women who are seeking work as screw-machine operators.

The bulk of the prospective postwar workers interviewed in this survey, or 86 percent, wanted their postwar jobs in the same industrial group as their wartime employment, and about the same proportion wanted to remain in the same occupational group. Postwar shifts to other industries were contemplated on a somewhat larger scale, however, among the wartime employees in restaurants, cafeterias, and similar establishments, as well as in the personal service industries in certain areas. In the Dayton area, for example, among the war-employed women who expected to remain in the labor force, fully 36 percent of those in eating and drinking places and 30 percent of those in personal service industries said they wanted jobs in other industries after the war. . . .

In the Mobile area almost a third of the women employed in the war period were Negro. In four other areas between 10 and 19 percent, inclusive, were non-white (including some oriental in San Francisco). In the remaining five areas less than 10 percent of the war-employed women were Negro or of other non-white races.

In each of the nine areas where there were enough non-white employed women in the war period to make comparison valid, a much higher proportion of the Negro women planned to continue work than of the white women. In six areas 94 percent or more of the Negro or other non-white women who were employed in the war period planned to continue after the war. . . .

Responsibility for the support of themselves or themselves and others was the outstanding reason given by war-employed women for planning to continue work after the war. As already pointed out, about three-fourths of the wartime-employed women in the 10 areas (excluding household employees) planned to keep on working after the war.

Fully 84 percent of them had no other alternative, as this was the proportion among them who based their decision on their need to support themselves and often, other persons as well. Eight percent offered special reasons for continuing at work, such as buying a home or sending children to school; and only 8 percent reported they would remain in the labor force because they liked working, or liked having their own money.

Virtually all of the single women and of those who were widowed or divorced (96 and 98 percent, respectively) who intended to remain in gainful employment after the war stated they would do so in order to support themselves or themselves and others, whereas 57 percent of the married wartime workers who expected to remain at work gave this reason. The remaining married prospective postwar workers interviewed offered reasons of the special purpose type, such as buying a home, about as often as those of the "like-to-work" type. Because married women differed so much on this issue from women in other marital-status groups, differences from area to area in the proportions of prospective postwar workers who offered each of the three sets of reasons reflect largely the relative concentration of married women in each area. . . .

That the need to work is just as pressing among some married women as among some single women was highlighted by the replies from the war-employed women on the number of wage earners in the family group. Out of every 100 married women who were living in family groups of two or more persons, 11 said they were the only wage earner supporting the family group. This was almost identical to the proportion of sole supporting wage earners among single women living with their families. The state of marriage, therefore, does not, in itself, always mean there is a male provider for the family. . . .

ECONOMIC CONDITIONS on the island of Puerto Rico produced a large migration to the U.S. mainland in this period. In 1945 air service between San Juan and New York City replaced the four-day boat trip, making the migration easier, and between 1950 and 1960 the number of Puerto Ricans in the states tripled. But conditions in the States were not easy for Puerto Ricans either, and there was also a large return migration to the island. Meanwhile, new forms of exploitation of Puerto Rico by U.S. capital have intensified the pace of industrialization there. This process has greatly affected Puerto Rican women, in some ways deepening their class oppression but in other ways stimulating their rebellion against traditional patriarchal oppression.

PUERTO RICAN WOMEN

Industrialization and economic growth in Puerto Rico . . . resulted in increasing participation of women in the labor force. In 1970, women constituted 27.1% of the total labor force, up from 22% in 1962, an increase due totally to non-agricultural employment. This difference would appear to be due to the fact that, at least in this early phase of industrialization in Puerto Rico, which emphasized light manufacturing, women were employed at a rate nearly equal to men. Thus, in 1970, women constituted 48.6% or nearly half of the labor force in manufacturing. They also constituted 44.8% of the persons employed in public administration, and 47.2% of those in service jobs, two other fast-growing employment sectors.

Women provided a cheap labor force for the start of industrialization in Puerto Rico. In the industries established through the Office of Economic Development, the salary differential was as high as 30.3% in industries where women predominated as compared to those employing mostly men. This reflected the fact that women were concentrated in the manufacture of nondurable consumer goods such as textiles, clothing, leather goods, and tobacco, where pay is considerably lower than in durable goods such as metal, stone, or glass products, where men predominate. The average salary for all women working full-time in 1970 was $3,006, compared to $3,382 for men. However, women were also concentrated in the lower-paid jobs, with 42.2% receiving less than $2,000 a year (compared to 26.7% of the men).

The recent concentration upon heavy capital-intensive industry in Puerto Rico as well as in other developing areas also threatens female employment. In these capital-intensive industries, labor tends to be reduced to a minimum and to be highly skilled, favoring the creation of a labor aristocracy in which men predominate. . . .

In the survey conducted in 1959 in Los Peloteros, a shantytown in the heart of the San Juan Metropolitan Area, 22% of the women were currently employed, while an additional 45% had been previously

Helen Icken Safa. "Class Consciousness Among Working Class Women in Latin America: A Case Study in Puerto Rico," *Politics and Society*, Vol. 5, No. 3, 1975, pp. 381–85, 387, 389–90, 392–93.

employed. Thus, the great majority of women in the shantytown have worked at some point in their lives, which completely contradicts the Latin American ideal of *la mujer en su casa* (the woman in her home). . . .

Paulita, now a young mother of seven children, recalls how she came to San Juan as a child together with her mother, two sisters, and a brother. Her mother worked as a domestic and only one child could live with her; the others lived in foster homes. Speaking of the difficulties women faced at that time, Paulita notes:

". . . At that time women who had a problem, who had left their husbands, the majority became prostitutes (paganas), right? Because they had no choice. If they were very young, they didn't want them working in families because they fell in love with the husband. And since they couldn't find work, those women went to sin because they didn't have any schooling . . ."

Many women in Los Peloteros continued to work as domestic servants, or in other service occupations, while the more fortunate were employed in factories, considered the most desirable occupations. The salary differential is substantial, with factory workers in 1970 earning an average annual income of $2,571 compared to $874 for domestic servants. In addition, domestic service is considered very demeaning, and places the woman in a completely dependent patron-client relationship, in which it is difficult to develop any class consciousness or collective solidarity. The domestic servant is one of the chief instruments by which elite women maintain their privileged status in capitalist society. She is as isolated as the housewife and more exploited. . . .

Flor gained much of her drive and initiative from her mother, who managed to raise a family of eight children on the sale of *cañita* or illegal rum. Flor's father was a chronic alcoholic who often beat his wife and children, and even turned his wife into the police out of sheer resentment over her economic independence. Even when he worked, most of his salary went for drink for himself and his friends.

Women . . . who cannot rely on a husband to support them are often forced to become the principal breadwinners for their family. In 1970, 47.6% of divorced women worked, compared to 22% of married women living with their husbands. Men who are separated from their wives cannot be relied upon for child support, and often migrate to the mainland to avoid family responsibilities. . . .

The growing number of female-based households among the working class in Latin America is an extremely important development for the formation of class consciousness among women. Women who are heads of households are more prone to develop a stronger commitment to their work role because they become the principal breadwinners for the family. They cannot afford to regard their work roles as temporary or secondary, as do most of the married women in the shantytown. This lack of commitment to a work role plays a crucial role in the absence of class consciousness among women in the shantytown, since women never identify with their work role, nor stay on one job long enough to develop a relationship with their peers. Thus, in the survey conducted in 1959, the great majority of women in the shantytown who had worked never saw their fellow employees after work, nor participated in union activities. The reason is clear: women must rush home after work to care for children and other household chores, whereas men are free to join their friends, and, as the survey demonstrated, often meet their best friends through work. Women in the shantytown tend to work sporadically, as the need arises, for which such menial occupations as domestic service and other service jobs are ideally suited. . . .

Economic instability is the most frequent cause of marital breakdown. There is no strong conjugal bond in the shantytown household to hold a man and wife together in the face of economic adversity. There is no investment in property, no status position to uphold, no deep emotional tie. The younger generation of women are less likely to accept the abuse their mothers stood for, including beatings, infidelity, and lack of financial support. Flor, Raquel's daughter, recalls how her father used to enter their house in the middle of the night in a drunken rage and begin to beat them all and chase them from the house. She said she would not stand for the same behavior from her husband: "En absoluto y si me pega yo no lo voy a soportar ni que me pege ni una sola vez. Aquí en esta época tantas formas que hay de resolver los problemas, que no me ponga ni un dedito encima." (Absolutely, and if he hits me, I won't stand for it, not even once. Here at this time there are so many ways of solving problems, that he doesn't lay a finger on me.) The younger generation of working class women clearly feel they have greater legal support and protection from male abuse. Nearly all our respondents, male and female, felt that women today enjoy more freedom and independence than previously.

Nevertheless, the abuse suffered by many women at the hands of their husbands makes them feel far more oppressed by men and marriage than by their class position. Nearly three-fourths of the women interviewed in 1959 felt that most marriages are unhappy, and blamed this largely on the man and his vices. . . .

There is also extensive mutual aid among families in the shantytown, particularly the women. They borrow from each other, including not only cups of sugar or electric irons, but even water and electricity or the use of a refrigerator. They also share in child-rearing. In the evening, children may gather in a neighbor's house to watch television. If they are hungry, they are fed. Neighbors will rush to comfort crying children, or try to entice them out of a temper tantrum with a bright new penny or a *lindbergh* (flavored ice cube). At the same time, they do not hesitate to scold a naughty child or ask a neighbor's child to run an errand for them. In this way, shantytown families avoid the intense and often strained relationships of the isolated nuclear family, where the woman has none of these sources of aid or friendship. In this sense the domestic role of the woman in the Puerto Rican shantytown is less isolating or alienating than that of the middle-class housewife. It may also be less tedious and exploitative than the occupational role of many shantytown men. . . .

The nature of family and interpersonal relationships in the shantytown can be compared to those in public housing, a planned community created by the government to house the urban poor. In public housing, the cohesion, built up over many years in the shantytown, breaks down; mutual aid is weakened and families become more suspicious of each other. Housing management begins to intervene in the internal affairs of the family, checking on income, furnishings, household composition, and other private matters, and the family no longer provides the refuge it could in the shantytown. The public housing family is alienated, not only because of their low socioeconomic status, which they share with the shantytown, but because family and community life has been disrupted by the agencies of the state. Public and private domains are blurred as the government begins to control the personal lives of public housing residents. . . .

According to Pico, working class women did demonstrate greater class consciousness in the earlier stages of industrialization in Puerto Rico. Pico has shown how prior to 1930, working class women, employed chiefly in tobacco, home needlework, canning, and other early manufacturing industries, were active in the union movement as well as the Socialist Party. The relative decline of these industries and the resulting dispersion of the female labor force into service as well as other marginal jobs apparently helped deflect this growth in class consciousness, as did the demise and eventual incorporation of the Socialist Party into the reformist Popular Party. The leadership of the women's movement was then taken over by petit bourgeois women, who found a growing source of employment in public education, and who were chiefly interested in legal and social equality, i.e., woman's suffrage and more education for women. . . .

The primary obstacles of the development of class consciousness among working class women in Latin America lie in the strict sexual division of labor, at home and on the job, their subordination within a patriarchal family structure, and their restriction to the private sphere of domestic labor. No simple solution will eradicate all of these obstacles. Rather, any attempt to develop class consciousness among working class women must attack all three areas where women are subordinate: work, the family, and the community. It must not only promote entry of women into the labor force, but end the sexual division of labor, which keeps women in poorly paid, low status jobs, and forces them to take on the dual burden of domestic responsibilities and employment. It must make men share in household responsibilities and socialize housework by creating public institutions which lighten the domestic role, such as free day care centers, laundromats, and communal eating places, with "take-home" foods. It must also encourage women to take a greater role in community affairs, on barrio committees and in political parties, so that their needs and interests as women will also be represented. . . .

By 1955 the expansion of the number of mothers of young children working began to attract the attention of social scientists, politicians, newspaper commentators and the general public. Vocal spokespeople argued that it was a dangerous trend and that pressure should be applied to force women back into their homes. One of the lynchpins in the argument against the working mothers was that if the mother worked, her children would become juvenile delinquents.

In this selection, from *The Militant*, newspaper of the Socialist Workers party, Joyce Cowley comments on "evidence" used against women. Her stories were printed in both Left newspapers and women's magazines. Cowley has been a trade unionist for over forty years, working as a waitress, textile worker, shoe worker, machinist and clerk, consistently concerned with workingwomen. She is now in her sixties and, under the name Joyce Maupin, active in a Berkeley, California, organization of trade-union women called Union WAGE (Women's Alliance to Gain Equality).

WORKING MOTHERS
AND DELINQUENCY

Ex-President Truman has a cure for juvenile delinquency. He's joined the judges and politicians and police officials who, with monotonous regularity, tell mothers to stay at home.

Several working mothers interviewed by the *New York Post* said they would be glad to stay home if someone would take care of their bills. . . .

Statistics don't back up . . . attacks on working mothers. . . . A recent article in *McCall's*, "Is A Working Mother a Threat to the Home?" tells about a study of 20,000 Detroit delinquents made over a period of eight years by social scientists at Wayne University in co-operation with the Detroit Police Dept.

This study indicates that children of working mothers have a delinquency rate 10% lower than that of children whose mothers stayed at home.

"Delinquency," *McCall's* explains, "is most prevalent in very low-income families . . . if the woman in such a situation has enough gumption and self-respect to go out to work—on top of her regular housework—it means she is still struggling. Her children have something to cling to. There is some hope in their lives. 'There are plenty of things that are worse for children,' says Judge Polier of the N.Y. Children's Court, 'than finding mother at work when you come home from school. Perhaps the worst is finding her resigned to hopelessness.' " . . .

The real question for the experts is: "Why are so many of our children not delinquent?"

I'm glad a great many young people have the physical and emotional fortitude to overcome what look like insurmountable difficulties, but instead of just wondering how they do it, I think we should give them some help. . . .

Of course, a police chief may urge that we get more cops but there is a possibility of self-interest involved here. You don't hear much from these people about over-crowded schools, slum clearance, playgrounds, clinics or guidance bureaus in the schools.

Right now in New York City there are 100 vacancies in the Bureau

Joyce Cowley. "Working Mothers and Delinquency." *The Militant*, September 12, 1955.

of Attendance which attempts to handle truancy problems and might be of some help in the earliest stages of delinquency. Salaries are so low that no one applies for the jobs.

The Bureau asked if a small increase in funds could be included in the new city budget. Of course, their request was brushed aside but I don't remember any judge or police official denouncing the Board of Estimate. A working mother, struggling to provide for her children, is a much easier target.

There is one thing wrong with this mother. She's working alone, and it will take the combined efforts of all parents to bring a real change in the conditions in which our young people grow up. The first step parents should take is to turn the heat on these politicians who are really responsible for the present mess and who condemn "working mothers" and "bad parents" so they won't have to admit their own failure and guilt.

BEGINNING IN the late nineteenth century, the American textile industry moved southward seeking a cheaper, nonunionized labor force. Runaway shops, plants closing in the North and reopening with nonunion labor in a Southern state, were common. Thus the bargaining position of the textile workers was constantly being threatened and undermined.

By 1950 the Southern textile industry had expanded to over 600,000 workers in nearly 2,250 mills, nearly 85 percent of whom were unorganized. In 1946, 1947 and 1948 the A.F.L. and the C.I.O. launched organizing drives in the South in the textile, chemical, oil and lumber industries. Over $1 million and 100 organizers were poured into the campaign, which nevertheless failed due to employers' violence and intimidation and legal harassment through use of the Taft-Hartley Act of 1947.

Because of the violence of the union struggles in the South, the U.S. Senate began investigation in 1950 on labor relations in Southern textiles.

THE KIDNAPPING OF
A C.I.O. ORGANIZER

Statement of Mrs. Edna Martin Concerning Her Abduction From Mrs. Pounds' Rooming House in Tallapoosa, Ga., on Monday, November 17, 1947

My name is Edna Martin and my home is in Athens, Ga. I was born in Madison County, Ga., and have lived in the State all my life. I am a widow and have raised six children. My oldest son was in the Army for 4 years, fighting in Italy and Africa.

I have worked in cotton mills all my life and have been a member of the Textile Workers Union of America, CIO, for 4 years.

Because I know what the union can do for cotton-mill people, I have been putting in all the time I could in the last 3 months as a volunteer CIO organizer.

One of the places I have been helping on has been the American Thread Mill at Tallapoosa. Kenneth Douty, State director of the union, assigned one of the organizers to Tallapoosa after a list of workers there who were interested in a union was sent in to the Atlanta office. There are about 300 workers in the mill and about half of them were on this list.

I have been going into Tallapoosa about 2 days a week for the last 2 months with one of the organizers, working especially with the women workers. I would return to Atlanta at night. . . .

I decided that if I could spend at least a week in there, full time, we could really help the people get their union started. . . .

One of the union members at the mill found a room for me in the rooming house of Mrs. George Pounds, 73 Meadow Street. I moved into this house on November 17 at noon. I paid Mrs. Pounds a week's rent in advance and told her that I was a CIO representative. . . .

While I was taking my things into the room, Mr. McGill, American Thread Mill superintendent, drove by the house, went down to the corner of the block, turned around and came back the second time, and eyed me very closely. . . .

U.S. Congress, Senate. Committee on Labor and Public Welfare. *Labor Management Relations in the Southern Textile Manufacturing Industry. Hearings before the Subcommittee on Labor-Management Relations of the Committee on Labor and Public Welfare*, 81st Cong., 2nd Sess., August 21, 22, 23 and 24, 1950.

After lunch I came back to my room and went to Mrs. Pounds' room and asked her if she would telephone and ask someone to send me some coal.

There were two ladies in Mrs. Pounds' living room. She introduced them to me as Mrs. H. O. McGill, wife of the American Thread Co. superintendent, and Mrs. Grimes, wife of the overseer of the card room. Mrs. Grimes and Mrs. Pounds were making a patchwork quilt and I sat down with them in Mrs. Pounds' living room and helped them quilt for a little while.

Soon after I joined these women Mrs. McGill left. Just before she left Mrs. Pounds took Mrs. McGill back into the kitchen. I imagine they were gone about 10 minutes, leaving Mrs. Grimes and me in the living room. Mrs. McGill went away from the back of the house and I did not see her again. . . .

At 4 o'clock I left my needle and thimble on the quilt and went down to Cliff's place to meet a group of our union people, because I had an appointment with them there.

When I went out the door to go down to Cliff's, there was a 1939 Ford sitting down below the house, and it turned around when I walked out on the porch, and when I got on the sidewalk it passed on. I walked on about half a block and the car passed me again. A man was driving the car. He went down about half a block and turned and came back and passed me the third time right at Cliff's place where I was supposed to meet the people.

The people were there, sitting outside Cliff's in a car, waiting for me. I walked up to them and said: "This car has been following me, do you know the man who is driving it?" One of them said "Yes, it is Mr. Davis, he is a deacon of the Baptist Church here in Tallapoosa, and Mr. McGill is a member of this same church." That was Mr. McGill, the thread plant superintendent.

I got in the car with this group of people and we visited all over the mill village. I guess we stopped at 8 or 10 houses, and I went in all of them, except one, and all were very friendly but that one. At this house, which was a Mr. Davis' home, the people were very cold and did not ask me in. They said they were not interested in unions and did not think they could better themselves by signing a union card.

After this last visit, the people I was with drove me back to the rooming house. I still did not have any coal to make a fire in my room and the people I was with went to their home and brought me some coal and kindling.

When I got in my room and looked around, it was approximately 8 o'clock and it was dark and I was by myself and wanted to fasten my room up. It was on the first floor (it was a one-story house). . . .

In my room there were four big, long windows that opened clear down to the veranda. . . .

There were no locks of any description on those windows. There were marks where locks had been, but there were no locks on the windows that night. I tried all four of them, and they opened very smoothly, a shove would push them all the way up.

There were no shades to pull down over the windows. There were little cheese cloth curtains that anybody on the porch could see through and see over. I had no privacy in my room at all.

There was no lock on my door, and Mrs. Pound had not at any time offered me a key or any means of locking my door.

After I had examined my room to see if I could fasten the door and windows, I took a pitcher that was on the washstand and went down to the back porch to the bathroom to get water. The bathroom had another door that opened into the kitchen. That door was open and Mrs. Pounds was in the kitchen cooking and Mrs. Grimes was still sitting in the room. I saw her when I walked to the kitchen door and asked Mrs. Pound for a glass to drink out of.

Mrs. Pounds said in a very unfriendly voice: "There is a hydrant in the front yard where you are supposed to get water." Then I asked her about the water she had promised me earlier in the day that she would heat for me to take a bath. She made no reply at all, just turned back into the kitchen.

I carried the pitcher of water back to my room and poured half of it in an old wash pan that was sitting in my room and put it on the heater to heat it for a bath. I had paid Mrs. Pounds 50 cents extra to heat water for me.

I began to wonder how I was going to take a bath in this room with no way to keep people from seeing through the windows. When the water got hot I put the light out and took a bath in the dark. The floor was so dirty I took towels from my suitcase and spread them on the floor. I then put on my gown, turned the light back on and sat down in a chair to read a *Saturday Evening Post*.

While sitting in that chair I had a sensation of being watched. I felt like there were eyes watching my every move. There was a big old timey wardrobe in the corner of the room—my clothes were hanging in this wardrobe. I got up and opened both those wardrobe doors and pulled my chair back in between those doors and sat there and read maybe 30 minutes.

Then I got up and got a notebook and made some notes of the happenings during the day, and wrote a card to my baby in Athens, and laid these on a table. I put this table against the door, because it did not have any lock.

Over by the front window I set one of the chairs, and at another window I put the only other chair in the room. At the third window I set the pan of water I had bathed in. The fourth window, at the foot of my bed, I did not have anything to put by it at all. I turned out the light and went to bed about 9. . . .

About midnight there was a knock on my door and a woman's voice called out: "Mrs. Martin," and I answered. She said: "I would like to talk to you." I got out of bed, turned on my flashlight and turned on the light in the middle of the room.

I said to the woman: "Are you by yourself?" She said: "No, I am not." I asked her: "Who are you?" and she did not answer. Then I said, "Well, you will have to excuse me." At this time, while I was talking to the women outside the door, four men came in at the windows as I was facing the door expecting somebody to turn the knob and come in, as there was no lock on the door.

One of the men crossed the room and opened the door and pushed the table in front of it back, and five women came in—three of them came on in the room and the other two stood in the door.

Each of the four men had a long shotgun. I remember I was looking in the hole in a single-barrel gun as it was pointed at me. At this moment I said: "I would like to put on a dress." The man who seemed to be leader of the mob said: "You don't need no God damn dress where you are going." . . .

Then an outspoken woman in the mob began talking. She said: "Mrs. Martin, you represent the CIO." I said "Yes." She said: "Well, we don't want no God damn CIO here, and we don't want no CIO representatives here." She said: "In fact we are not going to have a union here and you have got to leave."

I said: "It is your privilege if you don't want a union, but I am not going anywhere. My son went across the water to fight for freedom that I go where I want and stay where I please. I am not going to bother you."

The woman said: "Well you are not going to stay here in Talla-poosa." I said: "Well, if you want me to leave why don't you give me a fighting chance and go get a policeman and tell him I say come down here and carry me to Atlanta. I have no way out of here except walking."

Then the old man who was the mob leader said: "We are not bringing the God damn law in this—we are the law here." Then he said: "Where is that CIO man?" I said: "I don't know." He said: "Didn't a CIO man bring you here?" I said: "Yes." He said: "Where is he now?" I said: "Gone back to Atlanta." He said: "Are you sure he has gone back to Atlanta or Cedartown?" I said: "I don't know."

The old man asked me, "What is the man's name?" I said I did not know. He said: "You mean to tell me you don't know the name of the man that brought you out here?" I said: "I don't know." He said: "Lady, where are you from?" I said: "I am not from this part of the country." He said: "We are going to take you across the Alabama line." I said: "You might as well take me that way as any way because you will not carry me toward my home anyway you take me."

Just about this time the old man said: "Ain't you that damn CIO woman that was in Bremen about 3 weeks ago?" The outspoken woman said: "No, she ain't. I thought she was at first, she is about her size." The old man said: "It is a good thing you are not that damn CIO woman, or a man, or you would not even take a ride from here."

About this time the old man said: "There has been enough damn arguing. Go get the hemp rope from the truck." A man in the mob who had a crooked mouth went and got the rope. . . .

I asked them again to let me put on my dress; I did not have on anything but my gown, and the old man turned around and said: "Put on her God damn dress." I asked the men to get out while I put on my dress and they refused to get out. The woman put my dress on before all those that were present. I did not have on any underclothes.

Then one of the men tied my hands in front of me with the rope. . . .

As we left the room one of the men stuffed a piece of cloth in my mouth. I took it to be a man's dirty handkerchief. It made me gag and nauseated me.

All the time the argument in my room was going on, Mrs. Pound's living-room door was open and the light was on. As they took me out the outspoken woman said: "Thank you, Mrs. Pound." . . .

They took me out to the truck and pulled me into the back. It was an old truck with a built-on body of wood which brought the sides up to shoulder height. They kept the lights off when they started and the truck did not turn around. I don't know which way we went out of Tallapoosa. The whole mob went along, with most of them in back with me. One of the women was half sitting on me.

Before we left the room the people went through all my things and then pitched them together, carried them out and put them in the back of the truck. They threw my shoes in the truck, too, and I went out barefoot. They pulled me up into the truck. I was half lying down and could not see anything.

They did not turn on the truck's light and it was very dark. I don't know how they went out of Tallapoosa, but they did go in such a direction they did not hit a street light. I could have seen that, or the light from it. They went out on a dirt road. I don't know when and how they hit the highway. I didn't know where I was—I only knew they told me they were going to take me across the Alabama line. After while they put on the lights.

After we had gone a considerable time, and I know at a very fast rate, the lights were turned off and the truck turned into another road or a field—the place was rough and it was very dark.

I thought my time had come then. The truck stopped and a man in the back part where I was went to the driver and talked with him. I don't know what was said because I could not hear them and no one made any comment after the man got back in the truck.

Still without the light on the truck they turned back to the road. Then they put their lights on and rode what seemed a long time. I was very cold, in fact shaking all over with cold. I had nothing on but my dress and my coat thrown around me, no underclothes and barefoot.

Once I saw lights and that could have been a town; I don't know. The truck made a great many turns and I don't know in which direction we were going at any time. Part of the time I know we were on dirt roads.

After a considerable time they turned the lights off and made a very sharp turn. It seemed it was about 2 miles they drove down a dirt road, because I had to walk back over that same road.

When they stopped on that dirt road the driver, who was the watery-eyed old man, said: "This is about as good a place as any." Then I was pulled out of the truck and my things pitched out, including my radio. . . .

The truck started rolling and the man on the road had to run after it. Before he left he said: "Don't come back to Tallapoosa or you will be shot on sight." . . .

THE DAY-TO-DAY work of a labor organizer in the middle of an organizing drive is exhausting, slow and agonizing. In this selection, Sophie Stupek, an organizer for the American Federation of Hosiery Workers, an affiliate of the Textile Workers Union, reports to the union headquarters in New York about her progress in North Carolina. Her reports reveal not only her own work, but also the obstacles created by management and by divisions among the workers.

A THANKLESS JOB: UNION ORGANIZER

January 10, 1948. . . . I have made about 23 calls and 16 contacts the past week. . . . 14 were new contacts . . . all women except one knitter, only two were for the union and stated they would vote for it. This situation differs little from any I have worked on. . . . Claiming the company is very good to them. . . . Also that they are running the risk of this company moving their machines out of town, and although most of them have a farm which they tell me they can make a living out of, it is nice to have this extra money. . . .

January 19, 1948. . . . They [workers at the Wadesboro full-fashioned plant] are very scared and were not telling anyone how they would vote. The fear among all of these people is the worst thing about this situation. . . .

January 26, 1948. . . . One of the girls, Millie Burch, who is again at the union was called in to management's office a couple of times this week, latter tried to find out from the girls how they were going to vote. . . .

February 15, 1948. . . . The men have been keeping very much in the background not coming out to the meetings and by their attitude and remarks, they seem to be only interested in a knitters' unit. This is not very encouraging for the women. . . .

February 22, 1948. . . . In the third week here on the Mojud drive this is the 1st week it appeared like things are beginning to take shape. I have recontacted active people from all departments. . . . They have all taken cards and promised to help sign others. There is still some bitterness in one or two of the departments between the nonstrikers and those who were out.

    Papers of American Federation of Hosiery Workers, Organizers' Reports, Series 5, Wisconsin State Historical Society, Madison, Wisconsin (Reports and letters of Sophie Stupek to American Federation of Hosiery Workers, 1948).

February 28, 1948. . . . In contacting some women outside of the very active group but former members. . . . Some felt there is still too much bitterness between the two groups. . . . Some seamers and most throwing department girls said they would not even attend meetings until we could assure them that the knitters are really backing them, since they did not stick through the entire strike as well as the women. . . .

March 7, 1948. . . . I was also blessed out by the husband of Racheal Edwards who has married this fellow since the strike, he works in the shipping department at Mojud she is a seamer who was quite active during the strike but now said she could not join the union ever again.

March 13, 1948. . . . The company of course has been tightening up more in the departments where the women are than in the knitting department. . . .

March 20, 1948. . . . The women at the Mojud shop appear to be gaining more confidence each week and I am fairly sure will be ready to do a job when the knitters get started. Contacted a couple of knitters this week, they told me they are waiting for a proper break and feel it may not be too long in coming. . . . For that reason have not been pushing the girls too hard in getting cards signed. . . .

April 3, 1948. . . . Talked to Floyd Pegg, a knitter at Mojud who- . . . was put on 20 denier from 15 denier . . . which resulted in a cut in earnings, and made the knitters very dissatisfied. . . . The company is also putting in a new system in the examining department to take the shine out of the stockings and the girls are complaining that this will be an added operation for the inspectors without any extra in rates. . . .

April 10, 1948. . . . The forelady passed a notice around to all the girls telling them that they could only go to the washroom three times a day, and that if any of them found it necessary to visit the washroom more than three times a day they would have to ask her permission. This of course caused quite a disturbance among the girls. . . .

April 24, 1948. . . . In High Point. . . . Almost every one of the loopers I talked to work 8 hours in one mill and 4 hours in another mill. . . . On Friday distributed leaflets at the Mojud shop in Greensboro in the afternoon and night shift. I would say about one-third were thrown on the ground. The company officials were standing in the windows almost the entire time we were distributing. . . .

May 8, 1948. . . . A feeling of uncertainty prevails among most of the people in High Point due to the short time operations in almost all the mills. . . .

June 5, 1948. . . . The increase that was given to the people at the Pilot shop immediately following the last drive certainly changed the attitude of the majority of the people towards the union. It was especially evident in revisiting a couple of girls that appeared favorable in past drives, although admitting that no doubt our drives were responsible for them getting increases, one girl said: "We got the increase so I don't see any need for the union now." . . .

June 27, 1948. . . . On Saturday with the help of Matilda Pageant [in locating workers' homes]. . . . We called on seven people and contacted four. . . . It appears like the women don't like the treatment used in trying to get them re-signed. None of them said they would not re-sign. . . .

August 7, 1948. . . . Contacted the women working at the Francis-Louise the past week. . . . All of those who are signed that I talked to are very strong for the union. . . . They said they thought we had forgotten them since no one has been down to see them and they heard nothing mentioned about the union lately. . . . I then talked to this group about coming out to the meetings on Saturday or arrange-ing a meeting for the girls during the week. Most of them are married and if they don't work in the mill on Saturday they have house cleaning washing etc., and when I visit them they have a dozen things to do and can only talk to me for a short time. They were very receptive to the idea of a meeting of girls . . . almost all agreed on Thursday. . . . The Francis-Louise women who now are pulling the strongest for the union voted against it the last election. The company made all sorts of promises to the girls about the wonders they were going to do for them if they turned the union down. Not one of these promises were carried out. They say the company will not fool them that way again no matter what they promise. . . .

August 15, 1948. . . . [going] to have a meeting of girls on Thursday, August 19. It was suggested that we serve some kind of refreshments so we have decided on cake, ice cream and coke. . . .

August 22, 1948. . . . After arriving in Morganton . . . and talking to Frannie Littlejohn about the meeting on Thursday I sensed that something was wrong. She acted very discouraged regarding the girls' reaction. . . . One would say she would come if so-and-so was not invited for she didn't trust her, another would say the same about someone else. Following this discussion I contacted all the signed girls . . . four of them promised positively they would attend. The same was done on the women working at the Pine Burr shop, six of these promised to be there. I did not expect all of them to be there that

promised since most of them . . . are scared to death for fear someone would hear about this, and report them. Frankly I did feel pretty
sure about four of these girls and was very disappointed when only two
showed up. . . . Something will have to be worked out to enlighten
them and eliminate some of that fear. . . .

August 28, 1948. . . . Followed up some of the leads received from
Elise Tweety on the Chadbourn and it looks very ripe for organization
immediately. . . . The heat is so bad in that dept. the girls can't stand
it and they have done nothing to correct this situation. . . . In the
seaming dept. one of the girls that had worked there 12 years was fired
for staying home on Saturday for being sick, that incident has really
set the girls off in the looping and seaming dept. In the mending
department when the increase went into effect they got a cut from 56
cents a dozen to 46 cents on a dozen. . . . This is the first time in a
long while that I heard the girls say, yes we want a union. Faye Clontz,
Jessie Jones, and Myrtle Owens said they had tried reasoning with the
company and asked for cooperation from them in making it a more
pleasant place to work and got exactly nowhere, so they are ready to
help get the union in there. I had planned to go to Morganton on
Monday but the girls have asked that I stay at least that day so they
can meet with me Monday night and get more information on how to
get started. I told them I would arrange to stay if they were really
sincere in helping to get the union in there. . . .

September 11, 1948. . . . The deeper I get into the Chadbourn situation the more confusing it becomes. . . . There is no harmony among
the girls themselves any more than there is between the employees and
employer. . . . There is no doubt but that the company is responsible
and encourages this condition. . . . If the management hears about
any girl talking to a group regarding any pending grievance in respect
to doing something about this matter, she is called into the office and
asked to resign. Faye Clontz has been asked to resign on 2 different
occasions and refused. Myrtle Owens a looper was accused this past
week of being the instigator in deciding among the loopers that they do
not come into work last Saturday morning. The reason that the company will send them home early during the week and make them come
in on Saturday. She was called into the office the other day and asked
to resign, she refused. The grievances these girls have would fill a
book. . . .

October 10, 1948. . . . In talking to the girls from the Chadbourn
shop this week they informed me that Mr. Ingram the personnel manager had his desk moved where he could watch what goes on in the

girls' depts. The girls differ as why this was done. Some think it is to try and correct conditions, others think it is to spy on them. . . .

October 16, 1948. . . . Before we had a chance to tell the people at the Francis Louise mill that the election date was set the company was well on the way doing their informing by their own methods. . . . The forelady was questioning Franie Littlejohn as to how many girls were for the union, why they wanted the union etc. By Monday they had a couple girls who are anti-union with the help of a knitter (Jacmine) the foreman and some office man spreading a dozen different rumors. That the mill will shut down, the Drexel hosiery mill is shut down because of the union, that they will go on 3 days a week, that the Glen Alpine shut down when the union won and also that the company will know how everyone votes. The first 3 days F. Littlejohn had someone talk to her. . . . Of course all of this has scared some of the girls, and I had to talk like a "dutch aunt" to a few to explain away the rumors. By Friday they have worn themselves out, it was reported that hardly nothing was said by that time. As a result of this we will lose a few votes but I still think we have a good chance of winning. I have been concentrating on the women we are sure we can hold or thought we could hold and even these we still have to be with constantly to explain away the rumors. . . .

[Ed. note: In her next letter, dated November 1, Organizer Stupek reports that the Francis-Louise election was lost and by so wide a margin that she suspects its honesty—but is powerless to do anything about it.]

December 13, 1948. . . . Knitters . . . are blaming the officers in forcing them to accept the 2% dues. Claiming that when the local voted down the 2% at one meeting another meeting was called without mention on the notice that the dues question would again be taken up, as a result a small group voting for it had forced the rest of them to accept it. It appears that although some would now like to be back in the union the breach has become so wide between these people and the local officers that they don't want to give them the satisfaction. . . .

1955~1975

The years between 1955 and 1975 have been unique decades of social change and political protest. While many social commentators see only the '60s as the protest period, both the late '50s and the early '70s have been times of economic and social changes and radical political movements, many of which created a new situation for workingwomen.

One problem facing the American economy and particularly its women after World War II was how to maintain relatively full employment when war production ceased. One "solution" was through other wars—in Korea and Southeast Asia—and through an arms and space race that created governmental spending patterns and corporate subsidies similar to those in wartime. While unemployment has continued to be high, much of it is absorbed, or rather hidden, by its racial and sexual distribution. Black and other minority peoples bear the highest levels of unemployment, making poverty in America often "invisible" to middle- and upper-income people. Since women have a higher unemployment rate than men, the problem's severity is often hidden from men.

Underemployment, low wages and poor conditions are disguised by the channeling of women into the worst positions. So thoroughly is this done that many of these positions have become socially defined as women's work. Women accept these jobs for the same reason that men take bad jobs, because they need them. This has been the case for many decades. Contrary to the myth of perpetual progress and social improvement, in the last two decades sexual and racial discrimination have worsened. Today women's wages are lower in relation to men's than they were in 1955. Whole occupations (banking and clerical work, for example) have been increasingly stratified so as to keep most women on the bottom; and other occupations (like teaching and social work) have become increasingly bureaucratized, their workers transformed more and more into assembly-line participants with little control or initiative in their work.

The development of public higher education on a mass scale, sending more and more working-class youths to college, did not fundamentally alter these trends. It merely raised the educational requirements for the old kinds of jobs and in some cases even heightened employment discrimination by directing women, members of minority groups and poor students into vocational training programs. In addition, the cost of training has now shifted from private industry to the taxpayer and private individual, as more occupations (like health therapy and computer technology) require college rather than on-the-job-training. Prolonging education also functions to hide the inadequate number of jobs, as people are kept out of the labor market for a longer period of time.

Yet the number of women working has grown more in these years than in any other time period. Part of the explanation lies in the expansion of the clerical and service industries, two of the major employers of women. With increased job opportunities, more older married women have entered the labor market. Inflation and heightened consumption, mostly created by the vast advertising industry, make it necessary for women to work. Thus over the years the economic foundation for the ideology about women's subordination—that a wife must stay home and gain her definition and fulfillment exclusively by caring for her husband and children—has gotten shakier. In the 1970s it is considered normal, not exceptional, for married women to be employed.

The difficulties of the American economy have also affected women in their work as houseworkers and mothers. The last two decades have produced a steady expansion of consumer industries, not just those which produce tangible objects, but also those which sell "culture" in the form of television, fashion, rock music, and so on. Never before has such a large country been so integrated into a single homogenous mass culture. In Oklahoma, Alaska and Maine, women wash their clothes with the same detergent, buy the same instant coffee, watch the same television shows, which urge upon them the same deodorants. Installment buying enables working-class people to become consumers of these goods without their real wages being substantially increased. This mass consumerism has not only provided new sources of profits for industries, but has also increased the ideological unity of Americans around conventional political and social values.

However, to the extent that mass culture succeeded, it also produced a reaction. The nationwide organs of mass culture helped spread a youth culture that was to some extent an opposition culture. Changes in sexual and familial patterns have particularly affected young women, and not always for the good. The sexual exploitation of women has sometimes been heightened by the removal of traditional restraints, and the increased instability of marriages has left many women alone, lonely and overburdened with the double job of earning money and raising children.

Another factor that changed women's status in society was the birth control pill. By the mid-sixties for the first time most women in the United States had access to an effective method of preventing unwanted pregnancies. But the extreme health dangers of the pill exemplify a growing trend toward profiteering from women's sexual needs.

The economic and social difficulties of America in this period led to a virtual explosion of radical social movements. The civil rights

movement, for example, began primarily as a result of black people's experience in and just after World War II, encountering
intransigent racism just after having sacrificed so much for their
country. The civil rights movement was in many ways the source, in
ideas and people, of all the other movements of the 1960s: the anti-
war movement (although a ban-the-bomb peace movement existed
throughout the '50s), the student movement and the "New Left," the
women's liberation movement and the gay liberation movement. All
these movements had their own specific causes as well; they were
created by a collision of heightened expectations with heightened
frustrations. Women's hopes were raised by their increasing participation in the labor force, access to higher education and birth
control, involvement in other social movements and cultural alternatives which promised fuller lives and more respect. There was dis-
appointment on every level: the jobs were terrible, the education
alternative useless or boring, the new sexual freedom exploitative,
the relationships in the "movements" sexist.

The dynamic of expectation and frustration was undoubtedly felt
most sharply at first by educated women. It was these women who
created the women's liberation movement, as it was women of analogous class positions who created the nineteenth-century feminist movement. The women's liberation movement has created a greater consciousness and anger about women's oppression, the need for child
care programs, abortion, birth control and nonsexist gynecological
services, equal job and legal opportunities, women's history and
women's studies programs and a general equalizing of sex roles from
Little Leagues to housework. The ideas that were introduced in the
1960s have reverberated in the 1970s throughout all classes. Polls have
shown, for example, that while many working-class women do not
sympathize with the women's liberation movement, these same women
respond affirmatively to specific feminist demands—such as equal pay,
equal job opportunities and equal legal rights—in higher proportion
than do women of more privileged class positions. In their response to
such specific demands, black women statistically have been the most
feminist of all.

In the mid-1970s it is commonly observed that the women's liberation movement is receding in importance, as the "New Left" did a few
years before. But it would be more accurate to say that they have
been transformed as their ideas have found support in and been
changed by other social groups. If the 1960s reintroduced a kind of
romantic ideological and cultural opposition into the United States,
the 1970s seem to be reintroducing the possibility of a mass political
opposition based in the working class. There has been a marked increase in working-class struggles for better working and living condi-

tions. Both strikes and community struggles have tended to focus on demands that go beyond the economic, for an increase in the power of workers over their own situations and institutions. "Wildcats," in defiance of established leadership at both the workplace and the community, have become more common.

In all these battles, women have played an increasingly large role and have begun to make demands directly concerning their own lives. A potential example of this new militancy among working-class women was the overwhelming response to the establishment of the Coalition of Labor Union Women in March 1974. This and other developments suggest that the cause of women's liberation is being picked up by working-class women, who are most likely to make the profound social and economic changes necessary to achieve liberation.

HOME AND JOB: THE DOUBLE DAY

THE MAJORITY of American women do not earn wages, although almost all of them work very hard, and many of them perform necessary tasks. Indeed, many unpaid women working as housewives and mothers would not trade their work for other employment. Some wives and mothers have significant advantages in their working conditions: control over their own schedules, control over their environment, close contact with their children. But often these potential advantages never materialize due to poverty, overwork, children's and husband's demands. Furthermore, most houseworkers suffer from great isolation and are deprived of adult company many hours a day.

The following is the diary of two days in the life of Marion Hudson, mother of two, student at SUNY–Old Westbury and part-time employee.

DIARY OF A STUDENT-MOTHER-HOUSEWIFE-WORKER

7 rooms
2 children (1 girl 1 year, 1 boy 3 years)
Husband   Monday

Clock starts playing loud noise

5:30 Henry wakes up to go to work. "Trucking" by Marvin Gay can be heard all over the house at full volume. I'm awake.

5:35 Henry turns the radio down just a little.

5:40 Bathroom light is on. Kitchen light is on. Hallway light is on. (Why can't he turn off these lights when he's finished in a particular room!)

Diary of Marion Hudson.

6:00 Monique and Tracey are awake. (Who isn't after the troops have just been called out—meaning Henry.)

6:05 Gave Monique a bottle and changed her diaper.

6:06 Told Tracey he could not have a peanut butter and jelly sandwich at this *ghastly* hour. (Didn't say ghastly.)

6:15 Henry is off to the post office.

6:16 Get up to cut off the lights.

6:17 Settle down for some *sleep.*

6:30 Tracey is up—walking around in the house—scares me half to death.

6:31 Tracey starts pounding me on my back to wake up. He didn't make it to the bathroom. His pajamas are wet.

6:32 I tell Tracey I am going to beat him half to death if he doesn't change those pajamas.

6:33 Tracey gets in my bed.

6:40 We both finally doze off.

6:41 Tracey is awake again. He wants some Bosco.

6:42 I threaten him with a severe beating.

7:00 Thoroughly exhausted from scolding Tracey, I get up and make him some delicious Bosco. (Actually I feel like dumping the whole glass on top of him.)

7:05 It's no use. I can't get back to sleep. Tell Tracey to go upstairs and play with his trucks. Nothing else to do but daydream and think of what I have to do and wear.

7:25 Tracey wants a piece of pie.

7:30 I get up and turn on Tracey's TV so he can watch *Little Rascals.*

8:00 Monique wants to get out of her crib. I let her yell till 8:30.

8:30 I'm up and ready. The wheels begin to move into motion.

8:35 Head for bathroom—wash.

8:45 Wash Monique and Tracey. Get them dressed. Fuss with Tracey about what shoes he is going to wear. He wants to wear his cowboy boots instead of the black ones.

9:00 Feed them breakfast. Eggs, Spam and toast. Turn on *Sesame Street.* Tracey doesn't want his eggs. More confrontation.

9:05 Pack the kids tote bag to take over to Grandma's. Tell Tracey he cannot take his new trucks. "Yes, I have to go to school today." Clean off kitchen table and stove after Henry and myself.

9:10 Get dressed. Make up Tracey's and Monique's beds. Go into my room and make up the bed.

9:20   Pack my schoolbooks and coat. Gather Monique's and Tracey's coats and hats.

9:25   Start towards day. Run to freezer—take something out for dinner.

9:30   Monique just messed in her pants. Back to the bedroom. Change her. Put her coat back on. Meanwhile Tracey is hollering—he wants to go.

9:40   Get in car—head for Grandma's.

9:55   Drop them off at Grandmother's.

10:00 Head for the expressway—another rat race.

10:30 School. . . .

Friday

8:30   Get up—wash—get dressed. Made Tracey and Monique's bed while they watched *Sesame Street*.

9:30   Went outside and raked yard. Put mulch around shrubs. Planted one upright evergreen.

5 min. Helped Henry push car into driveway. (VW he just purchased.) Listen to him give me instructions on how not to push the car too fast.

10:05 Came inside and wiped Monique's nose. Scolded Tracey for being in refrigerator. Told Tracey his sweater was upstairs.

Went back outside for a second look at my shrubs.

10:15 Came inside—started cleaing kitchen which Henry left a mess after fixing his breakfast and the kids.
1. Cleared table of his schoolbooks.
2. Cleared table of his toast.
3. Cleared table of the glasses.
4. Cleared table of his bowls of half-eaten cereal.
5. Removed tape measure.
6. Also this morning's newspaper.

Threw garbage in can. Wrapped the bread up and put it back into breadbox. Cleaned off dishwasher where Henry left his cereal bowl on. (Bowl was left in his car from yesterday's breakfast on the way to work.) Also removed one comb and paintbrush. Closed kitchen cabinet which he just forgot to close when he came in looking for a screwdriver. Meanwhile he asks me to put batteries on my next shopping list. Before he finishes that sentence, he wants to know where the screwdriver is.

10:30 Start on dishes. Scraped hard cereal off kitchen table. Stacked chairs on top of table. Pick up Monique's pacifier off the floor. Search for more paper to continue this assignment. Henry sends

Monique inside because she is cold. Tells me to take off her coat. She immediately goes to his toolbox which he left in the middle of the kitchen floor. I have to repeatedly tell her to put the tools down. Put tools in the toolbox and close it. Take toolbox outside where he is working on the VW. (The toolbox should have been outside in the first place.)

Monique starts crying. "All right, Monique," I reply.

10:41 Back to the dishes. Monique is still crying. (I think Monique needs a beating.)

Henry comes in looking for something in the kitchen cabinet. He cuts in front of me where I am washing the dishes.

Leaves grease on my cabinet. Tracey comes inside and asks for a roll. Gave him a roll. Now Monique wants a piece of meat. Gave her a piece of cold chicken.

10:44 Back to the dishes. I tell Monique to stop slamming front door back and forth.

Wash dishes, clean off that grease spot on my door, wipe countertop and stove.

10:45 Swept kitchen floor. Henry comes in and asks, "What's up, Doc?" (I grin and bear it.)

Henry wants to know what I am going to do with this box. (Box located in laundry/boiler room.)

I reply, "Henry, do you want it?" He replies, "Yes." I reply, "Take it, Henry!"

He goes to toolbox and leaves it open. Monique is back into the tools.

I close toolbox. Monique starts crying again.

11:01 Make my breakfast.

11:15 Girl friend stops by. (Just what I need.)

11:16 Tracey wants another roll and a glass of juice. Goes back outside.

11:28 Finished breakfast and cleared table.

11:36 Finally finish second batch of dishes.

Now Tracey wants an orange. (One orange coming up.) Go into bedroom to check evening gown for an affair coming up. Sort clothes to wash.

1. Henry wants me to help him with the car outside.
2. Henry wants me to help him with the car again.
3. Put second batch of clothes in washer.
4. Swept laundry room floor.
5. Vacuumed Tracey's bedroom floor.
6. Went to the town of Babylon dump, 5 minutes away, to get rid of garbage.

1:36 Beat Tracey for playing with a knife.

1:40 Girl friend left.

1:44 Started cleaning in the master bedroom. Rearranged furniture. Put clothes in dryer. Put third batch of clothes in washer.
Sent Monique to bed to take a nap. Sent Tracey back outside.
Finished bedroom. Henry decides to go out. Asked him to take Tracey for a ride. Replies, "No."
Cleaned out my dresser. Went upstairs and cleaned out the bookcases. Tracey knocks on door. His gloves came off.

3:55 Start dinner. Tracey comes in. I remove his coat and gloves. Gave him some peaches. Put rice and meat in to cook. Took vegetables out of refrigerator and placed on stove to heat up.
Monique wakes up. Changed her diaper and wet clothes. Send her upstairs to watch TV. Monique comes downstairs—wants a slice of bread. I had to heat the bread in the toaster because it was in the freezer. She wants it right away, so she starts to cry.
Fill up empty water container in refrigerator. Drained macaroni. Took clothes out of dryer. Put final batch of wet clothes in.

5:00 Henry returns at dinnertime. Prepared dinner. He put paper down on table. As I reach for it, he takes it away and replies he bought it so he should look at it first. No reply.

5:30 We eat dinner.
Turn *Electric Company* on for the kids. Changed Monique's dirty diaper. Cleared table off. Henry decides he wants a cake for dessert. Believe it or not, I made a cake.

7:30 Watched *Let's Make a Deal.*

8:00 Read newspaper.

9:00 Collapsed into the bed.

PART OF THE "service sector" is the sale of sex. Some women sell the actual use of their genitals for a short time—prostitutes; some sell their overall beauty and stylishness—models; some sell views of their nakedness, enhanced by complicated routines of undressing—strippers. It is odd, perhaps, to think of this work as "service work" because it is of dubious value, but that is true of much that is sold. What constitutes service is defined by the dominant values of the society. If enough money demands a certain service, private industry is sure to provide it.

Other kinds of sexual services have increased in the last decades: massage parlors, pornography, the use of sex in advertising, and so on. The commoditization of sex—its presentation as something for sale, and its reduction to the level of technique—is proceeding more rapidly than ever. The "sexual revolution" of the 1960s does not seem to have given greater sexual self-determination to women. There remain economic and social pressures on women to use their sexual attractiveness as a means of exchange, whether to earn money by the hour or to buy a husband for years.

The following description was written by a waitress in a strip joint. It is taken from a long paper she wrote about her experience there, and her analysis flows from her sense that the entire atmosphere of the place was defined by the men's desire to look at women's genitals. At the same time, she is concerned with the working conditions of the waitresses specifically.

THE PARADISE LOUNGE: WORKING AS A COCKTAIL WAITRESS

The club opens at ten o'clock in the morning. From twelve noon until two in the afternoon, there are go-go girls, and from two in the afternoon until two in the morning there is a continuous show of strippers. Every night of the week—every day as well—men come into the Paradise to watch women take off their clothes. They sit around the stage, their faces set in dull stares, embarrassed, twitching smiles, drooling grins, or arrogant smirks. Men of all ages come, men from all walks of life.

The management requires that all the dancers mingle with the customers and hustle drinks. Some women are employed solely as "mixers." Generally, when mixing, the women will order a very cheap champagne, which they are not encouraged to drink, but rather to spit back in a frosted glass provided expressly for this purpose. A small bottle of this "champagne" (which would cost about 70¢ in a liquor store) sells for $5.00, of which the dancer receives $1.00 in commission. Larger bottles go for $15.00, $30.00, $60.00, $75.00, or even $100.00, the dancer receiving a 20 percent commission. (The price charged on the larger bottles may vary with what the management believes the customer is willing to pay.) Bottles going for $30.00 in the club cost under $5.00 in

Michelle Gubbay. "The Paradise Lounge." Unpublished paper.

the store. Dancers are not allowed to drink with customers except on commission.

The waitresses and the dancers work as teams. At certain cues—for example, when the dancer turns the bottle of champagne upside down in the bucket (which she may do even if it is not empty)—we waitresses rush over, trained to respond on signal just as secretaries are trained by executives to interrupt business appointments at the proper time with the proper excuse. We help the mixer to order more, more, more champagne, and she in turn makes sure that the customer gives us a nice tip.

The dancers vary in their attitude towards mixing. Some would rather not do it at all, would rather not face the game, the dirty remarks, the groping hands; they are continually hassled by the management because of their reluctance. Other strippers count on their mixing money as a major source of income, making several hundred dollars on commission each week. But it is always a battle, always a game, a hustle. The men are trying to get as much sex as they can from the women for the least amount of money, and the women are trying to make as much money as they can, for the least amount of time and effort. Some of the women insist on their right to do no more than talk with a customer who has bought them a drink or a bottle of champagne; others get by with a few light hugs and a promise to meet the customer later—a promise that they have no intention of keeping; still others will give the customers varying degrees of "action" for their money. But whether it's outrightly having sex with a customer in a dark booth (which we waitresses, at first quite shocked to see happening, soon enough accepted with a cynical, sophisticated, blasé amusement), or whether it's listening to a man's egocentric outpouring of complaints and problems—in order to make money mixing, a woman has to deliver the person that the man wants to be with. A dancer will be talking to me, her face strained by lines of anger or weariness; then she will approach a customer, and a smile will come on her face like a mask, a shield. Those mixers who provide little in the way of sexual service must often work the longest and the hardest, talking with the men, laughing at their jokes, building up their egos.

HATE

We speak jokingly of the "battle of the sexes," but there is more truth in this phrase than we would like to admit. The dehumanization, the objectification, that happens between men and women in the Paradise Lounge is only a reflection of these currents in society at large. If I ever doubted before that men hated women, I could never doubt that again after having worked at the Paradise. There I can see and feel the hatred exuding from the men; I can see it as they sit, watching the strippers; I can feel it when they interact with me. It is a hatred of the power of women's sexuality, a disgust and a contempt for beings they see as solely sexual creatures. And inevitably, of course, it is not just the men who stereotype and objectify the women: forced to be dependent on men, forced to hide behind the smiling act of service, women come to objectify men, seeing them only as sources of money; women find ways of making men pay.

Yes, of course, individuals may transcend this in part; sometimes individual men and women may love each other; but usually men and women must approach each other as strangers, as incomplete beings— and this is not a basis for love. Men come into the Paradise, and their distrust and objectification and hatred of women is confirmed—confirmed, mind you, it is nothing brand-new—and women working there have their anger and hatred of men confirmed. I cannot think of one woman in the club who has not at one time or another expressed some aspect of a deep bitter hostility toward the male customers, and by extension, toward men in general. How could we not feel hostile? They make comments at/about us, they try to grab and feel us, they humiliate us by deriding other women, they detract from our personhood by labeling us whores or bitches, by seeing us and judging us only in terms of how we please them. And is this behavior of the men in the club so different from the behavior of men on the street, on the subway, in the office, in our homes, in our beds?

We all have our defensive mechanisms for dealing with the hatred we feel for the customers. Some of the mixers get very drunk—"It's the only way I can put up with their shit." I find that generally I don't look into the customers' eyes when I wait on them, unconsciously avoiding having to partake in the sexual flirtation with them that they want and expect. Together we waitresses form a powerful group to vent our anger on the men who come to watch the show. We refuse to play the usual service role. We put the men on the defensive, loudly proclaiming our opinion of them as animals, jerks, assholes. We delight in playing tricks on them; gleefully we tell each other of our moments of revenge. A man trips over a step in the darkness. "Did you have a nice trip?" we say. I find myself watching with amusement. "I think hating men is an occupational hazard of this job," one of the waitresses remarked.

What has been gained in this battle of the sexes, this war? I look at the men sitting around the stage. Night after night after night they come; there is obviously some need, some hunger, being expressed, but it is hard to understand, so heavily has its form been distorted and perverted. There is plenty of grabbing and groping going on, but no real touching. There is never any joy in these men's faces, only a vision of a mechanical joyless sex, stressing human isolation rather than community.

In all the discussion about strip clubs this is never asked: Why can these men not satisfy their needs in other, more human contexts? In all the debates about pornography this is never discussed. Why is it that so many people cannot fulfill their sexual needs in the context of a relationship with another human being? Why must they turn to titillating cheap magazines or their higher-class equivalents to satisfy their sexual fantasies? Why is sex so much in the realm of the fantastical anyhow— why not closer down to earth, where we can reach out and touch each other?

LOVE

It is difficult to work in an atmosphere of such ugliness and hate. Of course, there are certain very tangible benefits of being a waitress at the Paradise. During periods of good business our nightly tips can be very high, and in a society where most jobs for women are low-paying, this is nothing to sneer at.

But in order to survive there, we know instinctively that we must laugh, and love. We do have an incredible amount of freedom on the job. We wear what we want to work. When we are not busy, we wander around, or sit and relax with our feet up in a booth. We have the freedom to refuse to comply with many of the rules governing most service relationships. We laugh at the idea that "the customer is always right." We make up our own rules. Perhaps we get more hassles than women in ordinary waitress jobs, but we can also deal with them more directly. We can take out our frustrations on our customers, we can sneer at them, be rude to them, laugh at them, do crazy things to them.

Many of us have been there for several years, and some can't even see the light at the end of the tunnel. We laugh hysterically at the thought that we will all be there when we are fifty, toddering about, What would you like to drink, sonny? What a feeling of insecurity is attached to the idea of having to venture into the outside, the real world, to find a real job, where we could not get away with yelling at the customers, cheating them out of their money, playing with their heads, partying on the job, running around madly, drinking, smoking, laughing.

We waitresses that work in the back room form a very close, tightly-knit group. We know we are in a hostile jungle, and we must adapt or perish. We turn toward each other to survive.

We have to sign in for work at seven o'clock, although we don't actually start work until eight. So we have an hour in which to relax, to be ourselves, before we must venture out into the hostile world of work, hiding behind a smile or a scowl or a vacant stare. Originally we spent this hour sitting at the back bar, passively drinking our coffee and smoking our cigarettes, making small talk. And then one night, out of nowhere, a small couch appeared against the wall in the ladies' room. It was a gradual transition, the change in our nightly ritual from sitting at the bar to congregating in the ladies' room, but it made a tremendous difference. We always valued the time we spent relaxing at the bar, but it was more impersonal, sitting there. Now, in the ladies' room, we could laugh more heartily, we could relax more, loosen ourselves up. Those of us who smoke grass began getting stoned. For that hour in the ladies' room it became possible to ignore the inevitable hassles ahead of us in the night about to begin.

It is incredible how much can happen in such a little space. A small physical space forces people to confront one another, to deal with one another, to touch one another. There is no room for hostile or indifferent feelings. When you are all falling all over each other, you just cannot retreat into yourself (as it was so easy for us to do when we sat at the bar, side by side).

Another territory which we adopted as our own is a back booth on a terraced back section of the club. No matter what section we are working, if we are not busy we are all drawn to this booth. We sit there and talk and laugh, drink coffee, eat sandwiches, make jokes at the customers' expense. To this booth we carry over from the ladies' room our warm, easy sense of friendship and familiarity.

Once our boss went through a phase of hiring new, unneeded waitresses, and at first we resented this strongly. Like animals snarling at intruders on their territory, we were hostile to anyone new, anyone foreign, ready to believe any hostile report about the new employee, ready to put a hostile turn on her every trait of character. But obviously this couldn't last for long. New waitresses became part of our close in-group; the ladies' room did it, if nothing else. It is absolutely impossible to continue feeling unfriendly to someone in such a small space; the bad vibrations just come right back and hit you in the face. Now we celebrate each other's birthdays with cakes and presents. We are a strong, brave little group. During the night we say to each other, "Come over and visit me," as if we were inviting a friend to tea.

It hit me once, how much support I derived from the group of waitresses there. Yes, certainly sometimes that place can be an irritant, unbearable when there are other things on your mind. But it can also function as a home, a refuge, a refuge of support, of friendship and warmth and laughter and belonging. Perhaps the darkness has something to do with it. It is a home because we can transform it into whatever we want it to be. In the dark we can mold it. Friendships are formed, and laughter is necessary. We learn to reassure ourselves of our own humanity by the love we bear for each other.

ONE OF THE persistent trends in the structure of work in America is the tendency for jobs to become more and more stratified. The reasons for this increasing specialization often have less to do with the division of work on a logical basis and more to do with, as sociologist Carol Brown has put it, the "division of workers."

In this case study, Susan Reverby traces the subdivision and its implications for nursing.

HEALTH IS WOMEN'S WORK

In the nineteenth century, hospitals were part of poor houses. There was no professional nursing; poor women, many times themselves inmates of the poorhouses, did what little nursing there was. Nursing as a distinct profession began on the battlefield where disease often killed more soldiers than did bullets. During the Crimean War of the 1850's, Florence Nightingale and a group of dedicated women proved that good nursing care could drastically decrease the mortality rate among soldiers. Nightingale returned to England after the war to introduce her concepts of professional nursing to English hospitals.

Stratification characterized the system from the beginning. The Nightingale system trained women in two categories which reflected English class divisions: "lady probationers" and regular nursing students. The lady probationers were to be gentlewomen of middle and upper class backgrounds who would have "those qualifications which

Susan Reverby. "Health: Women's Work." *Health Pac Bulletin*, No. 40, April 1972.

will fit them to become superintendents." The regular students were to be ". . . well-educated domestic servants and . . . the daughters of small farmers . . . tradesmen, artisans . . . who have been used to household work." These women would become regular hospital nurses.

Because medicine was still closed to women at this time, many headed for nursing. Nightingale was clear that nursing was to be a separate function, a coprofession to the doctors; but, she was not, she reassured the worried physicians, training "medical women."

U.S. DEVELOPMENTS

Hospitals in America quickly saw the advantages of training nurses. Student nurses could be used to fill the hospitals' nursing needs; and better still, they didn't have to be paid beyond room and board. Between 1880 and 1900 the hospital nursing schools in the U.S. grew from 15 schools with 323 students to 432 schools with 11,000 students. Since cheap student labor provided the bulk of nursing care, hospitals did not hire their students after graduation. Besides, most health care was delivered at home and thus graduating nurses tended to go into private duty nursing in the home.

As with medicine at this time, there was no uniformity or minimal standard for nurse training. The nursing leadership began to feel the need for uniform admissions standards and curricula in nursing schools. Above all, they sought the legal recognition of nursing through passage of nurse practice laws and the registration of nurses.

Thus, in 1894, leaders of nursing schools organized the Society of Superintendents of Training Schools for Nurses which in 1912 was to become the National League for Nursing Education (NLN). Recognizing the need for a more broadly based group, a Nurses Associated Alumnae of United States and Canada was organized in 1896. The NLN was primarily concerned with educational standards; the Nurses Associated Alumnae with work conditions and the registration of nurses on a state-by-state basis. In 1911, the alumnae group became the American Nurses Association (ANA). The overarching concern of both organizations was the establishment and upgrading of nursing standards and the recognition of nursing as a defined profession. The result of this professionalization was the creation of an internal hierarchy within nursing.

DIVISIONS BEGIN

Concerned with the increased costs of professional nursing, hospitals supported differentiation within the field. In 1907, the American Hospital Association (AHA) advocated distinction between three grades of nurses: the executive or teaching nurse, the bedside nurse, and the attendant or subsidiary nurse. The AHA suggested that all categories be licensed, but that the first two be classified as registered nurses, while the third be called by some other title. The AHA study had little influence at the time, but it clearly indicated the hospitals' interest in fostering the divisions within the nursing profession.

World War I increased the need for health workers and raised questions about their training. After the war, the Rockefeller Foundation convened a conference which led to a study of nursing and nursing education. Released in 1923, the study, called the Goldmark Report, suggested that nursing become part of a collegiate program. The report also recommended that auxilliary personnel be trained in shorter periods of time to carry on some of the less important nursing functions. The Goldmark Report attempted to do for nursing what the Flexner Report in 1910 did for medicine. The latter resulted in the upgrading and standardizing of medical training by putting it into a university setting. Following the Goldmark Report, nursing programs at Yale and several other universities were established.

During the Depression, droves of private duty nurses were unemployed and many hospital-based nursing schools closed. During World War II, hospitals began to hire nurses; the increased cost led to the creation of a new subdivision in nursing—the "practical or vocational" nurse.

By the post-war period, studies by the American Nursing Association recommended that there be a further increase in auxiliary nursing personnel on the one hand, and an upgrading of registered nurses on the other. Thus the hierarchy in nursing became more elaborate and rigid. Bedside nursing was to be done by the practical nurse and later by a new, lower category called the aide. Meanwhile RN's tried to separate themselves from "lower" nursing categories by greater specialization.

PROFESSIONAL VS. TECHNICAL NURSE

By 1964, seeds of the division planted by Florence Nightingale in the nineteenth century had come into full bloom. Indeed, divisions multiplied even within the ranks of registered nurses. The ANA recommended two different kinds of programs to train registered nurses: a four-year baccalaureate college program for "professional" nurses and two-year community colleges associate degree and hospital-based diploma programs for "technical" nurses.

The consequences of these new divisions were not long in coming. In the early 1960's 84 percent of all nurses had been trained in hospital-based diploma schools; by 1970 the figure was down to 52 percent. Hospital schools began closing while new associate degree community college programs expanded. In 1969, 27 percent of all nurses were trained in associate degree programs, 21 percent in the baccalaureate programs.

Nursing authorities see a wide difference in the functions of these two types of nurses. According to Martha Rogers, head of New York University's Division of Nurse Education, "Baccalaureate graduates in nursing are no more interchangeable with associate degree and hospital school graduates than are dentists with dental hygienists or medical doctors with physician assistants." Supervisory and administrative jobs go to baccalaureate nurses, even those fresh out of school. The divisions are racial as well as functional: In 1968–69, 10 percent of associate degree nursing students were black, while black students were only 5 percent of those in baccalaureate programs. Black graduates of these programs actually dropped from 9.7 percent in 1962 to 4 percent in 1966.

DIVIDED WE FALL

With expanding institutions and developing technology, division of labor in the health field has been irresistible, as it has in other industries. For the majority of health workers, this has meant specialized alienating, often low-paying jobs. This increasing division has threatened the nursing profession.

Rather than challenging this policy or the hospital hierarchy, the nursing leadership has sought, throughout history, to preserve the power and status of "professional" nursing by creating its own subdivisions and hierarchy. The result has been to divide the interests of all health workers, and to so narrow the functions of professional nursing as to threaten its existence.

Today the nursing profession feels it is being squeezed from all directions. The explosion of "new careers" and manpower training programs is turning thousands of technical and paraprofessional health workers onto the job market. There are now over 250 new job categories such as medical records technician, dietetic technician, social health technician and family health worker—many of which fill traditional nursing functions. . . . And many are low-paid, deadend jobs going, by and large, to third world women.

Many nurses are now turning to the gray area between traditional doctor and nurse functions—taking medical histories, screening patients, supervising routine care, etc. Nurses in this role are called nurse practitioners or "extended" nurses. There are now over fifty different training programs for "extended nursing" in pediatrics, obstetrics, anesthesiology, and other specialties.

The only problem with this tack is that it runs headlong into another new medical vocation—the physician assistant. Developed to utilize the experience of ex-military medical corpsmen, physician assistants "provide patient services under the supervision and direction of a licensed physician." Rather than advocating that nurses become physician assistants, however, the ANA has attempted to split the hairs that differentiate the two functions. "The term physician assistant should not be applied to any of the nurse practitioners being prepared to function in an extension of the nursing role," stated a December, 1971, ANA position paper.

In light of the pressures and threats to the profession, nurses are becoming more militant. Many are now turning to a union approach, although there is ambivalence about whether they should join traditional unions or make the ANA their bargaining agent. This approach may be more positive if it unites nurses with other hospital workers. But so far it has tended to be a defensive maneuver for nurses to tighten their professional status and to keep the rigid hierarchy.

UNTIL RECENTLY, few clerical workers were unionized. There was a myth that they couldn't be organized, due to the high turnover rate and the attitude of many women workers that they were only temporarily employed. This myth is rapidly being challenged. Today office work is one of the fastest-growing areas of union organizing.

Some of the first office workers to renew organizing attempts in the 1960s were more educated women influenced by the women's liberation movement. They found support from co-workers on such issues as dress codes, coffee making and disrespectful treatment. In several locales national unions have moved successfully into offices. While glad of this renewed attention to long-neglected workers, many women's groups have decided to maintain separate, nonunion women's organizations to fight not only for unionization but for the interests of women in unions. In New York there is W.O.W. (Women Office

Workers) ; in Boston, 9 to 5; in Chicago, W.E. (Women Employed) ; in the Bay Area, Union WAGE (Women's Alliance to Gain Equality). If the movement for unionization and autonomous, militant women's office workers' groups continues—as seems likely—office workers could become a powerful labor bloc. Today there are approximately 11 million office workers in the United States, 76 percent of them women and less than 10 percent of them unionized (most of that 10 percent are government employees). Their ranks are expected to grow to 20 million in the next decade!

Clearest proof of the reality of this possibility, perhaps, is in the reaction of those who have most to lose from it. Five years ago the *Harvard Business Review,* prestigious journal of the business community, published a report on the "problem" of clerical unionism and what businesspeople could do to prevent it!

YOUR CLERICAL WORKERS ARE RIPE FOR UNIONISM

While semiskilled workers are heavily unionized, clerical workers have traditionally resisted union overtures, relying instead on management responsiveness to their problems. But the foundation of this resistance to unions—positive attitudes toward management—is breaking down. The evidence comes from a recent analysis, performed by the Opinion Research Corporation. . . .

Numerous observers have pointed out the difficulties that face unions attempting to organize clerical employees. Some of the reasons are structural (e.g., the physical problem of reaching this group with the union message). But the majority of reasons for clerical workers' resistance are sociological: (a) the widespread feeling that unions are beneath their dignity and that they can bargain for themselves, (b) the belief that they, as members of the middle class, are identified with management and therefore should reject unions, and (c) the tendency to think of unions as unseemly, rabble-rousing organizations. Consider what clerical workers themselves have often said about unions:

"Unions are for the birds—for people without much education who can't stand on their own." (Oil company secretary)

Alfred Vogel. "Your Clerical Workers Are Ripe for Unionism." *Harvard Business Review* 49 (March–April 1971).

"Unions are undesirable and distasteful to people like me. I just can't imagine myself out on a picket line." (Young bank clerk)

"I don't need a union. I can handle myself. If I want a raise, I go see my boss." (Household-products company stenographer)

"What do I know about unions? No one has ever talked to me about them." (Insurance company clerk)

During the past decade, unions have had only modest success at best in organizing clerical workers and other white-collar employees. For example, while over one million nonmanagerial white-collar workers were recruited by unions from 1958 to 1968, the yearly level of this group's union membership has remained at about 11%. . . .

But beneath the surface there are signs that attitudes are changing, the clerical employees are becoming sufficiently provoked by management to take a second look at unions. Comments like the following are now commonplace:

"In my opinion, unions aren't desirable for my kind of employee, but they may come if companies don't treat us right." (Chemical company secretary)

"Unions kill all incentive, they help create mediocre people. But at the same time they furnish a much-needed bargaining power." (Electronics company clerk)

"Unions may be a necessary evil, despite the strikes and all. If companies recognized individual worth, unions would not be needed." (Electric utility telephone operator)

Clerical workers indeed *have* become much less satisfied on most key employee relations issues in recent years (1966 to the present) than in past years (1955 to 1965). . . .

Note too that clerical employees feel increasingly remote and shut off from management. . . . Clerical employees are beginning to feel like mere cogs in a great impersonal bureaucracy, and there is a growing tendency to see management as a nameless, faceless mask of authority and indifference. . . .

The attitudes of clerical employees have declined more sharply than those of any group for which we have similar comparative information. They have, for instance, sloped down considerably more than those of the heavily unionized blue-collar employees who have historically viewed management far less enthusiastically on a comparative basis. . . . It is important to point out that I am talking about relative declines in favorable ratings. Clerical employees currently have more favorable opinions of their employers and, on balance, still express less criticism than do blue-collar workers. But the gap is closing . . . and there are actually some issues where clerical attitudes are already less favorable than those of blue-collar employees. These include:

- Applying policies consistently.
- Letting employees speak up to higher authority.
- Telling employees what is going on in the company.

While the attitudes of clerical employees in the companies studied have moved, overall, in a more negative direction since 1966 than have the attitudes of hourly workers, this trend has not yet caused an en masse movement to unionization. For most companies, there is still time to act—time to find out how much discontent exists among clerical employees and what their major problems are.

Of course, it is possible that many companies will be lucky (we are presuming that most would prefer not to have their office employees unionized) and will avoid unionization of their clerical work force by ignoring the problem and doing business as usual. The traditional reluctance of office employees to join unions, for whatever reasons, may be a sufficient deterrent.

However, teachers, nurses, and other middle-class groups have already begun to turn toward unions, and, in view of what is happening to employee attitudes, it would be a bad bet, I think, for companies to depend on the historical reluctance of clerical workers to sign up.

TODAY AND TOMORROW

FREQUENTLY, women are alone with the double job of raising children and keeping a home while also supporting themselves and their families. In 1972, 22 percent of heads of households were women. Except in extraordinary cases of women with inherited money or exceptional earning ability, this double job is a great hardship in the United States. There is very little inexpensive or public child care; even the public schools do not keep children long enough to cover full-time working hours. One reason for high unemployment among women is that jobs are not flexible enough to let them cope with emergencies like sick children. Furthermore, most of the jobs available to women will not support a family. Thus the reason so many women—3 million in 1972—are "on welfare" has nothing to do with their individual failings; it is an institutional part of today's economic situation.

One way of looking at it might be this: welfare could be the salary women receive for raising children. Instead, welfare is seen by most people as charity given to the unfortunate, the incompetent and the lazy. This stigma reflects not merely uninformed attitudes about the situation of women but also some general myths about poverty in this country. For example, most welfare recipients are white, not black. Only one percent are "able-bodied" males, while 58 percent are children and 15 percent the aged. But if one bears in mind that children must receive welfare because their parents cannot support them, and that most children on welfare live in female-headed households, it is true that discrimination against women is responsible for a great deal of the need for welfare in this country.

Being "on welfare" in the United States is no fun. It usually requires submitting to indignities and invasions of privacy that would not be tolerated were not the welfare recipients worried about the welfare of their children. Despite these burdens, "being on welfare" has brought women in similar situations together, showed them the commonness of their problems and stimulated them to organize and fight collectively to improve their condition. The National Welfare

Rights Organization (N.W.R.O.) began with a local welfare rights group in 1963 and grew to be a powerful national women's organization.

In the interview below, Johnnie Tillmon, the first chairwoman of N.W.R.O., explains how she sees the welfare issue connected to the general question of women's work.

WELFARE IS A WOMEN'S ISSUE

I'm a woman. I'm a black woman. I'm a poor woman. I'm a fat woman. I'm a middle-aged woman. And I'm on welfare.

In this country, if you're any one of those things—poor, black, fat, female, middle-aged, on welfare—you count less as a human being. If you're all those things, you don't count at all. Except as a statistic.

I am a statistic.

I am 45 years old. I have raised six children.

I grew up in Arkansas, and I worked there for fifteen years in a laundry, making about $20 or $30 a week, picking cotton on the side for carfare. I moved to California in 1959 and worked in a laundry there for nearly four years. In 1963 I got too sick to work anymore. Friends helped me to go on welfare.

They didn't call it welfare. They called it A.F.D.C.—Aid to Families with Dependent Children. Each month I get $363 for my kids and me. I pay $128 a month rent; $30 for utilities, which include gas, electricity, and water; $120 for food and non-edible household essentials; $50 for school lunches for the three children in junior and senior high school who are not eligible for reduced-cost meal programs.

There are millions of statistics like me. Some on welfare. Some not. And some, really poor, who don't even know they're entitled to welfare. Not all of them are black. Not at all. In fact, the majority—about two-thirds—of all the poor families in the country are white.

Welfare's like a traffic accident. It can happen to anybody, but especially it happens to women.

And that is why welfare is a women's issue. For a lot of middle-class women in this country, Women's Liberation is a matter of concern. For women on welfare it's a matter of survival.

Forty-four per cent of all poor families are headed by women. That's

Johnnie Tillmon. "Welfare Is a Women's Issue." *Liberation News Service* (No. 415), February 26, 1972.

bad enough. But the *families* on A.F.D.C. aren't really families. Because 99 per cent of them are headed by women. That means there is no man around. In half the states there really can't be men around because A.F.D.C. says if there is an "able-bodied" man around, then you can't be on welfare. If the kids are going to eat, and the man can't get a job, then he's got to go. So his kids can eat.

The truth is that A.F.D.C. is like a supersexist marriage. You trade in *a* man for *the* man. But you can't divorce him if he treats you bad. He can divorce you, of course, cut you off anytime he wants. But in that case, *he* keeps the kids, not you.

The man runs everything. In ordinary marriage, sex is supposed to be for your husband. On A.F.D.C. you're not supposed to have any sex at all. You give up control of your own body. It's a condition of aid. You may even have to agree to get your tubes tied so you can never have more children just to avoid being cut off welfare.

The man, the welfare system, controls your money. He tells you what to buy, what not to buy, where to buy it, and how much things cost. If things—rent, for instance—really cost more than he says they do, it's just too bad for you.

There are other welfare programs, other kinds of people on welfare—the blind, the disabled, the aged. (Many of them are women, too, especially the aged.) Those others make up just over a third of all the welfare caseloads. We A.F.D.C.s are two-thirds.

But when the politicians talk about the "welfare cancer eating at our vitals," they're not talking about the aged, blind, and disabled. Nobody minds them. They're the "deserving poor." Politicians are talking about A.F.D.C. Politicians are talking about us—the women who head up 99 per cent of the A.F.D.C. families—and our kids. We're the "cancer," the "undeserving poor." Mothers and children.

In this country we believe in something called the "work ethic." That means that your work is what gives you human worth. But the work ethic itself is a double standard. It applies to men and to women on welfare. It doesn't apply to all women. If you're a society lady from Scarsdale and you spend all your time sitting on your prosperity paring your nails, well, that's okay.

The truth is a job doesn't necessarily mean an adequate income. A woman with three kids—not twelve kids, mind you, just three kids— that woman earning the full federal minimum wage of $2.00 an hour, is still stuck in poverty. She is below the Government's own official poverty line. There are some ten million jobs that now pay less than the minimum wage, and if you're a woman, you've got the best chance of getting one.

The President keeps repeating the "dignity of work" idea. What dignity? Wages are the measure of dignity that society puts on a job. Wages and nothing else. There is no dignity in starvation. Nobody denies, least of all poor women, that there is dignity and satisfaction in being able to support your kids through honest labor.

We wish we could do it.

The problem is that our country's economic policies deny the dignity and satisfaction of self-sufficiency to millions of people—the millions who suffer everyday in underpaid dirty jobs—and still don't have enough to survive.

People still believe that old lie that A.F.D.C. mothers keep on having kids just to get a bigger welfare check. On the average, another baby means another $35 a month—barely enough for food and clothing. Having babies for profit is a lie that only men could make up, and only men could believe. Men, who never have to bear the babies or have to raise them and maybe send them to war.

There are a lot of other lies that male society tells about welfare mothers; that A.F.D.C. mothers are immoral, that A.F.D.C. mothers are lazy, misuse their welfare checks, spend it all on booze and are stupid and incompetent.

If people are willing to believe these lies, it's partly because they're just special versions of the lies that society tells about *all* women.

For instance, the notion that all A.F.D.C. mothers are lazy: that's just a negative version of the idea that women don't work and don't want to. It's a way of rationalizing the male policy of keeping women as domestic slaves.

The notion that A.F.D.C. mothers are immoral is another way of saying that all women are likely to become whores unless they're kept under control by men and marriage. Even many of my own sisters on welfare believe these things about themselves.

On TV, a woman learns that human worth means beauty and that beauty means being thin, white, young and rich.

She learns that her body is really disgusting the way it is, and that she needs all kinds of expensive cosmetics to cover it up.

She learns that a "real woman" spends her time worrying about how her bathroom bowl smells; that being important means being middle class, having two cars, a house in the suburbs, and a minidress under your maxicoat. In other words, an A.F.D.C. mother learns that being a "real woman" means being all the things she isn't and having all the things she can't have.

Either it breaks you, and you start hating yourself, or you break it.

There's one good thing about welfare. It kills your illusions about yourself, and about where this society is really at. It's laid out for you straight. You have to learn to fight, to be aggressive, or you just don't make it. If you can survive being on welfare, you can survive anything. It gives you a kind of freedom, a sense of your own power and togetherness with other women.

Maybe it is we poor welfare women who will really liberate women in this country. We've already started on our welfare plan.

Along with other welfare recipients, we have organized together so we can have some voice. Our group is called the National Welfare Rights Organization (N.W.R.O.). We put together our own welfare plan, called Guaranteed Adequate Income (G.A.I.), which would eliminate sexism from welfare.

There would be no "categories"—men, women, children, single, married, kids, no kids—just poor people who need aid. You'd get paid according to need and family size only—$6,500 for a family of four (which is the Department of Labor's estimate of what's adequate), and that would be upped as the cost of living goes up.

If I were president, I would solve this so-called welfare crisis in a minute and go a long way toward liberating every woman. I'd just issue a proclamation that "women's" work is *real* work.

In other words, I'd start paying women a living wage for doing the work we are already doing—child-raising and housekeeping. And the welfare crisis would be over, just like that. Housewives would be getting wages, too—a legally determined percentage of their husband's salary—instead of having to ask for and account for money they've already earned.

For me, Women's Liberation is simple. No woman in this country can feel dignified, no woman can be liberated, until all women get off their knees. That's what N.W.R.O. is all about—women standing together, on their feet.

THE SOUTH has traditionally been an area difficult for unionization. Yet in Charleston, South Carolina, women hospital workers in 1969

won one of the most dramatic victories of the decade, after a strike
that lasted 116 days. The Charleston strike owes as much to the civil
rights movement and its transformation of black consciousness as it
does to the pride of workers as workers. One of the major issues at
the Charleston hospitals was unequal treatment and pay of black and
white workers. In 1968 one hospital arbitrarily fired five black LPN's
(licensed practical nurses). Workers organized and attracted up to
400 nonprofessional workers at meetings; their successes scared the
hospital administration into reinstating the workers. In March 1969,
when twelve black house aides were fired (on the grounds that they
"abandoned" critically ill patients to attend a grievance meeting),
workers struck. They sought aid from New York hospital workers'
union Local 1199, and organized their own local, 1199B.

The imagination and organizing ability of the workers and civil
rights leaders transformed the strike into a citywide issue with mass
demonstrations and school boycotts. Brutality used against strikers
by the police then transformed it into a national civil rights cause.
Many workers, almost all black women, were jailed and beaten. Their
stubbornness and solidarity forced the hospitals to negotiate, recognize the union and grant substantial wage increases.

The excerpts that follow are from letters of the strikers and from
a movie script based on actual speeches made by union and civil
rights leaders during the struggle. An important theme in the workers' consciousness is religion, transformed by them into a militant
and inspiring instrument for political struggle.

THE CHARLESTON HOSPITAL STRIKE

It all started when four hundred hospital workers decided to organize a
union. And when the Medical College fired twelve people, we just had
to go on strike. Of course, a week later, Country Hospital joined us in
the strike. Of the four hundred strikers, all but twelve were women. All
of us were black.

MRS. BESSIE POLITE:
We needed something that would help support us, that when we go to
these people and talk to them, and we didn't get no satisfaction from
them, we could go to our union and then and have them to come in

"I Am Somebody." Film script produced by American Foundation of Nonviolence;
1199 Papers. Letters from Charleston Hospital Strikers.

with us and—you know—and help get things straightened out. And so the next morning at five o'clock we met at the hospital and all of us—you know—walked and talked and sang and everything else. So the more we walked and talked looked like the tougher they got—the tougher they got with us, and they still—you know—wouldn't decide to give in.

We was women and we didn't have no weapons or nothing. I felt like they wouldn't hardly hit us with those big clubs and things because we didn't have no weapons and we didn't went out to fight them with no fist fight—we went to fight them—you know—with the law on our side you know, to try to win by the law, not with no fist fights.

Miss Mary Moultrie, President, Local 1199B:

In the hospital they have white workers doing the same work as blacks. You know, they might have a white nurse's aid and a black nurse's aid yet the white aide earns more money than the black. I want union recognition. I want to see that my people are able to enjoy something better than what they have been enjoying. . . .

Mrs. Ernestine Bryant:

When you're working around people who discriminate against you you just really feel like—you know—fighting all the time because—you know—"hey, girl," and they have these nicknames, they call you like "dooflotchie" and "monkey grunt" and all this carrying on and I think all of us are due respect regardless of age, race or creed. . . .

Mrs. Brown:

There were times when I was hardly ever home during the day. And, well, the children was left a lot of times to themselves, made a lot of sacrifices. My husband—well, he worked and—um—he would have to come home and see that the children were bathed and he would a lot of times cook, go to the grocery store. Matter of fact, I didn't see the grocery stores quite a few times during that period. And—um—well, a lot of times he got sorta upset and we would have to have a talk and I would try to make him understand that this was like my thing and something I had to do. You know. So—um—well, we worked it out and he beared with me until the end of it. . . .

Of all the folks who helped us in Charleston, I feel it was the students who did the most to really help us win the strike. They went out there and they did just what was necessary. More than a thousand of us went to jail during the strike. As a matter of fact, it was like a badge of honor to go to jail. I was in jail twice. My kids were in jail too. . . .

We realized if it's one thing that the white folks understand, and that's the dollar. All we bought was food and medicine. And do you know, it cost the business community over $15,000,000.

After a hundred days, the Medical College agreed to settle the strike. All of us went back to work at Medical College, including the twelve that the Administration claimed would never work in Medical College again. We won wage increases of thirty to seventy cents an hour. We won a real grievance procedure—one that we could really understand. . . .

It took another thirteen days before the county hospital strike was settled. So the workers just had to keep on, keeping on until it was settled. . . .

MRS. BROWN:

The strike was one of the hardest and most important periods of my life. We had to fight the whole power structure of Charleston and of South Carolina. We were up against Governor McNair, Mendel Rivers, Strom Thurmond. Just because we wanted to have a union. But we proved to everybody that we could stand and fight together. That we were ready to sacrifice and that we would go to jail.

And if I didn't learn but one thing it was that if you are ready and willing to fight for yourself, other folks will be ready and willing to fight for you. We learned that you gotta be together. That's what a union is all about.

We built a winning combination of 1199 union power and SCLC soul power. 1199B is here to stay in Charleston.

EXCERPTS FROM LETTERS

The meaning of this strike to me, can be summarized in two incidents.

First: one of my church sisters, whom I have much respect for, didn't understand why I saw fit to picket or join in a march. She said, "I would walk out but picketing and marching are against my religion. You should pray to God for what you want instead of picketing and marching."

Then one day as we demonstrated on King Street telling people not to shop, a black woman came bursting through the crowd with a package under her arms. Well, she was pretty mad but my soul Sister gave me some great advice. She said "I don't know what you fussing for, you ought to be out working for what you want." I think I got more out of that statement than all of the beautiful expression ever said in our strike.

"You ought to be out working for what you want." It can't get any plainer. Praying is not the only answer. You have to work for what you want. . . .

In church, the one thing I did learn was that salvation didn't come on a silver platter. There would be suffering and sacrifice like what Jesus spoke of and if wanted victory you had to work for it and hold out to the perfect end; keep your eyes on the prize! and Soul Power!

During this strike my eyes were open to new strength I didn't know I had. Now that it is over I pray that I never fall into the same old routine but that I be as new born and tell black people everywhere that our strikers stuck together. There was unity through love and respect for each other. This is the only way to survive; through each other.

Miss Virgie Lee Whack
Ward Clerk
Charleston County Hospital

This has been the most astonishing struggle in the history for poor black and poor white people in the world. . . .

At first I felt tense being with people that I didn't know. But after being with them, I got to know and understand and understand their problems; and try to listen to them. I really went through a struggle. During the struggle I met a lot of people of importance. I've seen interesting places.

I really enjoy the hit and run demonstrations. This was very effective to me, especially blocking the traffic on the historic Cooper River Bridge, finding out where the Governor was having luncheon; which I think was very funny.

The young girls and men with Civil War clothing on, you should have seen them.

The strike have taught me to take criticism and take a lot of kidding from other people. I have help other members from the medical establishment sign cards and even visit them in their homes. One member was so afraid of the boss it hurt very much to see how a person can be like that. Mr. Bradford and I would keep going and talk with them but so far I haven't succeeded as yet. We will keep on especially since we won our freedom from both Country and Medical College Hospitals.

One thing I enjoy, is that the community was with us and that no matter what we have done—Charleston, S.C. will never be the same. The historic sights will not be historic any more. The sacrificing Black people in Charleston has been historic.

I thank everyone for their help. I will start from 1199, SCLC and the community and the Concerned Clergy, we will remember that God takes care of his own.

Co-Chairman,
1199B chapter at County Hospital

Alma Harden
Aide
County Hospital

HISTORICALLY, women have repeatedly made the greatest gains in self-respect and the respect of others from participation in political struggles. When those struggles reach revolutionary proportions, women's consciousness often accelerates so fast that radical change occurs in the relations of the sexes (as in the French and the Chinese revolutions, for example). But even in smaller struggles, crises often propel women into work and even leadership that they and others might previously have thought beyond them. In American history, strikes have often had that effect, and we have seen examples earlier in this book.

The United Farm Workers' (U.F.W.) strike has not only strengthened the entire labor movement and the hopes of agricultural workers throughout the country, but it has also created a challenge to male chauvinism among the union members themselves. It has been an effective challenge because it has come from within their own community, and specifically within the particular culture of Mexican-Americans. Gains won in this kind of crisis are not secure and could be eroded. But no gains are ever completely lost. Changes as profound as the ones described in the interviews below cannot be erased.

THE WOMEN OF THE BOYCOTT

DOLORES HUERTA, vice president of the United Farm Workers, was standing on a flat-bed truck beside Cesar Chavez. She didn't show her eight-and-a-half months' pregnancy, but she looked very tired from the

Barbara Baer and Glenna Matthews. "The Women of the Boycott." *Nation*, February 23, 1974.

days and nights of organizing cross-country travel plans for the hundreds of people who were now waiting in the parking lot alongside the union headquarters at Delano, Calif. . . .

Dolores was the first person Chavez called upon to work with him organizing farm workers into a union. That was more than a dozen years ago. She became the UFW's first vice president, its chief negotiator, lobbyist, boycott strategist and public spokeswoman. . . .

When Dolores began organizing, she already had six children and was pregnant with a seventh. Nearly twenty years later, there are ten children, and Dolores is still so slim and graceful that we find it hard to imagine her in her youth, the age of her daughter. She has not saved herself for anything, has let life draw and strain her to a fine intensity. It hasn't made her tense, harsh or dry. She shouts a lot and laughs with people. She tells us she has a sharp tongue but it seems to us she has an elusiveness of keeping her own counsel, mixed with complete directness and willingness to spend hours talking. Her long black hair is drawn back from high cheek bones, her skin is tanned reddish from the sun on the picket line, and in her deep brown eyes is a constant humor that relieves her serious manner.

Contradictions in her life must have taken, and continue to take, a toll: her many children, Catholic faith and a divorce, her high-strung nerves and the delicate health we know she disregards. It must be that her work, the amount she has accomplished and the spirit she instills in others, have healed the breaks. We talked to Dolores Huerta for several hours in the union offices when the last cars had left Delano.

"I had a lot of doubts to begin with, but I had to act in spite of my conflict between my family and my commitment. My biggest problem was not to feel guilty about it. I don't any more, but then, everybody used to lay these guilt trips on me, about what a bad mother I was, neglecting my children. My own relatives were the hardest, especially when my kids were small; you know, they were stair steps—I had six and one on the way when I started—and I was driving around Stockton with all these little babies in the car, the different diaper changes for each one. It's always hard, not just because you're a woman but because it's hard to really make that commitment. It's in your own head. I'm sure my own life was better because of my involvement. I was able to go through a lot of very serious personal problems and survive them because I had something else to think about. Otherwise, I might have gotten engulfed in my personal difficulties and, I think, I probably would have gone under.

"If I hadn't met Fred Ross then, I don't know if I ever would have been organizing. People don't realize their own worth and I wouldn't have realized what I could do unless someone had shown faith in me. At that time we were organizing against racial discrimination—the way Chicanos were treated by police, courts, politicians. I had taken the *status quo* for granted, but Fred said it could change. So I started working.

"The way I first got away from feeling guilty about neglecting my family was a religious cop-out, I guess. I had serious doubts whether I was doing the right thing, giving kids a lousy supper to go to a council meeting. So I would pray and say, if what I was doing wasn't bearing fruit, then it would be a sign I shouldn't be doing it. When good things came out of my work, when it bore fruit, I took that as a sign I should continue and that the sacrifices my family and I were making were justified.

"Of course, I had no way of knowing what the effects on my kids would be. Now, ten years later, I can look back and say it's O.K. because my kids turned out fine, even though at times they had to fend for themselves, other people took care of them, and so on. I have a kind of proof: my ex-husband took one of my kids, Fidel, during the first strike. We didn't have any food or money, there was no way I could support him. He was eating all right, like all the strikers' kids, but on donations. So my ex-husband took the boy until he was 11. I got him back just last year. He had a lot of nice clothes and short hair, but he was on the verge of a nervous breakdown. When my ex-husband tried to take another boy, the judge ruled against him. You could see the difference when you compared the two kids—one was skinny and in raggedy clothes and with long hair, but real well, happy. Fidel is coming back now to the way he used to be, and he's got long hair too.

"We haven't had a stable place to live—I haven't been anywhere for more than two months, except in New York on the boycott—since 1970. But taking my kids all over the states made them lose their fear of people, of new situations. Most of us have to be mobile. But the kids are in school, they go to school and work on the boycott. Even the 10-year-olds are out on the boycott in the cities.

"My kids are totally politicized mentally and the whole idea of working without materialistic gain has made a great difference in the way they think. When one of our supporters came to take my daughter to buy new clothes in New York, she was really embarrassed. We never buy new clothes, you know, we get everything out of the donations. She said, 'Mama, the lady wanted to buy me a lot of new things, but I told her they didn't fit me.' You know, she came home with a couple of little things to please the lady, but she didn't want to be avaricious. Her values are people and not things. It has to be that way—that's why everyone who works full-time for the union gets $5 a week, plus gas money and whatever food and housing they need to live on, live on at the minimum they can."

How has it happened, we asked, that in the very culture from which the word *"machismo"* derives, the women have more visible, vocal and real power of decision than women elsewhere? Dolores told us that the union had made a conscious effort to involve women, given them every chance for leadership, but that the men did not always want it.

"I really believe what the feminists stand for. There is an undercurrent of discrimination against women in our own organization, even though Cesar goes out of his way to see that women have leadership positions. Cesar always felt strongly about women in the movement. This time, no married man went out on the boycott unless he took his wife. We find day care in the cities so the women can be on the picket line with the men. It's a great chance for participation. Of course we take it for granted now that women will *want* to be as involved as men. But in the beginning, at the first meetings, there were only men. And a certain discrimination still exists. Cesar—and other men—treat us differently. Cesar's stricter with the women, he demands more of us. But the more I think of it, the more I'm convinced that the women have gotten stronger because he expects so much of us. You could even say it's gotten lopsided . . . women are stronger than the men.

"Women in the union are great on the picket line. More staying power, and we're nonviolent. One of the reasons our union *is* nonviolent is that we want our women and children involved, and we stay nonviolent because of the women and children.

"One time the Teamsters were trying to provoke a fight to get our pickets arrested. Forty, fifty police were waiting with paddy wagons. We had about 300 people. The Teamsters attacked the line with 2 × 4 boards. I was in charge of the line. We made the men go to the back and placed the women out in front. The Teamsters beat our arms but they couldn't provoke the riot they wanted, and we didn't give in. The police stood there, watched us get beaten; the D.A. wouldn't even let us sign a *complaint*. But we had gained a lot of respect from our men. Excluding women, protecting them, keeping women at home, that's the middle-class way. Poor people's movements have always had whole

families on the line, ready to move at a moment's notice, with more
courage because that's all we had. It's a class not an ethnic thing."

We knew that the women of the UFW found themselves in a unique
situation. Unlike the sex-determined employment of the urban poor,
the jobs of farm worker women and men had always been the same.
They *had* to work, but it wasn't housework or even factory work,
separating them from men. Women had picked, pruned and packed in
fields, cannery and shed side by side with men. But would the women
decide to let the men organize the union? Dolores Huerta had spoken
for herself alone; the resolution of conflicts between family and political, union action, would come to each UFW woman in her own terms.

Lupe Ortiz has been an organizer in a union field office since she left
school. She is about 25, a natural leader, with a quality of making
people laugh to get work done. Yet for all her big voice and humor, she
didn't know how women could assert themselves at home as they did at
work. What she told us seemed the reverse of our more familiar, middle-
class feminism; here, by contrast, a woman insisted on work equality,
and in large part received it, but she wouldn't challenge the traditional
order of the family.

As Lupe directed her male co-workers in Spanish, she expounded to
us in English the differences between "Anglo" and Chicano women.
"You Anglo women, you do it your way, but I don't ever want to be
equal to my husband."

"You get the same salary; don't you want the same voice at home?"

"In work, but not at home. No, at home you have to know when to
open your mouth and when not to. You have to learn you can't go
places men go, like bars."

"Don't you want it to change? For men to act as though you're
equal?"

"It's not exactly equality. It's our culture. I don't want our Chicano
culture to change. Let men have the say-so." Lupe laughed, this time
openly, as she looked at the men in the office. "I bet *you* split up with
your husbands more often than we do because you make head-on conflicts."

Ester Yurande, a generation older than Lupe, showed a generation
difference in her appearance: she was as carefully, femininely dressed,
with lovely long hair and glittering earrings, as Lupe had been rugged
in jeans, sweatshirt and close-cropped curls. Ester had worked in the
fields until she became the bookkeeper for the Medical Clinic at Forty

Acres. She had been a UFW member from the start, been jailed in the early 1960s. How, we asked her, had the union changed the lives of the women who came to the clinic?

"A doctor treats us with dignity now. We don't get charity when we're having a baby, we get care. It's to do with pride. Mexican women around here used to do what the men said, but Dolores Huerta was our example of something different. We could see one of our leaders was a woman, and she was always out in front, and she would talk back. She wasn't scared of anything."

Dolores herself had told us that she didn't hesitate to argue. "You know, Cesar has fired me fifteen times, and I must have quit about ten. Then, we'll call each other up and get back to work. There have been times when I should have fought harder. When he tells me now, 'you're getting really impossible, arguing all the time,' I say, 'you haven't seen anything yet. I'm going to get worse.' Because from now on I'm going to fight really, really hard when I believe something. There have been times I haven't. I can be wrong, too, but at least it will be on the record how I felt."

When we asked Ester how she felt about fighting back herself, she didn't want to answer. We had become outsiders once more, women who didn't comprehend her way. Men have accepted strong women in the union, but there remains deeply engrained in these women a respect for their men's *machismo*. . . .

Dolores . . . told us that women were most important to the union because a woman determined the fate of a whole family. If a *wife* was for the union, Dolores said, then the husband would be, too. If she was not, if she was afraid or too attached to her home and possessions, then the family usually stayed out of the union, or it broke up. There had been a number of broken marriages that had cost the union the strength of a united family.

Maria-Luisa Rangel did not want to go out on the first boycott. At that time—in 1968—many women were staying in California while the men lived together in boycott houses in Eastern cities. The Rangels, parents of eight children, had saved enough money to own part of a family store, and they owned their home in the small town of Dinuba, near Fresno. They would have to part with both if they went to Detroit for two years. Hijino Rangel was determined to go. So Maria-Luisa went. Looking at her unsoftened features, her inaccessible but not unfriendly black eyes, we sensed the strength that had enabled her then to wrench herself away from everything she owned and keep her family together. She had a hard time in Detroit; she didn't know much English, the climate was completely strange and she had two operations in the city. But when they returned to the valley in 1970, the Rangels knew that they had helped win the boycott that secured the 180 union contracts with grape growers of the Coachella and San Joaquin Valleys. And the experience had worked on Maria-Luisa. She spoke out as a representative of the union about the present boycott. "It's just like it was then. The struggle is for the people to win, not the growers but the people. I know it, and *they*—the growers—know it."

Women have paid different prices for making the union part of their lives. The 100 women who spent many weeks in Fresno jails last summer (for violating anti-picket injunctions) ranged from minors to great-grandmothers. There were field workers and nuns, lay religious women and union officials. For some of the Chicano women, it was a reminder of previous jailings when no nuns had been present and the guards had beaten "the Mexicans." For others, it was the first time, and almost a vacation from their daily lives. Work-hardened baked hands became almost soft. All the women shared their experiences—the farm workers told city women like Dorothy Day, editor of the *Catholic Worker*, about their struggle, and learned from her about women's movements in the cities and in the Church.

Maximina de la Cruz and her husband, Juan, were born around 1910 in Mexico. Juan entered America on the bracero program, picked crops in Texas, and then in New Mexico, where Maximina worked in a clothing factory. They married, moved with their son to the San Joaquin Valley in 1960, and joined the union during the first strikes in 1965. Juan de la Cruz was killed last summer by a man who fired his .22-caliber rifle into the picket line from a truck. Maximina told us she remembers that many times the growers or the Teamsters put on deputy badges, joined in beating the farm workers, and then arrested them on grounds of self-defense. The man who shot de la Cruz has entered a plea in the valley courts that he shot defending himself from the picket line.

Maximina was observing the thirty-day mourning period when we came to her home in Arvin. Hearing us arrive, she and her mother, Porfiria Coronado, met us at their gate, and without a word, in the dark, she took us, with hands that felt like warm, worked clay, into her living room. Candles beneath pictures of saints and near a wedding photograph were the only light. As the night went on, she told us of her early life of hardship, the many moves, purchase of their small house, and the changes the UFW had made in their lives.

"We *know* the growers. They want to go back to the old days, the way it was before we had a union, when we got a dollar an hour, no toilets or water in the fields, no rest periods, and they could kick you out without any pay for not picking fast enough. A whole family earned less than one union man today. They fought us hard and dirty each time, but we didn't give in. We won't. This time we're out in the cities again to tell the good people what it is like to work here. I'm staying on here, and I'll be back at work in the fields, but not until the union gets its contracts back. I might have to wait a while but I know people will understand and help us win back our union. I'm proud to be a woman here. Juan was proud of the union. You know, on the picket lines, we were so gay, peaceful and *attrativas,* even the grandmothers. Until *they* shot their gun."

Except for the Catholic Church, the powerful and wealthy institutions of California have opposed the UFW at one time or another. Grower-biased central valley law enforcement and the courts have made a mockery of legal institutions; agri-business has never given up trying to break the union through legislation; Gov. Ronald Reagan has been photographed eating scab grapes; even the U.S. Government helped the growers by buying nonunion lettuce in great quantity to ship to troops in Vietnam. Yet the greater the odds, the more the union has come to represent poor people against the rich and mighty. Dolores Huerta fights best when the situation looks bleakest. . . .

"To tell the truth, I was prejudiced against women for a long time and I didn't realize it. I always liked to be with men because I thought they were more interesting and the women only talked of kids. But I was afraid of women, too. It was in the union that I lost my fear of being around women. Or put it this way, I learned to respect women. Cesar's wife, Helen Chavez, helped me more than anyone else. She was really committed to home. Actually, Cesar's toughest organizing jobs were on Helen, his wife, and Richard, his brother. They wanted to lead their own lives. Helen kept saying she wouldn't do anything, and she's so strong and stubborn you couldn't convince her to change her mind. She took care of the food and the kids, and while Cesar was organizing she was supporting them, too, working in the fields. Cesar, keeping his *machismo* intact in those days, would make her come home and cook dinner.

"We wanted her to learn the credit union bookkeeping. We yelled at her one night into the kitchen. 'You're going to be the assistant bookkeeper.' She yelled back, 'No, I won't either,' but we voted her the job.

Boy was she mad! But you should see her books. We've been investigated a hundred times and they never find a mistake."

The union had to teach its members—farm workers with almost no education or training—the professional skills it required. Marie Sabadado, who directs the R. F. Kennedy Medical Plan, Helen Chavez, head of the credit union, and Dolores, chief negotiator and writer of labor contracts, taught themselves. Dolores made it sound almost easy to learn very specialized skills in a week's time.

"When Cesar put me in charge of negotiations in our first contract, I had never seen a contract before. I talked to labor people, I got copies of contracts and studied them for a week and a half, so I knew something when I came to the workers. Cesar almost fell over because I had my first contract all written and all the workers had voted on the proposals. He thought we ought to have an attorney, but really it was better to put the contracts in a simple language. I did all the negotiations myself for about five years. Women should remember this: be resourceful, you can do anything, whether you have experience or not. Cesar always says that the first education of people is how to be people and then the other things fall into place.

"I think women are particularly good negotiators because we have a lot of patience, and no big ego trips to overcome. Women are more tenacious and that helps a great deal. It unnerves the growers to negotiate with us. Cesar always wanted to have an *all-woman* negotiating team. Growers can't swear back at us or at each other. And then we bring in the ethical questions, like how our kids live. . . .

"One of the reasons the growers are fighting us so hard is that they realize we're changing people, not just getting a paycheck for them. Without our militancy we wouldn't have a union. So we keep pushing our people, getting them out on other issues, like the tuition rise in California colleges, or the Presidential campaign. We had farm workers out door to door for McGovern. And when our people came back from the boycott, they will be stronger than ever."

We asked Dolores whether she had ever been scared, or lacked confidence in her ability to organize people.

"Of course. I've been afraid about everything until I did it. I started out every time not knowing what I was to do and scared to death. When Cesar first sent me to New York on the boycott it was the first time we'd done anything like that. There were no ground rules. I thought, 11 million people in New York, and I have to persuade them to stop buying grapes. Well, I didn't do it alone. When you need people, they come to you. You find a way . . . it gets easier all the time."

THE CIVIL RIGHTS Act of 1964, in its Title VII, prohibited discrimination in employment on the basis of sex (or race, color, religion, national origin). Under its provisions, an employee with a grievance appeals to the Equal Employment Opportunity Commission (EEOC), which can then bring suit against any employer with fifteen or more employees.

Like so much of our antidiscrimination legislation, however, the record of enforcement is not good. In October 1971, according to the *New Republic*, the EEOC had a backlog of 26,000 unsettled complaints. And the number of complaints is mounting. In the year ending June 30, 1972, women alone filed 10,500 complaints. The EEOC's powers and budget are very limited; it must go through years of investigation, mediating, and bargaining; only after all attempts at conciliation fail can it file suit, and it is not difficult for employers to keep this from happening by dragging out negotiations. Attempts to strengthen its powers were defeated in both House and Senate in 1971 and 1972.

In an attempt to act firmly against a major discriminator, and perhaps equally important, to convince complainants that it was acting firmly, the EEOC took on the American Telephone and Telegraph Co. in December 1970. Seeking a weapon with which to threaten the extremely powerful AT&T, the EEOC asked the Federal Communications Commission to refuse a rate increase that the phone monopoly was seeking until AT&T ended its discriminatory hiring policies. But the Federal Communications Commission insisted on handling the rate increase request separately—"on its own merits"—thus ignoring the merits of the women and minority employees trapped in the telephone company bureaucracy. Thus the EEOC was undercut by another government agency.

Nevertheless, in a record-breaking settlement, the EEOC ordered AT&T in early 1973 to pay $15 million in back pay and up to $23 million in pay increases, mostly to female employees. There is still room to question, however, whether AT&T in the long run lost money. Wilma Scott Heide of NOW computed that AT&T owes women $4 *billion*. Perhaps it was, despite everything, cheaper for them to underpay until forced to do otherwise by an enforcement agency.

Meanwhile, women workers in many workplaces are trying to use EEOC enforcement provisions to win equal treatment on their jobs. Lacking strong governmental support, however, women must continue to rely on unions, where they exist, in fighting discrimination. The following letter to a United Steelworkers local is an example of the constant pressure that women apply to their unions. It also illustrates the many ways in which women's working lives can be made miserable by sexist foremen.

FIGHTING SEXISM ON THE JOB

OPEN LETTER TO LOCAL #1299

Dear Union Representatives:

In the past four months since Great Lakes Steel was FORCED to hire women, they have followed a policy of rampant discrimination. Many women, especially Black women, have been fired for no reason at all. Before a woman really gets into the department she is told that the foreman doesn't want women in his department at all, and from that point on she is picked on until they find some "cause" to fire her. She is also forced to lift twice as much as a man just to prove that she can do the job.

Examples:

#1. This one woman's husband was a weight lifter and she could also lift weights. She worked in the masonry department. She could carry two buckets when most of the men carried only one. She got fired because she was too short and they said it was unsafe for her.

#2. The foreman's always complimenting the women on how good they work, and then they get fired for "not being able to do the work." Women really don't have a chance to pick their jobs like many of the men do, even if they might have more seniority than some of the men. One foreman would give out all the jobs before starting time. When the women got there he would turn to them and say, "All I have left is . . . !!"

There were two Black women working in the BOP #2, and although they had the most seniority in their department, a white woman was

Archives of Labor History and Urban Affairs, University Archives, Wayne State University, Detroit, Michigan (Open letter to Local 1299 of the United Steelworkers of America, n.d., probably 1973).

given a bid job, when the black women didn't know about it. They were given the impression you couldn't bid on a job until you got your 35 days in.

#3. In one particular case two Black women were given the job of rod straightening and were told to do 15. When the foreman came around to check on them they had already done eight. The foreman told them to stop. So they didn't do anymore. The next day they were off. The following day when they were supposed to go back to work, they got calls telling them they were terminated.

#4. In another incident one woman was told by one foreman to do a certain job in general labor. Then another foreman came along and told her to do something else. She got fired by the first foreman for leaving her job. So either way you lose, because there are too many people telling you what to do.

These are just a few examples of some of the women who have been fired. After all don't think any woman would be working in a steel plant if she didn't have to work. Most women are the head of their household just like the men working there. They have the nerve to apply there in the first place; and most of them work harder than some of the men there just to prove that they can do the job.

We call on Local #1299 to do its best to get these women their jobs back. Although many of these women weren't allowed to keep their jobs long enough to get in the union, we're asking the union Reps to please fight for these jobs, regardless of your specific contract obligations.

A failure to fight against such open discrimination will hurt all union efforts. Please don't allow the company to continue such divide and conquer tactics between women and men, Black and white.

Must women lift twice as much as men in order to keep their jobs?

Waiting For Our Jobs,
Women Fired by Great Lakes Steel

THE EQUAL RIGHTS Amendment is an attempt to provide a legal support for women's equality. It would write sexual equality into the U.S. Constitution and make literally hundreds of discriminatory state laws invalid (such as laws giving husbands control over children's and wives' property, laws providing for different, harsher treatment of woman criminals, laws providing separate salary scales).

Introduced into the U.S. Congress yearly since 1921, the ERA finally passed both houses of Congress, and as we write this lacks only the final states' approval for its final adoption.

There has been widespread controversy over ERA, some of it opposition from those who believe women's inferiority or separateness to be just and requiring enforcement. But, more interesting for us here, some of the opposition has come from those concerned with women's welfare. Especially among working-class women, there has been a concern with the fact that certain "discriminatory" state legislation—notably, protective labor laws creating slightly higher requirements for working conditions for women than for men—is valuable to women. While this point seems realistic on its face, it is difficult to evaluate it because we lack any objective overall survey of how protective laws really work in practice. Protective laws themselves can function to discriminate against women as well as to protect them from harm, and we do not know which is their main function in the majority of cases.

This controversy may be unresolvable at this time. But at this level perhaps it doesn't matter that much anyway, for the real significance will depend on how the laws are enforced. Just as the protective laws have been used to discriminate against women, so the ERA can be used that way too—by forcing women to compete against men in situations for which they are ill suited by training and other background factors. On the other hand, where protective laws have helped women it is because women have organized unions or other groups that gave them collective power. Similarly, where antidiscrimination laws have helped it has been for the same reason. The two excerpts that follow give a sense of the spectrum of views and issues involved in the controversy. Despite their varying opinions about ERA, they all indicate that only organization and group solidarity can ever give women the power—no matter what the laws—to resist employers' constant efforts to increase the rate of exploitation. The ERA, however, would provide a vital weapon for women to use, and the record suggests that working-class women will use it energetically if it is passed.

The excerpts are from hearings before the U.S. Senate Judiciary Committee in 1970. The first statement, by Myra Wolfgang, is representative of the position taken by A.F.L.-C.I.O. union leadership at that time—almost all were opposed to ERA. Since then, however, A.F.L.-C.I.O. unions have mostly reversed their position and come out in support of ERA.

THE EQUAL RIGHTS AMENDMENT

MRS. WOLFGANG. Thank you, Senator.

My name is Myra K. Wolfgang. I reside in the city of Detroit, State of Michigan, and am represented in this body by Senator Philip Hart. I am sorry he isn't here. I am the vice president of the Hotel & Restaurant Employees and Bartenders International Union, AFL–CIO, and secretary-treasurer of its Detroit Local No. 705. I am a member of the Michigan State Minimum Wage Board and I have served on the mayor's committee of human relations. I am, presently, a member of the Michigan Women's Commission (the Governor's Commission on the Status of Women), the first such State commission to be organized, and I have been appointed commissioner by the past three Governors of our State. I agree these credentials aren't as imposing as the judge from North Carolina. I am not a legal expert. I certainly can't interpret the law as would Paul Freund, but I think my credentials do qualify me to speak on behalf of the working women of America.

I am opposed to the enactment of the equal rights amendment to our Constitution. I state my position after long and careful consideration, in spite of the fact that we find sex prejudice parading in the cloth of tradition everywhere. We are aware that it is tailored to the patterns of ignorance and special interest.

The principle of equal pay for equal work is being violated throughout the breadth and length of this Nation. Women are being discriminated against unjustly in hiring and in promotion. Our social security laws remain discriminatory. Equal access to our educational institutions is still denied women. Qualified women are, in the main, excluded from the policymaking bodies of this Nation from the Cabinet down to our county institutions.

Fully aware of all of the inequities visited upon the women of America, I still appear here today to oppose the equal rights amendment. I believe that the amendment is not only undemocratic and its effect will bring frustration and tragedy, but that it will accomplish the exact opposite its proponents claim it will do. . . .

U.S. Congress. Senate. Committee on the Judiciary. *Hearings before the Committee on the Judiciary*, 91st Cong., 2nd Sess., September 9, 10, 11 and 15, 1970 (Statement of Myra Wolfgang) ; U.S. Congress. Senate. Committee on the Judiciary. *Hearings before the Committee on the Judiciary*, 91st Cong., 2nd Sess., May 5, 6 and 7, 1970 (Statement of Georgianna Sellers).

Until last week, I had many grave misgivings about the outcome of this legislation. I had seen the equal rights amendment run through the House of Representatives like a herd of stampeding cattle on a discharge petition maneuver. Never have so few business and professional women been so effective and done such harm. The hysteria created by bra-burning and other freak antics is not a justification for the action taken by the House of Representatives, nor is the fear of political reprisal. Let me assure you the threat is not borne of reality. It must have been this same type of hysteria that created the conditions for the passage of the Volstead Act. But now that the dust has settled and we begin to look around at the damaged past, the damaged present and the damaged future, more seasoned hands seem to be in the saddle.

Even though I appear here before you in my various capacities, capacities not usually associated by chauvinistic males with philosophical legislative considerations, I want you to know the women of America are not unaware of what Government is, what it means and what it should mean. . . . We know that the very foundation of all government worth having, is predicated upon laws designed to protect the unequal, those who are smaller and less strong from those who are larger and stronger.

We know that this concept is as American as squash and chitlins. . . .

Now, if one of the major and fundamental roles of government is this equalizing one, then the adoption of the so-called equal rights amendment will negate this same equalizing function under the guise of broadening it. The equal rights amendment will invalidate all the legislation, hundreds of pieces of it, which has been adopted over the last 100 years which were passed to permit a semblance of equality which had been denied women down through the ages.

There are various kinds of protection for women workers provided by State laws and regulations: (1) minimum wage; (2) overtime compensation; (3) hours of work, meal and rest period; (4) equal pay (5) industrial homework; (6) employment before and after childbirth (7) occupational limitations; and (8) other standards, such as seating and washroom facilities and weight-lifting limitations. It would be desirable for some of these laws to be extended to men, but the practical fact is that an equal rights amendment is likely to destroy the laws altogether rather than bring about coverage for both sexes. Those State laws that are outmoded or discriminatory, should be repealed or amended and should be handled on a case-by-case basis. . . .

The chief conflict between those who support the equal rights amendment and those of us who oppose it is not whether women should be discriminated against, but what constitutes a discrimination. We, who want equal opportunities, equal pay for equal work and equal status for women, know that frequently we obtain real equality through a difference in treatment, rather than identity in treatment. We think that democratic concept is an important part of our Constitution.

We believe that orderly legislative revision is the practical way to erase such "specific bills for specific ills." I oppose adoption of the equal rights amendment since I believe that the adoption of the amendment would jeopardize existing labor laws and standards that apply to women; that it would create endless confusion in the wide field of laws relating to property, personal status, and marriage. . . .

With unemployment on the increase, labor standards are under attack. The person who glibly states that no one has to work overtime, if they don't want to, does not understand that when there are not enough jobs to go around, people fight to keep those that are available. Thousands of women, because of economic necessity will submit to excessive hours without a law to protect them in order to obtain or hold a job. Thousands will work excessive hours, particularly when they see their employers calling for the nullification of protective legislation by urging passage of the equal rights amendment. They accede to this excessive overtime or quit the job. In the first instance, the children become the victims, in the second instance, the entire family suffers from the loss of that income or the mother and the family become public charges. This condition will adversely affect not only the women of America but the vast majority of all Americans.

Let me cite a perfect example of sex inequity. Is a man who works 60–72 hours a week confronted with the same home and family responsibility that, say the mother of three children working 60–72 hours a week is? Don't talk theory to me, tell me the practice. Don't tell me the man should help his wife. He doesn't. . . .

In Detroit, six Penn Central System office women were assigned to jobs as checkers of freight cars at the Detroit area railroad yards, after they complained about sex discrimination to the Michigan Civil Rights Commission. The women had been employed as clerks and typists. Climbing in and out of boxcars as railroad checkers, is a back-breaking job, but a company executive said "They asked for equal rights, so what are they complaining about?"

Eleanor Hannon, 51, a widow with five children said, "I can't afford to quit, but I don't know how long I can last on this job, particularly if I have to work a night shift." The transfer from the office pool to the freight docks was within the scope of the railroad's contract with the Brotherhood of Railway Clerks. . . .

Ironically, many of the business and professional women, most vocal in advocating the overthrow of hour limitations, would not be affected at all, since many of the States with hour limitations already exempt them from these restrictions. I must remind those who are influenced by the business and professional women that the equal rights amendment does not require equal pay for equal work, nor does it require promotion of women to better or decisionmaking jobs. It does not elect more women to public office. It does not convince men to help with the housework. . . .

MRS. SELLERS. Thank you, sir.

I am Georgianna Sellers of Clarksville, Ind., speaking on behalf of the Indiana and Kentucky unit of the League for American Working Women, known as LAWW.

I am acting chairman of this organization. LAWW is a new organization. Its basic purpose is to work for and achieve equality of rights for women. While our organization is not confined to working women, most of our members are employed as factory workers.

The members of our organization wholeheartedly support the equal rights amendment—and for many reasons. It would eliminate injustices to women in employment, educational opportunities, and other areas.

Since our major efforts have been directed toward achieving equality for women in employment, one of our strongest reasons for supporting the equal rights amendment is that it would nullify all State restrictive laws that limit women as to what work they can do, how long they can work, and what they can lift.

It is an insult to women that such laws or rules are referred to as "protective" when their sole function is to exclude women from the higher-paying jobs.

The experience of the women employees at the plant where I am employed, demonstrates the urgent need for the equal rights amendment.

Most of us working women are employed in factories on high-speed production lines. Some of us—including myself, are working for the Colgate-Palmolive Co. which has arbitrarily refused to concede that there is a Civil Rights Act of 1964, which prohibits discrimination in employment on the basis of sex.

The union supposedly representing the employees at this plant fails to see why it should recognize the minority group—women—and has made contracts since the advent of Title VII of the Civil Rights Act of 1964 that were just as discriminatory as were the previous contracts.

The women working for Colgate were denied the right to work on the better-paying jobs to which their seniority entitled them, simply because they were women and the jobs might occasionally require the lifting of over 35 pounds.

As a matter of fact, some women employees on the low-paying jobs lifted as much as 17 tons per day while men employees thumped buttons on automatic machinery. While Indiana has no so-called "protective" laws prohibiting women employees from lifting 35 pounds, the mere existence of such laws in other States was used as a phony excuse for this discrimination.

"Oh, no," our employer would say, "you are a woman. You can't do this job. You have to lift 35 pounds. Let George do it."

We were kept off of higher paying easier jobs for years because the company wanted to "protect" us. I say it did not protect, but exploited women. Used their hard labor for low pay, just as employers treated the Negroes for years. Keep them under foot, not on top."

Incidentally, the record that we sent to the Seventh Circuit Court of Appeals weighed 38.6 pounds. We did not have a man to carry it for us. . . .

The officials of Local No. 15, International Chemical Workers Union—our union—tell us that we should not fight for our rights because we are a minority. There are about 1,100 men employees and only 145 women employees at this plant. We need the equal rights amendment to eliminate restrictive laws and practices and to give us quicker and surer relief against both employers and unions.

The male representatives of the AFL–CIO who have appeared before the committee and argued that women should not be given their equality, should not be heard—they have no right to claim they represent working women.

[Applause.]

Mrs. SELLERS. There is not one single woman in the AFL–CIO executive council. Even the predominantly women's unions are governed and controlled by men. It is insulting for these males to use State restrictive laws as a gimmick for exploiting us by claiming they are protecting us. These males running the labor unions are merely trying to monopolize better jobs for themselves. . . .

American working women have learned the lesson that the black people have learned. There is no such thing as separate but equal. We do not want separate little unequal, unfair laws and separate little unequal, low-paid jobs. We want full equality. . . .

There is no one more aware of the power of woman than women—especially working women.

THE SPECIAL oppression faced by lesbians in the workplace is rarely written about. If it is discussed at all, it is generally in the context of professional jobs. In fact, lesbians are numerous in most working-class jobs too. Usually they are unnoticed because they are often forced to disguise themselves as "straight," or heterosexual, in order to keep their jobs. Recently the gay liberation movement has stimulated open challenges to that discrimination.

The first excerpt is from a discussion among gay men and women in the offices of *Workforce* magazine. The second is a report on gay organizing among nurses.

GAY WORKERS ORGANIZE

Our "Gay workers' " meeting this month drew a wide variety of participants: Elmer from Society for Individual Rights, Jill from Daughters of Bilitis, Laura from Whitman-Radcliffe Foundation, and three men—Michael, Joel and Michael—from the East Bay Gay Men's Political Action Group, who are organizing a Gay Workingman's conference in early October. . . . We spent considerable time talking about Gay civil rights and job legislation. Only nine cities, Jill pointed out, have included a sexual orientation clause in their affirmative action legislation.

Being a Gay woman is double jeopardy. Jill: "Even if Gay discrimination wasn't there, we're still going to be fucked over as women. Even in women's employment agencies and affirmative action programs, a lot of feminists discriminate against Lesbians, bowing to the 'sensitivity' of the issue." The anti-woman sexism of many Gay men has also inhibited women and men from coming together around Gay demands; besides, they are two very different cultures. Some contend, however, that work-

"Gay Workers Out of the Closet." *Workforce*, September–October 1974.
Carolyn Innes, R.N., and David Waldron, R.N. "Staying Gay, Proud . . . Healthy." *Workforce*, September–October 1974.

place organizing may be a vehicle for the development of functional unity between Gay women and men. One of our writers for this issue suggests, "The women and men in such a group have something in common besides being Gay."

There are additional problems Gay people face on the job. Jill: "One of the problems with organizing Gay workers is that they are *not* obvious. When my lover comes home from work, she's always saying that she may have seen somebody who's a Lesbian, looking for that moral support but being afraid to ask anybody." Laura: "Or always having to lie about that 'boyfriend' out there." . . .

There are certain social groups and professions where coming out at work is beginning to be possible. One participant said flatly, "It's basically a middle-class privilege to be out on the job." . . .

The Gay Nurses Alliance rode at first on the impetus of two RNs, David Waldron and Carolyn Innes. They met on the job, which is uncharacteristic of most of these groups, and points to a difference and advantage in organizing among white-collar workers. . . . As another of the discussion participants observed, "The prerequisite for any Gay worker organization is making space for Gay people to come out on the job, if only to each other."

Who's going to make this space? Most agree on the "Gay community," but that may be another way of asking the same question: who's the Gay community? Thus far, Gay activism has primarily expressed itself outside the workplace. . . .

Gay health professionals face a double dilemma: there has always been considerable prejudice and unequal (or not) medical treatment for people who are Gay or who have special medical or emotional needs because of their Gayness. Yet to speak out openly against these subtle discriminations is to bring massive denials, and to openly identify oneself as Gay is to risk the loss of license, job, family or friends. The Nursing profession particularly has been loath to admit that there are within its ranks a large number of Gay nurses. What it takes to change this attitude is a change of awareness among the Gay members of the profession who have preferred not to risk coming out, but who remain in the "closet." It also takes a re-education to and an indictment of the current health-care systems that exist for Gay patients. The Gay movement provided the support and incentive for these changes. Eventually the appalling care received by patients known or suspected to be Gay could no longer be ignored, and the discrimination evidenced against

Gay colleagues could no longer be suppressed or tolerated. The Gay Nurses' Alliance was formed out of this background.

In August 1973, after taking part in the 2nd Philadelphia Gay Pride Parade, David Waldron and Carolyn Innes, both professional nurses, decided that it was time to stop hiding, pretending, and playing the game and to start doing something constructive about their own liberation. Barbara Gittings, a Philadelphia resident and pioneer in the struggle for Gay rights had been encouraging Carolyn for a year to form a Gay caucus within the professional organization of nursing that would be similar to the group that Barbara had helped to found within the American Library Association. David and Carolyn met in 1972 while working at the same hospital and soon realized that they had similar views on many things. The more their consciousnesses were raised the less tolerance they had for hiding; they were also aware of the problems encountered by hospitalized Gays. They were disturbed at the lack of understanding and sensitivity shown by nurses toward patients who were identified as Gay and, sometimes worse, the total unawareness that there were valid alternatives to the "straight" life styles. David and Carolyn concluded that something had to be done and that they should get busy and do it.

After some agonizing and discussion about what being open would mean to their nursing careers, David and Carolyn decided to "come out" and formed the Gay Nurses' Alliance (the name suggested by Barbara Gittings). . . .

The decision that Carolyn and David, the co-founders of GNA, made to "come out" and their commitment to equal care for Gay patients and equal opportunities for Gay nurses has changed their lives completely. Their activity has brought them a great deal of satisfaction but also much hardship. All of their resources, financial and emotional, are tied up in GNA. They have not been fired from their jobs, but feel a lot of pressure, subtle and overt, from homophobics at the hospital and in their district nursing association. There is too much to be done and too few people willing to help, but GNA is here to stay, and isn't going to go away. State caucuses of GNA are springing up all over the country. One of the most activist is the Massachusetts GNA. Activist nurses there are providing health care to Gay people on Gay Health Night, held each week at a neighborhood health clinic. This is one example of the kinds of things that can be accomplished by Gay nurses and sensitive, professionally responsible straight nurses who advocate quality care for all patients.

THE FACT THAT the women's liberation movement began with college-educated women leaves open the question of its impact on the majority of working-class women. The elite nature of the movement has been exaggerated by the greater publicity commanded by the spokeswomen of the more conservative feminist organizations and projects; the sources of women's liberation as a mass movement lay in ex-students and working women from the working and middle classes. However, the alienation that many working-class women feel from the feminist movement itself has been wrongly taken to mean that they do not identify with its goals. This article by Susan Jacoby, dealing with working-class women over forty—for whom it is harder, perhaps, to change a life's patterns than younger women—illustrates how profound indeed has been the impact of women's liberation.

WHAT DO I DO FOR THE NEXT TWENTY YEARS?

. . . The life stories outlined by these women have many common elements. The women are all in their 40's; most grew up in first- and second-generation Italian or Jewish immigrant homes. A few have lived in East Flatbush since they were children and the rest came from nearby blue-collar neighborhoods. Most of the women graduated from high school, went to work for a year or two at poorly paid jobs, married by age 20 and quickly started having children. Only two of the 12 had any education beyond high school. Rose Danielli's background is typical; she worked as a telephone operator for a year before marrying Joe, a telephone installer, when they were both 19.

The husbands are blue-collar union men or white-collar workers employed by the city government; their general income range is between $9,000 and $14,000 a year. Most of the families have at least three children. Homemade soups and clothes are a necessary economy for them rather than an expression of the "traditional female role." Their houses represent the only important financial investment of their lives and are maintained with appropriate care—postage-stamp lawns raked free of leaves, living-room sofas glazed with plastic slipcovers and reserved for company, starched kitchen curtains, home freezers stocked with the specials the women unearth in numerous grocery stores on Saturday mornings. They worry in equal measure about the rising price

Susan Jacoby. "What Do I Do for the Next Twenty Years?" *New York Times Magazine,* June 17, 1973.

of ground chuck, the fact that so many of their grown children are leaving the old neighborhood, and how to get along with the blacks who are moving into the area. A movie and dinner in a local Chinese or Italian restaurant is a once-a-month event. Manhattan is "the city," a place to be visited on wedding anniversaries for dinner and a hotel floor show.

Whatever their problems, the women love their husbands and are not about to leave them. They do not expect to liberate themselves by living alone, although they understand why some younger women find marriage an unsatisfactory state. They have neither the education nor the work experience to be tapped as token women for high-powered jobs in high-powered companies. One woman in the group says she is waiting breathlessly for the day when the local 6 o'clock news will feature a broadcaster who is not only black and female but over 40, thereby providing on-screen representation for three oppressed groups instead of two.

Nevertheless, the women are convinced that they can build a future different from the traditional path laid out by their mothers and grand-mothers. The feminist movement is responsible in large measure for their belief that they can change the course of their middle-aged lives.

The movement was gaining strength and national publicity at a time when the women who make up the East Flatbush group began to face the void most full-time mothers experience after their children grow up and leave home. Their comments in the group sessions indicate that two main concerns spurred their interest in feminism: the feeling that society in general, and their husbands in particular, no longer viewed them as sexually interesting or even sexually functioning women, and the realization that they were "out of a job" in the same sense as a middle-aged man who is fired by his employer of 20 years. . . .

The most important decision at the first meeting was that the sessions would be held regularly on Tuesday nights. Except in emergencies, they would not be subject to interference by children and husbands who had other activities in mind. At the second session, several women reported with glee that the announcement of a regular meeting had caused a storm in their homes. "In our house, my husband expects me home every evening," explained one woman. "That is, unless he decides to go bowling. Then I can go to the movies by myself or out to a neighbor's."

Some of the husbands resented the decision to regularize the meetings because they had chosen to view the group as just another coffee klatsch. The reactions of the men included bitter opposition, secret sabotage, amused resignation and quiet support. "My poor man asked what he should tell the neighbors if they called and asked for me on Tuesday night," recalled a woman whose husband is part-owner of a Jewish delicatessen. "I told him to tell anyone who called the truth, that I'm working out what to do with my life. He said the hell he would, he'd tell them I was doing something for the temple."

Sarah Thomas, the 40-year-old wife of a policeman, had the biggest problem: Every time she planned to leave the house for her women's group, her husband had a minor household accident requiring her attention. The women were appropriately sympathetic when she arrived an hour late for the second meeting because her husband's ankle needed soaking after he twisted it on the front stoop. Before the next meeting, Sergeant Thomas carved a deep slice in his thumb with a potato peeler. When he poured boiling water over his hand, Sarah and the other girls began to suspect the acccidents were not entirely accidental.

At the fifth meeting, Sarah reported that "I told him since he was an experienced police officer he was used to dealing with emergencies and I was sure he could take care of a slight burn by himself. I figure if I just sail out of the house anyway, he'll stop having these accidents." (She proved a prophet, because she continued to attend the women's group meetings and, as of June, her husband was still chalking up at least two accidents a month.) . . .

"Life plays a dirty trick on women," said Ann Nussbaum, whose husband is a bookkeeper with the city Finance Administration. "The men think you're gorgeous when you're too young to know anything about life. How well I remember how hard it was to take any interest in my husband when I had been changing diapers all day. Now I have much more time and interest for sex, but my husband is the one who's beat. He does tax returns to make extra money on the side—I know he just feels like rolling over and going to sleep at the end of the day.

"One of the things I feel I have to get across to him is that being physically affectionate with each other doesn't have to mean sex; he doesn't have to feel all this pressure that men seem to feel about performance. I agree with Ruth that it's hard to talk about these things after a lifetime of being silent, but I don't see how we can get anywhere unless we speak up about what's bothering us." . . .

Ruth Levine, who had never worked outside her home, surprised the rest of the group by becoming the first to take the plunge into the job market. She applied for a job as a file clerk in a large advertising agency and was hired with a warning from the personnel department that "most of the girls on your floor will be 25 years younger than you are." . . .

"Well, I know it's not much of a job in the eyes of anyone else," she reported to her group after she had been working for a month. "Even the secretaries look down on file clerks—especially a file clerk in her 40's. And I agree with some of the stuff I read in *Ms.* these days—a man, even a dumb one, would never have to take one of these jobs. But to me the job is something. Someone has to do this kind of work. I never went to college, I never worked before I was married, and I don't really have the training for anything more. What do I get out of the job? For one thing, I get to meet a lot of different people who give me new things to think about. . . ."

The other important thing Ruth gets out of her job is money: She brings home more than $90 a week after taxes and Social Security withholding. "It makes me feel both that I'm independent and that I'm contributing something to the household," she said. . . .

Ruth is taking a shorthand course so that she can move into a better-paying secretarial job next fall. After she took the first step, four other women in the group found jobs. Two returned to the secretarial work they had done before they were married, one found an opening as a teacher aide in the Head Start program for preschool children, and another put her fluent Italian to work as an interpreter for older immigrants in their dealing with city agencies. Two women in the group decided they would go to college and were accepted in adult-education programs leading toward a bachelor's degree.

The women who plan to enter college are undergoing profound changes that have also made a deep impact on their husbands. "I don't think I could take file clerking," announced Alice Martino one night, "but I'm not prepared for anything else. I always wanted to go to college, and I think that's just what I'm going to do."

Unlike many of the women, Alice has no serious financial problems. Her husband, Rick, earns more than $16,000 a year as a construction worker; they live rent- and mortgage-free in a house Alice's mother left them when she died. Their children are between ages 18 and 24, and are either currently attending college or have graduated.

Alice is enrolling in the highly respected adult-education program at Brooklyn College. After considering several possibilities, she decided on teaching as a career because she felt it offered the easiest entree for an older woman. She plans to make a specialty of speech and reading therapy because there is a shortage of trained personnel in those areas despite an over-all teacher surplus.

Contradicting the hard-hat stereotype, Alice's husband turned out to be more favorably disposed toward the feminist movement than the other women's husbands. In fact, he decided to follow his wife's example. "He confessed he was jealous of my plans to go to college," Alice said, "and then he decided he was being stupid because he could do it too. College was never a possibility for him when he was younger —he was the oldest son and his parents needed money very badly. He's thought about architectural engineering for years; he always said he knew more about putting up buildings than the engineers on the job." . . .

Not all the women have had as much success in changing their own lives or the attitudes of their husbands. Judith Katz, who worked as a secretary before her marriage 20 years ago, encountered stiff opposition when she went back to work in the counseling office of a Brooklyn junior high school. Her husband especially resents the fact that she wanted a job enough to take an opening in a ghetto school with a tough reputation. As an expression of his disapproval, he refuses to ride the subway with his wife in the morning. Another of the women, an accountant's wife who is already attending classes at Brooklyn College, did not speak to her husband for several weeks after he told her, "You're too feather-brained to finish cleaning the house, much less four years of college."

In general, the East Flatbush men who disapprove of feminism express their reactions more openly than the professional husbands of upper-middle-class women who are the most vocal and visible participants in the movement. College-educated men are often reluctant to attack women's liberation in principle, but their practical behavior is another matter. Judging from the wide variety of male reactions described by the Flatbush wives, Middle-American men are no more or no less disturbed than other American men when the women in their lives try to break out of the traditional female pattern.

The East Flatbush women have considerable difficulty identifying with the widely publicized leaders of the movement. Said one: "I confess I don't feel much of a sense of sisterhood when I see pictures of Gloria Steinem with her streaked hair and slinky figure. I feel somehow that these people don't know how it is to be getting older with very little money and education. They have it a lot better than we do—it's not true that we're all in the same boat."

Another woman disagreed: "Well, there's one thing that we all have in common—we're all afraid of muggers and rapists when we walk down a dark street at night. And that's something we have in common

with the colored women who live right here in East Flatbush, even
though most of us are better off financially than they are."

The women do identify with the movement on a variety of specific
issues—child day-care centers, equal pay for equal work, the right to
abortion and contraceptive information, the need to educate young
girls to think of themselves as individuals in their own right instead of
viewing themselves only as future wives and mothers. Several of the
women now spend considerable time trying to introduce these reformist
ideas into the conservative environment of East Flatbush. One of their
immediate goals is a health information service for girls and women of
all ages; they feel that most East Flatbush women are unlikely to use the
referral services now available in Manhattan. Rose Danielli had hoped
to organize such a service through her church but ran head-on into a
clash with her priest over contraceptive information.

"My husband said, 'Oh, Rose, don't get into a battle with Father
——.' Then he said, 'I give up. If you were willing to do battle with
my mama you won't stop with the priest.' " . . .

ON MARCH 23–24, 1974, about 3,200 women from fifty-eight different
unions met in Chicago to found, with great enthusiasm and optimism,
the Coalition of Labor Union Women (CLUW). It promised to grow
into a mass organization of workingwomen. Within two years of this
auspicious beginning, however, by 1976 CLUW's promise has faded
and it has become merely another subdivision of the national AFL-
CIO bureaucracy (though some local chapters continue to assert some
independence). The reasons for this failure include the internal contradictions within the unions and the female labor force described
here by Annemarie Tröger, as well as divisions among the socialist and
feminist women who tried to organize within CLUW for rank-and-file
power against the union bureaucrats.

THE COALITION OF LABOR-UNION WOMEN: STRATEGIC HOPE, TACTICAL DESPAIR

The women's movement has reached a new level—in spite of itself. A new consciousness has reappeared in the labor movement—against the labor unions. The Coalition of Labor Union Women (CLUW) symbolizes both these developments. It signifies more than the intentions of its founders: It is women's liberation in the working class.

THE SOURCES OF CLUW

According to its founders, a group of trade-union officials, the stated objectives of this national coalition of trade-union women include organizing the 32 million nonunionized women in the work force; pressuring for affirmative action at the workplace; engaging in lobbying campaigns around issues concerning women; and encouraging women to move into policy-making positions within trade unions and political parties. Initially, rank-and-file women enthusiastically received the idea of an organization of women workers. They began immediately to organize CLUW chapters across the nation without waiting for the CLUW leadership to take the initiative. The concept of CLUW changed from that of a coalition of women in trade unions to a broader, more responsive organization of workingwomen—at least in the minds of the rank and file. This transformation due to rank-and-file and Left pressure is so threatening to union leaders, female and male, that they may well murder CLUW in its infancy. But the needs and the spirit which initiated CLUW will survive in other organizations, in a broader movement, because these needs express concrete historical forces and material needs which together are stronger than the Coalition and the Left factions or trade-union bureaucrats operating in and on it.

The growing economic crisis, the bankruptcy and male chauvinism of traditional unionism, the expansion of women's employment, especially in the service and clerical sectors of the economy, all contributed to the birth of CLUW, but its single most critical cause was the women's liberation movement. The ideas that the movement spawned,

Annemarie Tröger. "The Coalition of Labor Union Women: Strategic Hope, Tactical Despair." *Radical America*, Fall 1975.

though diffuse, created the consciousness essential for CLUW's beginning. . . .

The emergence of CLUW proves that the issues raised by the wom-
en's movement—sexual oppression and sex stereotyping—are not the
gripes of neurotic middle-class ladies, but rather are issues of great
importance to a broad spectrum of women workers. Although the wom-
en's movement's influence on working-class women has been diffuse,
abstract and distorted by the mass media, CLUW would not have been
created without it.

THE STRATEGIC QUESTION: A FEMALE PROLETARIAT?

Employed working-class women do not have a group identity. Women
who work outside the home do not yet see themselves as a class or part
of a class subjected to common forms of oppression. Most importantly,
they do not perceive themselves as a force which can act collectively,
and which, as a collective, has achieved something visible in the past.
Women wage laborers are not yet conscious of being a historical *subject*. "Workingwomen" remains only a sociological category, rather
than a designation for a political force.

"Female Proletariat?" What for? To drive another division into the
working class? Hidden or overt accusations of divisiveness have para-
doxically always been raised against those who struggled to abolish
real, economic divisions in the working class. There are innumerable
incidents in history where workingwomen fought for higher wages for
men. Where are comparable actions of the male proletariat? On the
contrary, men so often struck *against* equal wages and equal work for
women that it is historically correct to define trade unions as defense
organizations against the intrusion of women and other minorities, as
well as against capitalists. The most outrageous and divisive lie in
labor history, that at the beginning of the industrial revolution women
flooded the market with cheap labor and took the jobs away from men,
has been transported into a theory, ironically by many who called
fervently for proletarian unity. This call for "unity" by white, male-
dominated trade unions has as much credibility as the call for "industrial peace" by capitalists and governments. It means "Bow down and
we will forge unity (peace) on your backs!" History is to learn from,
not to "speak bitterness." We uncover the dirty side of the glorified
labor history to find out what to expect from today's labor movement.
To talk about the specific revolutionary potential of the female proletariat does not mean to map out a women's revolution ending up in
daydreams about a matriarchial empire. It also does not mean the easy

identity of interests announced traditionally by socialists and communists: "whatever is good for the male workers (i.e., "the Proletariat") is good for women anyway," with some extras thrown in for the "social duty," childbearing. Our strategy is to improve the social and economic position of women fundamentally and directly (and not indirectly as in socialist strategies). This means attacking the division of labor. . . .

DIFFERENT EXPLOITATION

What is the strategic position of the female proletariat? Its weaknesses have been noted again and again: less militancy and constancy due to responsibility for reproductive work, and as a result, "retarded consciousness"; the limitations of the female job market, and the size of the female reserve labor army; a lower skill level, and therefore easier replacements of women workers. The strengths of the female proletariat have rarely been thought about. Women workers are less divided by real or imagined pay status and qualification differences, which have been some of the strongest barriers to class consciousness among working-class men. Racial tensions and outright racism—although undeniably present—are less sharp, less antagonistic among women than among men.

One of the strategic goals of the female proletariat should be an attack on job classifications and wage differentials. Work on the production line is a qualitatively different, heavy job, not to be defined as a light, "less skilled" job with "less responsibility." Why should monotony and speed be paid less than more humane "skilled" jobs? The attack on the classification system must aim first at elevating the lower categories of jobs. But in the long run, it is a fight against the existing division of labor. For the female proletariat, "division of labor" is not an esoteric intellectual problem but the concrete condition of their work, the visible tool of their exploitation. The demand for equal work and admission to skilled jobs is a search for "better, more interesting work, a more fulfilling job," as a woman steelworker in a CBS interview put it, besides being a demand for decent pay and a stable job.

The present unequal division of labor is basic to the maintenance of the profit system, as much as the private ownership of the means of production itself. A struggle against the division of labor is not a "deviation from the major contradiction," but is aimed at its heart. The greater homogeneity of the female work force is a reason and a precondition for building a force unified enough to attack such a complex and far-reaching issue.

CLUW is certainly not the organization to confront the problem of division of labor, but it could be an agent for activating a collective sense of unity among workingwomen. The founding of CLUW was a step toward workingwomen uniting in the struggle to fulfill our own, self-defined economic and political needs. But a broad focus permeating all actions and politics of the Coalition, a collective awareness of unity, can grow *only* if rank-and-file women, rather than union officials, are the moving force in CLUW leadership.

DIVISION IN THE FEMALE WORKFORCE— DIVISION IN CLUW

The old, more ideological than economic, division between production workers and clerical workers has considerably diminished in the last decade. There remain a majority of white women in offices, although nonwhites are increasing. The artificial identification of secretaries with management, and the sexist and condescending attitudes of unions toward the "gals in the office," are giving way to the realization that office workers are workers too.

The real division within the female work force is between professional service workers (teachers, nurses, social workers, administrative employees, etc.) on the one hand and the rest of the women workers on the other. It is certainly true that the objective difference between these female professionals and the overwhelming male high professionals (doctors, lawyers, university professors, architects, etc.) is larger than that between the two parts of the female work force, or between males and females in industrial production. Therefore it is appropriate to identify the majority of female professional service employees as workers, and not as a new professional class. The famous "proletarianization of the middle class" seems to be nothing else than the unprecedented growth of the lower and middle skilled work force in the service industries. It was "proletarianized" since it began.

Yet, it would be dangerously misleading to assume unity under the banner "we are all workers" or through an emotional appeal to sisterhood. To begin with, educational differences are great, and professional service workers are better paid, have more job security and benefits, are less regulated and disciplined and even have some determination over their work—to a small, but for a woman on the production line to a great, degree. The differences are certainly not antagonistic, but they are real enough, and might function as specific group interests.

From these differences, unionization of professional service workers gets its political ambiguity. But compared with bourgeois interest groups and professional associations borrowed from higher professionals, unionization is progressive. Unionization reflects the realization that "professional" service employees are dependent, like all the other workers, and must unionize to protect their interests. In this context, unionization is a progressive step toward unifying all workers' interests.

On the other hand, rugged unionism which only battles for a bigger piece of the pie can be a reactionary battle for more professional privileges, making it a fragmenting force. Professional service workers still tend to identify with the ideology, and imitate the model, based on the status and privileges of the high professional strata such as doctors and lawyers. "Professional rights" have been, with few exceptions, partial rights to control and exploit those beneath as well as partial exemption from control from above. (The gains of such rights are minute for the individual professional workers, but considerable for the union leaderships in terms of political power in city governments.) By striving for the needs of one group at the expense of the other, a potentially unifying and progressive form of organization could turn into a powerful weapon for further dividing workingwomen.

CLUW has a single chance to counteract the reactionary tendencies of women who have been trained to see themselves as professionals. Currently, professional service workers, along with union officials, are overrepresented in CLUW. This overrepresentation occurs not so much in the membership as in leadership positions. New unionization as among the professional service workers creates a rather high level of political activity and awareness. Professional jobs require and reinforce certain superficial leadership abilities as rhetorical and organizational skills, some factual and procedural knowledge, self-assertion, and so on. Lack of these personal skills is a considerable disadvantage among some factory and clerical workers.

Yet, the most important factor is the nearly identical economic and political situation of professional service workers and of women trade-union functionaries, regardless of which union they represent, and whether they have been recruited as professional trade unionists or from the rank and file. Both groups of women are mostly stuck at the lower-middle steps of the career ladder dominated by old men, and often stepped over by young men with less experience and often less abilities. Women's personal, political and professional abilities and ambitions are constantly frustrated, sometimes with the threat of being degraded or dropped at an older age. CLUW is for both groups not only a political pressure group but also a way to gain a personal political visibility, which in turn could promote their professional careers. "The Coalition seeks . . . to encourage our leadership and our movement into policy-making roles within our own unions and within the union movement in all areas." And: "Whenever or wherever possible, CLUW urges union women to seek election to public office or selection for governmental appointive office at local, county, state and national levels." These passages from the "Statement of Purpose" are probably the most strongly felt. Without disqualifying these women as "petty bourgeois careerists," without denying the justice of their demands for equality, they do not represent the most urgent or the long-term needs of the majority of CLUW's membership of constituency.

CLUW must guarantee the leadership of blue-collar, rank-and-file women, if necessary through structural provisions. In order to insure their political influence, leadership bodies should be composed according to the size of the sectors of the female labor force, such as clerical, professional, blue- and white-collar service and factory workers. Although some may object that such a strategy would be divisive, sometimes we have to split now in order to unify later. Representation in CLUW in each region must be composed of both the organized and unorganized female labor force. Such a plan is the only way to guarantee a significant voice for the predominantly black and Third World women workers in unorganized factory and service jobs, and to prevent CLUW's blue-collar women from becoming mere adjuncts to skilled, "professional" women workers, and to trade-union functionaries.

THE MEMBERSHIP QUESTION
The conflict between a club of professional women trade unionists and an organization of workingwomen has been solved by a compromise: a coalition of women in trade unions. Difficulties began with the definition of membership: What is to be recognized as a labor union? What about women in organizing drives, or the unemployed unable to pay union fees? What about domestics and women who have to work for their welfare checks but are not allowed to unionize?

Membership is not primarily a question of the political aspirations of the women functionaries but rather a question of the control of union hierarchies over the new organization. To keep the membership confined to union members is probably one of the strictest obligations of the women bureaucrats toward their bosses. Politically experienced women such as CLUW president Olga Madar, former vice-president of the U.A.W., have no illusions about CLUW's inconsistencies and limi-

tations. Her prominent participation indicates the value the big industrial unions place on CLUW: To keep the growing unrest of the female
rank and file out of the union, and to give them an "independent"
organization to isolate disturbing women's issues. This way, craft locals
and other groups of skilled workers, some of whom are already on the
verge of seceding because of the black question, will not be further
alienated by the international having to take a stand on equal rights for
women. CLUW can only accomplish this if it remains under firm control. Otherwise it could, on the contrary, carry the unrest into the
unions instead of keeping it out. Control by the union hierarchies can
only be exerted through the leadership of their women functionaries;
their supremacy requires that CLUW elect its leaders through union
caucuses.

The problem of membership was a hot issue at the founding convention, and has threatened to get out of hand ever since. If a vote on the
question had not been blocked in the Chicago founding convention,
CLUW would be an organization open to all workingwomen. But there
is no force strong enough to pull such an organization together at this
point, over the aggressive resistance of most labor unions.

ASPIRATIONS OF RANK-AND-FILE WOMEN

Two of the few floor votes which could not be prevented at the founding convention indicate the aspirations of rank-and-file women. They
also illustrate that the rank and file is much more aware and militant
than the leadership seems to have expected. An amendment to the
Statement of Purpose from the floor called upon CLUW to fight for
democracy in all unions. The officials denounced this amendment as
antiunionism, because in their view it was critical of traditional union
politics, but it carried. This incident reiterated the tendency of officials
to silence members by accusations and pointed out the dichotomy between the concerns of the officials and of the members. The one side
wants to keep the unions an unquestioned authority, the other looks for
an authority capable of challenging the unions.

The second dispute in which the leadership lost overwhelmingly due
to a coalition of rank and filers and Leftists concerned a paragraph in
the Structure provision which read: "National CLUW and area CLUW
chapters shall not be involved in issues or activities which a union
involved identifies as related to a jurisdictional dispute." This provision would have barred CLUW from supporting the United Farm
Workers' campaign. In general, if CLUW is serious about organizing
the unorganized, it will invariably run into the conflicting interests of

individual unions, into so-called jurisdictional disputes. Declaring these cases irrelevant for CLUW is no solution. If CLUW fails to develop guidelines for its organizing drives based upon the interests of the *women concerned,* and on today's economic realities (conglomerates, runaway shops, etc.) rather than on the business perspectives of unions, it will fail in its primary reason for being.

A VIABLE DIRECTION

For CLUW to meet the needs and demands of workingwomen, it must operate at three different levels: the individual, the union and the multiunion. On the individual level, CLUW can actively support and advise women who have not been represented by their unions. Here CLUW will not act in place of the union, but will put pressure on the unions to do what they are supposed to do. For example, blatant cases of a union's refusal to defend and represent its women workers should be publicized within the labor movement. On this level, the knowledge and experience of union officials is invaluable.

On the union level, CLUW can organize women's committees in union locals. The advantages are obvious: women of a local union could legitimately unite to articulate their views on union matters and become a pressure group for women's issues in contracts, strikes, and so on. In addition, women's committees could become a potential organizing tool for CLUW. However, an aggressive women's committee will survive the inevitable attacks from union and management only if CLUW as a whole is willing to intervene in its behalf. At the same time CLUW must protect these committees against various forms of union co-optation in order to guarantee the continued presence of strong, internal pressure groups for women's interests. One way to protect these interests is to have the women's committee leaders elected by the rank-and-file women and supported by an independent operational fund from their union, rather than appointed by, and therefore accountable to, the male leadership.

The multiunion level strategy is the most complex and the most crucial one at this time. If CLUW is serious about organizing women in nonunion shops and supporting organizing drives, it will have to develop a set of principles to determine which of the unions contesting for representation should be supported. These principles should include not only the usual union demands such as pension, wage and health benefits, but also such problems as strike versus nonstrike contracts, the union's position or lack of one on the larger political-economic issues of inflation and progressive taxation, job classifications which discriminate on the basis of sex and race and internal union democracy. Candidate unions could be rated according to their "women's score" on: wage differentials within unions and shops; the percentage of women with seniority rights; the number of women in skilled jobs; and the union's active support in contracts and legislation for such women's demands as day care, maternity benefits and the ERA.

If CLUW becomes a mass organization of workingwomen, these principles will have a far-reaching educational impact on all workers by giving political direction to their strong but vague feeling of dissatisfaction with the unions. If it achieves these goals, it will have gone far toward effective action on behalf of women workers.

While there is certainly a need for a revolutionary mass organization of women workers, CLUW is unlikely to be it. Not only because CLUW was founded by the wrong people, or because it is now controlled by trade-union functionaries, but because the political preconditions are not yet present for such an organization.

First, while the economic homogeneity of the female work force is a fact, its social integration is just developing (aided by the unionization of service and clerical workers), and it has not yet any political cohesiveness. CLUW could be an important tool in fostering this social integration and under certain conditions could also be one of the first steps toward the creation of a political force of workingwomen, but these developments are now in an embryonic stage.

Second, there is not yet a revolutionary strategy for the female work force. The attempts of the women's liberation movement to develop revolutionary goals for women have been in the realm of reproduction, not production. Even these concepts, such as the socialization of housework and the abolition of the family, have been more abstract ideas than revolutionary goals with theoretical foundations and strategies. The Left continues to view women in general, and women workers even more, as adjuncts to the male proletariat. No autonomous revolutionary role has been envisioned for women workers within the Marxist tradition. Women workers have been seen as especially exploited, especially dominated, especially oppressed, but never in a situation with unique and sharp contradictions which would create the potential for a revolutionary outlook.

This article is an attempt to view the special conditions of the exploitation of women workers as the foundation of a specific revolutionary potential. One aspect of this potential has been sketched out: One of the main devices for exploitation of the female labor force has been the radical division of labor in social production and in society at large.

Women more than any other social group need the abolition of this division of labor. The ERA campaign, or any equal rights campaign for workers, has to be understood in this perspective. Such campaigns represent a political opportunity to fight against exploitation through the division of labor. Equal rights for all women means first and foremost the abolition of the lowest categories of labor.

Despite its limitations, CLUW is a sign of an independent movement of women workers. If this first move becomes a force strong enough and continuous enough to pressure for and set the standards for reform of the labor movement, it could be an important step toward the development of class consciousness among workingwomen, their self-consciousness as a collective historical subject, a female proletariat.

House & Garden

A Condé Nast Publication

WOMEN AT WORK . . . . . . BUILDING TOMORROW

In this issue:

...MORROW'S HOME
...w it will look and work

...UR WARTIME BUDGET
...Making it s-t-r-e-t-c-h

...N FALL COLOR SCHEMES

SEPTEMBER 1943

A World War II magazine cover of a woman worker.

Farah strikers.

San Francisco nurses' strike, 1974.

APPENDIX

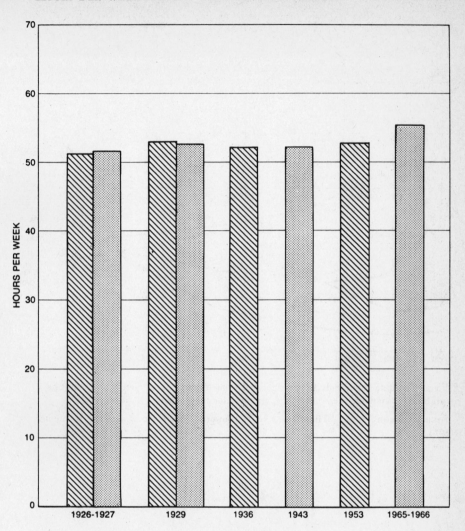

NOTE: Slanted column is hours for rural women, solid column is hours for urban women. Chart on the basis of surveys made in the years cited for women with no outside employment. Technological changes have increased women's productivity and shortened the hours necessary to do certain tasks (i.e., laundry), but the addition of new tasks and the creation of higher standards of cleanliness has meant that the hours necessary for housework have not noticeably changed.

SOURCE: Joann Vanek, "Time Spent in Housework," *Scientific American*, November 1974, p. 118.

DISTRIBUTION OF TIME AMONG VARIOUS KINDS OF HOUSEHOLD WORK

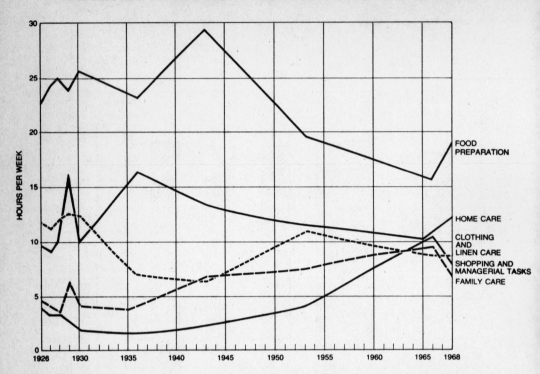

NOTE: The data relate only to nonemployed women, meaning women who did not have full-time jobs outside the household. Top curve includes cleaning up after meals.

SOURCE: Joann Vanek, "Time Spent in Housework," *Scientific American*, November 1974, p. 119.

THE FEMALE LABOR FORCE

Year	Female Labor Force as Percentage of Total Labor Force	Female Labor Force as Percentage of Female Population		Employed Married Women as Percentage of Female Labor Force
		Total	Married	
1890	16	18	5	14
1900	18	20	6	15
1910	21	24	11	15
1920	20	23	9	23
1930	22	24	12	29
1940	25	27	17	36
1950	29	31	25	52
1960	33	35	32	60
1970	38	43	41	63
1974	39	45	44	62

SOURCES: Peter Gabriel Filene, *Him/Her/Self: Sex Roles in Modern America*, New York: Harcourt Brace Jovanovich, 1975, p. 241; U.S. Department of Labor, Women's Bureau, *1975 Handbook of Women Workers*, Washington, D.C.: Government Printing Office, 1975, pp. 9, 11, 17, 18.

The Leading 10 Occupations of Women Workers 1870–1970
In order of size, and as reported in each census regardless of changes in definition

	1870	1880	1890	1900	1910
1	Domestic Servants	Domestic Servants	Servants	Servants	Other Servants
2	Agricultural Laborers	Agricultural Laborers	Agricultural Laborers	Farm Laborers (members of family)	Farm Laborers (home farm)
3	Tailoresses and Seamstresses	Milliners, Dressmakers and Seamstresses	Dressmakers	Dressmakers	Laundresses (not in laundr
4	Milliners, Dress and Mantua Makers	Teachers and Scientific Persons	Teachers	Teachers	Teachers (school)
5	Teachers (not specified)	Laundresses	Farmers, Planters and Overseers	Laundry Work (hand)	Dressmakers a Seamstresses (not in factory
6	Cotton-mill Operatives	Cotton-mill Operatives	Laundresses	Farmers and Planters	Farm Laborers (working out)
7	Laundresses	Farmers and Planters	Seamstresses	Farm and Plantation Laborers	Cooks
8	Woolen-mill Operatives	Tailoresses	Cotton-mill Operatives	Saleswomen	Stenographers and Typewrite
9	Farmers and Planters	Woolen-mill Operatives	Housekeepers and Stewards	Housekeepers and Stewards	Farmers
10	Nurses	Employees of Hotels and Restaurants (not clerks)	Clerks and Copyists	Seamstresses	Saleswomen (stores)

Sources: Decennial Census, 1870–1940; Janet M. Hooks, *Women's Occupations Through Seven Decades* (Women's Bureau Bulletin #218, U.S. Department of Labor); U.S. Dept. of Commerce, Bureau of the Census: Census of Population, 1960, Detailed Characteristics, U.S. Summary, Table 202; U.S. Dept. of Commerce, Bureau of the

20	1930	1940	1950	1960	1970
her Servants	Other Servants, Other Domestic and Personal Service	Servants (private family)	Stenographers, Typists and Secretaries	Stenographers, Typists and Secretaries	Secretaries
eachers chool)	Teachers (school)	Stenographers, Typists and Secretaries	Other Clerical Workers	Other Clerical Workers	Sales Clerks (retail trade)
rm Laborers ome farm)	Stenographers and Typists	Teachers (not elsewhere classified)	Saleswomen	Private Household Workers	Bookkeepers
enographers d Typists	Other Clerks (except clerks in stores)	Clerical and Kindred Workers (not elsewhere classified)	Private Household Workers	Saleswomen	Teachers (elementary school)
her Clerks xcept clerks stores)	Saleswomen	Saleswomen (not elsewhere classified)	Teachers (elementary school)	Teachers (elementary school)	Typists
undresses ot in laundry)	Farm Laborers (unpaid family workers)	Operatives and Kindred Workers, Apparel and Accessories	Waitresses	Bookkeepers	Waitresses
aleswomen tores)	Bookkeepers and Cashiers	Bookkeepers, Accountants and Cashiers	Bookkeepers	Waitresses	Sewers and Stitchers
ookkeepers d Cashiers	Laundresses (not in laundry)	Waitresses (except private family)	Sewers and Stitchers, Manufacturing	Miscellaneous and Not Specified Operatives	Nurses, Registered
ooks	Trained Nurses	Housekeepers (private family)	Nurses, Registered	Nurses, Registered	Cashiers
armers eneral farms)	Other Cooks	Trained Nurses and Student Nurses	Telephone operators	Other Service Workers (except private household)	Private Household Cleaners and Servants

Census: Census of Population, 1970, Detailed Characteristics, U.S. Summary, PC (1) D 1; U.S. Women's Bureau, "Occupations of Women, 1950, 1960 and 1970, Tables Reprinted from the Economic Report of the President 1973," 1973.

PROFILE OF THE WOMAN WORKER

1970   1920

AGE

39 years old.   28 years old.

MARITAL STATUS

Married and living with her husband.   Single.

OCCUPATION

Most likely to be a clerical worker.   Most likely to be a factory worker or other operative.

Many other women in service work outside the home, factory or other operative work, and professional or technical work.   Other large numbers of women in clerical, private household and farm work.

About 500 individual occupations open to her.   Occupational choice extremely limited.

EDUCATIONAL ATTAINMENT

High school graduate with some college or post-secondary-school education.   Only 1 out of 5 17-year-olds in the population a high school graduate.

LABOR FORCE PARTICIPATION

Almost half (49%) of all women 18 to 64 years of age in labor force.   Less than one-fourth (23%) of all women 20 to 64 years of age in the labor force.

Most apt to be working at age 20 to 24 (57%).   Most apt to be working at age 20 to 24 (38%).

Labor force participation rate dropping at age 25 and rising again at age 35 to a second peak of 54% at age 45 to 54.   Participation rate dropping at age 25, decreasing steadily, and only 18% at age 45 to 54.

Can expect to work 24 to 31 more years at age 35.   Less than 1 out of every 5 (18%) women 35 to 64 years of age in the labor force.

SOURCE: U.S. Women's Bureau, WB 70-127, April 1970.

INDEX

ABOUT THE EDITORS

ROSALYN BAXANDALL is teaching labor studies and women's studies at the New York State College at Old Westbury, Long Island, New York. She is a mother and has been very active in the feminist movement since 1967.

LINDA GORDON is associate professor of history at the University of Massachusetts at Boston. She is also the author of *Woman's Body, Woman's Right: A Social History of the Birth Control Movement in the U.S.*

SUSAN REVERBY is a graduate student in American Studies at Boston University and a fellow in the Milbank Multidisciplinary Program in Health Services, Research and Policy. She has been active in the women's and health movements and has written and lectured extensively on health, women's history, and labor issues.